PAGES FROM A BLACK RADICAL'S NOTEBOOK

African American Life Series

A complete listing of the books in this series can be found online at wsupress.wayne.edu

Series Editor
Melba Joyce Boyd
Department of Africana Studies,
Wayne State University

PAGES FROM A BLACK RADICAL'S NOTEBOOK

A James Boggs Reader

Edited by Stephen M. Ward

With an Afterword by Grace Lee Boggs

WAYNE STATE UNIVERSITY PRESS DETROIT

15 14 13 12 11   5 4 3 2 1

Library of Congress Cataloging-in-Publication Data

Boggs, James.
Pages from a Black radical's notebook : a James Boggs reader / edited by Stephen M. Ward ;
with an afterword by Grace Lee Boggs.
p. cm. — (African American life series)
Includes bibliographical references and index.
ISBN 978-0-8143-3256-6 (alk. paper)
1. African Americans—Social conditions—20th century—Sources. 2. African Americans—Civil rights—
Sources. 3. Civil rights movements—United States—History—20th century—Sources 4. Black power—
United States—History—20th century—Sources. 5. United States—Race relations—Sources.
6. Detroit (Mich.)—History—20th century—Sources. I. Ward, Stephen M., 1970– II. Title.
E185.615.B575 2011
323.1196'073—dc22
2010019760

Designed and typeset by Maya Rhodes
Composed in Avenir and Perpetua

For

Grace Lee Boggs

Sekai and Chaney

and

in memory of Aimé J. Ellis (1969–2009)

Contents

Preface xi

Introduction: The Making of a Revolutionist 1

Part I: *Correspondence* Newspaper

Introduction to Part I 37

Talent for Sale (1954) 42

Viewing Negro History Week (1954) 43

Negro Challenge (1954) 45

The Paper and a New Society (1954) 46

Sensitivity (1955) 48

The Stage That We Have Reached (1955) 50

A Report on the March on Washington (1957) 52

Who Is for Law and Order? (1957) 54

Who Is for Civilization? (1957) 56

The Weakest Link in the Struggle (1958) 57

Safeguarding Your Child's Future (1959) 59

Land of the Free and the Hungry (1960) 60

The Winds Have Already Changed (1960) 61

What Makes Americans Run (1960) 63

New Orleans Faces We Still Haven't Seen (1960) 65

The First Giant Step (1961) 67

A Visit From the FBI (1961) 69

FBI Asks Me about Rob Williams (1961) 70

Foreword to "Monroe, North Carolina . . .

    Turning Point in American History" (1962) 72

Part II: *The American Revolution:*
**   *Pages from a Negro Worker's Notebook***

Introduction to Part II   77

     Editors' Foreword to *The American Revolution:*
          Pages from a Negro Worker's Notebook   83

     Introduction   *84*

     1. The Rise and Fall of the Union   *85*

     2. The Challenge of Automation   *100*

     3. The Classless Society   *106*

     4. The Outsiders   *109*

     5. Peace and War   *120*

     6. The Decline of the United States Empire   *126*

     7. Rebels with a Cause   *130*

     8. The American Revolution   *139*

Part III: Black Power: Promise, Pitfalls, and Legacies

Introduction to Part III   147

Liberalism, Marxism, and Black Political Power (1963)   *157*

The City Is the Black Man's Land (1966)   *162*

Black Power: A Scientific Concept Whose Time Has Come (1967)   *171*

Culture and Black Power (1967)   *180*

The Myth and Irrationality of Black Capitalism (1969)   *185*

Manifesto for a Black Revolutionary Party (1969)   *195*

     Introduction to the Fifth Printing   *196*

     Preamble   *200*

     1. Racism and Revolution   *202*

     2. Who Will Make the Revolution?   *204*

     3. How Black Power Will Revolutionize America   *212*

     4. The Black Revolutionary Party   *220*

     Conclusion   *228*

The American Revolution: Putting Politics in Command (1970)   *229*

Beyond Rebellion (1972)   *251*

Beyond Nationalism (1973)   *253*

Think Dialectically, Not Biologically (1974)   *264*

Toward a New Concept of Citizenship (1976)   *274*

The Next Development in Education (1977)   *284*

Liberation or Revolution? (1978)   *293*

The Challenge Facing Afro-Americans in the 1980s (1979)   *306*

Part IV: Community Building and Grassroots Leadership in Post-Industrial Detroit

Introduction to Part IV   317

Letter to Friends and Comrades (1984)   *322*

Going Where We Have Never Been: Creating New Communities
   for Our Future (1986)   *324*

Community Building: An Idea Whose Time Has Come (1987)   *331*

Rebuilding Detroit: An Alternative to Casino Gambling (1988)   *341*

We Must Stop Thinking Like Victims (1990)   *347*

What Does It Mean to Be a Father? (1990)   *349*

Why Are We at War with One Another? (1990)   *351*

A "No" Vote Will Say Detroiters Want to Save What's Left (1991)   *353*

How Will We Make a Living? (1991)   *355*

Why Are Our Children So Bored? (1991)   *357*

What Can We Be That Our Children Can See? (1991)   *359*

Time to Act Like Citizens, Not Subjects (1992)   *361*

What Time Is It in Detroit and the World? (1992)   *363*

We Can Run But We Can't Hide (1993)   *365*

Beyond Civil Rights (1993)   *367*

Why Detroit Summer? (1993)   *369*

Afterword by Grace Lee Boggs   371

Notes   373

Index   387

Preface

James Boggs eludes singular classification. A southerner by birth and disposition, he maintained throughout his life the cultural outlook, sensibilities, and language (he refused to stop speaking his "Alabamese") of the rural black community in which he was raised. Yet, he lived nearly his entire adult life in Detroit, where he easily adapted to the rhythms of city life and immersed himself in political struggles emanating from the labor, racial, and class patterns of the urban, industrial North. He was a factory worker for twenty-eight years in a Detroit auto plant, and he loved to work with his hands—fixing the plumbing, painting the house, helping a neighbor repair a car, or doing housework—but he was also a writer. During and after the years he spent in the auto industry, Boggs wrote two books (and coauthored two others) as well as dozens of essays, pamphlets, reviews, manifestos, and newspaper columns. He therefore exemplified the organic intellectual.[1] We should not, however, allow this label to elide his tireless activism or downplay the mentorship he provided to younger radicals both black and white. Indeed, a variety of labels have been assigned to him, including union militant, revolutionary Marxist, theoretician, Black Power activist, radical author, and community organizer. Each describes a particular moment or dimension of his political work, but none of them alone fully captures his activist career or his significance as a historical figure.

This volume invites readers to discover James Boggs—his ideas, the depth of his political commitments, the character of his intellectual engagement—through his writings. The works collected here span many facets of his intellectual and political work from the 1950s to the early 1990s. They document his personal trajectory, following him through some of the most significant political currents and movements of the mid- and late twentieth-century United States, particularly as they unfolded in Detroit. In the process, this volume offers a unique angle from which to view and interpret the history of political struggles following World War II. Specifically, his body of work illuminates at least three important dimensions to the study of this era: the role that ideological debate played in the evolution of black political movements during this period; the issues, objectives, and tensions faced by grassroots activists (particularly in Detroit) who organized and mounted local struggles; and the ways in which such local struggles related to and at times helped forge larger national movements. Furthermore, Boggs's writings (and organizational work) during the 1960s and 1970s help us better understand the origins and development of the Black Power movement, while his work during the 1980s helps clarify the movement's complex legacy.

We can also enrich our understanding of the historical and theoretical development of twentieth-century radicalism through an engagement with Boggs's ideas and the political struggles out of which they developed. His critical encounter with Marxism places Boggs in a long line of black thinkers—figures such as Hubert Harrison, W. E. B. Du Bois, and Oliver C. Cox from the first half of the twentieth century, as well as Boggs's contemporaries such as Harold Cruse—who confronted Marxism as a theoretical framework for black political action and in the process critiqued, revised, and eventually rejected key tenets or theoretical propositions of Marxism.[2] Boggs embraced Marxism in the 1940s as a critical theory of capitalist development and a useful guide for political struggle. However, as important contours of the postwar world took shape through the 1950s—anti-colonial revolutions in the third world against the backdrop of the cold war; the rise of the modern black freedom struggle concomitant with the ascendancy of American global economic and military power; and the wide-ranging impact of technological change on American industry and the labor movement—he ultimately found Marxism insufficient as a theory of revolution in the late twentieth-century United States. The selections in this volume reveal Boggs's critical assessment of Marxism and document his attempt to grapple with the challenges and opportunities for radical action in his own time.

Finally, James Boggs's writings offer a compelling grassroots perspective on the transformation of postwar Detroit. Scholars have recently begun to explore important questions about the causes and consequences of urban change in postwar America.[3] Some of the most compelling examples of this work directly explore the relationship between black political mobilization and changes in urban economic and political dynamics.[4] As a historical figure, James Boggs shines a clarifying light on this relationship. From the dual lens of an activist (and thus participant) and as an astute and critical observer, Boggs's writings from the second half of the 1960s through the early 1990s consistently raised challenging questions arising from the interconnected developments of deindustrialization, economic decline, shifting racial demographics, and black political power in Detroit. These writings are of various types: theoretical pieces about political organizing in cities with growing black populations (and black mayors); analytical assessments of urban social, economic, and political changes; and personal, passionate reflections on the challenges facing urban youth in post-industrial (and increasingly dangerous) Detroit. While diverse in form, all of these pieces share a desire to create new ideas for what he saw as a new and pressing struggle: to rebuild community life and to revitalize and re-spirit the city. His work therefore provides a record of thought and activism (community-building efforts, organizations created, struggles mounted) that documents how African Americans engaged and struggled with (rather than only being victimized by) urban economic collapse and social inequality during the postwar period. By focusing our attention on the ways in which activists in one city understood, analyzed, and challenged urban decline, his writings show how Black Power politics evolved into community-based attempts to fashion a new vision for the post-industrial city.

This is the first published anthology of James Boggs's writings. His contributions to black political thought and to Detroit movement politics have been recorded in both scholarly works and popular settings, but Boggs has yet to receive in-depth scholarly attention.[5] This volume, therefore, seeks to introduce him to a new generation of thinkers and activists, as well as to general readers. Another goal of this work is to facilitate future research into Boggs's work and the broader historical, political, and theoretical currents within which he participated. The book's introduction, which explores Boggs's intellectual and political influences while setting out the contours of his thinking, is designed to provide contextual information and a historical framing within which the reader may productively engage Boggs's ideas.

The selections are organized chronologically into four sections that show the evolution of his thought and political activity. Part 1 presents some of his columns from *Correspondence* newspaper written during the 1950s and early 1960s. These writings reflect his simultaneous engagement with the organized left, the labor movement, and especially the burgeoning civil rights movement, and they show him beginning to work out an analysis of the African American struggle that moved fluidly between local, national, and international political developments. Part 2 presents the complete text of Boggs's first book, *The American Revolution: Pages from a Negro Worker's Notebook.* Originally published by Monthly Review Press in the summer of 1963 (just a month before the historic March on Washington), this book marks Boggs's emergence as a significant intellectual and political figure at a critical juncture in the evolution of the civil rights movement and American liberalism. The writings in part 3 show Boggs's engagement with major intellectual discourses and political developments from the mid-1960s through the end of the 1970s. In particular, these essays, pamphlets, and speeches reflect his participation in and analysis of the origins, growth, and demise of the Black Power movement. Part 4 contains pieces written from the early 1980s through the early 1990s, the last decade of Boggs's life. The writings in this section illustrate how his political experience and evolving vision of a world transformed had led him to engage the challenges of post-industrial Detroit. Some of these selections are being published here for the first time; others had previously gone out of print or were relatively obscure and difficult to access.

As these writings reveal, James Boggs had a profound respect for ideas. He sought to develop new ways of thinking about society, thinking that would generate new concepts for how people might relate to each other and open new paths of social organization and human activity. The selections that follow reflect the concerns and challenges of particular historical moments—as Boggs wrote in the preface to his second book, these pieces were "not written for all time but for our time."[6] But his writings also project a vision for an ever-expanding humanity, a vision, therefore, that speaks to the ongoing struggles to realize our better selves and a better world. This book is offered as an entry point, a window into James Boggs's evolution as a thinker and activist who thought and cared deeply about those struggles.

INTRODUCTION

The Making of a Revolutionist

Asked during a 1975 interview how he identified himself, James Boggs replied, "I describe myself as a revolutionist." This was for Boggs a characteristically bold pronouncement, but it was not the posturing or empty rhetoric of a self-aggrandizing militant. In claiming to be a "revolutionist" Boggs did not mean to simplistically situate himself alongside Mao Tse-Tung, Ernesto "Che" Guevara, Amilcar Cabral, Ho Chi Minh, or the other revolutionary icons of the day. Nor was he suggesting that he possessed insights or abilities unique to himself—"everybody," he told the interviewer, "has the potential to be a revolutionist." Rather, Boggs's self-ascription reflected his vision of an activist and theoretician who self-consciously assumed responsibility for grappling with fundamental social and political challenges. He had, by the mid-1970s, derived this self-concept from more than three decades of political activity, and by calling himself a *revolutionist*—as opposed to a *revolutionary*—he was making a clear distinction, one that his activist experience had taught him was important. "A lot of people are revolutionary," he explained, "that is, they have radical views they think ought to be interjected into society and they believe that society should be motivated by these views." However, a revolutionist not only is "revolutionary" but also accepts the responsibility of leadership. This, he said, involves projecting a philosophy of change, developing a method or form of struggle based on a new ideology, and organizing to change society along the lines of this new ideology.[1]

Boggs's self-definition as a revolutionist is a useful starting point for an assessment of his historical significance because it highlights two important dimensions of his intellectual and political work. First, his readiness to claim the label revolutionist is an example of his intellectual confidence and self-assuredness, characteristics that led him to take bold political positions and make grand theoretical projections. Speaking to a university class in 1991, he shocked his youthful audience by asserting: "I don't believe nobody in the country knows more about running this country than me." The students immediately broke out in laughter, causing Boggs to pause for a moment before he went on to explain: "I'm not being egotistical, I'm saying you better think that way." He had an unwavering belief in his capacity to not only analyze but also help transform society, and he encouraged the same in others, particularly young people. "Everyone is capable of going beyond where they are," he told the class, "and I would hope that everybody in this room thinks that, OK? That's going to be one of the biggest challenges, to believe that you can do what has not been done yet."[2]

Second, Boggs's identification as a revolutionist reflects the centrality of revolutionary change in his thinking and political practice. As we will see, a consistent objective in his activism and writing—perhaps the driving theme of his work—was his attempt to develop a concept of revolutionary change appropriate for the late twentieth-century United States. With his wife, workmate, and comrade, Grace Lee Boggs, he came to see revolution as reaching a new stage in the evolutionary advance of humanity. They arrived at this conception through their participation in the labor movement, the left, and the post–World War II African American freedom movement, decades of activism and theoretical work in which the Boggses steadily refined their thinking about revolutionary change. Ultimately, they understood revolution as more than a struggle to take power, to claim rights, or to improve material conditions; it was a struggle toward the conscious creation of a new expanded human identity. "A revolution is not just for the purpose of correcting past injustices," they wrote in their 1974 book, *Revolution and Evolution in the Twentieth Century.* "A revolution involves a projection of man/woman into the future. It begins with projecting the notion of a more human human being, i.e., a human being who is more advanced in the specific qualities which only human beings have—creativity, consciousness and self-consciousness, a sense of political and social responsibility."[3]

The writings in this volume chart James Boggs's development as a thinker and activist who continually pushed toward an ever greater understanding of revolutionary possibilities and who particularly concerned himself with the purpose and means of an American revolution. These selections also necessarily document the remarkable intellectual and political partnership he shared with Grace Lee Boggs. As they worked and struggled together over the course of forty years, they generated a rich body of ideas, writings, and organizations. To contextualize this body of work, we turn now to a brief snapshot of James Boggs's political style. This is followed by a review of his early experiences and influences. The remainder of the introduction lays out the major political currents within which he participated and illuminates the contours and central concerns of his thinking.

The Man Who Would Not Be King

While his intellectual and political work was fixed on the revolutionary transformation of society in the broadest sense, the foundation of James Boggs's activism was essentially local. That is to say, he was rooted in the experiences, problems, and struggles of the specific communities to which he belonged, and his activism grew from those realities. From the 1940s to his death in 1993, Boggs cofounded or helped build dozens of organizations, participated in countless marches, picket lines, and meetings, wrote numerous essays, leaflets, and manifestos, and touched many struggles large and small. He shared platforms with Malcolm X and Stokely Carmichael, though his political meetings typically took place in living rooms, in basements, or around kitchen tables. During the 1950s and 1960s he built organizations with well-known figures such as C. L. R. James and Rev. Albert B. Cleage Jr., but he derived equal if not more satisfaction from his work with lesser-known activists and the groups he founded with them, such as the National Organization for an American Revolution (NOAR) in the 1970s and 1980s and Detroit Summer, the youth program founded the year before his death. He carried on political dialogues with international figures, including Kwame Nkrumah and Bertrand Russell, but these were secondary to the discussions and debates he carried on with neighbors, fellow Detroit activists, and grassroots organizers in numerous community settings. His books reached a wide audience among leftists and black activists and were translated into several languages, but this was not the whole of his intellectual production. Indeed, books represented only one dimension of his intellectual output: one might just as likely encounter his ideas through his self-published pamphlets, his contributions to community newsletters or letters to the editor, his articles in local black nationalist newspapers or obscure leftist periodicals, or the many speeches he gave to university students and other audiences. Even when engaged in national movements, Boggs's activism was rooted in local experience and generally operated through grassroots struggles, community-based relationships, and activist networks that he continually built over decades.

Another important dimension to Boggs's political practice was his generous and compassionate way of engaging people. "Jimmy," as many people called him, was a decidedly political person, but his political passions were frequently and perhaps most clearly expressed through social interactions and interpersonal relationships. Detroit poet Willie Williams captured this in his poem "The Man Who Would Not Be King (for James Boggs)," a tribute to Boggs written for his memorial service. Williams described Boggs in the following way:

> The right question asker
> in a closed-mouthed society
> asking them even of himself
> Activating activists
> across state lines
> across gender lines
> across generational lines
> even beyond the grave
> A hate hater
> lending love to the struggle
> by example.[4]

Many of Boggs's political collaborators have similarly commented on the centrality of love to his political work. Indeed, such commentary can provide specific insights into the character of Boggs's political activism, so it will be instructive to review the remarks of various people—activists representing distinct stages and sites of struggle over forty years—reflecting on Boggs's life and legacy. These statements testify to Boggs's downhome manner, the power of his plainspoken yet profound ideas, the wide array of people and movements he touched, and the imprint left by his many years of activism.

Consider the powerful reminiscences from two of Boggs's former comrades from the 1950s. Selma James (the third wife of C. L. R. James) praised Boggs as "that rare being, a civilizer in politics." Thinking back to when they first met in 1952, she recalled that "Jimmy's wealth of information about how society actually functioned, his warm and sweet temperament and his enormous social gifts were all already prominent then, and these clearly never left him. He was in training to be the community teacher others knew later."[5] Filomena D'Addario, whose association with Boggs extended over decades, praised him as "a rare human being" and spoke in particular to his humanizing leadership style and the ways in which personal relationships and a communal sensibility consistently undergirded his intellectual and political work.

[H]e was a leader in thought and action. But I believe his distinction as a leader was reflected in his deep concern and feelings for the human condition. His writings speak to us about the human condition in general. But anyone who met Jimmy and was moved by him can speak of how he touched their lives in particular. We are accustomed to hearing that the foremost quality for leadership is charisma. But charisma is lackluster when compared to Jimmy's genuine concern for everyone he met and with whom he unhesitatingly compared and shared ideas.[6]

The historian, activist, and theologian Vincent Harding, whom Boggs met in the 1960s, also noted Boggs's balancing of political questions and human relationships. He appreciated that Boggs's "powerful politics never overcame [his] powerful humanity" because he "always found time to be the loving compassionate uncle, brother and constant friend to us all." In the process, he "constantly reminded us that one of the central purposes of all our political struggles was to create space, time, and environment for that kind of profound and humane caring."[7]

These qualities were especially evident in Boggs's relationships with and mentorship of younger activists. One of these was Bill Strickland, an activist and radical intellectual who was active in the civil rights and Black Power movements during the 1960s and 1970s and who spent time with the Boggses throughout the period. "Few memories are as lasting, or as fond, or as important to me intellectually," Strickland wrote, "as are my memories of those talks on the phone or talks in Jimmy and Grace's living room; grappling with the latest developments in 'The Struggle.' These discussions enlarged my capacity to know and think and act less blindly. They also gave me a lesson in how a revolutionary intellectual thinks with clarity, reflects with humor, and speaks out in courage." Referring to the Boggses eastside Detroit home, Strickland added that "[t]he Boggses University on Field Street was a great place to learn and be warmed in the fire of a politically exciting intellectual hospitality whose like I have not encountered since."[8]

Activist and poet Gloria House (Aneb Kgositsile), who was a member of the Student Nonviolent Coordinating Committee (SNCC) when she met Jimmy and Grace Lee Boggs "in their warm expansive house" in 1966 or 1967, gives further evidence of Boggs's role as movement elder and mentor.

What was it about Jimmy that made it possible for him to give such inspiration to fellow-fighters? It was his deeply-rooted belief in himself and the kind of life he had chosen that enabled Jimmy to support others who made revolutionary choices. Fully centered in the integrity of his own cultural heritage, his political direction, his personality and character, Jimmy was free to be intensely involved with social problems, emerging ideas and proposed actions. He seemed to be striving always to understand, respond to, be a part of social change that moved us closer to fulfilling our humanity.

As a revolutionary Jimmy showed us that one's life can be an integration of physical labor, grassroots activism and intellectual production—a way of living that challenges the traditional elitism of the American left, thrives on the love and support of family, friends and comrades, and points the way to the community building of the future.[9]

It was this combination of attributes that drew many activists to Boggs and that allowed him to lead by example, to teach and instruct and challenge people to grow and continually push themselves to new frames of thought and new levels of political commitment. This was especially the case during the 1970s and 1980s, when the end of the Black Power movement and a general rightward shift in the nation's political culture seemed to stifle the exploration of radical ideas and foreclose the possibility of progressive social change. With his nearly four decades of movement experience and his continuing commitment to revolutionary change, Boggs could offer counsel and perspective to the younger activists he encountered and worked with, activists who had come of age in the 1960s and wanted, either implicitly or explicitly, to extend the struggles of the black movement and the new left. Boggs helped them develop a practice of critically examining and learning from previous struggles to fortify their analysis of contemporary conditions for the purpose of projecting a new vision of change. It was in this context and for this purpose that Boggs and others created NOAR, through which Boggs influenced and nurtured many activists.

Kenneth Snodgrass, a Detroit activist who began working with Boggs as a teenager in the late 1960s, was one of them. Over the course of two-and-a-half decades they "developed a close relationship—one that, at varying times, was father-son and mentor-mentee," through which Snodgrass came to value the impactful roles Boggs played for him and others, "from giving advice to providing leadership to developing ideas."[10] Another NOAR member, Rich Feldman, was a 1960s student activist turned Detroit auto worker and radical community organizer who met Boggs in the early 1970s. He similarly cherished his experiences with Boggs, who grew to be a friend, mentor, and teacher to Feldman. Among the lessons he took from Boggs, Feldman recalled that whenever Boggs spoke, "at the university or at a high school, a church or a union hall, in a living room or on TV or radio, [he] respected each individual and squeezed out a lesson to teach, inspire, and empower." Feldman also learned from Boggs "to demand the highest human standards of all people" and to build political analyses and programs that were "always looking forward."[11]

Sharon ("Shea") Howell, who also met Boggs as a young radical in the early 1970s, is another NOAR member who counts Boggs as a passionate and powerful teacher as well as a dear friend. She became one of the Boggses' closest comrades ("we were inseparable," Grace recalled),[12] and the time they spent together, both in political work and socially, impacted her in multiple ways. Here she highlights the role of love in Boggs's political vision and practice.

Jimmy taught me that revolutions are made out of love for people and for place. Love isn't just something you feel. It's something you do every day when you go out and pick up the papers and bottles scattered the night before on the corner, when you stop and talk to a neighbor, when you argue passionately for what you believe with whomever will listen, when you call a friend to see how they're doing, when you write a letter to the newspaper, when you give a speech and give 'em hell, when you never stop believing that we can all be more than we are. And he taught me that love isn't about what we did yesterday; it's about what we do today and tomorrow and tomorrow.[13]

By the mid-1980s another generation of activists gained mentorship, inspiration, and political wisdom from James Boggs. Errol Henderson, who had been a student activist at Wayne State University and later a community activist, worked with Boggs in Save Our Sons and Daughters (SOSAD), a grassroots organization combating youth violence in Detroit during the 1980s and 1990s. Henderson remembered Boggs this way:

Mr. Boggs remained relevant to each subsequent generation he came into contact with. He would consistently challenge you on your own terms and then transcend your terms. He understood and practiced a philosophy that even the most militant and adversarial conflicts must be organized around principles rooted in love, mutual respect, and freedom from all relationships of domination. He never rested on the laurels of struggles past. He would never accept, especially in his later years, those who spoke of struggling in their time. He felt any time and all time was our time, and he seized it, shaped it, and helped to mold so many of us into conscious agents of human liberation.[14]

It is appropriate to turn finally to Grace Lee Boggs for insight into the ways that relationships grounded James Boggs's political activism and community-based work. "People in the community came to him for advice on community issues . . . [and] with their personal problems," she recalled in her autobiography. "[H]e helped them write for their birth certificates or process a grievance at work. They listened to his advice on how to cope with their cars, their children, or their spouses as if he were their minister. He loved being a notary public so that he could certify documents for friends and neighbors, never accepting payment."[15] Throughout their four decades of marriage and political partnership, Grace observed Jimmy's unwavering commitment to a community-based political practice.

Jimmy was especially caring toward young people and elders. We watched three generations of young people grow up on Field Street, where we lived for more than thirty years. He called them "my girls" and "my boys," kept track of how they were doing in school, and was always ready to help them with their homework or with advice about a summer job or how to get a loan. . . . During the Vietnam War he counseled hundreds of young Detroiters on how to register as conscientious objectors. To this day I receive phone calls from some of those whom he counseled, asking if there is anything they can do for me because they have never forgotten what he did for them.[16]

These statements attest to a generosity of spirit at the heart of James Boggs's political commitments. This generosity had many sources. Its root lay in his southern upbringing, where it was nurtured and fortified. It then flowered through his experiences in the labor movement during the 1940s, his participation in black struggles of the 1950s, 1960s, and 1970s, and his involvement in community-based struggles during the 1980s and early 1990s. In 1992, a year before his death, the *Detroit News* ran a profile on James Boggs celebrating this long record of committed activism. It dubbed him "An American Revolutionary" and both Boggses "philosopher kings of Detroit's social left."[17] For his part, Jimmy reconfirmed the identity he had claimed for himself decades earlier: "I call myself a revolutionist." To elaborate, and to explain the wellspring and foundation of his many political efforts, he added: "I see myself as a person imbued with the mission of advancing humanity. My ideology is changing with one constant cornerstone: it must always advance humanity."[18]

His ideas for advancing humanity were by this time, with the twentieth century coming to a close, focused on rebuilding communities in post-industrial Detroit. But he had learned his first lessons on community building and social struggle in a very different setting: rural Alabama during the early part of the twentieth century.

Southern Roots: Making a Way out of No Way

James Boggs was born on May 27, 1919, in Marion Junction, Alabama, about twelve miles west of Selma in Dallas County.[19] He often described his place of birth, then a mostly black town of about 1,100 people, as a place "where white folks were gentlemen and ladies by day and Ku Klux Klanners by night." It was a place, he added, where "they hung someone nearly every weekend so that we would be nice fellows the rest of the week."[20] If Boggs exaggerated the frequency of lynching in his hometown, he nonetheless captured the pervasive threat of such violence in the world to which he was born, one marked by racial terror. Across the country, seventy-eight black people were murdered by lynching in 1919, the year of Boggs's birth. Indeed, his birth occurred at the beginning of what came to be known as the "Red Summer" of 1919, when white mobs attacked black citizens and communities in twenty-five cities and towns across the nation between April and October.[21]

But racial terror was not the sole or even the dominant force in James Boggs's young life.[22] His family and community provided a nurturing environment in spite of and as a counter to the oppressive social climate of Jim Crow and white supremacy. The youngest of four children born to Ernest and Lelia Boggs, young James picked blackberries and worked in cotton fields as a child. He attended school in Selma and then Bessemer and at an early age became something of a scribe, penning letters for elderly people in the community who had not learned to write.[23] Throughout most of his adult life as an activist, he credited the community in which he was raised for instilling in him a sense of responsibility and an appreciation for struggle, a sensibility that is captured in the African American folk saying "making a way out of no way."[24] Speaking to a group of friends and fellow activists in Detroit at the beginning of the 1990s, Boggs recalled: "The environment which I grew up in said to me very early that listen, 'you have to make a way out of no way.'"[25] He credited this lesson from his childhood with instilling in him a personal and communal sense of struggle, a resolve in the face of seemingly insurmountable obstacles. Reflecting a sensibility forged in the post-emancipation and Jim Crow South and passed down through subsequent generations, the phrase "making a way out of no way" signifies both a collective cultural consciousness and a credo of individual behavior built upon a shared experience of faith, resilience, and hope in African American communities.[26] Boggs's invocation of the phrase not only highlights the importance of this tradition in his early life but also signals that it was a central ingredient of his political identity.

The person in his life who perhaps most exemplified this tradition was his great-grandmother Big Ma. She was born into slavery during the early 1850s and lived into her nineties. Thus, her life had been touched by the brutalities of slavery, the coming of emancipation, and the many hardships that arrived in its wake. And she shared these experiences through an intergenerational dialogue with young James and his siblings. She told them about the spirituals sung by the enslaved and about the brutality of masters toward enslaved children. She told them about the origins of the "buck dance," when "white people would come up and say 'N——r, dance', and then start shooting around the feet of blacks so that they would dance like everything."[27] As an elder, she was a source of historical knowledge and an important presence in James's childhood and adolescence. She was able to give him a unique and powerful sense of historical change, and he learned from her the centrality of struggle in the lives of African Americans. "When she talked about slavery," Boggs recalled, "she always talked not about how they freed the slaves, but about how [slaveholders] surrendered. There was a big difference. She saw the change as something that had been won by somebody, not something that had been given. She realized that there had been a struggle and that somebody had to lose."[28] This historical sensibility—and especially an understanding of the continuity of struggle in black people's lives—proved to be a foundation for Boggs's intellectual development and political thinking.

Urban Groundings: Coming to Detroit

If James Boggs learned his initial political lessons from his family and rural community in the black belt of Alabama, he came of age politically and intellectually in the rapidly expanding urban black community and industrial landscape of Detroit. In 1937, at the age of eighteen, Boggs decided to trade Jim Crow for a chance in the big city. Well over one million black southerners had made that decision during the preceding two decades, many of them during the World War I–era Great Migration. This mass migration had already propelled enormous growth of black urban communities outside the South. The existence of these communities and the experiences of migrants—related through letters, visits home, and reports in the black press, among other ways—seemed to provide irrefutable evidence that in the North could be found a new racial order and prospects for a better life. Thus, for Boggs and many like him, the decision to leave the South came relatively easily. "Every time someone went north," Boggs explained years later, "they came back talking, telling a bunch of lies about how good things were there . . . you didn't come back until you had a big car and other stuff to let people know you were doing well up North. I believed all those lies, too."[29]

Of course, the promise of the North was reinforced by its corollary: southern repression. "You have to remember," Boggs told an interviewer, "I was born in the South and could see, on a day-to-day basis, the oppressive conditions and the aggressive measures that whites used in order to instill their form of domination in the minds of blacks. It's out of that context that I became a rebel. Or, to be more exact, a renegade from the South. By 'renegade,' I mean that I was one of those who left."[30] Among the renegades preceding him were his two older brothers and some of his uncles, who settled in Detroit and found work in the auto industry.

Early one June morning in 1937, James Boggs arrived at the home of his uncle in the African American enclave on Detroit's lower east side. Weeks earlier, after their graduation from Dunbar High School in Bessemer, Alabama, Boggs and a friend from Marion Junction, Joe Perry, climbed aboard a freight train headed north. With no change of clothes and one dollar between them (they ran out of money on the second day), Boggs and Perry "bummed" for food in places like Cincinnati and St. Louis as they "hoboed" their way to the Motor City. This is how Boggs describes his arrival: "I came in on a train from Toledo. Got off at the Ford River Rouge plant, and I walked down Michigan Avenue to downtown Detroit, asking the police in Dearborn and all down that route where was Theodore and Hastings. That's where my uncle was living." On his way to his uncle's home on Hastings Street, the heart of Detroit's black community, Boggs immediately became aware of the scale and novelty of his surroundings, the place that would be his new home. "This is the first time I had ever been to a big city," he reported. "I had been to cities like in Alabama, but they wasn't nothing like Detroit. Detroit was the first big city I'd ever been to."[31]

Indeed, Detroit was "the big city." When Boggs arrived it was the fourth largest city in the nation and was in the midst of a tremendous period of growth. At the beginning of the twentieth century, Detroit ranked thirteenth in population among American cities with 285,704 residents. A decade later, the city had the ninth largest population, at 465,766 people. Between 1910 and 1920, the population more than doubled to 993,675, and during the 1920s the population continued to grow, adding nearly 600,000 people. By 1940 Detroit was home to 1,623,452 residents; only New York, Chicago, and Philadelphia had more people. Both black and white migrants from the South fueled the city's population boom, and while the number of whites was larger, African Americans migration significantly changed their proportion of the city's total population. Between 1910 and 1920, which includes the World War I–era Great Migration, the black population increased nearly eightfold from 5,741 to 40,838. During the 1920s the black population in the city tripled to 120,066, and during the depression years the number climbed to 149,119. In 1910 African Americans made up 1.2 percent of Detroit's population; by 1940 they constituted 9.2 percent of the city.[32]

The driving force of this surge in population was Detroit's booming industrial economy, led by the automobile industry. When auto production in the city began at the turn of the twentieth century, plants required relatively little capital and were operated by small-scale designers and assemblers. Before 1913, when Henry Ford first deployed the assembly line, most auto workers were skilled workers. Over the next two decades, however, technological innovations transformed the automobile industry and demand for automobiles skyrocketed. The industry came to be dominated by large manufacturing companies and skilled workers were replaced by low-skilled and unskilled assembly-line workers. By 1920, the auto industry employed 135,000 workers, many of them at wages well above the national average, and the city's economic and social landscape was transformed.[33]

While Detroit earned its label as the Motor City during the first two decades of the century, it was in the 1930s that the city established itself as a union town. During the economic boom of the 1920s Detroit remained a solidly "open shop" city with a fragmented and relatively weak union movement, but the massive unemployment and economic malaise of the depression—along with the active mobilization of the Communist Party, among others—fueled a rising militancy and spurred collective action. The emergence of Unemployed Councils in 1930–31, the Ford Hunger March in 1932, and a wave of strikes in 1933 signaled the arrival of mass labor activism in Detroit and helped set the stage for the consolidation of industrial unionism with the formation in 1935 of the United Auto Workers (UAW) union and the Congress of Industrial Organizations (CIO).[34] The next year, the UAW launched a "sit-down strike" against General Motors in Flint, about sixty miles north of Detroit. Workers occupied plants of the leading auto producer for forty-four days, resulting in a union victory in February 1937. The Flint sit-down further galvanized the labor movement in Detroit, as a wave of sit-downs spread across the city in March 1937. Thousands of UAW members and supporters occupied Detroit's major automobile plants as well as nearly 130 offices, stores, and factories in a range of industries throughout the city, large and small. On May 26, 1937, just days before Boggs's arrival in Detroit, the escalating conflict between labor and employers found bloody expression in the "Battle of the Overpass," where UAW organizers attempting to leaflet the Ford Rouge plant suffered a severe beating at the hands of Ford Service Department men.[35]

Thus, when James Boggs hopped off a freight train in Dearborn and walked into Detroit in June 1937 he faced the great promise and potential peril of a major American city. It was a city of sprawling factories and newly constructed skyscrapers—two very different symbols of the city's recent economic boom—but it was also a city bursting at the seams, straining to meet the basic needs of its expanding citizenry. It was undoubtedly a city of opportunity, but many of the newcomers were unemployed and hungry, nearly all of them jostling for space. It was, too, a city soon to be swirling with racial tension and antagonism as the mass migration of African Americans into the city pushed against (and would eventually transform) the city's racial boundaries.

Indeed, the two terminus points of Boggs's initial trek into the Motor City—the Ford River Rouge plant and Hastings Street—were especially apt symbols of the city's competing and contradictory realities. The Rouge plant, situated in the city of Dearborn on the southwestern edge of Detroit, was a grand icon of the automobile industry and an awesome symbol of industrial might. Built between 1917 and 1925, the massive Rouge factory complex stood as a ready example of the promise of mass production. The Rouge plant would also come to symbolize Detroit's powerful labor movement, as it was the site of the bloody Battle of the Overpass and the target of the UAW's bitterly fought but ultimately successful drive to organize Ford workers in 1941 (which was largely responsible for solidifying the city's labor movement). Moreover, the Rouge was home to UAW Local 600, one of the largest and most progressive local unions in the nation.[36]

Hastings Street, meanwhile, was both sign and substance of black Detroit. It was the major thoroughfare and economic lifeline of Black Bottom, Detroit's main African American neighborhood. Located on the city's increasingly cramped lower east side, Black Bottom showed a distinctly different face of Detroit's industrial economy. Beset with the vice and squalor of a segregated black ghetto, the area also boasted a thriving business community and the bustling nightlife of Paradise Valley, the black entertainment and commercial district. Hastings Street, which ran through Paradise Valley and extended northward for several blocks, represented all these aspects of black life in Detroit.[37] Along Hastings could be found bars and nightclubs, churches and grocery stores, apartment buildings and hotels, funeral homes and illegal gambling houses—nearly all manner of business activity, entertainment, and social life.[38] Celebrated and memorialized in the artistry of blues musicians and poets, Hastings became black Detroit's most famous street.[39] It both resulted from and symbolized a rapidly growing urban black community, women and men building institutions and cultural life in the context of—and against—the adversity of racial discrimination and economic privation.

Black Radicalism in the Big City

This was the black community in which James Boggs would make his home and, ultimately, make his mark. His first destination in the city, his uncle's home at Theodore and Hastings, sat just a few blocks north of the renowned Forest Club, a sprawling entertainment complex at the corner of Forest and Hastings. Under the ownership of Paradise Valley icon Sunnie Wilson, the Forest Club was one of the area's most popular destinations throughout the 1940s. But it was not the city's nightlife that brought Boggs to Detroit; it was the promise of good wages in the auto industry. His uncle had been the first African American to be hired at the Budd Wheel plant on Charlevoix, and Boggs expected to land a job there as well. He did not, however. Employment in Detroit's auto industry during the depression proved hard to come by, especially for African Americans. Instead, he found occasional employment doing day work, painting houses, and at car washing establishments before eventually landing a Works Progress Administration (WPA) job digging curbstones in the northwestern area of the city. He returned to Alabama in 1938 to marry to his first wife, Annie McKinley, and then came back to Detroit where he continued working for the WPA. As part of the WPA work program he completed eighteen months at the George Washington Trade School where he trained to be a template maker.[40]

In 1940 Boggs took a job at the Chrysler assembly plant on Jefferson Avenue, where he would work for twenty-eight years. Boggs's opportunity to work in the auto industry did not come from his trade school training but from the economic impact of World War II. As he would later say, "Hitler and Tojo put me to work in the plant."[41] His seemingly sympathetic reference to the leaders of Nazi Germany and Imperial Japan was not meant to signal approval or endorsements of the Axis Powers of World War II but to highlight the link between the conflict abroad and the sweeping changes in the American economy, specifically in employment practices in Detroit's auto industry. In his first book, *The American Revolution: Pages from a Negro Worker's Notebook,* published in 1963, Boggs laid out the analysis more explicitly.

With the coming of the Second World War, Negroes up North made use of the opportunity created by the weakness of American capitalism to organize the March on Washington movement. Out of this movement came Executive Order 8802, opening up jobs in defense industries to Negroes. Negroes did not give credit for this Order to Roosevelt and the American government. Far from it. Recognizing that America and its allies had their backs to the wall in their struggle with Hitler and Tojo, Negroes said that Hitler and Tojo, by creating the war which made the Americans give them jobs in industry, had done more for them in four years than Uncle Sam had done in 300 years.[42]

This passage is noteworthy for two reasons. First, the incisive language provides an example of Boggs's rhetorical style. Second, the passage suggests Boggs's sense of historical development, which was an important element of his intellectual and political work. He identifies his own experiences as part of broader changes in society, namely the impact of World War II on black workers in Detroit, and constructs historical meaning for African Americans out of these developments. Indeed, the tremendous demand for military production during the early 1940s led Detroit's automakers to convert their plants to the mass production of military goods such as airplanes, tanks, and other equipment. As a major center of wartime production, Detroit became an "arsenal of democracy," and one consequence was the opening up of industrial jobs to African Americans in much greater numbers than in any previous period. Historian Thomas Sugrue describes World War II as "a turning point in black employment prospects" in Detroit's industrial economy as a "chronic shortage of labor forced manufacturers to hire blacks and women for jobs that had been restricted to white men."[43]

In addition to a tight labor market, the agitation and activism of civil rights organizations, black community leaders, and the UAW helped open up jobs for African American workers during the war years.[44] Indeed, the early 1940s saw the emergence of an alliance between black Detroit and the UAW. This alliance proved critical for the consolidation and success of the union and was an essential feature of an increasingly strong and visible black working-class political presence.[45]

Thus, James Boggs's entry into factory work and Detroit's industrial economy coincided with a pivotal historical juncture in the development of the labor movement and black politics in the city. He joined Chrysler Local 7 of the UAW and became active in union politics. He was a member of the local's organization committee, generally known as the "flying squadron," which provided protection and support for striking workers throughout the city. According to B. J. Widick, members of UAW flying squadrons were "colorfully garbed union militants chosen for their aggressiveness in defending picket lines."[46] Boggs was also very active in the anti-discrimination efforts of Local 7's Fair Practices Committee, for which he served as secretary throughout the 1950s and early 1960s. By the early 1960s, Boggs was a strident critic of the UAW and the labor movement, but he was nonetheless clear that it was in the labor movement that his politics took root and began to flourish. "My early experience was in the union," he told an interviewer decades later, "and that's where I got my real organizing skills—in strikes, wildcats, picketing, goon squads, stuff like that."[47] And he was not alone. The labor movement provided an important space for many black activists.

"Black workers," Boggs continued, speaking of the World War II era, "began to create a new social milieu and an arena of struggle inside the plant."[48]

More broadly, the overlapping and intersecting political worlds of 1940s Detroit—industrial unionism, left-wing politics, civil rights activity, and a black community growing in size and militancy—provided the space for Boggs's political development and maturation. Boggs was part of a generation of black workers who found in the UAW a platform for various forms of working-class black activism. They developed organizing skills, gained exposure to many currents in radical thought, and used the union as a political base from which to mount efforts to address racial discrimination both inside and outside the plant. Boggs thus joined other black UAW members who, as they moved in and out of other black institutions, constructed significant networks of black political activity.[49]

Boggs's participation in the NAACP's efforts during the 1950s to fight racial discrimination in restaurants and other public places serves as an illustration of how these networks formed and operated, while also providing a window into Boggs's political trajectory and development. In October 1949, after receiving numerous complaints of discrimination in restaurants along Woodward Avenue and in the downtown area, the Detroit Branch of the NAACP formed a committee on restaurant discrimination (popularly known as the Discrimination Action Committee, or DAC). Many black UAW members, including Boggs, joined the committee. Combining direct action tactics with legal challenges, the committee met Friday evenings at the St. Antoine YMCA to organize interracial teams of volunteers sent to challenge the practices of restaurants known to refuse service or otherwise discriminate against African Americans. The DAC eventually expanded its efforts to include other public spaces such as roller rinks, bowling alleys, bars, and hotels, ultimately forcing dozens of establishments to comply with Michigan's public accommodation statute, the so-called Diggs Act barring discriminatory treatment by public facilities.[50]

Ernest Dillard, a member of the NAACP board of directors as well as a General Motors employee and active member of UAW Local 15, organized and chaired the DAC.[51] Dillard's leadership in this effort (as well as the participation of Boggs and other UAW members) points to a defining feature of black politics in postwar Detroit, namely the overlap and exchange between civil rights agitation and the labor movement. Furthermore, both Boggs and Dillard were associated with the Socialist Workers Party (SWP), one of the groups active in the Detroit left. That these (and other) black auto workers were simultaneously involved in these seemingly disparate political arenas—the NAACP, the labor movement, and the left—was not especially unique or surprising. Rather, it reflects the fluid activist community and political environment in which black workers and others operated. This is not to say that no ideological differences or class divisions existed among these political formations; certainly they diverged in key aspects of their analyses and proscriptions. But these differences were not insurmountable—at least not in this particular historical moment—and did not preclude some measure of overlap and even collaboration.[52]

Explaining his participation in the DAC to an interviewer years later, Boggs remarked that he and the other UAW members "called ourselves infiltrating the NAACP in order to make them carry out a more aggressive campaign."[53] Thus black workers such as Dillard and Boggs—who lived and worked and struggled within the mutually reinforcing racial economy and political economy of postwar Detroit—apparently felt no contradiction in going back and forth between meetings of the middle-class-led NAACP, the working-class culture of the union hall, and the revolution-minded SWP. More to the point, they saw each of these as a viable vehicle or means of struggle.[54]

This, then, gives us a snapshot of the intellectual and political milieu in which James Boggs developed into a radical. Indeed, through his affiliation with the SWP, Boggs came in contact with and eventually joined a small Marxist collective known as the Johnson-Forest Tendency (JFT). As a member of JFT and its successor group, Correspondence, he would develop some of his most important political influences and collaborators—most notably Grace Lee Boggs.

Correspondence and Grace Lee Boggs

Taking its name from the pseudonyms (or "party names") of its two leaders, Trinidadian C. L. R. James (J. R. Johnson) and Russian-born Raya Dunayevskaya (Freddie Forest), the Johnson-Forest group began in the early 1940s as a faction within American Trotskyism (initially in the Workers Party and later in the SWP). James, the group's most prominent figure, was one of the foremost Trotskyist theoreticians as well as a major international participant in Pan-African politics. Dunayevskaya, who had served a translator and personal secretary for Leon Trotsky, and had been active in radical politics since the 1920s was an impressive intellectual and Marxist theorist with a profound understanding of political economy. With their innovative formulations of Marxist theory, these two formidable intellectuals drew adherents of the Tendency (who were also known as Johnsonites), forming an energetic collective based in New York City with a loose network of members in other cities, including Detroit.[55]

A key figure in the group, in effect its third leader, was Grace Chin Lee (whose "party name" was Ria Stone). The daughter of Chinese immigrants, Lee was born in Providence, Rhode Island, in 1915 and raised in New York City. At the age of twenty-five, she earned a Ph.D. in philosophy from Bryn Mawr College. Rather than pursue a career in academia, she moved to Chicago in 1940—the same year that James Boggs began working in the auto industry—and quickly plunged herself into the intersecting worlds of World War II–era racial and radical politics in the nation's second largest city. Lee lived near the University of Chicago on the edge of the city's south side, the so-called black belt where the vast majority of African American Chicagoans lived, and she was greatly influenced by powerful mass black political mobilization that she observed. She was especially influenced by the March on Washington Movement. She joined the Workers Party (WP) and worked with its South Side Tenants Organization. In the WP she met C. L. R. James. He was the group's leading theoretician on the "Negro Question" and had recently formed JFT. By 1942 Lee had moved to New York to become an active member of the Tendency. Over the next decade, she played a central role alongside James and Dunayevskaya as the group engaged in a rigorous and sustained study of Marxist theory and philosophy. Collectively they produced a dazzling body of writing on revolutionary theory, the Soviet Union and the development of international socialism, the labor movement, the American working class, and the revolutionary potential of the independent struggles of African Americans for democratic rights.

James Boggs became an active member of the group after it broke from the Trotskyist movement and relocated its base to Detroit in the early 1950s. As a newly independent Marxist organization, the group renamed itself Correspondence (taking its name from the Committees of Correspondence from the American Revolution) and began publishing a newspaper of the same name. To be written, edited, and circulated by its readers, the paper was conceived as a unique experiment in democratic participation and intellectual exchange. As the editorial statement in the first issue states: "CORRESPONDENCE is a paper in which ordinary people can say what they want to say and are so eager to say. Workers, Negroes, women, youth will tell in this paper in their own way the story of their lives, in the plant, at home, in school, in their neighborhoods, what they are doing, what they are thinking about."[56] The paper's orientation and focus on these social groups reflected the organization's political analysis of American society and its position that revolutionary social change could only come about through the self-activity and mass mobilization of the working class—led not by organized labor but by rank-and-file workers with the active participation of other marginalized or disaffected groups, namely African Americans, youth, and women. Jimmy Boggs, therefore, was an ideal member of the organization and the perfect candidate to work on the paper.

For his part, Boggs found in the JFT and especially in Correspondence, an organization that was ideologically consistent with his experiences and his primary political concerns. Indeed, he was witness to the sapping of revolutionary potential of the labor movement that Correspondence theorized: he had been in the left-wing caucus of the UAW led by George Addes and R. J. Thomas; he saw the rise of Walter Reuther's faction after World War II and the subsequent purging of radicals from the union; and he experienced the Reuther group's heavy-handed steering of the UAW, riding the waves of McCarthyism and cold war liberalism toward the Democratic Party and away from the insurgency of the union's recent past.[57]

Grace Lee moved to Detroit in 1953 to work on the paper, and the next year she and James Boggs, whom she had met two years earlier in New York, were married. In midcentury Detroit, a city with a small Asian American population and still quite resilient patterns of racial segregation, James and Grace Lee Boggs no doubt made an unlikely and uncommon couple. Nonetheless, they settled in a black neighborhood on the city's east side—where they eventually became well-known community activists—and were recognizable figures in Detroit radical politics. Over the next four decades, James and Grace Lee Boggs created an unconventional yet amazingly generative personal, intellectual, and political union.

If socially theirs was an uncommon paring, the Boggses were also somewhat of a political anomaly. As a black factory worker from the rural South and a New York–raised Asian American woman with a Ph.D. in philosophy, neither of them fit the standard profile of

Marxist radical. Certainly, they were unlikely candidates for leadership of a small revolutionary socialist organization. Yet, by 1957, with C. L. R. James living in London and Raya Dunayevskaya no longer a member of the group, the Boggses assumed the primary leadership of Correspondence. Grace was by then editor of the paper, which comprised the group's primary activity, and Jimmy[58] was elected the group's chairperson.[59] He also did a substantial amount of the writing for the paper, including a column he wrote under the pen name Al Whitney, which appeared on the "Special Negro News" page.[60]

Through these columns Boggs presented commentaries and analyses of black political life, both in Detroit and nationally. A common thread in nearly all of his columns during the mid-1950s was a focus on the everyday struggles of ordinary black people, and he frequently asserted that through such struggles, "Negro rank and filers" were bypassing an inept, self-serving black elite leadership (which he often called "the talented tenth"). Some columns connected contemporary political dynamics to historical subjects, such as resistance to slavery (one column refers to the case of Margaret Garner, whose act of infanticide in the 1850s inspired Toni Morrison's 1987 novel *Beloved*).[61] Boggs also wrote about the relationship between African Americans' struggle for democratic rights and the labor movement. He frequently used his column to criticize the UAW for its failure to adequately respond to the demands of black workers, chiding the union for failing to close the gap between its anti-discrimination rhetoric and its dismal record on actually rooting out discrimination in the union and in employment.

His condemnation of the union was in part a reflection of the ideological position of Correspondence, but it was also born of experience. The organization's particular interpretation of Marxism (especially its theory of revolutionary change) and analysis of the American labor movement led its members to reject unions and all bureaucratic structures in favor of the "self-activity" of the working class as the true agent of change. For his part, as an auto worker and union activist since 1940, Boggs witnessed firsthand the UAW's steady retreat from the great promise of cross-racial worker solidarity heralded by the CIO's militancy during the late 1930s, the apparent triumph of interracial trade unionism in the 1941 Ford organizing drive, and the World War II upsurge of black demands for defense jobs and industrial democracy. Furthermore, he served for several years as the secretary of his local's Fair Practices Committee, which tried to push the union toward stronger anti-discriminatory action. Thus, he knew well the UAW's failure in the eyes of black workers during the 1950s. As he recalled years later, with the struggles against Jim Crow intensifying during this period, black "UAW members began to kind of transfer their interests from the union to working in the civil rights movement."[62]

With the dramatic civil rights campaigns of the early 1960s—namely, the sit-ins in 1960 and the freedom rides in 1961—Boggs emphasized not only the failure to eliminate discrimination in the union but also the union's lackluster and conditional support of the broader civil rights struggle. For example, his June 3, 1961, column, "The First Giant Step," chastised the "great American labor movement" for "standing by, doing nothing" as others in the nation mobilized to support and aid the freedom riders. Boggs sent a telegram to UAW president Walter Reuther (which was reprinted in Boggs's column), urging the union to actively support the Freedom Rides.

In the name of common humanity and as an expression of labor's support of the cause of freedom and equality at home, urgently request that the UAW-AFL-CIO immediately organize and send a fleet of integrated buses of freedom riders to Alabama.

James Boggs, Chrysler Local 7

Fair Practices Committee[63]

It is doubtful that Boggs expected Reuther to implement his idea or that he believed his telegram would compel the UAW to find other ways to more actively participate in the black struggle for full citizenship. More likely, Boggs's aim was to publicly register his contempt for the union's anemic commitment to racial democracy. Also, Boggs's call to the union to engage in the civil rights struggle was an implicit statement of his view that the UAW was no longer, as it had been in the 1930s, a force for social change.[64]

Indeed, as strident as his critique of the UAW's racial politics was, Boggs's strongest indictment of the union was his declaration of its obsolescence. In April 1961 he gave a speech titled "The State of the Union—The End of an Epoch in the UAW," which outlined, as he saw it, the rise and fall of the union. Anticipating the analysis he would make in *The American Revolution,* Boggs told his Detroit audience that during the 1930s the CIO dealt a "crippling blow" to "the domination of American life by the Almighty Dollar" when it organized militant workers ("the ranks on the shop level") to take control of the factories and in the process create new relations between workers and management.[65] But these gains were eroded during and after World War II when a series of developments, including the no-strike pledge and collective bargaining, transformed the union from a vehicle of worker insurgency and progressive social action into a bureaucratic interest group.

Perhaps the most significant development responsible for the union's growing futility and eventual demise, according to Boggs, was the advent of automation. As large-scale manufacturers increasingly automated their production facilities during the 1940s and 1950s, this labor-saving technology allowed them to increase production while decreasing their workforces, resulting in the reduction and in some cases elimination of job categories in a range of industries. The problems of displaced workers and unemployment consequently grew into national concerns, and by the early 1960s a national debate among politicians, labor leaders, business executives, and intellectuals emerged over the impacts of and appropriate responses to automation.[66] Boggs argued that the technological advances represented by automation signified a new mode or stage of production in American industry that was eliminating the need for the mass worker. In this "new Age of Abundance," he boldly proclaimed, "enough could be easily produced in this country so that there would be no need for the majority of Americans to work."[67] But the UAW and other labor unions were stuck in the framework of a dying era. "Today in the Sixties," Boggs wrote, "the American labor movement has reached the end of the road."[68]

Boggs's commitment to dialectical thinking drove his analysis of automation and led him to his conclusions about the end of the labor movement. "To think dialectically," he explained, "is to recognize that reality is constantly changing and that new contradictions are constantly being created as old ones are negated."[69] He therefore insisted on the need to create new concepts to fit new realities and political circumstances, and he argued that ideas which at one point are progressive can become reactionary at another point. Thus, he could conclude in March 1963 that labor unions' call for full employment was "as reactionary today as 'rugged individualism' was in the 30s."[70] He believed that automation was ushering in a new stage of economic development. Indeed, he saw it as a new era of production in the process of replacing the system of mass production (and mass employment) from which industrial unionism sprang. The need for mass labor was vanishing, he said, and the union had no answer to this profound change.

The American Revolution

Boggs's dialectical thinking led him in the early 1960s to break with Marxist orthodoxy. Based on his analysis of the political and economic development of the United States during the years following World War II, including in particular his assessment of automation, organized labor, and the rising African American struggle for democratic rights, Boggs argued that changes in the United States called into question Marxist concepts of class formation and revolutionary change. Specifically, he came to reject the idea that the industrial working class (and the American working class in particular) would be the agent of revolutionary change, a basic tenet of Marxist theory. Boggs saw the decline of the labor movement and the upsurge of the civil rights movement as simultaneous developments of the postwar United States, which together signaled a profound shift in political alignments and possibilities. He was convinced that whatever revolutionary initiative the labor movement claimed during its heyday of the 1930s had now passed to the black struggle. That is, Boggs argued that African Americans, through their organic struggle for equal rights and full citizenship, were bumping up against the basic structures of American society in a way that could potentially shatter the entire social, economic, and political system; during the postwar era the black struggle, he said, had usurped the American working class as the agent of revolution.[71]

Boggs presented his critique of Marxism, along with his analyses of automation and the black struggle, in *The American Revolution: Pages from a Negro Worker's Notebook*.[72] Published during the summer of 1963, this book reflects Boggs's attempt to explore, in his words, "the potentialities of the American revolution."[73] He said that the traditional Marxist scenario of revolution was appropriate for the nineteenth century (when Marx and Engels made their analyses of capitalism) and had even been able to some extent to predict the rise of the CIO during the 1930s. But it was inadequate for the mid- and late twentieth-century United States. Given its economic and military power, the United States stood as "the citadel of world capitalism today,"[74] a counterrevolutionary behemoth at a time of growing social upheaval at home and revolutionary ferment abroad. Marx and Engels foresaw a long period of industrialization that would produce a constantly growing and increasingly concentrated working class whose conflict with capital would lead ultimately to social revolution. But this scenario had to be updated, Boggs argued, in light of capitalism's recent development. "Today when automation and cybernation are shrinking rather than expanding the work force," he said, "a new theory must be evolved."[75]

He was in effect grappling with the emergence of what we have now come to call the "post-industrial" economy. He recognized the process of deindustrialization as it was happening in Detroit and elsewhere in the country, and he attempted to analyze not only the social impacts of these changes but also their political implications. He wrote of a "growing army of [the] unemployed" made up of production workers displaced by automation as well as a new generation of young people without work "who have never been and can never be involved in the system."[76] This was not simply a problem of temporary or structural unemployment to be addressed through job-training programs, public works projects, or similar means, but the much more severe problem of a large group of people for whom there is quite literally no place within the economic order. Boggs labeled such people "outsiders." While he may have overstated the impact of automation, or perhaps he failed to foresee American capitalism's ability to adapt and reconfigure itself into an information and service economy, Boggs nonetheless captured an important development and enduring dynamic, namely, the transformation of social and economic life as a result of the severe reduction in mass industrial employment. "This," he wrote, "is the dilemma of the United States: What is to be done with the men and women who are being made obsolete by the new stage of production?"[77] To face this dilemma, he asserted, required "a much bolder and more radical approach to society."[78]

Boggs found the seeds of this radical approach in the post–World War II African American freedom struggle. Tracing the development of the civil rights movement from the 1940s through the early 1960s, he concluded that "the development and momentum of the Negro struggle have made the Negroes the one revolutionary force dominating the American scene."[79] Its revolutionary content, he stressed, was not simply in seeking rights or addressing economic grievances but in the ultimate directions that the struggle would be forced to turn and objectives it would pursue: "The strength of the Negro cause and its power to shake up the social structure of the nation comes from the fact that in the Negro struggle all the questions of human rights and human relationships are posed."[80] In particular, Boggs anticipated that the civil rights struggle would soon identify the need for political power as a central task.

The struggle for black political power is a revolutionary struggle because, unlike the struggle for white power, it is the climax of a ceaseless struggle on the part of Negroes for human rights. Moreover, it comes in a period in the United States when the struggle for human relations rather than for material goods has become the chief task of human beings.[81]

This statement is suggestive of two significant strands of James Boggs's thinking: it points to his theoretical engagement with the Black Power movement as it emerged during the mid-1960s; and it forecasts the concept of revolution that he and Grace Lee Boggs would develop over the next decade culminating in the publication, in 1974, of their jointly authored book, *Revolution and Evolution in the Twentieth Century.*[82] In that study, the Boggses synthesized and refined ideas about revolutionary struggle that they developed through their participation in the labor movement, the JFT and Correspondence group, and especially the "black revolution" of the 1960s and early 1970s. Indeed, the path they traveled organizationally and theoretically during the decade between publication of *The American Revolution* and *Revolution and Evolution* provides a revealing map of black political developments of the era. For example, tracking their intellectual and political activities helps us see how the civil rights movement transformed during the middle of the 1960s into a movement for Black Power. Furthermore, their work through the end of the 1960s and into the 1970s—and the networks of activists and organizations that it touched—reveals some of the often obscured dynamics of the Black Power movement that lay beyond the sensationalized images of gun-toting, would-be revolutionaries, dashiki-clad militants, and central cities up in flames. As the writings in this volume demonstrate, the Boggses' intellectual and political trajectory saw them assume the interchangeable roles of activists, analysts, and even architects of Black Power. We can therefore gain valuable insights into the movement's history—its sharp rise and great promise, its intense ideological debates, and some of its stumbling blocks—by tracing the Boggses' trajectory.

Seen in this light, *The American Revolution* represents both an ending and a beginning for James and Grace Lee Boggs. Their ideological break with Marxism led to an organizational break within Correspondence in 1962, and the publication of the book the following year served as a public expression of the end of the Boggses' political relationship with C. L. R. James. At the same time, the book inaugurated a new stage of their political activism. From the early 1960s onward James and Grace Lee Boggs were what we might call movement intellectuals; that is, their intellectual activities grew out of and responded to their specific political activities, and they consciously and consistently carried out the type of intellectual work they deemed necessary to build a social movement.

By the early 1960s, even before the publication of *The American Revolution*, the Boggses had developed an ever-widening network of black activists in Detroit and nationally. In Detroit this included Rev. Albert B. Cleage, Milton Henry, Richard Henry, and their organization, Group on Advanced Leadership (GOAL), as well as the young activists associated with the group UHURU.[83] Local collaborators also included Reginald Wilson and Conrad Mallet, politically conscious teachers who were attracted to the Boggses' analysis of American society and racial oppression and began working with them during the late 1950s. By the beginning of the 1960s, they along with their wives, Dolores Wilson and Gwen Mallet, had joined the Boggses in writing and publishing *Correspondence*.

Among their national political connections of the early 1960s, perhaps the most noteworthy is Robert F. Williams.[84] The Boggses' relationship to Williams began in 1959 when *Correspondence* started their extensive coverage of Williams and the struggle he led in Monroe, North Carolina. This coverage continued through 1961 and included carrying reprints from Williams's own newsletter, *Crusader*, and other writings by Robert as well as his wife, Mabel Williams. The Boggses helped organize support efforts, among other things by sending members of Correspondence to Monroe, both to report on the black community's efforts and to bring supplies (including weapons).[85] After Williams and his family fled the country in 1961, the Boggses continued their support efforts as leaders of the Detroit Committee to Aid the Monroe Defendants (CAMD) and in collaboration with activists and organizations in New York.[86] In 1962, *Correspondence* published a pamphlet on Williams and the Monroe story consisting of two speeches by Conrad Lynn, a mutual political ally of the Boggses and Williams and the attorney for Williams and the other Monroe defendants. Titled "Monroe, North Carolina . . . Turning Point in American History," the pamphlet began with a foreword by James Boggs. The foreword mostly rehearses ideas that Boggs articulated in his writings of the period (particularly *The American Revolution*), but Boggs is nonetheless clear regarding the importance he assigned to the Monroe case: "Monroe, North Carolina, is not the whole United States; neither was Emmet Till the only Negro boy ever killed in Mississippi. But just as Till's lynching and the barefaced acquittal of his lynchers in 1955 were the signal for the Negro people to start their offensive for rights in this country, so Monroe represents the turning point at which Negroes have decided that they must convict their attackers on the spot."[87]

This turning point that Boggs identified—a new militancy reflected by the rejection of nonviolence and the embracing of self-defense—was indeed in ascendency in the early 1960s and by mid-decade helped transform the civil rights movement into a movement for Black Power, a transition both Williams and Boggs helped envision during the early 1960s. Williams's exile, first in Cuba and then in China, prevented a closer collaboration between him and Boggs as Black Power emerged, but they maintained a connection to each other as they continued along parallel and at points intersecting paths within the larger black radical network of the 1960s.[88] From their respective locations, each man played an important role in the development of the Black Power movement—Williams through his historic example of armed self-defense, as a powerful icon of international solidarity, and as a figurehead for the Revolutionary Action Movement (RAM) and the Republic of New Africa (RNA) while abroad; Boggs through his writing, the organizations he helped build, his mentoring of younger activists, and other efforts in Detroit. All of this grew his reputation as an important voice of revolutionary change and his ability to bridge generations of black radicals.

Black Power and Beyond

The publication of *The American Revolution* brought Boggs national (and to some extent international) recognition as a provocative and original thinker, and this helped further expand his network of fellow activists and thinkers. This notoriety also led to numerous invitations for Boggs to speak, participate in forums, and publish his writings. As a consequence, he became an increasingly active figure within mid-1960s black radical political circles, contributing to ideological debates and helping build organizational networks that pushed against the boundaries of civil rights discourse. Indeed, while media attention focused on the efforts of national civil rights organizations to dismantle segregation during the first half of the 1960s, an emergent political perspective among many black thinkers and activists across the country challenged the efficacy and even legitimacy of liberal integrationist politics. In his speeches and writings during the years 1963–66, as the civil rights movement was transforming into a struggle for Black Power, Boggs set out to do the theoretical work for this next stage of the black struggle.

He was also an activist. Along with his intellectual work, Boggs participated in or helped form several political organizations during the 1960s. Indeed, his writing and organizing frequently went hand-in-hand, one being influenced by or growing out of the other. And he undertook most of these efforts in collaboration with Grace Lee Boggs. During November 1963, they helped organize the Northern Negro Grassroots Leadership Conference in Detroit, a gathering of black militants and radicals from across the country, where Malcolm X gave one of his most famous speeches, which has come to be known by the title "Message to the Grassroots." Grace was named secretary and James chairman of the continuation committee. The next year, they were key figures in the Michigan branch of the Freedom Now Party (FNP), an all-black political party based on the principle of independent black political action (a principle that would become, within two years, one of the primary political commitments of Black Power). In 1965 the Boggses convened a meeting of activists and leaders from several radical black organizations to build a coalition group that could push the civil rights struggle in new directions. The two-day affair, which took place in the basement of the Boggses' east-side Detroit home, led to the formation of the Organization for Black Power (OBP) in May 1965—a full year before the Black Power slogan erupted onto the American political scene. During 1964–65 the Boggses also worked closely with Max Stanford (Muhammad Ahmad) and RAM, whose internationalist and revolutionary nationalist program prefigured and in some ways helped launch Black Power.[89]

Each group was short-lived and, if measured by the size of its membership roles or its immediate impact on the movement, could be judged unsuccessful or ineffectual. However, such an assessment misses the significance of these and similar efforts. They were important attempts to work out new political forms, develop and implement new ideas, and devise coordinated strategic approaches. Furthermore, they were forward-looking attempts to assess the new political circumstances emerging from the gains (and failures) of the civil rights movement. Thus, these activities were important steps in the process of movement building and the emergence of Black Power.

Their experiences in organizing the Grassroots Leadership Conference, the FNP, and the OBP informed the Boggses' jointly authored essay "The City Is the Black Man's Land." Published in April 1966 in *Monthly Review,* the essay argued that, with African Americans soon to become a majority in many of the country's largest cities, the black movement should focus on establishing urban political power.[90] In addition to these demographic changes, they cited the recent expansion of the civil rights movement beyond the South and the Watts uprising in August 1965 as significant changes requiring the movement to develop new strategies, programs, and objectives. Moving beyond the call for self-determination and community control of black areas within cities (which would be heard frequently during the late 1960s and early 1970s), the Boggses called for black people to claim control over the administrative functions of cities as a whole (as opposed to black sections or communities within cities). "The war is not only *in* America's cities," they asserted, "it is *for* these cities."[91] Essentially, they theorized a program of black political power in the nation's urban areas as such: "self-government of the major cities by the black majority, mobilized behind leaders and organizations of its own creation and prepared to reorganize the structure of city government and city life from top to bottom."[92] The essay was, in effect, an attempt to deepen the movement's theoretical basis by formulating a revolutionary theory of black urban struggle that would reorganize not just black communities but American society.

"The City Is the Black Man's Land" was the Boggses' first published collaborative work, and as such it is an important marker of their intellectual and political partnership. The essay is an early example of what Jennifer Jung Hee Choi has characterized as the Boggses' "increasingly inseparable ideological and political collaboration."[93] Grace Lee and James Boggs shared a fundamental political outlook, but they frequently differed on specific political questions and at times took opposing positions. Also, their divergent backgrounds and distinct styles often produced compatible but different analyses. This resulted in a generative process of give-and-take in which they learned from and challenged each other. Thus, the nature of their collaboration was such that by the mid-1960s, if not sooner, ideas and concepts flowed freely between.

The essay also reveals another essential component of the Boggses' collaboration, namely the fluid and reciprocal relationship between their theoretical work and political activism. That is, their intellectual and theoretical work was organically connected to their political work, with each informing the other in a dynamic process of mutual generation. Because it both grew out of and critically assessed OBP and other political developments, the essay is a ready illustration of how the Boggses' intellectual and political work fused together. The essay is among those collected in Jimmy's second book, *Racism and the Class Struggle: Further Pages from a Black Worker's Notebook* (several of which, including "The City Is the Black Man's Land," are included in this book). Published in 1970, the book includes essays and speeches from 1963 through the end of the decades, and together they provide informed commentary and critical analysis from within the Black Power movement as it was unfolding.

The Black Power slogan erupted onto the American political landscape in June 1966, two months after the publication of "The City Is the Black Man's Land." Many saw the introduction of the slogan during the Meredith March by Student Nonviolent Coordinating Committee (SNCC) activists Stokely Carmichael (Kwame Ture) and Willie Ricks (Mukasa Dada) as sudden and dramatic, instantly drawing sharp and antagonistic responses. But for people in black communities across the country, the slogan captured a mood that already existed and a political perspective already in the making. Cutting even deeper into an already fractured American racial order, the introduction of Black Power and the emergent militancy that it represented marked the beginning of the end of the civil rights movement. In the turbulent weeks and months to follow, black activists across the country quickly took Black Power as their mantle. New formations such as the Black Panther Party, which was formed in October 1966, sprung up almost immediately, while existing grassroots groups across the country continued their work with renewed vigor under the banner of Black Power. At the same time, two of the most prominent national civil rights organizations, SNCC and the Congress of Racial Equality (CORE), declared themselves Black Power organizations. SNCC and CORE had already begun to question their commitment to nonviolence and liberal integrationism, and both organizations were in the midst of an ideological transformation by the summer of 1966. So the arrival of the "Black Power" slogan put a name to a sentiment that was already there; it articulated for many members of SNNC and CORE—and for the countless others who joined the movement—a new political perspective already in the making.

Commentators of all stripes immediately seized upon the slogan, and within weeks a national debate emerged over its meaning and its impact on the civil rights movement and on the nation. Opinions varied widely, even as to the definition of the term, but all recognized that Black Power represented a fundamental challenge to the precepts and goals of the civil rights movement—that is to say, however amorphous and slippery the concept of Black Power was, it nonetheless represented a new movement. James and Grace Lee Boggs emerged as active and influential participants in the new movement. In an era that produced larger-than-life personalities, the Boggses certainly were not recognizable Black Power figures. Nevertheless, by mid-decade they were widely known within movement circles. Indeed, the Boggses had helped lay the groundwork for the emergence of Black Power both theoretically and organizationally during the early 1960s, particularly in Detroit.

James Boggs emerged as one of the most thoughtful and insightful theorists of the movement. He wrote several articles during the second half of the 1960s, engaging in and trying to shape political and ideological debates of the movement. For example, in "Black Power: A Scientific Concept Whose Time Has Come" and "Culture and Black Power," both originally published in 1967 and collected in *Racism and the Class Struggle*, he foresaw some of Black Power's ideological pitfalls and urged its adherents to base their struggles on a serious analysis of historical and political dynamics, not just the immediacy of the moment. He saw Black Power as a new stage in the historical development of the black movement, and in much of his writing he attempted to develop a theoretical framework for understanding that new stage and advancing the struggle toward revolutionary action. In "The Future Belongs to the Dispossessed: King, Malcolm, and the Future of the Black Revolution" (1968), he exhorted Black Power adherents to recognize that

[w]hen Black Power took over the center stage of the revolution, it was not just a new stage of development. It also required new insights into the positive objectives of the movement different from those defined by King, and a concrete organization to achieve these objectives which Malcolm did not have the time to organize. Black Power now has the responsibility to structure and state its demands and to organize its struggles just as King did for his stage of the movement. When a movement moves from a reform stage to a revolutionary stage, it requires not only people who have developed out of the past but a clear concept of the further development of goals and struggles to achieve these goals.[94]

While James Boggs wrote these and other essays for national audiences, and he intended them to engage broad debates within the movement, he and Grace also attempted to apply and refine their ideas through local grassroots organizing. For example, in October 1966, the same month the Black Panther Party was formed, the Boggses teamed up with Rev. Albert Cleage, one of Detroit's most militant and high-profile Black Power activists, to form the Inner City Organizing Committee (ICOC). The Boggses had worked with Cleage since the beginning of the decade on several efforts, including the Freedom Now Party, and the ICOC grew out of this relationship and their continuing efforts to build a grassroots political movement in Detroit. It also represented one of the many localized expressions of Black Power politics that arose across the nation in the wake of the Meredith March. Conceived as "a disciplined organization whose responsibility shall be to promote the welfare, organize the power and expand the rights of the people of the Inner City,"[95] the ICOC expressed this emergent political consciousness of the historical moment. Like many other local groups that would emerge during the Black Power era, the ICOC attempted to identify and deal with the specific needs and circumstances of black urban communities. However, the group was somewhat unique in that it asserted that residents of the inner city not only had "the right and responsibility . . . to organize for their power, protection and benefit" but also that their struggle took on a broader political and historical significance. This task had "never been more urgent," stated the group's constitution, "than at this stage in history when the vast majority of the population in this advanced country have become urban residents and when all the problems that face mankind in the Twentieth Century are concentrated in the Inner City."[96]

The organizing of the ICOC during the fall and winter of 1966 was part of a wider network of activity among activists building a grassroots movement for Black Power in Detroit. Indeed, the political and cultural activity among African Americans in Detroit leading up to and during 1966 suggests the concept of Black Power had arrived in Detroit before the slogan became a part of the political landscape in June 1966. Expressions of this activity included a militant student group named UHURU ("freedom" in Swahili), GOAL led by Richard Henry, Milton Henry, and Reverend Cleage, an active presence of RAM, Vaughn's Bookstore and its black nationalist collective and study groups, Forum '65, Forum '66, and Forum '67, and Cleage's militant community newspaper, *Illustrated News.*[97] Furthermore, by the summer of 1966 Detroit had also emerged as one of the centers of the Black Arts movement, which was described by Larry Neal, one of the movement's key figures, as the "aesthetic and spiritual sister of the black power concept."[98]

For these activists, as well as for the city (and to some extent the nation) more generally, the concept of Black Power achieved a new level of intensity with the Detroit rebellion in July 1967.[99] Sparked by a police raid of an after-hours drinking establishment (called a blind pig) in the 12th Street area, one of Detroit's largest black neighborhoods, the disturbance lasted five days and claimed forty-three lives (thirty killed by law enforcement officers).[100] In the immediate aftermath of the rebellion, city officials and civic leaders scrambled to make sense of the violence, anger, and deep-seated resentment unleashed during the nearly weeklong uprising, and they quickly crafted a range of responses designed to ensure that the city did not experience a recurrence going forward. Meanwhile, the uprising had squarely focused the city's attention on the various "black militants" who were now seen as an unavoidable if unsettling and even frightening piece of Detroit's social and political landscape. In a series of columns on the rebellion in the *Detroit News*, Louis Lomax, a relatively prominent black journalist, identified six people as most responsible for Black Power activity in the city: James and Grace Lee Boggs, Reverend Cleage, Milton Henry, Richard Henry, and Ed Vaughn.[101] Ostensibly written to explain why the uprising occurred, Lomax's columns were an inflammatory and factually flawed effort, succeeding only in adding to the speculation among newspapers, police, city officials, and others who thought (incorrectly) that the civil disturbance might have been the result of a conspiracy or an organized effort by Black Power militants. The Boggses were in California during the July 23–28 eruption, and they certainly played no role in instigating the rebellion, nor did they have any impact on its course or direction. The rebellion did, however, have an effect on them, as it did activists throughout the city.

The rebellion galvanized Black Power sentiments and political energies in Detroit. Over the next two years several new Black Power groups were formed in the city, many of them organized by people who had been collaborators and allies of the Boggses in local Detroit struggles. For example, in 1968 former members of UHURU and other black auto workers formed the Dodge Revolutionary Union Movement (DRUM), which by 1969 had grown to form the city-wide League of Revolutionary Black Workers (LRBW). Also in that year, the Henry brothers (taking the names Gaidi and Imari Obadele) formed the Republic of New Africa. In yet another expression of black nationalism and Black Power militancy, Rev. Albert Cleage rechristened Central Congregational Church as the Shrine of the Black Madonna Church. Already a center of movement activity, the church and its doctrine of black Christian nationalism was emerging as an important institution in post-rebellion black Detroit. These and other expressions of Black Power politics reflected the intensity and variety of movement activity in Detroit following the July 1967 uprising.

As for the Boggses, Grace recalled that the rebellion "forced us to rethink a lot of philosophical questions."[102] The Detroit rebellion erupted just days after the Newark, New Jersey, uprising, and both took place in the still ominous shadow cast by the Watts uprising in 1965. Together, they demonstrated the powerful impact of urban uprisings on Black Power politics. The urgency, anger, and outrage embodied in these rebellions led the Boggses to reevaluate and further develop their understanding of the revolutionary process and the place of urban black youth and spontaneous rebellions in that process. Thus, as they watched events unfold nationally and in Detroit, the Boggses felt the need "to draw a clear distinction between rebellion . . . and revolution."[103]

Meanwhile, Jimmy continued to receive invitations to speak at universities and conferences across the country. In addition, *The American Revolution* had been published in Italian, Spanish, Japanese, French, Portuguese, and Catalan, bringing his ideas to an ever-widening international audience. In June 1968, as plans were under way to publish a collection of Jimmy's essays in Italian, the publisher invited him to speak to university students in several Italian cities. Thus, in the wake of the student and worker revolt in Paris, the Boggses traveled to Europe, observing political developments and sharing ideas with students and activists throughout Italy and in Paris.[104] From there, they spent a week with African revolutionary Kwame Nkrumah in Conakry, Guinea, where he had been living in exile since being deposed as president of Ghana by a 1966 military coup. In 1967 the Boggses had begun correspondence with Nkrumah, whom Grace had known since 1945, to arrange their visit. The week in Conakry gave them the opportunity to discuss the political situation in both Africa and the United States, which they continued through correspondence and the sharing of writings until Nkrumah's death in 1972.[105]

When the Boggses returned to the United States at the end of June 1968 they revisited their concern with the theoretical difference between rebellion and revolution. The fast-paced and powerful developments within the Black Power movement (including the assassination of Martin Luther King, the subsequent wave of urban rebellions, and the rapid rise of the Black Panther Party) led them also to concentrate on "projecting and initiating struggles that involve [the oppressed] in assuming the responsibility for creating the new values, truths, infrastructures, and institutions that are necessary to a new society."[106] Shortly after returning to the country, they spent time with their longtime comrades Freddy and Lyman Paine on Sutton Island in Maine, where they had wide-ranging conversations about these issues. Through these discussions (which the four continued every summer for several years), the Boggses began working through the theoretical concepts that would inform their next intellectual and political effort.[107]

It was in this context, and responding to these circumstances, that Jimmy wrote, in early 1969, a pamphlet titled *Manifesto for a Black Revolutionary Party*.[108] The pamphlet continued his (and Grace's) efforts to develop a revolutionary program for the Black Power movement. The *Manifesto*'s primary objective was to advance the proposition that a black revolutionary political organization—a "vanguard party"—was necessary to provide revolutionary leadership to the Black Power movement. The *Manifesto* begins with a preamble stating in brief the rationale and general tasks for a black revolutionary party, and then provides in four concise chapters a systematic analysis of the historical development and revolutionary potential of black struggle. Read carefully, and in light of the Boggses' intellectual and political work up to this point, the *Manifesto* is both a record of the ideas they developed through the decade and a manifestation of their commitment, self-consciously as theoreticians, to grapple with the changing circumstances, challenges, and opportunities facing the Black Power movement.

By 1970, Grace and Jimmy were putting into motion their plans to build the type of cadre organization they had projected in the *Manifesto*. Such an organization would address the need to develop new kinds of leadership—leaders who were grounded in a revolutionary ideology and rooted in local communities rather than itinerant, larger-than-life public leaders such as Stokely Carmichael and H. Rap Brown. Toward this end, the Boggses led "revolutionary study groups" with young radical black activists in Detroit. This led to the formation of an organization called the Committee for Political Development (CPD), which later took the name Advocators. CPD/Advocators worked in conjunction with a group of radical black activists in Philadelphia called Pacesetters. The two groups sought to assess the inability of the Black Power movement to respond to the various emerging crises in American political and social life during the first half of the 1970s. To advance their analyses, CPD/Pacesetters wrote and distributed statements on such topics as the Angela Davis case, the Attica prison uprising, Watergate, and the energy crisis. The primary goal of CPD/Pacesetters was to develop revolutionary ideology and disciplined leadership for the Black Power movement.[109]

Also in 1970, the Boggses gave a series of lectures titled "On Revolution" at Wayne State University's Center for Adult Education. These lectures, which grew out of the revolutionary study groups, probed the historical and theoretical lessons to be gleaned from a variety of revolutionary situations, including the Russian, Chinese, and Cuban revolutions, several instances of "the African Revolution" (Ghana, Kenya, and Guinea-Bissau, among others), the "People's War in Vietnam," and "the Black Revolution in the U.S." These lectures led to the publication of the Boggses' jointly authored book, *Revolution and Evolution in the Twentieth Century.* Completed in 1973 and published the following year by Monthly Review Press, the book presented an original and provocative assessment of revolutionary movements at a historical moment that many people considered to be ripe with revolutionary possibility the world over.

Indeed, one of the key arguments of the book, which in some ways the Boggses began developing in the JFT and reworked through the Black Power period, is that those who would make a revolution in the United States should learn from other revolutionary situations but must also and always attend themselves to the specific character of the United States so as to build a revolution appropriate for the United States. "The revolution to be made in the United States," they wrote, "will be the first revolution in history to require the masses to make material sacrifices rather than to acquire more material things."[110] In this forward-looking analysis, they anticipated a strain of thought regarding the nature of progressive social change that has gained increasingly wider acceptance during the four-and-a-half decades since the publication of the book: "We must give up many of the things which this country has enjoyed at the expense of damning over one-third of the world into a state of underdevelopment, ignorance, disease, and early death."[111] Given the prominent role of U.S. consumption and production patterns in creating our current environmental and ecological crises, and with these patterns shamefully implicated in an increasing economic disparity between the global North and South, this passage is especially prescient.

The National Organization for an American Revolution (NOAR)

Revolution and Evolution arrived as the Black Power movement was coming to an end. By the mid-1970s, most expressions of the movement had either succumbed to the harassment and repression of law enforcement agencies, collapsed under the weight of corrosive organizational dynamics and internecine leadership rivalries, or fizzled out as activists moved on to other endeavors. The Boggses believed as well that the movement's inability to project a new vision for society in the face of significant changes in the nation's political economy contributed to the collapse of Black Power. For example, by the mid-1970s black mayors in Detroit and other major urban centers had come to power largely on the strength of black political mobilizations and continued migration to urban centers during the 1950s and 1960s. Yet, these electoral victories and emerging black urban regimes seemed powerless in the face of the disinvestment and deindustrialization that devasted central cities. They similarly lacked a political program to deal with the persistence of urban poverty alongside an increasingly visible black middle class riding a wave of opportunity to suburban neighborhoods and professional careers—a wave that was created largely by struggles for integration *and* for black power. More broadly, by the 1980s—with the election of Ronald Reagan, the deepening of urban crisis, and the radicalism of the 1960s and 1970s safely muted—radicals confronted a dramatically different and at times seemingly futile political landscape.

In this climate and context, the Boggses reconfigured and redoubled their efforts to build a revolutionary organization during the second half of the 1970s, culminating in the formation of the National Organization for an American Revolution (NOAR). Formally organized in 1978, NOAR's origins lay in previous groups such as the Committee for Political Development and Pacesetters, and it grew out of the networks of organizations that the Boggses had developed during the preceding decade and a half. Thus, NOAR in some ways was an organic continuation and extension of their Black Power activism, building on their experiences and theoretical work over the preceding two decades. Yet it was also an attempt to create a new organizational form and to forge a new movement. In NOAR, the Boggses and their comrades sought to build, on a national scale, a "cadre" (as opposed to a mass) organization composed of disciplined and dedicated members. Accordingly, the group was devoted to developing the potential of every member to give leadership and, collectively, to the patient development of revolutionary theory. With "locals" across the country, NOAR envisioned its task as laying the groundwork for dual or parallel power structures and localized self-government. They held public forums, carried out local organizing campaigns, and wrote pamphlets and short statements on contemporary issues and local concerns.[112]

NOAR produced an impressive body of literature of political and social analysis, which they distributed through self-published pamphlets, statements, leaflets, and occasional newsletters.[113] The following statement appeared on all NOAR material:

We are American citizens who have chosen to become revolutionists out of our deep concern for the future of our people and our nation. Our members reflect the rich ethnic diversity of our country. At the same time we place special emphasis on developing Black Americans and other Americans of color into revolutionary leaders—because we know that there will be no American revolution unless those at the bottom are involved in the struggle for a new America.

We believe that eventually we will have to take power away from the capitalists who, in their determination to increase profits, are destroying our right and responsibility to govern ourselves. At this point, however, our main task is to create a movement in the hearts and minds of the American people—so that we can stop seeing ourselves as victims and start exercising the power within.[114]

Implicit in this statement are two ideas that emerged from James and Grace Lee Boggs's theoretical and political work during the 1960s and 1970s and which, along with their comrades in NOAR, they continued to articulate and further develop. One is the concept of "two-sided transformation," which emphasized the need for personal transformation along with structural transformation. For example, they said that revolutionary change required changes in capitalist values as well as institutions. Thus, both the oppressed and radicals, all who would struggle to change the system, must confront their own individualism and materialism while simultaneously engaging in struggles to transform social structures. This idea was embodied in the phrase "Change Yourself to Change the World," which served as the title of a NOAR pamphlet and which members frequently invoked. Second, NOAR called for "a new self-governing America" in which people accept responsibility for making social, economic, and political decisions rather than leaving these to politicians and corporations. This notion of a self-governing America—based on group members' individual and collective experiences in the civil rights, Black Power, and antiwar movements, as well as a reflection of the Boggses' evolving concept of revolution—was an attempt to push beyond the familiar activist frameworks focused on struggling for rights or articulating grievances. It was also an explicit rejection of the Marxist- and anti-colonial-inspired models of revolution as a struggle solely to take power (as in taking over the state). Instead of thinking of themselves only as victims making demands on others (i.e., the system or those in power), citizens must make demands on themselves as well. Through these and other ideas, NOAR attempted to articulate a vision of revolutionary change in which people transform themselves into more socially and politically conscious citizens; the entire society is thus enriched by an expansion and deepening of human identity.

NOAR enjoyed a successful period of intense and effective leadership development, but by the mid-1980s the organization was falling apart.[115] The collapse of the organization was a painful and bitter experience for many members, including the Boggses.[116] They did not, however, despair or retreat from political activity. Just as they had done after the breakup of previous organizations, the Boggses used the NOAR experience as a guide to build new organizations and spaces within which they could continue their political work, seeking again to create new ideas and political practices to meet new circumstances. As NOAR wound down between 1983 and 1985, the Boggses engaged in other activities, including community organizing with the Michigan Committee to Organize the Unemployed and working to close down crack houses. This activism soon grew to full-fledged involvement with grassroots groups and struggles, as they turned their attention squarely to these social and economic challenges that they saw in their own east-side neighborhood and all over the city.

These challenges—the unemployment, poverty, and crime of a city devastated by the flight of industry, an epidemic of youth violence, and the frightful ravishes of crack cocaine—marked the post-industrial landscape of 1980s Detroit. From the mid-1980s to Jimmy's death in 1993, he and Grace participated in or helped found a series of small, community-based organizations that responded in some way to an aspect of the crisis facing the city's residents, who during the 1980s and 1990s were increasingly black and poor. Their efforts helped weave a tapestry of grassroots struggles in post-industrial Detroit.[117] In the mid-1980s they helped organize seniors (primarily women) in a group called Detroiters for Dignity. In 1987 they became involved with Save Our Sons and Daughters (SOSAD), a new organization committed to mobilizing communities to combat youth violence founded by Clementine Barfield, who had lost her sixteen-year-old son in a shooting in the summer of 1986. Throughout the rest of the decade and into the 1990s the Boggses worked with SOSAD to reduce violence, foster a culture of healing and hope, and create meaningful pathways for young people's development.[118] In 1988 the Boggses joined with Dorothy Garner and other local activists to form WE-PROS (We the People Reclaim Our Streets), a city-wide network of neighborhood groups that held regular anti-crack marches in different neighborhoods across the city. Around the same time, they joined a coalition of groups named United Detroiters Against Gambling (UDAG), which successfully defeated Mayor Coleman Young's proposal to legalize casino gambling in the city.[119] The group evolved into Detroiters Uniting (DU), a multiethnic coalition advocating a vision for Detroit based on neighborhood empowerment and opposition to Young's developer-driven model of urban revitalization.[120]

In each of these efforts James Boggs brought his movement experience and his sense of politics as individual and collective human development to the specific struggles being waged. The practice of community building—the need to repair social connections and use these ties as the basis for tackling community problems and meeting community needs—was perhaps the guiding principle of his activism during this period.

Impact and Legacy

Boggs engaged much of this activity as he faced deteriorating health. In 1988, at the age of sixty-nine, he was diagnosed with cancer of the bladder, which required frequent medical tests and several operations, and in 1991 his doctors discovered a cancerous tumor in his left lung. He underwent chemotherapy, which successfully eradicated the cancer in his bladder, and radiation treatment sent the lung tumor into remission. However, another tumor in his lung appeared in 1992. Boggs nonetheless remained active. He gave support and counsel to community activists engaged in local struggles, wrote letters to the editor and columns for the SOSAD newsletter, and continued to speak to audiences of young people, sharing the lessons he had learned from five decades of activism. He shared with them his commitment to revolutionary change and his conviction that ordinary citizens have both the ability and the duty to bring about that change.

These exchanges and interactions with young people during the final years of his life reflect important qualities of James Boggs's political legacy. In particular, it is worth briefly highlighting two characteristics that were central to his intellectual and political identity. The first is his intellectual boldness. He saw himself as a theoretician capable of tackling the most pressing political problems and of projecting grand ideas. Second, he understood political struggle—that is, the task of imagining and shaping society—as available to everyone. Each member of society, he said, had the capacity—indeed, the responsibility—to participate in the life of the community and the broader society. In his final years, Boggs increasingly sought not only to teach and inspire young people but also to empower them, helping them see themselves as agents of change.

Perhaps the most enduring expression of his commitment to empowering young people is Detroit Summer, an "intergenerational multicultural youth program/movement to rebuild, redefine, re-spirit Detroit from the ground up."[121] In January 1992 (just a year and a half before his death) Jimmy, Grace, and a few others developed the idea for Detroit Summer out of their analysis of what was needed to address the city's contemporary political and social crisis and, specifically, their belief that rebuilding communities was an essential component of rebuilding the city. As Grace recounts in her memoir,

Thinking back to how Mississippi Freedom Summer raised the civil rights movement to a new plateau by bringing young people from the North to assist in the Voter Registration Drive in 1964, Jimmy came up with the idea of bringing young people to Detroit to work with local youth in order to dramatize the idea that rebuilding our cities is at the heart of the new movement that is emerging as we come to the end of the twentieth century.[122]

This provides another example of the important role that historical analysis played in Boggs's political vision. It also points up again his use of dialectical thinking. Especially attentive to historical change, he constantly assessed contemporary realities and political challenges and then devised new modes of political activity to bring about change.

Boggs's belief in the importance of dialectical thinking was part of his profound respect for ideas, which he frequently tried to impress upon young people engaged in their own struggles. This was the case right up to his last days. In February 1993, he was put on oxygen. The next month, however, he participated in a SOSAD workshop on movement building. Frail and moving slowly, he nonetheless spoke with a passion and conviction that conveyed his sense of commitment. "I believe ideas are life and death questions, and peoples oughta struggle over 'em," he told the group, in his customary "Alabamese." "My concept of what the duty of a human being is, the chief responsibility and duty of all human beings," he continued, "is to advance human kind to another level of evolution."[123]

Four months after the SOSAD workshop, James Boggs died of lung cancer. His death was not sudden nor did it come as a surprise. In the middle of May he had entered a hospice program. Despite this, he continued to write, speak, and organize into the summer, though at a slower pace.[124] During his final days, his family and close friends attended to him while he received visitors. He passed away at home on the morning of July 22, 1993. His body was cremated, and two memorial services were held on July 31, the first a small family service and the second a larger gathering of family members and dozens of friends.

Three months later, friends and comrades from across the country gathered in Detroit for another memorial, this one a joyous celebration of Jimmy's long commitment to community building and activism. The memorial was called "Celebrating a Life" and included music, poetry, and remarks from friends, all of which was followed by a reception and a roundtable discussion titled "The Struggle for the Future," hosted by Detroit Summer.[125] Grace and two of Jimmy's Detroit comrades, Nkenge Zola and John Gruchala, composed a tribute booklet for the celebration titled *James Boggs: An American Revolutionary* that included dozens of messages from Jimmy's friends and comrades across the country. Their words expressed sadness and a sense of loss, but they also gave testimony to the broad impact of his five decades of political and intellectual work. They spoke of his plainspoken yet profound ideas, his down-home and compassionate manner, and the many ways in which he taught and inspired people. Many of them recalled how he constantly challenged them to think in new ways. And nearly all of them said that, above all, he touched people because he was a kind, warm, and loving person. The booklet vividly captures the interpersonal relationships at the heart of James Boggs's political practice.

Among the attendees of the memorial celebration were Ruby Dee and Ossie Davis, the artists and activists who had been friends of the Boggses since the mid-1960s. Dee and Davis, of course, were themselves a compelling study in marital, artistic, and political union. Over the course of their storied careers and marriage they carefully calibrated their shared commitment to being artists as well as principled and politically engaged citizens. In their remarks at the memorial, they credited the relationship they built with Jimmy and Grace as an important part of their journey. Just days before Jimmy's death, Dee had penned a long poem in his honor titled "For James, Writer, Activist, Worker" that expressed her gratitude for his political passion, theoretical insights, and generosity of spirit. By relating the affections that animated Jimmy's relationship with her and her husband, Dee's poem, especially the following stanzas, eloquently underscores the sentiments expressed throughout the tribute booklet.

> You, dear James, you and Grace, represent
> The nobleness of life
> Stalwart cheerleaders of the
> BETTER WAY contingent
> Water on the seed bed of exciting and
> Necessary choices
> You have certainly opened us—Ossie and me
> To horizons of thought and theory that
> Underline and
> Strengthen so much of what we have done and
> Hope to do in our remaining minutes in the
> Arts. You have taught us ways of thinking
> And looking at Life and its challenges
> That without you
> May have escaped us.
>
> When you move through the glory tunnel
> My heart will track the journey with you
> Shouting
> LOVE, LOVE, LOVE. WE TRULY LOVE YOU.
> Best we so far know how.[126]

These words, along with the many testimonies from others who worked with and were touched by James Boggs, invite us to consider the life and work of a self-proclaimed "revolutionist," an activist and thinker who, though relatively unknown today, was involved in some of the most profound movements for social transformation in the twentieth century. He spent decades thinking, writing, and acting to bring about the next American revolution. His understanding of this revolution—what its objectives will be, who will bring it about, how it will transform society, what struggles it will call forth—grew and evolved into something quite different from previous examples of revolution or standard visions of revolutionary change focused on seizing state power, claiming rights, or increasing material well-being. "The only struggles worth pursuing," he was often heard saying, "are those which advance the whole society and enable all human beings to evolve to a new and higher stage of their human potential."[127] By exploring how he came to this conclusion, we will not only gain insights into the historical periods of which he was a part but we might also open up new perspectives from which to fashion our own visions of transformation in light of the challenges we face today. The writings in this volume offer a place to begin this exploration.

PART I
CORRESPONDENCE NEWSPAPER

Introduction to Part I

Correspondence newspaper played a significant role in James Boggs's intellectual and political development. He worked on the paper throughout its nearly eleven-year existence (from October 1953 to the spring of 1964), serving on the editorial board and writing dozens of articles. He also expended considerable energy soliciting subscriptions, discussing the paper with coworkers and neighbors, and engaging in other efforts to sustain, promote, and build the paper. His work on *Correspondence* proved to be (along with his union activity and local civil rights activism) a central site of Boggs's political work during the 1950s and early 1960s. Writing for the paper gave him an early outlet for his ideas and a venue to develop himself as a writer and political thinker. Additionally, he used the paper as a vehicle for interacting and connecting with people in ways that engaged political and social questions on a personal basis. Indeed, in some ways working on the paper may have been his most intellectually and personally rewarding political activity of the period. "Jimmy loved *Correspondence*," Grace Lee Boggs recalled. "It gave him the opportunity to write, which he loved to do, [and] it gave him the opportunity to get stories from workers, which he loved to do." She recalled further how the two of them would "go out and visit people to get subscriptions and sit around and talk to them. So it was a way of linking up with the community."[1]

Boggs's multiple roles in the production of *Correspondence,* and in particular his direct engagement with potential readers (who were also coworkers, neighbors, and friends), reflect the unique format and purpose of the paper. The idea for the paper emerged in 1951 when the Johnson-Forest Tendency left the Socialist Workers Party and reorganized itself into an independent Marxist organization, taking the name Correspondence and relocating its base from New York to Detroit.[2] Solidifying its break with Trotskyism, the group set out to publish a newspaper based on their vision of socialist revolution led by the self-activity of the working class (rather than organized labor or radical political parties). The paper was to be a new type of workers newspaper, serving as an outlet for the views and experiences of rank-and-file workers. In addition, the paper sought to give voice to three other segments of society—women, youth, and African Americans—whose voices were marginalized in or absent from the mainstream press and the political spaces of "official society." Attempting to distinguish itself not only from the mainstream press but also from other radical papers, the Correspondence group (which eventually took the name Correspondence Publishing Company) organized the paper as a vehicle for the full expression of these four groups. As the masthead of early issues of the paper announced, it was to be "A Paper That Is Written—Edited—Circulated by Its Readers." The conversations that Boggs and other members of the group (which numbered approximately seventy-five at the paper's founding) had with fellow workers and others about *Correspondence* or topics to be discussed in its pages did in fact result in short articles and letters that appeared in the paper, though the group ultimately achieved little success in getting readers to regularly write for and edit the paper.

Correspondence experienced a somewhat turbulent publishing history owing primarily to its chronic lack of resources, both financial and human, but ideological tensions within the organization also contributed to its volatility.[3] It is difficult to know the paper's circulation or the extent of its readership—not only because *Correspondence*'s records are incomplete but also because the paper experienced an irregular publication pattern and because personal relationships figured significantly in how it was distributed—but it seems likely the distribution never grew beyond five thousand.[4] To contextualize Boggs's writings in *Correspondence,* it will be helpful to briefly outline four relatively distinct stages of the paper's nearly eleven-year history.

The first stage spanned eighteen months, beginning with the inaugural issue, which appeared on October 3, 1953, as a twelve-page newspaper published every two weeks. In keeping with the goal of creating a workers' paper, Ford employee Johnny Zupan served as editor, while another Detroit auto worker, Simon Owens (writing under the pen name Charles Denby), wrote a column titled "Worker's Journal" that appeared on the front page of every issue. These early issues also devoted one section each to the four social groups that the organization hoped to attract to the paper—labor, youth, women, and African Americans—treating readers to a lively if at times uneven mix of columns, news stories, first-person accounts of events, and the ruminations of readers on topics relevant to that particular group. Take, for example, the African American section, which was called "Special Negro News." A typical issue would have a column by James Boggs (written under the pen name Al Whitney), news stories on local and national civil rights activities, and a range of first-person articles: someone would recount experiences with discrimination on the job, share thoughts on interracial marriage, or describe a trip down South to see relatives. Three additional significant and distinguishing features of the paper during this period bear mentioning: the "Readers' Views" section, which appeared on the editorial page and was filled with comments from readers on past issues (generally culled from the conversations initiated by Boggs and other members of the group); a strong interest in popular culture, including a section called "Viewing and Reviewing" full of enthusiastic engagement with television, movies, and music; and clever political cartoons that, among other things, frequently mocked labor bureaucrats.

The paper entered its second phase in the summer of 1955, when a split in the organization left it with a diminished publishing capacity and forced those remaining to reevaluate the paper's form, function, and future. McCarthy-era repression proved to be one source of the conflict and dissension that produced the split.[5] The U.S. Postal Service deemed the July 24, 1954, issue of *Correspondence* "un-mailable" because "it tended to incite murder and assassination" (though no specific articles or passages were identified), and in late 1954 the U.S. attorney general placed the organization on its subversive list.[6] This exasperated existing tensions in the group, and in the spring of 1955 Raya Dunayevskaya broke with the organization. Along with her, Zupan, Owens, and approximately half the group's roughly seventy-five members left. This organizational crisis forced *Correspondence* to cease publication during April and May 1955. It resumed in June but in a drastically differ-ent format. For the next two years, the paper experienced an interim phase during which the organization had to regroup and reassess its publishing project. In fact, during this pe-riod it in effect ceased to operate as a newspaper, functioning instead more like a journal of commentary and political theory. Carrying the designation "Discussion Bulletin" in the masthead, these issues appeared only every other month and in a truncated format (some issues were eight pages, others four). Much of the content during this period consisted of theoretical or historical pieces written by C. L. R. James, examinations of factory life in various industries, and articles by or about European workers, radical organizations, and political developments. Many of the features of previous issues—such as the Special Negro News—no longer appeared in the paper, and James Boggs, while he was still an active presence in the organization and production of the paper, wrote very little for the paper. This interim period ended in August 1957, when *Correspondence* ceased its Discussion Bulletins and resumed regular publication.

Thus, in the fall of 1957, *Correspondence* entered the third phase of its development. With Grace Lee Boggs now serving as editor, the paper attempted to return, with some modifications, to its original format and frequency. In March 1958 it began appearing monthly and a year later went to bimonthly. The Special Negro News was gone (as were the sections on labor, youth, and women), but James Boggs again wrote regular columns. While the paper continued to devote the bulk of its space to workers and labor matters, its identity as a workers' paper began to loosen over this period as *Correspondence* gave regular and increasing coverage to African Americans and, in particular, to developments in the rising civil rights movement. For example, the paper ran many stories throughout 1959 and into 1960 on the activities of Robert Williams and the struggles of the black community in Monroe, North Carolina. The most dramatic national developments—most notably the 1960 student sit-ins and the 1961 Freedom Rides—similarly garnered significant space in the paper, both in news articles and analyses. Indeed, under the leadership of Grace Lee Boggs as editor and James Boggs, who in addition to writing for the paper was now the chairperson of the organization, the paper shifted its focus away from workers and working-class struggle to African Americans. By the summer and fall of 1961, this shift precipitated another organizational crisis. Some members of the organization—including, notably, C. L. R. James, who lived in England but exerted a considerable influence over the group and the paper, and Marty Glaberman, a member of the organization since the early 1940s, a loyal comrade to James, and the paper's managing editor since its founding—perceived this shift as reflective of a distancing from if not outright rejection of the principles upon which the paper was founded.

This crisis resulted in another organizational split, marking the fourth and final stage in *Correspondence*'s publishing history. The Boggses left the organization in the beginning of 1962. However, with their longtime comrades Freddie and Lyman Paine (who also left the group), the Boggses retained control of the paper and continued to publish it for the next two years. While the paper maintained the same general look and format of its previous years, its political focus and ideological basis were unmistakably changed. The paper now devoted itself to interpreting and advancing the struggles of African Americans (with a secondary focus on anti-colonial and revolutionary movements in the third world). During this period (from early 1962 to the spring of 1964) *Correspondence* consistently and perceptively chronicled the rising surge of black protest activity, providing its readers with coverage and analysis of the civil rights movement as well as other, less visible, and often more militant or radical strands of African American thought and activism. The Boggses and their now quite small circle of collaborators argued through the paper's editorials and its analysis of political developments that black Americans, not the working class, held the capacity to forge revolutionary change. Among these collaborators was a group of four dynamic young Detroit black activists—two married couples, Dolores and Reginald Wilson and Gwen and Conrad Mallet—who had been drawn to the Boggses in the late 1950s and soon began working on the paper. By the fall of 1962 they played pivotal roles in nearly every dimension (writing, editing, finances, and cartoons) of publishing *Correspondence*, and their involvement helped solidify the paper's political turn away from worker struggles and toward the revolt of black Americans.[7]

Thus, in its final two years *Correspondence* completely shed its identity as a workers' paper and established itself as a journal of black activist politics, or what we might call a *black movement* paper. That is, *Correspondence* now devoted itself to recording and analyzing black protest activity, and it focused, in particular, on the events, organizations, individuals, and ideas that proffered the most radical direction for the black movement. As such, the paper documented a stream of black political activity during the early 1960s, operating largely outside of (and sometimes as a challenge to) the main organizations and ideological contours of the civil rights movement. This stream—characterized by a rising nationalism, strident anti-colonialism, and a challenge to nonviolence, among other things—was barely visible to the mainstream press, but it was a significant force in the evolution of black protest and helped lay the foundation for the emergence of the Black Power movement in the middle of the decade. *Correspondence*'s coverage of this stream aligned it with similar publications of the era such as the monthly magazine *Liberator*, the quarterly journal *Freedomways*, and the Detroit biweekly newsletter *Illustrated News*, all of which were established in 1961 (the year that *Correspondence* transformed into a movement paper). *Correspondence* developed a collaborative relationship with *Liberator* and *Illustrated News*, both as allied and mutually supportive publications and as linked nodes in a growing network of black radical activists in the early 1960s. Through their work on *Correspondence*, James and Grace Lee Boggs deepened their activism, expanded their connections to other activists and intellectuals, and heightened their status as respected figures within black radical circles.

Somewhat paradoxically, the Boggses' increased involvement as grassroots activists during the early 1960s eventually diminished their capacity to publish *Correspondence*. For example, in November 1963 the Boggses were key organizers of the Grassroots Leadership Conference (where Malcolm X gave his now famous "Message to Grassroots" speech), with Jimmy serving as chairperson and Grace as secretary. The next year they were active in building the Freedom Now Party, with Grace serving as coordinator of the organizing effort to get this all-black political party on the ballot in Michigan. In addition, Jimmy published his first book, *The American Revolution: Pages from a Negro Worker's Notebook,* in the summer of 1963 (while working full-time at Chrysler). This brought him greater notoriety, and by 1964 he was in high demand as a writer and speaker and was also increasingly being called upon by other activists to lend his support to or partake in specific protest efforts. This was the backdrop for their decision to cease publication of *Correspondence* in the summer of 1964.

The selections presented in this section, which are a sampling of the dozens of columns James Boggs wrote for *Correspondence,* are meant to provide multiple lenses on his thinking from the early 1950s to the early 1960s. These writings chart his evolution during this ten-year period, which saw considerable shifts both in his own political location (organizationally and ideologically) and in the social movements with which he identified and engaged. At the beginning of this period, he was part of a small Marxist organization that theorized struggle of African Americans for democratic rights as an autonomous spark to the coming socialist revolution to be led by the self-activity of the industrial working class. By the end of this period, he had come to question and even reject central tenets of Marxist theory, forcefully argued that African Americans, not the working class, were the social force best situated to lead an American revolution, and he was helping lay the ideological and organizational foundation for the emergence of the Black Power movement. At the same time, the writings gathered here reveal some continuity in the coordinates of his intellectual and political work by documenting Boggs's consistent engagement with particular themes and concerns, some of which would remain central to his work well beyond the life of *Correspondence.* While his columns over this period addressed a relatively wide field of topics (families' struggles to obtain welfare, civil rights milestones, international developments), they generally fell within one of four areas of concern: life in the plant; expressions of a rising determination among the black masses not only to claim their democratic rights but to forge new social relations; the increasing moral and political failure—and thus futility—of organized labor; and the impact of technological changes on the industrial economy and social relations. Additionally, this selection of James Boggs's *Correspondence* columns documents growth in his writing. As the reader will notice, the later pieces have a quality of exposition and depth of analysis not found in the earliest columns. Finally, these writings present a picture of Boggs's thinking leading up to the publication of *The American Revolution: Pages from a Negro Worker's Notebook,* his first and most enduring work, published in 1963.

Talent for Sale*

Walter White typifies the same thing as Walter Reuther.[†] The CIO is supposed to fight for labor, the class struggle. Walter White is supposed to fight for Negroes, the Negro struggle.

Walter Reuther pretends that he has to beg. Not only does he pretend. He has to because he doesn't use all force of the workers behind him. If the problems of workers were solved, Walter Reuther wouldn't have any job. The same thing applies to Walter White. If it wasn't for the racial question, White wouldn't have anything to do.

All of the so-called Negro spokesmen and Negro leaders are somebody on the basis of fighting for Negro rights. But at the same time, their basis is not reaching these goals, which they blame on the people themselves.

Those people up there are actually individualists. They would sell anybody out just to stay in that atmosphere. Bill Oliver,[‡] Reuther's right-hand man among the Negroes, doesn't make any bones about it. If it is a question of Negro rights vs. his job, he takes his job any time. He told that to three thousand people one time. He said he had a bone to protect and he was going to protect that bone. The same thing about Walter White. Any time the pressure for Negro rights endangers his position, he capitulates. Walter White comes into a Negro meeting and makes a big speech, just like Walter Reuther makes a big speech. And then he walks out of that room, meets some big shots, white and black, and he just lives in that society. And his whole prestige is on the basis that he represents Negroes.

[January 23, 1954]

---

* This is Boggs's first column (it appeared under his pen name Al Whitney). —Ed.

† Walter White was the executive secretary of the National Association for the Advancement of Colored People (NAACP), and Walter Reuther was the president of the United Auto Workers (UAW). —Ed.

‡ Oliver was an African American unionist named by Walter Reuther as the head of the UAW's Fair Practices Department in 1947 after Reuther dismissed black labor lawyer George Crocket from the post. Oliver was relatively conservative and ineffectual, particularly compared to his left-leaning and popular predecessor. —Ed.

Viewing Negro History Week

I can see the speakers everywhere squaring off for annual Brotherhood week and big preparations being made for banquets on the special occasion of Negro History Week.*

I'll always remember my school days when on this week there would be much preparation, just as there is for Christmas. This was the only time I had an opportunity to really find out about Negro people, their accomplishments, and their struggles for recognition of their human dignity. But somehow, after this week I never noticed any change in Negro and white relations.

Every year at the school, there would be two or more speakers who were invited to speak on Negro history that week, generally one was a Negro and one was white. Each speaker would go back into history and pick out some Negro figure and praise him to us. Most of the time it was Booker T. Washington or George Washington Carver, the scientist.

Always, I would feel very proud when they talked about their accomplishments but I would be very confused when it was all over. Always, they would talk about him or her from the standpoint of their personal behavior and this I was much upset over.

DISPROVING A MYTH

The same thing happened to me in later life in relation to Joe Louis. I had a swelling pride in him as a fighter, especially when he was in the ring fighting a white. I would be so nervous, I would be trembling until the fight was over. I felt proud of him for he was a Negro and he was disproving everything that was said about Negroes' inability to do things and proving Negroes were equal to all in every way.

But whenever he was talked about by white society for what he meant to Negroes, they always talked about his role in relation to Negro behavior and that he advanced his race from his personal conduct. His personal conduct I never cared for. He had a "place."

I never wanted to think I had a "place." Negroes detest the idea that they have a "place." Capitalist society has a standard policy to never mention any Negroes who do not accept its idea that they have a "place." To me a Negro's "place" is any place.

---

* Negro History Week was founded in 1926 by Carter G. Woodson. It is now Black History Month. Brotherhood Week was sponsored by an interfaith organization called the National Conference for Community and Justice (formerly the National Conference of Christians and Jews). Both took place during February. —Ed.

I am proud of Negro History Week and what it is supposed to represent. It is the corrupt way of white society that I detest, which uses certain Negroes to portray what they would like Negroes to be.[*]

[February 20, 1954]

---

[*] Next to this column was an editorial titled "On Negro History" that criticizes both "the Communist and official American versions of Negro history." It ends by saying "We are taking this opportunity of Negro History Week to start as a regular feature of this page the *real* history of the Negro people." (Emphasis in original.) Also on this page was a box titled "Negro History" with an article on Crispus Attucks, the black man who escaped from slavery and fought and died at the Boston Massacre. —Ed.

Negro Challenge

It has been over one hundred years since Margaret Garner, a Negro mother, tossed her son into the Ohio River, giving him back to his Maker rather than give him to slavery.*

Everywhere today, where Negroes gather, one hears the common expression, "I'm fighting and working that my son will not have to go through what I had to endure." It is the expression of a fighting race, not to be subdued under the footsteps of slavery and servitude.

Take all the arguments against tyranny, communist or fascist. I know nothing any worse than the argument against equal rights. Yet we find everywhere this age-old argument going on.

In Constant Struggle

Some say it will always be, some say it's something that will be with us for some time, but the Negro every day is in a constant struggle to end it once and for all.

No longer do they contemplate how it should be ended or what time. The question is, "Why should it be at all?"

Negro rank and filers aren't looking to leaders to accomplish this for them but in their everyday way are demanding the right to work, to eat where they please, to talk to whom they please, to go where they want to go and say what they want to say. It is not just that they know they are as good as other races, but that they are showing other races they had better follow suit. This fight for equal rights will tear up the *whole* system of dividing and conquering. Workers of other races have only to look in countries where there are no Negroes to find this same division.

Have to Choose

You cannot have your cake and eat it, too. You cannot be for segregation and discrimination and have a new human relation based on the worker running things the way they should be run.

You have to choose a side. Negroes are not accepting the old phrase, "I like colored people, but . . ." and dozens of reasons, and "but," which end up saying, "the time is not ripe, yet."

Negroes have no particular plan or method. When and where it shows itself, be it in the factory or the street or the neighborhood, they are challenging it.

[August 7, 1954]

---

* See note 61 of the introduction. —Ed.

The Paper and a New Society

Since time immemorial man has fought for certain rights, one of the main ones being the right to freedom of speech. *Correspondence* feels that in this issue that right has been somewhat curtailed. This issue we have only eight pages.*

Thirteen months ago and twenty-eight issues back seventy-five people decided to publish a twelve-page paper. We had a conception drawn from experience and history that the common people needed a paper where they could say what they thought about their government, the way it should be run, what they thought about their jobs and homes, every aspect of their lives. Never in history has there been such a paper. There have been labor papers, but *man's life is more than labor*. It is a full life. It takes in the totality of a *human being*.

This cut means to us that somehow, although we seventy-five contributed over $750 a month and went out and met over a thousand people and got subs from them, somehow we haven't got across to these people what the paper means to us and what it means to them. This paper in a sense is *our whole life and purpose*.

People who never thought that what they said meant anything are saying it. It's being read by thousands of others. We who put out the paper have gained strength. Those we have met have gained strength. They found out that what they felt and thought mattered.

Basis for a New Society

If what *Correspondence* has published could be put into action, it would be the basis of establishing a new society, a society based on what the majority feels. What our readers think would mean the best society that ever was. No society has ever existed before that the bulk of the people have run. Society has always been ruled by the other folks.

If this paper could get the active support of its readers it could get to be a daily. A daily wouldn't just be what poor folks say about society. It would force society to change to what they think it should be.

Your Strength Is Needed

Most of our subscribers are convinced, to one degree or another, that there is a need for such a paper. But we haven't met enough of them and the seventy-five of us can't ever do it. So the only way it can be done is if you, one of our thousand subscribers,

---

*The paper had just completed its first year and was struggling to raise its level of support, both financially and in terms of readers participating in the production of the paper. —Ed.

begin to take the steps of coming to meet us at our editing meetings and at our parties, sending *Correspondence* to your friends, shop mates, and neighbors in your community, sending in your own dimes, quarters, dollars, and subscriptions and asking your friends to send in theirs.

The strength and roots to spread the paper is in you readers. You are in a thousand neighborhoods and have thousands of friends and shop mates that we seventy-five will never be able to reach.

On Your Terms

It isn't a question of "Have we done enough?" We have done as much as our small number will allow us to do. Now, whether we continue is a decision that the readers have to make, based on whether they want a new society on the terms they think it should be, not on the other man's terms. Because that is what *Correspondence* stands for. A new society on the ordinary people's terms.

We are urging everyone, subscriber, contributor, and supporter, to write in, even those who disagree, what they think about this paper and how we can solve this financial problem.

We hope that, along with their criticism, they will send a donation, so that even those who disagree will continue to have a place to say what they think in this period where the right to say what one thinks and feels is threatened more than ever before.

[October 30, 1954]

Sensitivity

The Negro in relation to American society has the sensitivity of an animal that can sense danger, something man can't do. This comes not of his own making but out of the pressure of society against him. A little kid six years old senses first from his parents that there is something different in life that he has to go through that other kids don't have to go through. If he is in the South he finds out the first day he goes to school or even before in the neighborhood he lives in. In the North, too.

That is the early stage. This sensitivity develops more rapidly than anything else about him. Even before he can read or write it develops. In the South the Mr. and Mrs. handle he has to put before white people's names makes him sensitive.

The man, particularly, as the years go by, becomes conscious and more conscious. I think it is when you start going places around the age of ten or twelve that the pressure really begins to bear down. You find the places you can't go to. Whites don't put much pressure on kids, but at this stage they begin to let you know you don't belong.

The Danger Stage

At this stage they begin to separate the sexes, particularly Negroes and whites. They don't play together anymore. In the North that's when they separate boys and girls too.

When you get around fifteen or sixteen you take on a sensitive feeling like people take on age. It grows on you. That is the danger stage too. More than ever, now, you want to challenge.

You get to thinking about your career. What are you going to do after you get out of school? In choosing your trade or your course, you choose on the basis of race first of all. You try to choose a field that Negroes are already in, because you are conscious of the pressure of breaking into a new field.

The real pressure begins when you start looking for a job. You meet a white owner and he asks all kinds of questions. You begin to know where to go, what kind of job to ask for if you want to get hired. You know what restaurant to go in if you want to eat. You know what neighborhood to walk in if you don't want to be molested by police.

Negro Knows More

You know how the birds get still when human beings walk in a forest? Well, you get the same feeling when you walk into a restaurant. Everything stops.

Talk about sensitivity. A Negro can pass with whites but he can't pull it off with other Negroes. And no white could pass as a Negro with Negroes.

It is funny how these things come to you. Whites telegraph it to you. But then one advantage a Negro gets over whites is that he knows more about whites than they know about him. They become insensitive and he becomes sensitive. It is this sensitiveness that is going to make it increasingly difficult every day for whites to pull anything over on Negroes. He watches their every move. In fact, he often can predict this move before they make it.

[January 22, 1955]

The Stage That We Have Reached

All labor leaders, liberals, and radicals always say that the solution to the Negro question is with the class question. In theory that is true. But I think that if you look at the history of the United States from the very beginning, the formation of this country was on a class basis. The people who came over from Europe, the settlers who were getting away from Eurpope, were what we would call today class-conscious people.

But the one thing that makes the Negro question such a dual thing, as I have pointed out before in this column, is this: Even though the Negroes are working-class people, they are at the bottom of the class *as human beings*. Today even though we have had the historical struggles of the CIO, which is the closest thing to a total class struggle that we have had in the United States, you find more and more that the independent struggle of the Negroes goes far beyond the CIO.

Pressure on the CIO

The advancement of the Negroes at this point is far beyond what the CIO itself wishes to cope with. So much so that the CIO at this point has taken just a liberal viewpoint, no more advanced than other classes in society and similar to the liberals back in Reconstruction times who wanted to protect the Union in order to save the country rather than to give everybody human rights. That is the condition which the CIO is in today, while Negroes, even within a working-class organization, are constantly pressuring them to go beyond where they want to go.

Every move the CIO makes at this point is being challenged and questioned by Negroes because Negroes do not expect to find in the CIO what they found in other organizations. At first they saw in the CIO an amalgamation of races. But at this point they begin to question how much the CIO has been using them. What appeared in 1937–39 to be a total social reorganization now seems to them just a way to gain economic means. And the reason the Negroes see this so clearly is that the Negro question goes far beyond just gaining economic means.

An Independent Role

The Negro question means recognizing everybody as a human being. That cannot be bought with nickels and dimes and quarters. More and more the tendency now is that the Negro struggle will take on an independent role, accepting those who give unquestioned concrete support rather than those who talk but still operate on the "big But" and "step by step."

Like on the Supreme Court decision,* anybody now who does not demonstrate that he is wholeheartedly in favor is automatically classed as an enemy of the Negroes. It used to be a common characteristic of Negroes to say, "I heard a white man say this or that," as if the white man had authority on a particular subject. But that no longer prevails. The Negro today is saying, "I think so and so."

This in itself means that the Negro question in the United States is reaching a very new stage, a stage where it is put up or shut up. All the ifs, ands, buts, and hesitations will have to be reckoned with. The initiative has been taken by the Negroes themselves. No amount of intimidation, Klan organization, or reactionary elements will be able to stem the tide. In the minds and hearts of all Negroes is the idea that the solution to the Negro question lies fundamentally with them and that the answers and solutions can only come from their demonstration.

NOT ASKING

I wouldn't ask a white person anymore what he thinks is the answer to the Negro question. Few Negroes are asking. They are telling white people now. The only Negroes who consult with whites about what should be done are those who are scared of the masses of the Negroes themselves and what they will do. And in their concern with whites, these Negroes are doing it because of the pressure of Negroes rather than from the pressure of whites. The whites have lost the initiative. Negroes figure they have had it long enough. From now on Negroes are going to be aggressive, demonstrative, demanding.

American society is today in the position where it can run but it can't hide. So sensitive are Negroes to the Negro question that the minute whites open their mouths, Negroes know what they are going to talk about, how far they are going to go. The minute a white guy gets up on the rostrum, I can figure when the "But" is coming in. Nobody can deceive anyone anymore.

[February 5, 1955]

---

* Boggs is referring to *Brown v. Board of Education.* —Ed.

A Report on the March on Washington

Colored people streamed into Washington by every mode of transportation possible.[*] Old women with run-down shoes, old women well dressed, kids with the South written all over their faces. New York sent eight thousand by chartered bus and car. The most significant of all was the determination of the southern colored women and men.

The NAACP and CIO had hoped to keep the crowd down—the CIO in particular—but they are through on the colored question. They were minor cogs on the platform. The NAACP is something to be watched and studied, for in their loose makeup is room for all types of action.

Television systems were set up for full coverage. All policemen and National Guardsmen were on full duty. Washington was tense. After the singing of the National Anthem, the invocation, a wreath was laid at the Lincoln Memorial by James and Theresa Gordon, who had been in the Clay County riots in Tennessee.[†]

Roy Wilkins cautioned the white American of the danger that exists in the Negro who has been trampled on and the possibility of waking up one morning with a black man superior to them. Three-fourths of the world is black. "Go home South, never despair, the universe is on our side. Keep pressing forward in every school, on the theater, on the sidewalk, on the job." Powell[‡] gave the usual rabble-rousing speech demanding work stoppage, boycott, and a new third party.

REV. MARTIN LUTHER KING

Finally Rev. Martin Luther King came and the hands went up like unto Gandhi. King spoke with the feeling of the crowd. He said only the judicial branch had spoken but the executive branch of Ike and Nixon was quiet. Both political parties have betrayed

---

[*] Boggs is describing the Prayer Pilgrimage for Freedom that culminated with a rally on the steps of the Lincoln Memorial. The pilgrimage was led by Martin Luther King and the Southern Christian Leadership Conference (SCLC) and held on May 17, 1957, the third anniversary of the *Brown v. Board of Education* Supreme Court decision. The pilgrimage was designed to compel President Eisenhower and Congress to support civil rights reforms including the implementation of the *Brown* decision. This was the first major activity of the newly formed SCLC, and King's speech was his first national address. —Ed.

[†] African American brother and sister involved in a school desegregation effort in Clay, Kentucky, during the preceding September. Boggs incorrectly identifies the location as Clay, Tennessee; he likely was conflating the Kentucky case with a similar one in Clinton, Tennessee, that also took place during September 1956. —Ed.

[‡] The Reverend Adam Clayton Powell Jr., a local black community leader in Harlem, New York, pastor of Abyssinian Baptist Church, civil rights activist, and politician. In 1957 he was serving in the U.S. House of Representatives. —Ed.

the cause. Now it is too late. Destiny is ticking out. We must be calm and positive. We shall have the victory and in it all America will gain. History will show that the quasi-liberal is through. There is but one side, the right side, and God is on that side.

The crowd began to disperse after he spoke for he had given them the twentieth-century Karl Marx. Here in America where the Bible is a household product, he used the Bible the same as Marx used capital.

This is the crux: The Bible for the Negro is, in the United States, as of now, his best weapon. The CIO was not even mentioned. Moral principle is the issue; moral principle or the United States will perish. It is this which the leaders sense the masses will fight on.

The southern people went home determined beyond the expectations of even King. No one in the South is big enough to stop this march of the people and no one can call it off.

[August 1, 1957]

Who Is for Law and Order?

The Little Rock school riot* by the white people of that city raises the most serious question in U.S. history.

If white people defy the Constitution, who then are the law-abiding citizens of the United States and who is for democracy?

For years untold numbers of colored people have been forced to maneuver in all directions, trying to avoid a head-on collision over the issue. They have allowed white people to name them "Negroes," by which the whites mean a thing and not a person. They have stayed out of the public parks, restaurants, hotels, and golf courses, walked on the cinder path when meeting whites on the sidewalk, gone to separate schools, worked on the worst jobs under the worst conditions, smiled and acted unhurt when abused in public places. They have fought in two world wars and one Civil War when told by the whites they were fighting for democracy and the American way of life.

All of this bowing and scraping was done to preserve and promote unity between the races.

For years the colored people in the South accepted this way of life. Then suddenly they made an about-face and began pressing for the human rights the Constitution says the American people have a right to. Through their pressure and the legal work of the NAACP, the Supreme Court ruled in 1954 that the Constitution of the United States is valid even if it has never been upheld by the white citizens of the United States.

They began to denounce the use by the whites of the word "Negro" and began forcing whites to call them "colored." Because when whites say "colored," they have to say a colored man or colored woman, and when they use the word "man" or "woman" they are beginning to accept colored people as human beings. They started legal battles for the right to use public parks and public places. They began to go to white schools on the grounds that a country cannot be united and yet separated.

---

* In the fall of 1957, nine black students (who became known as the Little Rock nine) attempting to enroll in the previously all-white Central High School in Little Rock, Arkansas, faced the opposition of white mobs and Arkansas governor Orval Faubus, who ordered the National Guard to prevent the students from enrolling. Following weeks of negotiations, mob violence, and finally Faubus's refusal to comply with the federal court order, President Eisenhower was forced to send federal troops to Little Rock, opening the way for the students' admission to Central. This was the first use of federal power to enforce equal treatment of African Americans in the South since Reconstruction, and the weeks-long crisis became a flashpoint in the civil rights movement as well one of the earliest major news stories of the still young television era. Boggs's column was one of three (the other two were unsigned) in this issue of *Correspondence* that discussed the Little Rock desegregation crisis, all under the banner "Events in Little Rock Mark the End of an Era." —Ed.

They denounced the idea that they must have the approval of whites before they can act and denounced the liberals who straddled the fence and said whites have to be educated into accepting colored people as equals. They have denounced the reasons why they should have fought in the last war for democracy when no democracy exists for them at home.

In every instance where colored people have defied the status quo, they have been the first to ask for law and order. From Clinton, Tennessee, to Sturgis, Kentucky, from Nashville to Little Rock, the colored people have asked that they be given protection of the law in the form of city police or state or federal troops.* It has been the white people in every instance who have defied these troops.

The Little Rock crisis has put an end to the era of the white man's burden to preserve democracy and to bring the colored man up to the white man's standards of civilization. The white man's burden now is to prove that he believes in democracy and that he can follow the example of the colored people in upholding law and order.

[October 1957]

---

* In each of these places, black children and their parents attempted to desegregate their local schools and were met with resistance from local whites during 1956 or 1957. —Ed.

Who Is for Civilization?

While the white southern segregationists are squirming and trying to work out a new approach to further segregation, the colored people are quietly watching and waiting to see what the next move will be. To contrast the fanatical excitement of these southerners with the calmness of the colored people is to show the whole world who at this time is the most uncivilized in the United States.

For years and years historians have shouted about the backward and uncivilized black peoples of the earth. When the history is written of the colored people sending their children to school in the face of a white mob, as in the Little Rock school incident,* it will have to say that a savage bunch of white people in a modern American city gave evidence that those who were considered to be the most civilized were in reality the most uncivilized.

When governors of a state and senators and congressmen encourage their citizens to deny other citizens' rights, which they have sworn to uphold, barbarism takes the place of civilization. The mob and the instigators of the mob had no shame, felt no shame, and yet to this day consider themselves the defenders of liberty and justice in the United States.

Who Is a Citizen?

The question of who is a citizen and what is a citizen is looming larger every day in the United States. From Virginia to the Deep South the leaders of the government in every state are campaigning on the promise that they will keep the races separated. They are encouraging the white people to do the same.

Quietly but with determination the colored people are pushing them into a frantic stage. Openly they are laughing at these whites because they know the arguments put forward by them are the silliest that a person calling himself civilized could put forward. The colored know that the only support the segregationists have are the police force and the National Guards, which have been used on them since time immemorial. So naked and brutal have been these forces that they have disgraced the nation they are supposed to be representing. This has forced the president to intervene, against his wishes, to try to save the nation's face, at a time when the United States is in its most perilous position as a leading world nation.

[December 1957]

---

* See "Who Is for Law and Order?" —Ed.

56

The Weakest Link in the Struggle*

A grim battle is taking place daily inside the shop between the company and the men. With thousands of men and women laid off and no demand for its products, the company is turning the heat on the workmen. Few workers have worked a full forty-hour week since Christmas. No worker knows whether or not he will work next week, nor how many hours he will work each day when he gets work—four or six or eight.

In every plant the company is demanding more production from the workforce. Dodge and Chrysler workers have been sent home twenty-three days before completing an eight-hour day. The company says they are not producing up to their new work standards. Over a hundred men have been fired or given days off for not meeting these standards. The only difference from company policy before the union is that in the pre-union days the company would take a man to the window and show him how many people were waiting for his job at the employment gate.

Men Pinpoint Blame

The union at each of these plants has taken a strike vote, but every worker in the shop knows that the union isn't going to strike. The company knows that the union isn't going to strike. Because if the union does strike, the men can't collect compensation and a strike wouldn't hurt the company now because the company has no business anyway.

The men are discussing what they could have done to avoid this situation. So far they emphasize two things. (1) The union should have never let the company put in automation. Not that they are against automation, but the union should have known how dirty the company would be and how it would use automation against the men. (2) The union should never have let everybody work all that overtime last year. The union should have known what every worker knows: that in the auto industry, working overtime one year means you are working yourself out of a job next year.

Out of this chaos there is one definite piece of education that is coming to the workers. That is that the company is only interested in production for production's sake. On skilled and unskilled the pressure from the company is being exerted day after day. Foremen, lead men, utility men are being cut back and laid off. Men who had always felt that there would be a place for them in the shop are finding out that in the eyes of the company they are no more than the lowest sweeper.

The chief stewards who are arguing with the company are finding that the contract is only a contract to work, not to solve any of the workers' problems and that the weakest link in the struggle is the union.

---

*This column appeared with the dateline: Detroit, Mich., Feb. 15. —Ed.

Whenever the steward tries to negotiate a grievance over these high production rates with the company, the company always says that it has the right to run production as it sees fit and this is the way it sees fit. The steward can't tell the men to resist because he would be penalized by the company for violating the contract and by the union for telling the men not to get the work out. The only policy that the union has is exactly the policy of the company: Stay on the job and get out production.

[March 1958]

Safeguarding Your Child's Future

There is an old superintendent in my plant who comes by every now and then and calls out to me, "Hi, boy." It isn't that he is hostile. As a matter of fact, he wants to be friendly. Up to now he has gone by so fast that I haven't had a chance to tell him what I think. But one of these days, very soon, this is what I am going to tell him.

"Look, man, I know you don't mean any harm but it is time you learned a few things. Maybe you're too old and won't live to see it. But the people I'm thinking about are your grandchildren and the young folks coming up.

"I am quite sure that when you think of security for the younger generation, you think in terms of defense against Russia, and keeping the communists from taking over the country, and prosperity and things like that, as if that is all that is necessary. But the main problem of their future, their relations with people in the world we live in, you are not thinking about at all.

"Because you're white and I'm colored, you consider me a minority and that I will just keep on being a minority. You don't stop to think that only a few years ago the idea of colored ambassadors and colored prime ministers never occurred to anybody in this country. But today there are colored ambassadors and colored prime ministers and ten years from now there are going to be a lot more. And your grandchildren and those of their generation whom you old folks have been trying to protect from associating with colored kids in schools and parks, these same grandchildren of yours are going to have to face these colored folks. And it isn't going to be enough for them to say that the reason they didn't associate with me and my children was because their parents wouldn't let them.

"Right now, to you I look like a minority, but what looks like a minority is really a majority and I happen to be one of that majority. Ten years from now I might stomp on somebody, and I won't be stomping on him because I'm mad or full of hate but just because I won't be able to get out of my mind all the time you called me 'Boy.' It might just happen that one of your grandchildren is that somebody."

[November 21, 1959]

Land of the Free and the Hungry

A group of English City Council women, led by Mrs. Theresa Russell of Newcastle-on-Tyne, has started an airlift of free baby food for Negro children in New Orleans, Louisiana. These Negro children have been purged from the state welfare rolls by a new law against "immorality." In reality, as these Englishwomen and most Americans know, the purge is motivated by a Dixiecrat determination to stop at nothing to cripple the southern Negroes' drive toward integration, now reaching the stage of desperate conflict in Louisiana.*

Not only is the food being welcomed with open arms by the hungry children and their mothers. It is hailed by many Americans as a Marshall Plan in reverse, since unlike the State Department's Marshall Plan, this airlift is not for the purpose of gaining power or prestige but only to help those who are denied the elementary necessities of life in a country that boasts of plenty.

Meanwhile, in Cleveland, Ohio, Jim "Mudcat" Grant, the young Negro pitching star of the Indians, has been suspended from the team by manager Jimmie Dykes. It all came about this way. While players and spectators were standing and singing the National Anthem before a recent game, Grant said the words, "This land is not so free, I can't even go to Mississippi" in place of the usual "Land of the free and home of the brave." The rhyme was not so good but the sentiment was indisputable. However, he was overheard by Coach Wilks, who called Grant a "black so and so." Grant retorted that Texas is worse than Russia and walked off the field.

Dykes's reason for suspending Grant was that Grant had left the field during a game. Legally, Dykes was within his rights but the rights Grant was singing about go much deeper.

In a country the size of the United States incidents like these may be shrugged off as minor. Certainly the politicians who are making the spectacular speeches wish they would go away. But they are not minor and they will not go away. All the talk of American greatness and all the talk at the UN about American readiness to help underdeveloped nations are only encouraging Negroes to fight to make this country truly the land of the free and the home of the brave.

[October 8, 1960]

---

* In the summer of 1960, the all-white Louisiana state legislature passes a series of bills ostensibly aimed at curbing illegitimacy but were clearly part of a counterattack launched by the most extreme segregationist forces in state politics against the movement for civil rights. The laws criminalized common-law marriage, made it illegal to have more than one child out of wedlock, and ended state welfare payments to the parents of illegitimate children. By July, 23,000 children (most of them children of color) had been dropped from the state's Aid to Dependent Children Program. The laws also restricted voting rights, disenfranchising people in common-law marriages and parents of illegitimate children (along with several other categories of people) and requiring prospective voters to pass both a literacy test and a constitutional interpretation test. —Ed.

The Winds Have Already Changed

Every once in a while you see and hear things in this country that you wouldn't believe a large majority of people thought and believed in.

Ever since the Congo got its independence people here have been making jokes about the names of the Congo leaders.* Each day they joke about them as if they were dance tunes, but very few realize that though the sound of their names may remind people of a dance, Kasavubu and Lumumba (whether they remain leaders or not) are the sounds of the winds of change.

The other day in the United Nations, Khrushchev made an idiot of himself by proposing the UN secretary be removed from his post. The African nations voted against him and for the first time in a long time the United States was in a favorable position with the new African nations. But when Nkrumah, president of Ghana, spoke and emphasized that no nation should control Africa but the Africans, Mr. Herter put the United States right back where they were before the Russian blunder. Herter said Nkrumah was leaning to the left, whereupon Nkrumah had to remind Mr. Herter that for ten years he has been saying that the Western powers do not understand the African problem at all. The United States can't understand the idea that Africans do not want to be dominated by either bloc or pressure group, just as they can't understand that the colored people who are marching and demonstrating all over the United States have finally gotten tired of waiting for the United States to understand what they want.

It is time for some people in the United States to separate themselves from the jokes and laughing and underestimating the new African nations and their expression of total freedom.†

A few years ago it was possible to say that anyone who thought Africans would achieve freedom was indulging in some wishful thinking. Today those winds of change that people have been talking about have become a tornado as one nation after another

---

* The former Belgian Congo became independent on June 30, 1960, establishing itself as the Republic of Congo (now the Democratic Republic of Congo) with Patrice Lumumba as prime minister and Joseph Kasavubu as president. Almost immediately after the independence ceremonies, political, military, and diplomatic crises engulfed the Congo. On September 5 military forces under the command of Joseph Mubutu (who would become the country's long-ruling despotic head of state) captured Lumumba, leading to his execution on January 17, 1961. The CIA had some involvement in Lumumba's arrest, imprisonment, and assassination. His murder remained secret for nearly one month, but as soon as it became public protests erupted worldwide. In the United States, black activists in New York mounted an unprecedented protest at the United Nations, which helped announce a rising black nationalist politics in the early 1960s to which James and Grace Lee Boggs were connected and which they closely covered in *Correspondence*. —Ed.

† Seventeen African nations gained independence in 1960. —Ed.

and these same people who a few years ago could be joked about and passed off arrive at independence.

Only a few years ago, the English people had a habit of not renting rooms to Africans who came up to London because they were black. Suddenly in 1957* they realized that they were playing with fire. The blacks they were refusing accommodations to might some day become prime minister of their countries and thus become powerful figures.

Today all one has to do is count heads in the UN and see how many heads are of color and how many people they represent. Anyone seriously doing that will be rudely awakened. There are already some new names around the world, names not to be so callously spoken about. They have been blown in on the winds that have already changed.

[October 22, 1960]

---

* This is the year that Ghana (formerly the Gold Coast colony) achieved independence from Britain, making it the first sub-Saharan country to free itself from colonialism. ——Ed.

What Makes Americans Run

When people talk about the exodus of the Hungarians and the East Germans from behind the iron curtain, everyone understands they are running away from terror and brutality, perpetrated by a government determined to impose its will upon the people.

When we talk about the Puritans and Pilgrims coming to America to get away from religious persecution in old Europe, we think about this being historical and the fundamental basis of our country's conception of freedom.

Today in America when we see people frantically driving themselves in the pursuit of the dollar, we call it progress. We call it progress because we have succumbed to a philosophy that progress is to own things and that the more we own, the freer we are.

Every day in any factory, auto shop, steel shop, office, or department store everyone is running as if his very life depends on outrunning the next man. Big shots and executives run to impress the bigger shots that they are go-getter types and best fitted to run the company to make it profitable. Plant managers run to impress the executives that they are going to keep all the superintendents and departments heads running, carrying out orders. Plant or office superintendents run to impress on all the foremen and workers below that if they aren't running, they aren't working for the best interests of the company. The workers are running because if they don't run, they will be fired by the foreman or superintendent for not running to keep up with production.

Union officials are running to get away from the workers who have grievances they can't resolve because the big national union had contracted away all the grounds they formerly had to fight the company on. Finally, the steward is running because he has to impress upon the company that he has so many grievances that he hasn't time to do work the contract says he is supposed to do.

All this running is not disconnected from other reasons why Americans are running. In every big plant or office, even if business is at a standstill and warehouses jammed with finished and unsold products, every one is still running as if the next hour the world will stop unless they keep up this mad pace.

Executives are running because if they don't they will lose that little summer cottage or suburban home they ran to in order to get away from the Negroes and lower-class whites.

The foremen and workers are running because of the notes still due on the house, TV, refrigerator, or used car, even though repairs are already needed by the inferior product put out by a company that had the workers running so fast they couldn't do a good job when they built it.

Running has become a way of life and each is afraid not to run because everyone is caught up in a mad race to run away from each other.

Then to top it all off we have Kennedy and Nixon running for president. Each one promises he will make America run a little faster than it is already running.

[November 12, 1960]

New Orleans Faces We Still Haven't Seen

Every year thousands of people from all over America flock to New Orleans for the annual Mardi Gras. White and black put on their masks and go out to celebrate.

This year the Mardi Gras has started early. Already New Orleans faces have been flashed on TV news all over the world. These faces are not behind masks. We don't have to guess who is behind them.*

We have seen two sets of faces. We have seen those of white women, twisted with hate, coaching their little ones to say "I don't want to go to school with N———rs" before they can even say "Mama." These women have made clear that they not only hate the little Negro children being escorted into school by towering U.S. marshals. They also hate white parents like Mr. and Mrs. Gabrielle and Rev. Foreman† and the few others who have run the gauntlet of their jeers and threats. They hate the judge who made the decision that the school board must desegregate. They hate the school board members who have complied with the law. They hate the Constitution of the United States. But most of all, they hate these black Americans who have had the courage to challenge their pitiful little havens of white superiority.

These hateful faces are not strange to the American scene. We have become accustomed to them. We have seen them everywhere in America, although seldom as unmasked as in New Orleans today. The faces we have not become accustomed to are those like the Gabrielles and the Foremans, whose actions give hope that the colored people of America may be able to take their place inside the American family of nationalities without wholesale bloodshed.

The faces we have still not seen on the TV screens, although actually the ones we are most accustomed to, are those of the great majority in New Orleans, the respectable citizens who have nothing to say in public but who privately threaten a white par-

---

* During the fall of 1960, a long-simmering struggle over school desegregation in New Orleans grew into open confrontation as staunch segregationists (including the state legislature and the White Citizens Council) fought the school board's court-mandated plan for open schools. White parents mounted a boycott, removing their children from school in an effort to derail the entry of black students into formerly all-white schools. Newspaper and television reports captured groups of enraged white mothers, usually between forty and two hundred, who gathered daily to launch invectives at the black children and all who dared not respect the boycott. —Ed.

† Jimmy and Daisy Gabrielle refused to withdraw their daughter from a school slated for desegregation. They were taunted and harassed and found it difficult to find work. The couple and their six children eventually had to leave the state. Lloyd A. Foreman, a Methodist minister, was blocked and shoved as he escorted his daughter to the same school in defiance of a boycott mounted by white parents opposing school integration. —Ed.

ent with loss of his job if his child goes to one of the integrated schools. We have not seen any one of these respectable citizens come forward and say that he will fire the husband of any woman who continues her "Jeerleading."* We have not heard any one of them admit that New Orleans is one of the South's most racially intermixed cities—at night.

The faces we still have not seen in New Orleans are the true face of today's America. Like Eisenhower who refused for six long years to disclose his views on the rightness of the Supreme Court decision, they are still behind their masks.

[December 24, 1960]

---

* The most vociferous of the mothers came to be called "the cheerleaders." Displaying an unrestrained racism, they screamed obscenities, hurled jeers, and issued threats in their daily mobs outside the schools attempting to integrate. Boggs is mocking this name. —Ed.

The First Giant Step[*]

Busloads of Freedom Riders are now rolling across Alabama and Mississippi, and Negroes are determined to keep them rolling despite Kennedy's appeal for a "cooling-off period," an appeal in the same spirit and for the same purpose as Walter Reuther's constant appeals to the workers to "cool off" strikers against the company.

The news of the riot in Montgomery on Saturday, May 20, came as no shock to me. I had been forewarned by what happened in northern Alabama, in Anniston and Birmingham, the previous Sunday. In fact, only three days earlier on May 17, speaking to a group of students in Ann Arbor, I had ended with the warning, "If in the morning paper you read that a revolt has erupted in Mississippi, don't be surprised. That is how belligerent and indignant the colored people in the United States are today over the race issue."

However, just listening to the news bulletins over radio and TV, a person feels so helpless. You ask yourself what you would do if you were there, and since you aren't there, what you can do anyway. In the meantime friends begin calling you on the phone, people stop by and obviously don't want to leave. Everyone feels something should be done, if only to indicate support, but no one is sure just what.

After dinner you call some members of various Fair Practices Committees of UAW locals in the city. As you talk to them it begins to dawn on you that the labor movement is standing by, doing nothing. In fact, the news bulletins are about evenly divided between reports of the Montgomery riot and of Reuther's negotiations over the prisoners in Cuba. Very strange, you feel. This great American labor movement can't organize the South because of the race prejudice there and can't put up a decent fight against the companies in the North because they can run South with their plants. Yet, "in the name of common humanity," it can rush off at a moment's notice to the rescue of counterrevolutionary prisoners in Cuba.

The 11 o'clock news bulletin reports that Reuther is keeping Solidarity House open all night for a reply to his cable from Castro. So at 11:30 P.M. you send off a telegram to Reuther at Solidarity House as I did:

IN THE NAME OF COMMON HUMANITY AND AS AN EXPRESSION OF LABOR'S SUPPORT OF THE CAUSE OF FREEDOM AND EQUALITY AT HOME, URGENTLY REQUEST THAT THE UAW-AFL-CIO IMMEDIATELY ORGANIZE AND SEND A FLEET OF INTEGRATED BUSES OF FREEDOM RIDERS TO ALABAMA.

JAMES BOGGS, CHRYSLER LOCAL 7
FAIR PRACTICES COMMITTEE

---

[*] This column carried the dateline: Detroit, May 25. —Ed.

The next morning you call preachers in the city to ask them to raise the proposal with their congregations. The friends who had gathered the day before are also on the move, going to churches, telephoning their friends. The response is enthusiastic among the thousands who hear the proposal. It is not you who have aroused people. They have been aroused by the events, are anxious to act, see immediately what the effect of such an action would be.

In the shop on Monday there is surprisingly little talk about the riots; only some people saying that blood has been mixing in this country for a long time. Now this is the forerunner of more blood mixing but on a different pattern.

Tuesday night there is a meeting of representatives of UAW Fair Practices Committees from all over the city. They pass a resolution making a similar demand upon the UAW leadership and appealing to all locals to do likewise.

What the UAW will do I don't know. But as of now the buses are still rolling, and it is up to the labor leaders whether common decency is enough to bring them to act. The Negroes themselves have no other choice but to act, and they are not waiting on the labor movement. They have taken the first giant step.

(Under pressure and trying to buy his way out of direct action, Reuther on May 26 announced a $5,000 UAW contribution to CORE.—Ed.)

[June 3, 1961]

A Visit from the FBI

Friday evening, September 1, two FBI men visited me. They wanted to know whether I knew Robert Williams* and where he was. I told them that I had met Williams, that I knew of him and what had been happening in Monroe, North Carolina, in the last few years, but that I didn't know where he was. I then added immediately, "But I want you to know this. I don't know where Williams is. I wouldn't harbor him or even one of my own children if they had committed a crime. But I want you to know I have a feeling in regard to this. If I did know where he was I would not tell you. I am no stool pigeon."

In a coming issue I shall go into detail about my conversation with these two young men and the questions I had to ask them. For the present let me just say that when I told my friends about this visit, practically everyone said, "If they call on you again, send them to see me, I have plenty of questions to ask them."

[*September 9, 1961*]

---

* For information on Williams and his relationship to Boggs, see pp. 20–21. —Ed.

FBI Asks Me about Rob Williams

In the last issue I promised to go into more detail about my visit from the FBI on September 1.

With their crew cuts the two young men looked like insurance agents or time-study men as they entered. But they flashed badges and said briskly, "FBI." I asked them to sit down.

One of them, the talkative one, asked me if I knew Robert Williams. When I said that I did, he said, "I guess you know what he has done and why we're looking for him. Do you know where he is?" I replied that I didn't know where Williams was, that I would not harbor him or even one of my own children if he had committed a crime, but that I wouldn't tell them if I did know. "All I know about the riot," I said, "is what I read in the papers. But I know a lot about the background in Monroe and I want you to know I'm an admirer of Williams."

Then he began explaining about the "harboring law," so I said *I* wanted to ask some questions. "How is it," I began, "that the FBI is so interested in Williams and yet in all the other cases . . ." Before I could finish, the other young man, who had said nothing up to now, interrupted, "You mean Till?" Obviously it had occurred even to him that there was a big difference between the FBI rushing into this matter and its refusal to get involved where whites were accused.

I replied, "Not only Till, but Parker and all the other cases where whites have been known to lynch Negroes and the FBI said it couldn't intervene."

The talkative one began holding forth about the kidnaping law, the crossing of state lines, etc. "All we are interested in is turning Williams over to the local authorities," he said. Whereupon I asked, "How do you know Williams has crossed the state lines? I have a feeling he may still be in North Carolina."

At about this point it was obvious that the conversation wasn't getting them anywhere. The talkative one changed the subject, asking, "Are you working?" When I replied that I was, he asked if we were going on strike and whether we wouldn't lose a lot of money by doing so. I replied that I wouldn't mind striking and losing money if it meant something but that Reuther's strikes don't mean anything for working conditions, which is all we are interested in. "Talk about behind the iron curtain," I said. "In the shop we work worse than any Russians. There's a real reign of terror and not just for us poor slobs. Young guys like you who would be time-study men in the shops are also running around like crazy."

They got up to leave and the talkative one asked if I would call them if I got any information about Williams or if I minded if they called me. I said that they could call me if they wanted to, but I wasn't going to tell them anything even if I knew. "I am not going to fool you," I said as they went out the door. "I am proud of Williams and I don't care who knows it. As for you and me, let's not fool each other. I have nothing for you and you have nothing for me."

[*October 1961*]

Foreword to "Monroe, North Carolina . . . Turning Point in American History"*

Conrad Lynn is a lawyer who speaks not only for Robert Williams and the Monroe defendants but for millions of Americans in the most explosive trial of our day: the Negro people vs. the United States of America. That is how closely related his words are to their true thoughts and actions.

Monroe, North Carolina, is not the whole United States; neither was Emmett Till the only Negro boy ever killed in Mississippi. But just as Till's lynching and the bare-faced acquittal of his lynchers in 1955 were the signal for the Negro people to start their offensive for rights in this country, so Monroe represents the turning point at which Negros have decided that they must convict their attackers on the spot.

It has been said that when the lowest stratum of any society begin to revolt, the whole society has to be changed. The Negroes, who have always represented and still represent the great mass bloc of the lowest stratum of workers in this country, are now in the early stages of revolution. In these speeches Conrad Lynn is telling their story, stating their case. He is posing before the American people the cold fact that the old Negro organizations that for so many years have led the Negro struggle with the cooperation and support of white liberals and the labor movement have already been bypassed. They can no longer act as a cushion between the Negro people and American white society. The Negroes are going to speak for themselves, act for themselves.

How can the labor movement speak for the Negroes in this age of automation when, for example, 76 percent of Negro youth in Detroit are unemployed and therefore completely outside the control of organized labor?

When American liberals talk about how many Russians were killed behind the iron curtain in the concentration camps it doesn't move the American Negroes at all. The reason is very simple. The same thing happened in this country. The American workers who weren't Negroes didn't have to go through what the Russian workers went through under Stalin because the Negroes went through it for them on the cotton plantations of the South, first as slaves and then as sharecroppers under a caste system as brutal as that of slavery itself. Every immigrant who walked off the gangplank to make his way in the land of opportunity was doing so off the Negroes' backs.

---

* This selection is the foreword that James Boggs wrote for a pamphlet of this title that *Correspondence* published in 1962. The pamphlet consisted of two speeches by Conrad Lynn, the attorney for Robert Williams and the other defendants from the kidnaping case in Monroe in 1961 that resulted in Williams's exile. —Ed.

The Negro question in the United States has therefore never been purely a question of race, nor is it purely a question of race today. Class, race, and nation are all involved. The American nation has become the giant of industry that it is today on the backs of the Negroes. The white workers were an aristocracy that benefited first and always from the exploitation of the Negroes and in between by the exploitation of each immigrant group. While the workers in Western Europe were forming labor parties, the American workers did not form a mass party of labor because they were ready to allow the landed aristocracy in the South to exploit the Negroes as long as the white workers could go their way, settling on the free lands of the West and working as free labor in the new industries of the East. Thus the concept of "Black and White, Unite and Fight" has never had any basis in fact in this country.

When the Civil War ended in the bargain of 1877 between northern capital and the southern landed aristocracy, which returned one section of the workers to serfdom on the basis of color, it was the first major defeat of the class struggle in this country. From that time on Americans, including the radicals, have regarded the Negro question as a race question. Until the Civil War the Negro struggles were called rebellions and revolts. But after the Civil War and the formal emancipation of the Negroes, any violent action by Negroes was just called a "race riot" even when these actions were based on economic grounds, such as jobs, housing, or prices.

So long have the American people lived with this contradiction that it has become a way of life. That is why the issue as to what the Negro struggle really represents, what should be done about it, what is right and what is wrong, is shaking the United States more than any other issue.

What began as a class issue and was made into a race issue by the simple act of separating the Negroes on the basis of color has now in fact become a national issue, the great, the pervasive, the all-American question that is shaking up every organization, every institution, and every individual inside America and affecting the relationships of all these to the rest of the world: labor, the professions, the church, the courts, war, foreign policy, industry, space flight, employment, transportation, the family, marriage, schools, hospitals, neighborhoods, cities, suburbs, government at all levels, police, firemen, social welfare, political parties, press, TV, radio, movies, and sports.

The list is endless. So is the guilt.

So long as the contradiction remains that everybody in this country is supposed to be free and equal but the Negroes are unfree and unequal, this country is the living denial of itself and its claim to be a classless society.

When the historic Supreme Court handed down its decision eight years ago in 1954, a lot of labor leaders, liberals, and Negro leaders thought that the decision itself would lead to integration. Today it is a known fact that at the present deliberate speed of desegregation, it will take another hundred years before there is integration of schools, which will mean two hundred years since the alleged emancipation of the Negroes in 1863. The question of questions that remains in the United States is not *whether* the government will challenge the whole white South even if it means war. That is coming, whether the government likes or not. The only question is *which* government and *when*. For if this or that government doesn't carry through this challenge, then a war is inevitable anyway, just as the war between the Algerian nationalist and the French army was inevitable yesterday and a war between the Muslims and all European elements in Algeria is becoming more inevitable every day.

[May 17, 1962]

PART II

THE AMERICAN REVOLUTION
PAGES FROM A NEGRO WORKER'S NOTEBOOK

Introduction to Part II

The American Revolution: Pages from a Negro Worker's Notebook is James Boggs's best-known and most enduring work.[1] Published in the summer of 1963, the book arrived at a pivotal moment in the civil rights movement, and its thought-provoking assessment of the movement's meaning and possible trajectory established its author as an original and penetrating analyst of the black freedom struggle. The book, however, is not only or even principally about the civil rights movement or black protest. Its starting point, both narratively and analytically, is the labor movement. Specifically, Boggs begins his analysis by tracing the decline of the labor movement and its failure in the face of changes in the industrial economy brought on by automation. He then moves to an analysis of the economic as well as social implications of automation. This proved to be one of the most celebrated features of the book, catapulting him into a national debate during the early 1960s about the effect of automation on employment and the future of the industrial economy. The book argues that automation was making black labor obsolete, turning a generation of young people into "outsiders"—a group of people who had no real prospects of entering the system—which, he said, would shape the meaning and future directions of the civil rights movement. Amid an eruption of books on "the Negro revolt" and a similarly exploding body of writing on poverty and economic production, *The American Revolution* was unique in the way it linked the technological and economic changes of automation to the social and political changes being forged by the black struggle and showed how they were related historical processes. The automation debate had already identified increasing job loss among African Americans as a central concern, but Boggs looked beyond the relationship between automation and black joblessness and identified a deeper connection—both historically and sociologically—between changes in the industrial economy and the unfolding of the black struggle for democratic rights over the preceding two decades. His understanding of the civil rights movement and automation as related social phenomena of the 1960s remains a distinguishing feature of the book.

The book also marks a significant point in Boggs's intellectual and political trajectory. It rather suddenly raised his profile as a thinker and activist. Widely read in both black radical and Marxist circles, as well as around the world through translations in six languages,[2] the book opened up new opportunities for intellectual and political engagement for Boggs. In this sense, *The American Revolution* marked a new stage in his activist career. The book also marked a shift in Boggs's relationship to the labor movement and to Marxism, both of which had been central coordinates of his political life during the preceding two decades. During most of the 1950s, even as he was an active unionist, Boggs had been a vocal critic of the UAW and the labor movement in his *Correspondence* columns and elsewhere. By the early 1960s his critiques grew especially strident, culminating in *The American Revolution*, which put forward a devastating indictment of the American labor movement. He argued that it had irreversibly devolved into a special interest group bearing no relation to its origins in the 1930s, when industrial unionism represented a genuine movement for social change.

Similarly, the early 1960s saw Boggs move away from Marxism, rejecting, in particular, the Marxist vision of the industrial working class as the agent of revolution. In *The American Revolution* Boggs argued that Marxism could not account for the new stage of capitalist production and social relations in the United States and was therefore inadequate as a guide for revolutionary transformation in late twentieth-century America. This break with Marxism was at the heart of Boggs's break with C. L. R. James and the disintegration of their organization in 1962. Through *The American Revolution* and his subsequent writings, Boggs sought to develop the new theory he saw as necessary for this new stage; at the same time, he founded or helped build a range of grassroots organizations with fellow activists in Detroit and nationally. Thus, the book announced new directions for Boggs both ideologically and organizationally.

Indeed, the following brief review of the timing and circumstances of the book's publication shows how the book marked a major pivot in James Boggs's half century of activism and writing.

The origins of the book lay in the organizational conflict within *Correspondence* in 1961. During the spring and summer the appearance of Boggs's ideas about the American working class, Marxism, and the rising black struggle in *Correspondence* caused tension and ideological debate within the group. This included a clash between Boggs, who was the group's chairperson, and C. L. R. James, who though living in London maintained considerable influence within the group as its founder and most dominant intellectual force. C. L. R. James saw Boggs's challenge to Marxist theory, especially his rejection of the industrial working class as a revolutionary social force, as a wrongheaded and unacceptable departure from foundational Marxist ideas and the guiding concepts of the organization. During the fall, Boggs began writing an internal document to clarify his position and to make the case for the direction he thought the organization should take. It outlined, in the most coherent and sustained form yet, his thinking about the development of American capitalism, the need to go beyond Marxism to project a new revolutionary vision for the late twentieth century, and the potential role of the black struggle (and not the American working class) in this vision. Completed at the end of 1961, the extensive document (more than eighty single-spaced pages) carried the title "State of a Nation: 1962" and was circulated to members of the organization for discussion. In fact, it deepened the ideological impasse in the group and assured that the only resolution was for Boggs and those who agreed with him to leave the organization, which they did in early 1962.[3] In this sense, "State of a Nation: 1962" was a "split document," meaning it articulated the emerging philosophical and political differences in the group and set out the basis for the split.

But that was only the first incarnation of the document. After the split James and Grace Lee Boggs began sharing "State of a Nation" with various people in their widening network of associates and friends, including W. H. "Ping" Ferry, vice president and cofounder of the Center for the Study of Democratic Institutions and initiator in 1964 of the Ad Hoc Committee on the Triple Revolution in Cybernation, Weaponry, and Human Rights (of which Boggs was a member). In April 1962, Ferry brought the manuscript to the attention of Leo Huberman and Paul Sweezy, the editors of the socialist journal *Monthly Review*. They contacted Boggs, and by August they reached an agreement to publish the manuscript. Over the next eight months Boggs revised the manuscript for publication, giving it the tentative title "But Only One Side Is Right: The Industrial and Social Revolution in America." During the editing process, it acquired a sleeker and more assertive title: "The American Revolution: Pages from a Negro Worker's Notebook."[4] It appeared first as the ninety-six-page special double summer issue (July and August) of *Monthly Review* in 1963 and ultimately as a paperback book published by Monthly Review Press in October.

The response from readers was immediate and overwhelmingly positive. In the very next issue of *Monthly Review*, the editors reported that readers had written them describing *The American Revolution* as "the best thing *MR* has ever done." "The demand for copies has been so great," wrote Huberman and Sweezy, "that we have decided to do a second printing of the issue as a $1 paperback."[5] Letters commending the book for its clarity and insight into the history and future of the labor movement, the left, and the black struggle came from across the country and from abroad. Perhaps the most surprising of these was a letter from Bertrand Russell, the British philosopher and internationally renowned peace activist, who wrote to Boggs shortly after the book was published saying he was "greatly impressed" with the "power and insight" of his "remarkable book."[6] Russell's letter initiated an improbable but remarkable correspondence between the two men over the next several months in which they discussed such topics as the March on Washington (which occurred eight days after Russell wrote his first letter to Boggs), the efficacy of nonviolence in the civil rights movement, the impact of automation on the consciousness of American workers, and the internal dynamics of and divisions in the civil rights struggle.

Artist and activist Ossie Davis was similarly taken by *The American Revolution*. When this "little book came into my life," Davis recalled years later, it left him with the sensation of being "born again."

I read every word of it and it opened my mind, my thoughts. It was immediately apprehended by me in every possible way. When I read it, I said, "Yes, of course, Amen. Even I could have thought of that." Immensities of thought reduced to images so simple that coming away from the book I was indeed born again. I could see the struggle in a new light. I was recharged, my batteries were full, and I was able to go back to the struggle carrying this book as my banner. Ruby and I bought up copies and mailed them to all the civil rights leaders, Martin Luther King Jr., Malcolm X, Whitney Young. We thought all of them should have access to this book. It would give them an opportunity to be born again.[7]

While there is no direct evidence that any of these national figures were influenced by or even read the book as Davis and his wife, Ruby Dee, hoped, Davis's comments nonetheless shine light on the ways in which the book propelled Boggs into national discussions and activist networks. Davis's remarks also provide a vivid example of how the publication of the book brought Boggs's analysis and ideas to a broader audience while also opening up new relationships—including the decades-long friendship that James and Grace Lee Boggs shared with Ossie Davis and Ruby Dee.[8]

The responses from Russell and Davis, situated as they were in distinct spheres and political spaces, suggest the wide reach and impact of the book. *The American Revolution* stretched across conventional realms of political analysis and appealed to a varied readership that included radical trade unionists, civil rights activists, longtime leftists, young internationalist-minded black radicals, and people watching current trends involving technological and economic changes. Indeed, while readers like Russell and Davis found themselves drawn to the book primarily for its analysis of the rising black struggle, the book's examination of automation, the meaning of work, and the failure of the labor movement spoke to other readers. For example, Wyndham Mortimer, a major figure in the formation of the UAW and CIO during the 1930s, wrote to Boggs "having just finished reading your very fine and thoughtful book."[9] Mortimer agreed with and appreciated Boggs's critique of the union. As a participant of the storied Flint sit-down strikes in 1937, the veteran gave the highest praise to his younger comrade: "I think your book is the best thing that has happened to the UAW since the sit-down strikes."[10] Another reader, Minnie Livingston of Technocracy, Inc., in the state of Washington, wrote to congratulate Boggs "on your excellent analysis of America's economy," while a radical labor activist in Chicago appraised the book as "one of the most important, if not the most important, and one of the most lucid books produced by the American left in generations . . . [this] book surely belongs at the top of the list of works of the 'New Left.'"[11]

Despite this acclaim from readers, the book was not widely reviewed. The highest-profile review appeared in *The Nation,* where black poet and cultural activist A. B. Spellman reviewed it with Robert Williams's *Negroes with Guns* in June 1964.[12] Spellman was sensitive to the role of each book and its author in sharpening divisions of black protest, identifying both authors as "Negroes who, from their understanding of their own experience, have no faith in America to do anything except perpetuate itself as the most reactionary power in the world. Both Robert Williams and James Boggs are angry in a way that James Baldwin is not."[13] With this allusion to Baldwin, Spellman was situating Boggs and Williams on the militant end of a continuum of black thought. (Spellman placed Baldwin, whose *The Fire Next Time* appeared to much acclaim in early 1963, next to Martin Luther King and Roy Wilkins on the moderate end.) Spellman praised *The American Revolution* as a "series of brilliant and startling insights into the American past and the probable American future,"[14] citing in particular Boggs's view that black aspirations for freedom cannot be realized under the system as presently constituted. This praise notwithstanding, the review devotes most of its space to *Negroes with Guns* and leaves much of Boggs's analysis unaddressed.

Most reviews appeared in small local or radical publications. A reviewer for the *Los Angeles Sentinel,* an African American weekly newspaper, found the book "full of startling ideas" written "with perceptive clarity" and declared each "exciting chapter is an education in miniature."[15] *Soulbook,* the Northern California–based "quarterly journal of revolutionary afroamerica," carried a lengthy review essay of *The American Revolution* written by two of its editorial board members, Ernie Allen (who in the early 1970s would be involved in Detroit activist politics, including as a member of the League of Revolutionary Black Workers) and Kenn M. Freeman. Allen and Freeman lauded the book for, among other things, laying waste to Marxist premises and exposing "old myths" about the working class. They also found the book valuable for its account of the failure of the union and the lessons black Americans can "learn from the experience which our brother, James Boggs, has obtained from the union movement." And while they found that "Boggs'[s] solution to this problem of automation vs. income is tinged with ambivalence," Allen and Freeman concluded that book offers an analysis "that we feel will greatly aid Black Americans in their task of providing a viable program for total Black liberation on a worldwide scale."[16]

There is another measure of *The American Revolution*'s reception. Almost immediately after the book's publication, Boggs began receiving speaking invitations and requests for his writing. In September 1963 alone, letters arrived with the following invitations: to participate in a conference at Princeton University; to give an address on "the revolution of the unemployed" at McGill University in Montreal; to address a community group in Toledo, Ohio; and to be one of the speakers at a forum at Town Hall in New York City called "Where Is the Negro Liberation Movement Going? How Will It Get There?" In December Richard Gibson, editor of *Revolution* magazine, asked Boggs to contribute an article on "the latest developments in the Afro-American struggle." In each case the person extending the invitation had read *The American Revolution* and cited its power and insight as the impetus for the invitation. Such invitations continued into 1964, and Boggs increasingly found multiple and varied platforms to share formulations from the book and to interject himself and his ideas into the deepening discourse during the mid-1960s about the future directions of black protest. Thus, the book's novel ideas and sharp analysis of converging social phenomena brought instant recognition to its author and helped establish his reputation as a respected interpreter of (and participant in) the Black Power movement and veteran black radical.

The American Revolution:
Pages from a Negro Worker's Notebook

Contents

Editors' Foreword   83

Introduction   84

1. The Rise and Fall of the Union   85

2. The Challenge of Automation   100

3. The Classless Society   106

4. The Outsiders   109

5. Peace and War   120

6. The Decline of the United States Empire   126

7. Rebels with a Cause   130

8. The American Revolution   139

Editors' Foreword

The fact that we are devoting an entire double issue of *Monthly Review* to one man's assessment of our present national condition does not mean that we agree with everything James Boggs has to say, any more than publication of this work in *MR* means that Mr. Boggs shares all the views of the editors. Our reason for publishing these pages is that we think Mr. Boggs has things to say that all Americans, and especially Americans of the left, ought to listen to. He knows the American labor movement from the inside, and he knows the mood of working-class Negroes because he is one. When he speaks of the American Revolution, he is not using a figure of speech. He means it quite literally. In fact he thinks that the American Revolution has already begun. He also thinks that it will be a protracted, painful, violent process in which not only will Negroes clash with whites but Negroes will clash with Negroes and whites with whites. And there is no end in sight and will not be until Americans finally come to realize that their responsibility is nothing less than the building of a classless society capable of making use of the prodigious powers of modern technology for genuinely human ends. They will not come to this realization and assume this responsibility except to the extent that they purge themselves of the accumulated corruption not of years or decades but of centuries, and this can be achieved only through struggle, suffering, and sacrifice. To this, we can only say amen.

Where we tend to differ from Mr. Boggs is in his analysis of the economy. He looks at the current economic scene through the eyes of a production worker, and he sees clearly that he and his fellow production workers are a "vanishing herd," being made obsolete by rapidly advancing automation. He also knows that automation is invading other areas of the economy—the store, the office, the bank. He concludes that the United States today is headed not for the liberal utopia of full employment but for full *un*employment. We must, he tells us, learn to build not only a classless society but also a workless society.

There is no doubt of the reality or the force of the trends which Mr. Boggs highlights in this analysis. What he neglects or underestimates is a certain countertrend. As productive labor becomes ever more fruitful and less needed, the frantic search for profits drives the great corporations which dominate the American economy to create, directly and indirectly, other areas of employment—in salesmanship, entertainment, speculation (legal and illegal), personal service, and so on. Some of the jobs thus provided also succumb to automation, but the process of proliferation is not halted. To be sure, it is not rapid or vigorous enough to prevent the steady rise of unemployment, as the experience of the past eight years so convincingly shows. But it does brake the rise of unemployment. Mr. Boggs's concept of "full unemployment" is an enlightening exaggeration, but it can be misleading if it is taken too literally.

Do not misunderstand us. We see nothing healthy in the job trends just referred to. For the most part, the American economy creates new jobs through organizing waste which is at best harmless and at worst poisonous and destructive. Not only are millions of Americans unemployed today; more millions are engaged in basically antihuman activities (this is the aspect of our society which is so effectively exposed by Paul Goodman in his book *Growing Up Absurd*). The net effect is twofold: to add to the corruption which James Boggs rightly sees as our most basic problem and to make it easier for the old illusions to live on a while longer. If we were really headed for full unemployment, the hour of truth could not be long postponed. As it is, who knows? The American Revolution may be more protracted, painful, and violent than even a man as perceptive, sensitive, and courageous as James Boggs is yet able to imagine.

LEO HUBERMAN
PAUL M. SWEEZY

Introduction

There are two sides to every question but only one side is right. I believe in democracy, but I don't believe in being too damn democratic. In other words, I believe that everyone has a right to his opinion, but I don't believe he has a right to be hypocritical or sly about it, and I believe that it is my responsibility to fight and right those opinions that are wrong.

People are not born with opinions. Their opinions are shaped by their environments and their teachers, and they can be shaped by the wrong environment and the wrong teachers. A baby is not born with hate, but a lot of babies in the United States are taught hate.

Those who have the most power can do the most shaping and the most teaching, and if they are teaching what I believe is wrong, then I believe their power should be taken away from them.

That is what I hope this book will help to achieve. I especially recommend it to the FBI and the CIA and all those who plan to save and secure the world on the false premise that the world can be made safe and secure by freezing the ideas and creativity of man.

I am a factory worker, but I know more than just factory work. I know the difference between what would sound right if one lived in a society of logical people and what *is* right when you live in a society of real people with real differences. It may sound perfectly natural to a highly educated and logical person, even when he hears people saying that there is going to be a big riot, to assume that there will not be a big riot because the authorities have everything under control. But if *I* kept hearing people say that there was going to be a big riot and I saw one of these logical people standing in the middle, I would tell him he'd better get out of the way because he sure was going to get killed.

Reforms and revolutions are created by the illogical actions of people. Very few logical people ever make reforms and none make revolutions. Rights are what you make and what you take.

JAMES BOGGS

DETROIT, MAY 1, 1963

Chapter 1

The Rise and Fall of the Union

In the last twenty years an industrial revolution has been taking place in the United States at a pace faster than that of any country in the world, transforming social layers of this country on a scale never before dreamed of. So fast has this industrial revolution been developing that 60 percent of the jobs held by the working population today did not even exist during the First World War, while 70 percent of the jobs that existed in this country in 1900 don't exist today. Not only have work classifications been fundamentally altered but the workforce has multiplied from 20 million in 1900 to 40 million in 1944 to 68 million today. The change is not only in numbers. Over 20 million of those working today are women, and by 1970 it is expected that women workers will have increased to 30,000,000—a workforce of women that will be one-and-a-half times the entire workforce of 1900.

The United States has transformed itself so rapidly from an agricultural country to an industrial country and as an industrial country has undergone such rapid industrial revolutions that the question of who is in what class becomes an ever wider and more complicated question. Today's member of the middle class is the son or daughter of yesterday's worker.

When I was a child, my mother's chief ambition was to learn how to read and write, because if she had been able to read and write she could have become a first-class cook for some rich white people. That, for her, would have been success and the realization of what was, for her and in her day, a high ambition. Her ambition for me was that I should obtain an education so that I would not have to do the things she had to do. In

America, more than in any other country, the revolutions in the mode of production have been accompanied by changes in the composition and status of classes. Today most workers in the plant have been to high school and quite a few have even been to college. All either plan or wish to send their sons and daughters to college—their sons so they won't have to work in the factory on what they call a dull and automated job, their daughters (get this!) so that they won't have to marry some bum but can make their own living and be free to decide whether they want to marry or not marry, un-hampered as they have been in years gone by, when the big aim was to raise a girl so that she'd be able to meet and marry a good hardworking man who would provide for her and the children.

America is therefore at the stage where no class is a homogeneous segregated bloc as in the early days in Europe when, fresh out of feudalism, everything was controlled by a few large owners of estates and factories while the rest of the population were the direct servants of the ruling class, whatever the form in which they worked for it. Nor is it like the United States in the period before the Civil War when, in the South, you had the big landowners with millions of slaves watched over by a few straw bosses, while in the North you had craftsmen in small shops, farmers, and textile millworkers. Nor is it like the 1920s when the farms were being mechanized and the rural popula-tion was pouring into the big cities to man the machines and the assembly lines of the mass production industries that had grown up since the First World War.

In the 1930s, with the country in a deep economic crisis, the old craft unions went into a state of decline, and people in panic and disillusionment began to create new forms of organization. They were spurred on by an administration that called itself the New Deal and, in order to save the country from total collapse, initiated certain reforms, thereby creating an arena in which the people could act. This led to a wave of further social reforms and the birth of the CIO, which at that point was the biggest social reform movement that had ever taken place in America. Radical groupings for the first time had a mass force in action within which they could propagate and agitate for their theories and ideas, ideas that were predominantly based on European con-cepts of organization and on Marx's, Lenin's, and Trotsky's theory of the class struggle. Thousands of young intellectuals, most of them the sons and daughters of European immigrants, began to take part in and become part of the labor movement. At that time the validity of their approach was strengthened by the fact that the bulk of the American workers were still "raw workers" and not at all articulate—sharecroppers, auto workers, textile workers, rubber workers.

What has transpired since then? The sons of the factory workers and coal miners have become teachers, engineers, draftsmen, scientists, social workers. In fact today, even the radicals no longer think of their children replacing them on the assembly line, or with the pick and shovel in the coal mine, or behind the tractor. Today the largest bulk of organized workers in this country is made up of truckers, dispatchers, etc., in the transport industries. The other large bulk, mainly unorganized, is composed of teachers. There is a growing army of technicians and engineers who today have the same status in industry as did the plumbers, carpenters, and skilled workers in yesterday's industries. That is all they are, nothing more, nothing less.

Even in the South this transformation is taking place and not only among whites but among Negroes. There are many tens of thousands of Negro youths in the colleges today, and they are the ones leading the freedom struggles in the South. They are the sons of ex-GIs, men who have worked in the steel mills, on railroads, in factories, in the mines, but are determined that their children shall not follow in their footsteps.

Today the working class is so dispersed and transformed by the very nature of the changes in production that it is almost impossible to select out any single bloc of workers as working class in the old sense. Today something like 15 percent of industrial employment is in war industry—in the production of missiles, tanks, guns, rockets—and the men and women in these industries hold all kinds of positions. Some of these positions in years gone by would have classified them as middle class; some make salaries that exceed those of the executives of some corporations. The sons and daughters of yesterday's ditchdiggers are today's engineers, scientists, toolmakers, electronic specialists, nuclear physicists, schoolteachers, social workers, time-study men, cost-analysis experts, laboratory technicians, hospital nurses, and secretaries to big executives, as well as typists, file clerks, dictaphone operators. Only the mothers and fathers are still left in those jobs that were once considered the testing ground of the pure working class. And each year these pure working-class jobs become fewer and fewer as automation moves in and takes over.

However, it is not only diversification of work that has changed the working class. The working class is growing, as Marx predicted, but it is not the old working class that the radicals persist in believing will create the revolution and establish control over production. That old working class is the vanishing herd. There are only twelve million of these production workers left in American industry out of a total workforce of sixty-eight million. Moreover, since the Negroes were the last hired into these bottom jobs, over 30 percent of these twelve million production workers (or about four million) are Negroes. So the Negroes, whom the radicals do not ordinarily think of as workers, form a large proportion of this working-class force, which is usually considered the revolutionary force, while the native-born whites who have been able to move up with every change in production are less and less inside the working-class force.

By examining the history of the CIO, the industrial revolution, and unemployment, we can get some idea of the revolutionary changes that have so rapidly developed in America, directly leading to changes in the nature of work, the social composition of various strata of the population, the classes within it, and the culture of the population.

The CIO came in the 1930s. It came when the United States, which had fought in the war of 1917 and built up large-scale industry out of the technological advances of that war, was in a state of economic collapse, with over twelve million unemployed. The workers in the plant began to organize in the underground fashion which such a movement always takes before a great social reform—in the cellars, the bars, the garages; in the same way that the abolitionists had to organize—a minority against the sentiments of the community. Involved in getting the movement under way were communists, socialists, Wobblies, radicals of every type, along with preachers and a new layer of militant workers. Sit-down strikes erupted all over the country. All auto workers, except those of Ford, were involved, and the movement spread to allied industries.

To grasp the social significance of the CIO it must be clearly understood that the workers in taking hold in the plants did not take power. They only took hold of the plants. They did not take over the state government, or the national government, or the city police, or the National Guard, or the army. But in their struggles with the police and often with state troopers, they mobilized the section of the population that was not directly involved but felt it also had a stake in the struggle. People from all strata of the population began to support these struggles centering around the workers and often participated in them, both physically and financially.

It should also be clearly understood that all the workers did not act as one, nor did they all sit down as one, nor did they all join the movement as one. When the sit-down movement began in the shops, some workers stayed in while others went home and waited to see how it would all come out. The great Ford plant at River Rouge, where more workers were concentrated than in any other plant in the country, did not erupt at all. It was only four years later, in 1941, that the Ford Motor Company was brought into the union. It is necessary to realize that more workers were organized *into* the union than themselves spontaneously organized the union. The struggle for the union was also the battle against the scabs. There were workers who had to be forced to join by those who had seen and felt the benefits of this great social organization.

From 1935 to the entry of the United States into the war in 1941, we saw in this country the greatest period of industrial strife and workers' struggle for control of production that the United States has ever known. We saw more people than ever before become involved and interested in the labor movement as a social movement. Those who worked in the plants under a new Magna Carta of labor, the great Wagner Act, not only had a new outlook where their own lives were concerned. They also had the power to intimidate management, from the foremen up to the top echelons, forcing them to yield to workers' demands whenever production standards were in dispute. When management did not yield, the workers pulled the switches and shut down production until it did yield. So extensive was their control of production that they forced management to hire thousands and thousands of workers who would not otherwise have been hired. Yet it should be remembered that even at this point, at the height of its greatest power at the point of production, the CIO never solved the question of unemployment. It took the Second World War to put back to work the millions who had been unemployed throughout the 1930s. At the height of CIO power, we had more unemployed than we do now, both absolutely and proportionately.

The first serious contest of the CIO came in 1938, and it expressed itself in contractual language in 1939. That was when the union agreed with management to outlaw sit-downs inside the plants.* The workers, not to be outdone by the union contract, quickly devised a new way that would later prove to be the path of opposition to both union and management. They began to walk out *without union authorization.* In 1939 and 1940, with the shadows of war hovering over Europe, the contract stated that the union would not cause or instigate sit-downs or walkouts in the plants. The NLRB [National Labor Relations Board] was set up in Washington and then, following Pearl Harbor, the War Labor Board. The union leaders gave the government the no-strike pledge, and there followed one of the biggest debates that has ever taken place in the union over the question of whether or not the unions should abide by this pledge. Although thousands and thousands of militant workers, realizing that their newly won freedoms were being curbed, put up a protest, the CIO and all the other unions except the miners' succumbed. But throughout the war, the workers continued to wildcat over production, even though many had sons in the armed forces. It was here also that the union leaders began to use other forces from outside the unions, including members of the War Labor Board, to persuade workers to return to work for the sake of the war effort.

However, in the flux of the Second World War, the workers created inside the plants a life and a form of sociability higher than has ever been achieved by man in industrial society. For one thing, the war meant the entry into the plants of women workers, Negro workers, southern workers, and people from all strata, including professors, artists, and radicals who would never have entered the plant before because of their race, sex, social status, or radical background. With the war going on, you had a social melting pot in the plant, a sharing of different social, political, cultural, and regional experiences and backgrounds.

Side by side with what was taking place in the shop there was also growing up the union organization and what is today the union bureaucracy. With only one problem

---

*When I speak of "the union" without further qualification, I mean, unless the context indicates otherwise, the UAW. This union displays in clearest form the main trends and developments in the CIO as a whole, and it is the union I know best from long personal experience.

at hand—to keep the workers at work—the labor leaders began to sense their power. Yesterday workers at the bench, they now sat at the table with management and with representatives from Washington. If in Washington, on the top level, Roosevelt was clearing things with Sidney* and vice versa, on the local level labor leaders with thousands of workers under their control were also feeling their oats. These labor leaders often used the radical intellectuals as advisors in strategy and tactics. They found these radicals useful in presenting a militant face to the workers. On the eve of the war, the union bureaucracy received the union shop contract that required every worker in the plant to become a member of the union. For the first time the political machine of a plant was organized by the union itself, and the company set up private rooms in the plant for union officials.

Throughout the war period the workers continued to defy the union on its no-strike pledge to the government. Thousands upon thousands of unauthorized strikes took place. (In 1943 and 1944 alone, there were 8,708 strikes involving four million workers.) These strikes took place over such issues as the right to smoke a cigarette (the companies for the first time were forced to allow workers in the big plants to smoke so that tobacco chewing was no longer necessary); the right of management to fire guys who were accused of sleeping on the job, or who laid off too much, or who didn't keep up with production; the right to eat on the job, read on the job, and even to cook on the job. Although workers officially had no right to strike, they achieved by these unauthorized strikes such human rights in the shop as to give them the ability to utilize their talents as never before and the opportunity to develop such an understanding of production as no group of workers in history has ever had the leisure to acquire. With the War Labor Board settling the matter of wages, the union leadership spent most of its time at the bargaining table trying to finagle job classifications that would bring a few cents more, hoping thereby to prove to the workers that they were doing something. It was only the miners' union under John L. Lewis that officially took any position with regard to workers' rights during the war. It did this by calling the only strike of national significance, the strike that brought into the labor movement the "No Contract, No Work" slogan.

It made little difference to management, which was making record profits through the government's cost-plus contracts, how many hours workers worked or even how many workers were on the payroll. So corrupt were both union and management that a government study at Packard Motor Company revealed hundreds of workers sitting

---

*The phrase "Clear it with Sidney" originated at the Democratic Convention in 1944 when Roosevelt said labor leader Sidney Hillman should be consulted on the choice of a vice presidential candidate.

around and gambling while others worked. The workers were frozen on the job and had no way to leave unless they could harass management into firing them. So some of the more ingenious workers carried on individual wildcats, refusing to work in order to be fired, whereupon they would go to another plant for a few cents more. In this way many workers moved from job to job and saw the inside workings of many plants.

Then as suddenly as had come the war, came V-J Day. An era had ended and a new era inside the union movement began. The control of production and the human relations inside the plant which the workers had achieved were now shunted aside by the union. The struggle was shifted from the plane of relations on the job to the economic plane, where it had never been up to then. For although the coming of the CIO had meant wage increases for most workers, these increases had not been big. The average wage in the plants throughout the war was $1.00–$1.25 an hour. It was the long hours of work that made the paychecks big enough to meet the black market prices and the rising cost of living.

The great General Motors strike of 1945–46 was the opening gun in the new vicious circle in which wage increases and fringe benefits would be won by the union and hailed as great social progress, only to be followed by concession of some part of the control over production that the workers had won. But flushed with the freedom they had gained inside the shop during the war, the workers almost unanimously supported the early postwar strikes for economic benefits. It was not until 1948 when the union gave management the "security clause," handing over the right to run production as it saw fit, that dissension began to spread.

Reuther had come to power in 1947 and with him a new kind of labor statesmanship that was to set a pattern for the whole CIO. Riding the crest of the popularity of his "Open the Books" slogan (which he had raised as director of the 1945–46 GM strike), Reuther pushed aside all the militants and radicals who in the sit-downs and during the war had built the UAW up into a model for the CIO. The historic escalator clause the Trotskyites had projected and GM had rejected in 1946 was now accepted by GM. A new pattern of a sliding scale of wages was adopted, which became the foundation of the union's "Sliding Scale of Socialism" strategy. The year 1948 also saw the further development of the union's Political Action Committee, whereby the schemers of the Reuther bureaucracy and the CIO leadership in general hoped to take the militancy away from the shop and focus it on the halls of Congress—to do through legislation what the workers had not done through the sit-downs: exercise political power.

In 1950 the UAW launched its historic pension scheme, and the 117-day Chrysler strike took place. In the contract that emerged from this strike, Reuther (to use one of his favorite phrases) "nailed down" a scheme for the workers to get pensions and holiday pay. It was with this contract that the workers began to realize how nailed down they really were to the company and how they were being made into a part of it. The contract evoked from the workers, particularly the younger ones who were unable to see any benefits for themselves in the pension schemes, the first serious opposition from the ranks. The pension pattern quickly spread to other unions. Again the UAW had established itself as the model for the labor movement.

But 1950 also brought something else—the five-year contract. GM hailed it as a guarantee of five years of industrial peace. From the workers' standpoint it was the beginning of the stalemate, and a rash of wildcats began, which were to continue until the expiration of this contract and even up to the expiration of the next contract, in 1958. During these eight years, from 1950 to 1958, the workers used the wildcat as a defensive weapon to fight off encroachment on their control at the point of production, while the companies gradually wore them down with the help of the union.

During this period, management's strength began to assert itself in conjunction with the Republican administration in Washington. The economic pace of the country was beginning to slow down as Truman's "police action" in Korea was being brought to an end. But the United States was still moving from a welfare state to a warfare state: the cold war was on, the McCarthy era was here, and the radicals and militants were on the run, pushed out by Reuther's insistence that all opponents were "parlor pinks." The Taft-Hartley Act, enacted under Truman, the friend of labor, was now being enforced by Eisenhower. Merger of the AFL-CIO to centralize labor's strength was being talked about everywhere. No one said that the CIO, which represented the most radical point yet reached by labor in the United States, was now going back to join those whose only contribution to the labor movement had been the conservatism of business unionism. All that mattered now was a bigger organization. Strength was measured by size.

The wildcat movement reached its peak in 1955. In that year the Ford and GM workers, who up to that time had more or less supported the Reuther machine, believing that thereby they were supporting unionism, erupted in nationwide wildcats while Reuther was still celebrating the "Guaranteed Annual Wage" contract (which was to turn out to be only a supplementary unemployment benefit). The wildcatters all over the country raised the slogan of "Specific Local Grievances" and forced the union to give them the right to local strikes over these grievances. For the first time Reuther and his associates were really scared. They had been warned by the workers that control of the machine was one thing and control over the workers quite another, that a contract between the union and the company is not necessarily a contract between the workers and the company.

However, a new force had now entered the picture, a force the union had given up its claim to control when in 1948 it yielded to management the sole right to run production as it saw fit. With the decline again of auto production after the Korean War, and with the signing of the 1955 contract, management began introducing automation at a rapid rate.

Automation is a change in the mode of production that is more radical than any since the introduction of the assembly line. But unlike the assembly line, which was to increase the manufacturing workforce over what it had been, automation is an advanced form of technology that replaces individual human controls with electronic controls. What had already happened to the coal miners with the mechanization of the mines was now catching up with the CIO in chemicals, rubber, steel, glass, autos, machinery, etc.

As the companies began to step up their pressure for higher job standards from the workers, the union itself began to try to persuade the workers that automation would provide more jobs for them. Caught squarely between the union contract and the company, the workers continued to wildcat against every attempt to reduce the workforce, but each time they were forced to return by the union officials. New plants with new automated machinery began to spring up all over the country. The workforce in the old plants was broken up, scattered to the new plants. Thus the machine shop work that had been done by 1,800 at the old Chrysler Jefferson plant was now being done by 596 in the new Trenton, Michigan, plant, which supplies not only the old plant with machined parts but all the other plants of the corporation. Layoffs followed by the hundreds as more was being produced not only by the new automated machinery but by forcing workers to tend more of the old machines—man-o-mation. With the building into the automated machines of more controls, thus reducing or eliminating breakdowns, even skilled workers were no longer needed for repair work.

The workers wildcatted, held meetings of their locals, voted not to work overtime, all in an attempt to stem the tide. But the union continued to send them back, and so the layoffs continued, reaching into every section of the plant, and including office workers, time-keepers, and paymasters. As the office workers found their places taken by IBM machines and computers, high-heeled and silk-frocked women began to join the production workers on the picket line.

Finally, after 137 wildcats at U.S. Rubber in one year and 700 wildcats in the Chrysler plants in three years, the union agreed with the company that any worker who wildcats should be first warned and then summarily dismissed. That put an end to wildcatting. Then came what was for all practical purposes the end of the union when, in 1958, under the pressure of the company and for a period of four months, the union insisted that the workers continue on the job without a contract. Meanwhile, the company introduced new work standards when and how it pleased, daring the union to strike. When the 1958 contract was finally signed, there were few workers in the plant who did not realize they had returned to fully company-controlled plants. Time-study men and work layout specialists roamed the plants like sniffing bloodhounds, spying, taking pictures, watching over the workers' shoulders, while the shamed union representatives hid behind pillars or in the toilets.

The cooling-off period the union had devised in the 1955 strike over local grievances was now in full contract effect. After a certain number of workers' grievances had been accumulated, a strike vote could be taken. Then a sixty-day wait was in order. Then, if the International Board considered the grievances worth a strike, a strike might be held, etc., etc. Meanwhile, the company was free to keep the work standard in effect and get out all its production.

So ridiculous has the union become as a workers' organization that in 1958 when the contract with Chrysler was being ratified on a Sunday, the union authorized the workers to take a strike vote the next day.

Once again the workers devised a method to hit back, but this time not against the company. In December 1958, the unemployed began to picket both the plant and the union against overtime. When this happened, the union, in cooperation with the company and the courts, saw to it that a ruling was handed down that any picketing by the unemployed of a plant would be a violation of the contract. Not satisfied with this outlawing of actions by its unemployed members, the union at its next convention decided that unemployed workers could only retain their membership and the right to vote if they reported to the local union during the last ten days of each month. Thus the union has itself drawn the line between the employed and the unemployed. Today unemployed workers march around the Chrysler plants protesting overtime, but the union does not allow them to do so during hours when the workers are actually going into the plant. They may only march when the workers are already inside working.

All that is now left to the workers is the picketing of the union itself.

From 1955 until today the workers have made it absolutely clear that man does not live by bread alone. They have insisted that the question of wage raises or money benefits in any form is not what concerns them but rather the conditions of work in the shop. In 1961 the union bureaucracy negotiated new contracts with the "Big Three" and American Motors. If you take the word of the workers themselves, you will see that not one of the issues that they consider the major ones was settled by the new contracts. The overtime they insisted must go and the shorter work week they wanted have been tossed out the window. In fact, before the ink was dry on the new contracts and before the workers had even ratified them, the plants were scheduling six days a week, ten hours a day. Not only was nothing done to improve working conditions. Management now had another three-year contract under which it can legally pursue the merciless speed-up and intimidation that have been developing since 1955. Even the small representation of stewards and committeemen that workers retained at Chrysler has been reduced. At American Motors wash-up time has been cut out. Faced with the question of unemployment and accepting it as permanent, the union has now embarked on an all-out program to ease as many workers out of the plant as possible, through severance pay, pensions, and increased unemployment benefits. At the same time, it is pushing a profit-sharing plan to incorporate those still left in the plant into management itself. When American Motors workers made it clear that they didn't want the profit-sharing plan, the union manufactured a new definition of democracy: the holding of one election after another until the workers vote the way the union wants them to vote. Joining hand in hand with management, it conducted an intensive educational program to brainwash the workers into line. At General Motors, where local union after local union, with the Pittsburgh local in the lead, refused to go back to work until their local grievances had been settled, the International simply brought all dissident local officers to Detroit where, together with management, it whipped them into line. In the Chrysler setup, where the Twinsburg, Ohio, stamping plant is the key to continued production, the International came to a settlement with the company over the *unanimous* opposition of the entire local bargaining committee.

The UAW is just one union among the major CIO unions. But it has been considered the most advanced, the most progressive, the model of the labor movement that arose in the 1930s. If this is what the UAW has done, it is not difficult to imagine the state of the other CIO unions that failed to reach the heights of militancy and social advancement of the UAW.

Thus, after twenty-five years, the UAW has given back to management every right over production won in the movement of the 1930s and the war years. Today the workers are doing in eight hours the actual physical work they used to do in twelve. At 6:30, a half hour before the day shift begins, you can see workers setting up their operations so that they will not fall behind during the hours for which they are paid. They are afraid to go to the toilet, to get a drink of water, to take time off to go to the funeral of a relative. If they refuse to work overtime, they are written up and sent home on a regular working day. They are afraid to walk around with a newspaper in their pockets for fear that they will be accused of reading on the job. Whenever the company wishes to work the men more than forty hours a week, all it has to do is "schedule" overtime. Here is an example of how "scheduling" works: Recently a worker at one of the Chrysler plants refused to work through lunch when asked to do so by the foreman. The foreman took him to Labor Relations. The Labor Relations man asked the foreman, "Did you tell him the work was scheduled or did you just ask him to work?" The foreman replied that he had only asked the worker to work. Whereupon the Labor Relations man said, "Next time tell him the work is scheduled, and then if he refuses you can fire him because we have the sole right to schedule production as we see fit."

Anyone listening and talking to workers in the auto plants today can tell that the workers are through with the union. In the early days of the union, the most common expression in the shop was, "Now that we have a union we don't have to take a lot of the stuff that we used to take." Now the expression is, "When we had a union we didn't have to take this stuff." For over four years now it has been obvious that the workers themselves have drawn the curtain on the era of the union.

When the situation has reached such a stage, all questions of what the union should have done or could have done, or what some other leaders might have done or should have done, or what might have been achieved if some other policy had been followed—all these questions become completely irrelevant and abstract. To continue to think in such terms is to repeat the mistake that the Trotskyites made for thirty years as they tried to formulate an alternative policy and leadership for Stalin, while Stalin himself was going ahead and building not only the Russian bureaucracy but a Russia that no longer bears any resemblance to the Russia of 1917.

The end of the CIO is not necessarily due to the advent of automation, although it is automation that has made clear its helplessness. It is due to the fact that all organizations that spring up in a capitalist society and do not take absolute power but rather fight only on one tangential or essential aspect of that society are eventually incorporated into capitalist society. *The fact, the key to the present situation, is that from the beginning the union did not take absolute control away from the capitalists.* There was no revolution, no destruction of the state power. The union itself has therefore become incorporated into all the contradictions of the capitalist system and is today fulfilling the same functions for the American state as the Russian trade unions do for the Russian state.

But what about the experiences that the organized workers have had in the last twenty-five years and what is going to happen to the workers who were organized into the CIO, now that automation has arrived and the assembly-line system and mass production by mass production workers are coming to an end as the typical mode of production?

First of all, these workers have undoubtedly made certain very substantial gains not only for themselves but for society, as all workers have who have carried on the class struggle.

The CIO movement gave the American public its first real taste of class consciousness and social thinking, establishing in the American mind for the first time the idea of democracy on the job, in the factories, in the offices, and every place where people work. The whole idea of human relations at work, which has since become the subject of innumerable studies by industrial relations experts, is the product of this movement. The CIO, in conjunction with the war and the activities of the Negroes themselves, established a framework within which Negroes could fight for equality inside the plant. It has done the same for women workers. Over the years it has provided a focal point for the energies of tens of thousands of idealistically minded young people who found in the labor movement a cause that they could serve. The theory that America has a class structure, so long disputed, was finally recognized after the CIO was organized. It was the CIO movement, and following it the Second World War, which established the production worker as a citizen of American society rather than just a beast of burden.

But the question is: What is going to happen to the workers who established these values now that automation is cutting so sharply into their ranks? What is going to happen to the steel, auto, rubber, aircraft, and coal workers who are today the vanishing herd? This is a burning question, not only to these workers themselves but to all who for so long have looked to these workers to save American society as a whole.

These workers will not just fade away, although their numbers will be constantly diminishing both relatively to the rest of the working population and absolutely as older workers die or are pensioned off and no replacements are hired. Those who remain have undergone a very rich economic experience. They are not only educated in the meaning and nature of modern production, but through this they have acquired a certain wit that they will use to evolve tactics of self-defense, prolonging their tenure as long as possible. They have also had a very rich political experience—with the union, with management, and with the government—from which they can draw as they join other strata of the workers in the struggles that will inevitably develop as the pressure is transferred to these new workers. But above all, they have learned a great lesson for all future workers: the lesson that those in whom they put their trust to serve them have wound up as their masters. From now on these workers are going to fight these new masters every step of the way, sometimes advancing, sometimes retreating, but always antagonistic. Their fights will clarify for the new revolutionary forces what a struggle entails.

But what about all the unemployed? What will society do about them? This would be one question if we were talking about a socialist society. It is another question when we are talking about a capitalist society, which is what the United States is today. The capitalists will take care of them. The capitalists, you say? Aren't they the most inhuman people on earth? Aren't they the ones whom these workers have been fighting tooth and nail all the time?

Here is one of the greatest contradictions of capitalism itself. Today the capitalists have to feed these untouchables instead of being fed by them. Faced with an economic crisis or industrial change, as after a war or when a new mode of production is introduced or when the market is glutted with goods, the first thing that the capitalists say is, "We have a cushion." What is the cushion? It is the very thing that these capitalists refused to give for so long and which the workers forced them to yield only by long and bitter struggles—social security, pensions, severance pay, unemployment benefits, supplementary unemployment benefits, charity, welfare. But the capitalists are not going to pay for these, you say. You are so right. The workers have paid and are still paying for them.

Today over one hundred thousand UAW workers are on pension—the product of the new method of silent firing the companies have devised to get rid of one set of workers without having to hire new ones. Even more coal miners, steel workers, rubber workers, iron ore workers, and railway workers have been eased out in this way. In fact, the railroads have made the process clearest of all. They will hire no new firemen, they say, but those still working can continue to ride like dummies in the cabs until it is time for them to retire. In the auto shops one of the methods of silent firing involves the use of the physical rating code. Workers are required to take a physical examination each year and are coded accordingly. Any worker over sixty who cannot keep up with production is forced to retire on the basis of physical fitness. Those under sixty are laid off, draw unemployment benefits until they are exhausted, and then go on social security disability.

What about those millions of unemployed who have never been called back to work and have exhausted their compensation? Well, the government can periodically extend compensation a few weeks longer whenever it fears these unemployed may be getting desperate, and then finally there is welfare, where the bulk of them wind up. But won't this cost the state, the country, the city, the manufacturers a lot of money to take care of all these people? But the people pay for that also, through taxes on those still working. It is among these taxpayers that the tempo of revolt is accelerating.

What about the young people to whom the doors of industry are closed because there are no more semiskilled jobs and because they have not been trained for the new technical jobs? There is always the mass army, the mass peacetime army which, like automation, we didn't have in the United States in earlier periods. This army, the biggest peacetime army in the world, is the modern equivalent of the Civilian Conservation Corps of the 1930s. It is the place where a part of the unemployed youth are now regularly dumped and where periodically even some of the employed are transferred in order to make room for others to take their jobs. Only now it is not civilian, it conserves nothing, and it is paid for out of the taxes of those still working and excludes the most handicapped and underprivileged—the illiterate and the physically unfit.

It is clear that this growing army of the permanently unemployed is the ultimate crisis of the American bourgeoisie. But the American bourgeoisie is a powerful bourgeoisie, and it will take every step in its power to moderate, cajole, and temper the revolution that this condition will undoubtedly provoke. It is also clear that the most organized workers in this country, the members of the old unionized strata, the vanishing herd of production workers, have learned that in the actions they will take or may take from now on, they will have to be joined by other forces. Today, the problem of control over production and the solution of their specific local grievances will have to be dealt with by larger sections of the population. These are now, more than ever before, questions that require the taking on of the union, the city government, the state government, and the national government. That these workers can or may revolt is not the question. Even one worker can revolt. But workers are not fools. They want to win sometimes too, and this is true of American workers more than of any other workers in the world. When they struggle, they like to know that they can achieve some immediate success. And understanding the structure of society as they do, they know they are going to have to join with others in order to win. They will have to move on a scale of revolt powerful enough to smash the union, the company, and the state which, under the guise of national security and national defense, denounces every move they make on their own behalf as irresponsible and irreconcilable with the system itself.

Why don't they take over their own organization, their union? Looking backward, one will find that side by side with the fight to control production has gone the struggle to control the union and that the decline has taken place simultaneously on both fronts. As the company regained control of production through bargaining with the union and through automation, the workers have been losing control of the union. Just as the workers today know that they have to challenge more than the plant management for control over production, they know that merely taking over the union today would gain them very little. Historically, workers move ahead by the new. *That is, they bypass existing organizations and form new ones uncorrupted by past habits and customs.* In the 1930s the workers did not take over the AFL. They formed the CIO, a new organization, adapted to the new forms of industrial struggle. It is also significant that when the AFL and the CIO finally joined together in 1955 with the aim of strengthening the American labor movement, they did not become stronger but rather declined in numerical membership and influence. Millions of workers in the South have never been organized by the unions and never will be because the unions no longer have the social power to overcome the resistance of the southern industrialists who control the local sheriffs, judges, police, politicians, and agents of the federal government. Millions of unemployed have been run out of the unions because they are afraid that these unemployed may explode in some action that would disrupt the cooperation between union and management. Thus with every day more people who can be classified as workers are outside the labor organizations than inside them.

Chapter 2
The Challenge of Automation

Since 1955 and the advent of automation, overtime has been detrimental to the workers. Again and again workers have been faced with the decision to work overtime or not to work overtime, and the decision has usually been: "To hell with those out of work. Let's get the dollar while the dollar is gettable." The amazing thing is that this has nothing to do with the backwardness of these workers. Not only can they run production and think for themselves, but they sense and feel the changes in conditions way in advance of those who are supposed to be responsible for their welfare. But with all these abilities there is one big organic weakness. Over and over again workers in various shops and industries, faced with a critical issue, only divide and become disunited, even though they are well aware that they are being unprincipled and weakening their own cause as workers. Since the advent of automation there has not been any serious sentiment for striking, particularly if the strike was going to come at the expense of material things that the workers already had in their possession, like cars, refrigerators, TV sets, etc. They were not ready to make any serious sacrifices of these; they would rather sacrifice the issue. Between the personal things and the issue, they have chosen the personal. Most American workers have geared themselves to a standard of living that is based on a five-day week *plus*—either in the form of overtime or another job, part- or full-time. And any time this standard of living is threatened, it is a personal crisis, which means that more and more decisions are being personalized and individualized rather than collectivized and socialized.

What then happens to the class struggle? At this point the class consciousness of the workers tends to shift from what has traditionally been considered its main quality, hostility to the class enemy outside, and to focus on antagonisms, struggles, conflicts among the workers themselves. Fights among the workers begin to sharpen, although they no longer take the form they did in the 1930s when the workers were divided by race and nationality prejudices ("Dagos," "Wops," "Polacks," "Niggers," "Buffaloes," etc.). The division is now between two groupings. On one side are the brownnoses, stooges, and workers who are only looking out for themselves, those who are complacent because of the fringe benefits they assume they have won through the union, particularly those near to retirement, and those who would revolt but are afraid of the union bureaucracy or of being fired and then forgotten or branded as "nuisances" and "troublemakers." On the other side are those who emphasize issues, who raise a cry about rights, who call upon workers to make decisions on principles and issues. Among the latter are the unemployed who picketed the union for agreeing to overtime work and who continue to picket the plants against overtime even at the risk of being considered nuisances and troublemakers by those inside the shop, showing that the only ones who are seriously concerned about unemployment today are the unemployed themselves.

Yet these same workers who call the principled ones "nuisances" know exactly what their own chances are. In the average auto plant today, for example, ex-foremen make up nearly one-third of the workforce. Although these ex-foremen know they'll never get back on supervision, they still keep hoping and trying to make an impression on the bosses by their work. The same thing is true of a lot of other workers. They know that the speed-up is going to get worse and worse, but they continue to keep up with it rather than sacrifice a few days' pay to show the company how much they resent it. Instead they take the easy way out and blame it on the union. It is true that contract-wise the union has made all this possible. But at a certain point the union simply becomes an excuse, a pretext for not taking a stand on issues. The sellout that has taken place in the contract between the union and the company does not change the fact of the corruption that has taken place in the workers.

These struggles among the old workers, which are creating such antagonisms among them, are really only delaying tactics on the part of the old herd. They do not touch the real question. It is automation that is the reality facing them and everybody in American society today. America today is headed toward an automated society, and it cannot be stopped by featherbedding, by refusal to work overtime, by sabotage, or by shortening the work week by a few hours. America today is rapidly reaching the point where, in order to defend the warfare state and the capitalist system, there will be automation on top of automation. The dilemma before the workers and the American people is: *How can we have automation and still earn our livings?* It is not simply a question of retraining or changing from one form of work to another. For automation definitely eliminates the need for a vast number of workers, including skilled, semi-skilled, unskilled, and middle-class clerical workers.

It is quite obvious that the attitudes and relations to their work of the new strata of workers who are already deeply involved in automation are different from those of the old workers. It is these new relations to their work that have already made it impossible for the union to organize these new workers or for the old herd of workers to establish any relation to the new workers. The old workers regard the new ones as close to management and as part and parcel of the process that is eliminating them. The union can only approach these new workers in terms of economic demands or job classifications. But their salaries are high enough so that they are not concerned about a few cents more an hour. They start at salaries much higher than the old skilled workers ever dreamed of attaining. But they do not think like the old skilled workers in terms of job classifications. Not at all. Rather, they welcome constant changes in production as a challenge to their ability, knowledge, and ingenuity. Automation to them is as fascinating as going to school and tackling new problems every day. This interest in their work also makes them quite unconscious of the effect that their work is having on the old workers. But there is more than that. These new workers are not like the old inventor-geniuses who were hired by the company only so that their brains could be picked (e.g., as Henry Ford hired George Washington Carver at the peak of his abilities). These new workers are part and parcel of the new *process* of production, and at the same time their ideas are so crucial to the direction of the work that they are inseparable from management and the organization of the work. In their attitude to work and in the process of their work they have invaded management to the point of actually controlling the flow of production itself. But at the same time, in much the same way as the semiskilled workers of the CIO era failed to seize political control, these new workers are leaving the political direction of their work, the purposes for which it is intended, to the old management. And because they lack any experience of struggle, even in getting their jobs, it is unlikely that any initiative for political struggle will come from them. Yet they are the new workforce coming into a position of strategic power in production at a time when all the social problems of American society are being posed.

Automation replaces men. This of course is nothing new. What *is* new is that now, unlike most earlier periods, the displaced men have nowhere to go. The farmers displaced by mechanization of the farms in the 1920s could go to the cities and man the assembly lines. As for the work animals like the mule, they could just stop growing them. But automation displaces people, and you don't just stop growing people even when they have been made expendable by the system. Under Stalin the kulaks and all those who didn't go along with the collectivization of agriculture were just killed off. Even then, if they had been ready to go along, Stalin could have used them. But in the United States, with automation coming in when industry has already reached the point that it can supply consumer demand, the question of what to do with the surplus people who are the expendables of automation becomes more and more critical every day.

Many liberals and Marxists say that they should be used to build schools and hospitals and be sent to foreign countries to aid in their development. But such a proposal has as its premise that this is a socialist society when it is in fact a capitalist society, and what motivates a capitalist society primarily is the return on its investment.

There is only a limited number of these old workers whom capitalism can continue to employ in production at a pace killing enough to be profitable. The rest are like the refugees or displaced persons so familiar in recent world history. There is no way for capitalism to employ them profitably, yet it can't just kill them off. It must feed them rather than be fed by them. Growing in numbers all the time, these displaced persons have to be maintained, becoming a tremendous drain on the whole working population and creating a growing antagonism between those who have jobs and those who do not. This antagonism in the population between those who have to be supported and those who have to support them is one of the inevitable antagonisms of capitalism. And it is this antagonism, brought to a climax by automation, which will create one of the deepest crises for capitalism in our age. In this crisis one section of the population will be pitted against another, not only the employed against the unemployed but those who propose that the unemployed be allowed to starve to death rather than continue as such a drain on the public against those who cannot stand by and see society degenerate into such barbarism. On both sides there will be members of all strata of the population.

Thus automation not only poses the questions of poverty and employment and related economic questions. It brings into sharp focus that element the Negroes always bring with them when they struggle for their rights. It makes the question social because it poses the relations of man to man.

As automation spreads, it will intensify the crises of capitalism and sharpen the conflicts among the various sections of the population, particularly between those working and those not working, those paying taxes and those not paying taxes. Out of this conflict will grow a counterrevolutionary movement made up of those from all social layers who resent the continued cost to them of maintaining these expendables but who are determined to maintain the system that creates and multiplies the number of expendables. This in turn will mobilize those who begin by recognizing the right of these displaced persons to live and from there are forced to struggle for a society in which there are no displaced persons.

Thus automation is the stage of production that carries the contradictions of capitalism to their furthest extreme, creating and sharpening inside capitalist society the conflicts, antagonisms, and clashes between people that make for social progress and the inevitable struggle that goes with it.

The fact has to be faced. Automation is the greatest revolution that has taken place in human society since men stopped hunting and fishing and started to grow their own food. It is capable of displacing as many productive workers from the workforce as have been brought into the workforce since the invention of the automobile at the beginning of this century. (Today an estimated one out of every six American workers depends, directly or indirectly, on the auto industry for employment.) In fact, so devastating would be the immediate effects if automation were introduced in one fell swoop that those who would appear to benefit most from it (the capitalists) are as afraid of its introduction as the workers threatened with displacement.

Up to now the Marxists have more or less gone along with the old herd of semiskilled and skilled workers who have resisted automation, at the same time reassuring themselves that private capitalists themselves would not have sufficient capital to go all-out for automation. What they have failed to recognize is that it is not private capital as such that is introducing automation. The great bulk of the capital invested in automation today comes from the government and is paid for by every member of the American population, whether he is a worker, a member of the middle class, or rich. This is all done in the name of research and defense, but, whatever it is called, the benefits are as great to the capitalists as if they had put out the capital themselves. Thus the capitalists have found a way to get around the high cost of automation as well as the high cost of scrapping still productive machinery.

One of the major aims of the Kennedy administration is to encourage automation by granting subsidies to companies who go full-speed ahead on it, both directly and in the form of tax write-offs. Therefore, when workers fight the introduction of automation, they are taking on not only private capitalism but the federal government itself. Yet so great is the contradiction generated by automation that the government, while giving it such encouragement, must at the very same time set up a new committee to study what is going to happen to the millions of displaced workers.

There is continual talk of new training programs. Yet those making these suggestions know that training is not the answer. In the very period when individuals are being trained, new machinery is being introduced that eliminates the need for such training. Take, for example, the draftsman. With the old methods the engineer used to present his ideas to a draftsman who would make a rough sketch of these ideas, which would then be given to another draftsman to refine. A third draftsman then drew the final blueprint, incorporating in it the exact size, the appearance, and the correct fittings to the millionth of an inch. Today all that this same engineer has to do is talk his ideas into a tape recorder that plays into a computer and the ideas are transformed into a design; the design in turn is fed into a developer and, once developed, can be handed over to the work foreman for building. The three draftsmen have been eliminated from the work process, and only the engineer and the toolmaker remain, each having to know more than before about the other's job.

Marxists have continued to think of a mass of workers always remaining as the base of an industrialized society. They have never once faced the fact that capitalist society could develop to the point of not needing a mass of workers. But this is the dilemma of our time in the United States, and as of now only for the United States. The question before Americans is whether to be for the technological revolutions of automation despite all the people who will be displaced, or to be opposed to this advance, sticking with the old workers who are resisting the new machinery, as workers have done traditionally since the invention of the spinning jenny.

When Marx was writing in the middle of the nineteenth century, he was dealing with the most advanced countries of his day. But even these countries were underdeveloped in the sense that the great bulk of the people were still engaged in farmwork. A large part of the labor force was still needed to produce the foodstuffs for people to eat and the raw materials (e.g., cotton) for industry.

Today if you told the average worker in a big American city that he ought to go back to the farm, he would give you all kinds of arguments. The only reason why he might go back is to get away from the bomb. He wouldn't think of going back in order to make a contribution to society in the way of production. He knows enough about the food that is rotting in the warehouses and the taxes he has to pay to store it. He knows enough about the great change that has taken place in the technology of farm production so that farmwork is no longer socially necessary for the great majority of people.

But as yet few people have been ready to face the fact that, with automation and cybernation, we are reaching the stage where work in the factory is also no longer going to be socially necessary for the great majority. It is easy to accept that a man should move from one form of labor to another form, but it is hard to accept that there will no longer be a mass demand for *any* labor. It is so taken for granted that the production of goods is man's fundamental role in society that, even when technology is making this unnecessary, most people from the politicians and economists down to the man in the street still try to dream up schemes that will require a lot of people to play a material productive role.

Yet, unless the bomb falls and throws what is left of mankind back to the stage of hunting and fishing, society can't go backward technologically. Once man has gone on from the stage of hunting and fishing to that of agriculture, it makes no sense for him to go back to hunting and fishing as a means of making his livelihood. If man no longer needs to drive a mule in order to live, you just can't make him drive a mule. Why then should people keep looking for work in order to justify their right to live if there is no longer a social and economic need for them to work?

Marx envisaged a long period of industrialization during which the number of workers would be constantly growing. He believed that in the course of the conflict between labor and capital in the productive process, a new force would be created with human values of organization, cooperation, and discipline, in sharp contrast with the individualism, competition, and greed of the capitalists. This new force he called "socialized labor," and he said that it was the new society growing up within the old.

In this country during the 1930s Marx's perspectives were realized to an astonishing degree in the organization of the CIO. The workforce had grown in numbers to meet the needs of the mass industrial production, and now came its cooperation, organization, discipline, and revolt. True, this workforce did not actually take over power from the capitalists, but in the crisis of the depression the pressures it exerted compelled the capitalists to establish the welfare state with many of the social benefits that Marx had advocated.

That was a generation ago. Today when automation and cybernation are shrinking rather than expanding the workforce, many people still think in the same terms. They still assume that the majority of the population will be needed to produce material goods and that the production of such goods will still remain the heart of society. They have not been able to face the fact that even if the workers took over the plants they would also be faced with the problem of what to do with themselves now that work is becoming socially unnecessary. They have not been able to face this fact because they have no clear idea of what people would do with themselves, what would be their human role, or how society would be organized when work is no longer at the heart of society.

I don't think Marx would have had any difficulty in facing this fact if he were living today. Marx saw more clearly than anybody that men's ideas are determined by the stage of production. However, Marx is dead and one cannot continue to quote him as an all-time solution for social problems brought on by the development of production. A new theory must be evolved, and it is likely to meet as much opposition as Marx's has met.

Chapter 3
The Classless Society

The United States is a warfare state.

The United States is an inseparable part of Western Civilization.

The United States is the citadel of world capitalism today.

The basic philosophy with which all radicals have approached the analysis of the United States has been centered around what the workers would do, ought to do, would have to do, etc., usually ignoring the power of the state and the bureaucracy, which are today such an essential part of American capitalism; ignoring the fact that when Marx wrote a hundred years ago, and even up to thirty years ago, there was no mass standing army, navy, and air force, and no universal draft in this country; and sometimes realizing but more often forgetting that their own ideas are shaped by no less a fact than that they themselves are by-products of Western Civilization.

Today this philosophy is at the crossroads. The emerging nations of Asia and Africa, which have all these years been dominated by a little corner of the globe known as Western Civilization, are clashing head-on with that civilization. The Marxists themselves, who have done very little since the time of Marx to understand the rest of the globe, merely pigeonholing it in their minds as colonial and semicolonial, must now do some serious reevaluating.

American Marxists, like Marxists all over the world, believe in Karl Marx's ideology. They believe, first, that capitalist production and capitalist society are organized for the benefit of the capitalists and against the masses, and second, that at a certain stage in the development of capitalism, the people living under it will be forced to revolt against it because their conditions will become intolerable and because there will grow up inside this society the embryo of a socialist society, united, disciplined, and organized by capitalist production itself.

In America, the Marxists have found their role more challenging than in any other place on the globe. For inside this country are all the necessary material ingredients that could make socialism possible, and yet it all seems so remote.

It is not a question of whether socialism can or cannot be imported. It is only the specific conditions of a country at a particular time that make people struggle. The fundamental point is that it is impossible for an American Marxist movement to build itself on the ideas of mass poverty and the abolition of private property, which have played such an important role in the development of the European Marxist movements. This alone makes the challenge to American Marxist groups more severe than in any other country. For although the poverty-caused misery of the American masses has by no means been eliminated, it is so dispersed and scattered among various segments of the population that it does not constitute a fundamental and unifying issue to mobilize the masses of the people in struggle.

Thus the question, "What is socialism?" finds the American Marxists constantly seeking a new formula to fit in with the ever-changing conditions of the country. So that today when one asks an American Marxist point-blank, "What is socialism and why should the people struggle for it?" he is baffled and has to fumble around for an answer.

Marx in the nineteenth century said that there would have to be a transitional society between the class society of *capitalism* and the classless society of *communism*. This transitional society, which he called *socialism,* would still be a class society but instead of the capitalists being the ruling class, the workers would rule. It was this rule by the workers which, for Marx, would make the society socialist. As the ruling class, the workers would then develop the productive forces to the stage where there could be all-around development of each individual and the principle of "from each according to his abilities, to each according to his needs" could be realized. At this point there could be the classless society or communism.

In the United States the forces of production have already been developed to the point where there could be the classless society Marx said could come only under communism. Yet ever since the Russian Revolution, all kinds of socialists have differentiated themselves from the communists in terms of political policy and political organization but have never tackled this question of Marxist theory that socialism is just a transitional society on the way to communism and that only under communism can there be a classless society.

How have the revolutionary socialists arrived at just being for socialism while still claiming to be Marxists? The turning point was the Russian Revolution. If the Russians had never won the revolution, socialism and communism, with communism as the ultimate goal, would have remained a part of Marxist ideology, and Marxist organizations all over the world could have kept on struggling against capitalism without having to clarify what they were struggling for.

It was after the Russian Revolution and on the basis of examining what emerged from it that American Marxists began to split and decline. They were always splitting over the question of the correct policy for the socialist—i.e., the workers'—state in Russia, instead of advancing their theory to keep step with the advances of capitalism which, in the United States in particular, were creating the productive forces to make possible a struggle far beyond what was possible in Russia. They tried to make the Russian blueprint fit the United States when the United States was developing productivity to the point where the workers, through economic, political, and social pressure but without political power, were deriving from capitalism the economic benefits that elsewhere the workers would have had to take political power in order to achieve.

What then is still lacking in the United States where capitalism has achieved its highest form? What is it that the American people want, which they find lacking in capitalism and which will mobilize them to fight against capitalism and for another society, call it what you will?

A social revolution in the United States has to mean control of production by the producers. A social revolution in the United States has to mean production for the use of those who need it. But beyond these goals the social revolution in the United States has to mean the classless society—a society in which the antagonisms and divisions between classes, races, and people of different national backgrounds are eliminated and people can develop among themselves civilized and cooperative relations, relations that are possible today as never before because there need no longer be any problem of scarcity of material goods and services. All the problems of scarcity that up to now have required the exploitation of various races and immigrant groupings have now been outmoded by the technological advances of production.

The horizons that the social revolution in America opens up are more tremendous than anywhere else in the world. But the path the revolution will have to take in this country is also more difficult and vicious than anywhere else in the world. First of all, it is the warfare state with its huge forces that has to be challenged. And second, inside each American, from top to bottom, in various degrees, has been accumulated all the corruption of a class society that has achieved its magnificent technological progress first and always by exploiting the Negro race, and then by exploiting the immigrants of all races. At the same time the class society has constantly encouraged the exploited to attempt to rise out of their class and themselves become exploiters of other groupings and finally of their own people. The struggle to rid themselves and each other of this accumulated corruption is going to be more painful and violent than any struggles over purely economic grievances have been or are likely to be.

Chapter 4
The Outsiders

Many people in the United States are aware that, with automation, enough could be easily produced in this country so that there would be no need for the majority of Americans to work. But the right to live has always been so tied up with the necessity to produce that it is hard for the average person to visualize a workless society. The result is that when people face the perspective of their jobs being eliminated by automation, all they can think of is learning a new trade or a new profession, hoping that in this way they can maintain their right to live.

As long as this country was in the situation that most underdeveloped countries are in today, it was natural to tie together the right to live with the ability to produce. But when a country reaches the stage that this country has now reached, productivity can no longer be the measure of an individual's right to life. When you travel around this country and see new automated plants springing up in one area after another, it becomes apparent that the era when man had to earn his right to live through work is rapidly drawing to a close. Within a few years, man as a productive force will be as obsolete as the mule.

It is in this serious light that we have to look at the question of the growing army of unemployed. We have to stop looking for solutions in pump-priming, featherbedding, public works, war contracts, and all the other gimmicks that are always being proposed by labor leaders and well-meaning liberals. Nor is there any solution through production to aid the underdeveloped countries. Perhaps this would be a possibility if we lived in a world society where the whole world was working in a unified way to advance the welfare of all. But the fact is that we are living in a nation-state society in which millions of dollars' worth of goods rot away unless they can be used abroad to further the foreign policy of this particular nation-state.

So there is no way to avoid facing the fundamental problems. What we need today is a new Declaration of Human Rights to fit the new Age of Abundance.

This nation cannot long endure short on rights and long on goods. We must accept the plain fact that we are moving toward an automated society and act on the basis of this fact.

The first principle that has to be established is that everyone has a right to a full life, liberty, and the pursuit of happiness, whether he is working or not. The question of the right to a full life has to be divorced completely from the question of work.

Society must recognize that the magnificent productive tools of our day are the result of the accumulated labors of all of us and not the exclusive property of any group or class. Now that our productive machinery has been developed to the point that it can do the tasks that have heretofore been done by men, everyone, regardless of class, regardless of background, is entitled to the enjoyment of the fruits of that development, just as all men are entitled to warm themselves in the heat of the sun.

Once it is recognized that all men have the right to a full life, liberty, and the pursuit of happiness, whether they are working or not working, have worked or have not worked, it will be necessary for society to create a completely new set of values. Up to now, because productivity has been low, a man's value has been determined by his labor from day to day, by how much he could produce both to sustain himself and to permit investment in new machinery. Now that man is being eliminated from the productive process, a new standard of value must be found. This can only be man's value as a human being.

Up to now it has always been possible if not always easy to cast aside the productive forces that have become obsolete. Work animals were put to pasture; tools, machinery, factories, and even whole industries have been simply scrapped or put to the torch. It has been said that capitalism wages wars so that it can get rid of surplus manpower that has become obsolete. Whether or not this has been true in the past, no capitalist in these days of nuclear warfare would be foolish enough to take this way out. The key question, therefore, is what should be done with man who is being made obsolete by the new stage of production. Obviously no ordinary solution is possible. This is the social dilemma of our time.

No one understands better than a worker the humiliation and sense of personal degradation that is involved when some big shot is coming through the shop and the superintendent tells him to "look busy" in order to prove that there is useful work going on. That is what our whole society is like today. By all kinds of gimmicks—including war work, which may end up killing off those for whom jobs are being created, and a host of government agencies set up to study the problems of "full employment"—the American government is now trying to make work when we are already on the threshold of a workless society.

In the fall of 1961 as Chrysler workers were streaming out of the plant, they were telling one another: "This could be a long strike because the company don't need us at all. They got plenty of cars in storage." That these workers practically to a man felt this way is a sign of the work situation in the United States, not only in the auto plants but in the TV plants, appliance plants, the furniture industry, the clothing industry, and in every domestic industry. It is a known fact that one single auto company like

GM or Ford, or a single refrigerator company like General Electric or Westinghouse, or any major steel firm like U.S. Steel or Bethlehem, could produce enough so that all their competitors could close down. All they would have to do is bring in a little more automation and cybernation (automation plus computers). What they are doing today is "competing" with one another and splitting up the profit. Only in war work, and particularly in missiles, can workers feel sure that if they go on strike they will be missed. *This* is the dilemma of the United States: What is to be done with the men and women who are being made obsolete by the new stage of production?

The American economy is kept going today by the pump-priming of war contracts. This kind of work produces no goods that will reach the consumer market, because what is produced is blown up or stored—some of it at the bottom of the sea. However, by this means money is put into the hands of the large corporations to pay out to their employees, who in turn buy consumer goods.

It is when you begin to think of a peacetime economy that everybody, from the average worker to the labor leader, from the government official to the big capitalist, begins to have nightmares. Each may have a different view of what should happen to the unemployed, but they all have one thing in common: they believe that man must work.

The average worker believes this because that is the only way he or she has been able to live. The labor leaders believe it because if workers didn't have to work, labor leaders wouldn't have anyone to lead. The government official believes it because the role of the government has become that of regulating relations between management and labor, both of whom must exist in order for government to play its part. Thus, as Kennedy's speech to the UAW convention and his overtures to industry show so clearly, government alternately appeases and rebukes both wage earners and capitalists. Finally, the big capitalists can only see themselves growing richer and more powerful if they are in control of the destinies of the workers and the means whereby they must earn a living.

None of these people, and this includes the liberal economists who propose public works and foreign aid as a substitute for war contracts, has left behind the eighteenth-century philosophy that man must earn his living by the sweat of his brow and that anyone who can't or doesn't work (unless he happens to own property) is a misfit, an outcast, and a renegade from society.

None of these people is ready to admit that with automation and cybernation we have to have a much bolder and more radical approach to society. The change we are facing is more radical than the change that five thousand years ago transformed men from roving bands of tribesmen and hunters into forced laborers on the irrigation projects of the early states.

Today the creative work of production is being done by the research engineers, the program planners, the scientists, the electronic experts. Already there are over 850,000 scientists in industry, not counting all those outside industry who are working toward much the same goals. What they are creating is a mode of production which, as long as the present system continues, excludes more and more people from playing any productive role in society. This means that our society, as we have known it, is just as finished as feudal society was finished by the time capitalism arrived on the scene. It means not only that hundreds of thousands are yearly being displaced from production but also that millions are outsiders to begin with. These millions have never been and never can be absorbed into this society at all. They can only be absorbed into a totally new type of society whose first principle will have to be that man is the master and not the servant of things.

Today in the United States there is no doubt that those at the bottom are growing in numbers much faster than the system will ever be able to absorb. This reflects the population explosion taking place right here inside the United States. Already there are millions of young men and women who have never held any jobs at all and who live from hand to mouth, either by charity or by petty crime—in other words, at the expense of those who are working. They cannot be integrated into society unless they work, and there is no prospect of any work for them. What is more, the social measures that made work for such people in the days of the New Deal are completely silly in an age when you can dig ditches, lay bridges, and build buildings merely by pushing a few buttons.

All this means that there can be no smug plan for reforming this system. Because when you add to those who are daily being displaced from the plant the millions who have never even had a chance to work inside a plant, what you have is no longer just the unemployed and the castaways but a revolutionary force or army of outsiders and rejects who are totally alienated from this society.

We must have no illusions that there will be any easy unity between these outsiders and those who are inside the system because they are still working. Already, as we have noted above, the labor organizations themselves are separating off the employed from the unemployed for whom they can do nothing. The present workforce is itself a product of the old society and struggling to survive within it. This means that we must look to the outsiders for the most radical—that is, the deepest—thinking as to the changes that are needed. What ideas will they have? They have not yet expressed them clearly, but their target is very clear. It is not any particular company or any particular persons but the government itself. Just how they will approach or penetrate this target I do not know, nor do I know what will happen when they have done what they must do. But I know that the army of outsiders that is growing by leaps and bounds in this country is more of a threat to the present "American way of life" than any foreign power.

Ask the average American what is the biggest threat to our way of life and the chances are that he will blurt out, "Communism." He sees the threat as coming from a foreign power. Yet the fact that, after all these years of capitalism, he is so afraid of another system means that capitalism has definitely not proved itself to be the system man must have to live his life as a full and equal human being.

If you can once get the average American to stop blaming everything on the communists (or the Negroes, or the Jews, or the Italians) and finally face up to the fact that there is a crisis in his own country, and then ask him what the real crisis is, the chances are good that he will say, "Automation." But when he says this, he still has a distant look in his eyes as if automation, too, is something that will pass without creating or demanding too great a change in the present system of having to work for a living.

But for the outsiders who have never been and can never be involved in this system, regardless of how much free enterprise or initiative they show, automation means something much deeper. It means that they have to find a new concept of how to live and let live among human beings. A new generation of these "workless people" is rapidly growing up in this country. For them, the simple formula of "more schools and more education and more training" is already outmoded. We already have with us a generation of youth who have completed high school and had some kind of training and yet have found no mode of production into which they can fit. Because as fast as they are trained for a higher technical stage of production, just as fast does a new technical revolution take place. Whereas the old workers used to hope that they could pit their bodies against iron and outlast the iron, this new generation of workless people knows that even their brains are being outwitted by the iron brains of automation and cybernation. To tell these people that they must work to earn their living is like telling a man in the big city that he should hunt big game for the meat on his table.

This means that the new generation, the outsiders, the workless people, now have to turn their thoughts away from trying to outwit the machines and instead toward the organization and reorganization of society and of human relations inside society. The revolution within these people will have to be a revolution of their minds and hearts, directed not toward increasing production but toward the management and distribution of things and toward the control of relations among people, tasks that up to now have been left to chance or in the hands of an elite.

There are some people among the older generation who recognize that this is the threat or promise contained in automation and cybernation, but most of them are afraid to face the reality and continue to hope that the old house can still be patched up. The outsiders, in contrast, owe no allegiance to any system but only to themselves. Being workless, they are also stateless. They have grown up like a colonial people who no longer feel any allegiance to the old imperial power and are each day searching for new means to overthrow it.

I am not saying that this new generation of outsiders is as of now an organized force. It is not as simple as that. In fact, no existing organization would even think of organizing them, which means that they will have to organize themselves and that the need to organize themselves will soon be forced upon them as they grow in numbers like the beggars on the streets of India. The big difference between them and Indian beggars is that in India the means to live without having to work are not available, while in the United States these means are all around them, before their very eyes. The only question, the trick, is how to take them.

The forces of a cold war are thus taking shape inside the United States: the war between those who are setting up all kinds of social agencies, training bureaus, and the like to head off the stateless and workless people, and those who are learning every day that these stopgaps offer no solution to their problems. Just as the natural wealth and technical advances of this country have meant that a lot more people here can share in the material things of life than anywhere else, so the eruption of this new group will pose radical concepts beyond the imagination of us all but certainly founded on the principle that people should be able to enjoy everything in life and from life, without being fettered or limited by any system.

These radical concepts cannot come from organized labor. In the 1930s the class struggle of the American workers, united, organized, and disciplined by the process of production, reached its greatest height in the organization of the CIO. Today in the 1960s the American labor movement has reached the end of the road. In the face of the social and ideological adjustments that are necessary to meet the revolutionary changes that have taken place in technology, organized labor is as reactionary today as organized capital was thirty years ago. The fundamental reason for this is that organized labor continues to cherish the idea that man must work in order to live, in an age when it is technologically possible for men simply to walk out on the streets and get their milk and honey. To talk about full employment and getting the unemployed back to work at this point when we are on the threshold of the workless society is as reactionary as it was for the "rugged individualists" to say in the 1930s that the only reason why a man wasn't working was that he didn't have the initiative to go out and get himself a job.

Even in their best days, it should be remembered, the CIO and AFL were not able to do much about unemployment. In 1939 when the Second World War began, there were still more than nine million unemployed, well over twice today's official figure. With the war, millions of old and new workers went into the plants and the last layer of the population, which had up to then been completely outside industry—the Negroes—was finally brought in. Following the war the pent-up purchasing power of the population kept employment high for several years. But after the Korean War management started a two-pronged attack, automating the plants and tightening up on work rules. At about the same time, unemployment began creeping up again.

Organized labor, instead of facing the challenge inherent in automation and the potentiality of material abundance, responded by continuing to seek ways and means to achieve full employment—ranging all the way from demands for a shorter work week and retraining programs to appeals for bigger tax cuts and fatter war contracts.

Why is organized labor unable to face the issues posed by the 1960s? To answer this question we have to look at the changes that have taken place in this country, industrially and socially, over the last quarter century.

As long as the vast majority of a population has not begun to acquire the consumption goods that are possible under conditions of modern technology, the employers are producing not only for profit but also for social use. The people actually need the goods that are being produced—the refrigerators, the cars, the radios, the TVs. These goods provide the material base so that the people can live like human beings. But once the point is reached where the vast majority have acquired these goods, then the manufacturers are no longer producing for social use. Apart from a reduced need for service and replacement, they are producing for a market that has been created not by the needs of the people but by the needs of the manufacturers. They continue producing so that they can continue to make profits and to stimulate the necessary demand, they produce shoddy goods, plan obsolescence, and above all "sell" the population, stimulating its appetite for more and more useless commodities, propagandizing and corrupting it.

Organized labor shares the concern of the employers to keep production going. Its motive is different but the aim is the same. The manufacturers want to maintain production for the sake of profits; the unions want to maintain it to keep up their memberships. Thus the labor organizations have in effect become partners with management in a system of corrupting the population. Each needs the other because each is faced with the same insoluble predicament of capitalism today—that through the use of machines enough can now be produced for everybody without any need either for millions of dollars in profits or millions of people at work.

In order to continue with its philosophy of full employment, organized labor has become part and parcel of the "American way of life." It has become partners with the military in establishing and maintaining a war machine, the only purpose of which is to threaten the destruction of all humanity.

The philosophy of "Solidarity Forever" on which the labor movement was built is today in rags and tatters. There is a never-ending dog-eat-dog fight going on between international unions over the available work—who is going to build a new factory, who has jurisdiction in a new construction project, who is going to do the electrical work or transport the equipment. There is a never-ending dog-eat-dog fight going on between locals of the same union over which plant is actually going to get a particular operation or which local will have jurisdiction in a new construction project, who is going to do the electrical work or transport the equipment. There is a never-ending dog-eat-dog fight going on between workers who want to work only forty hours a week and the money-hungry ones who spend all their time catering to the boss and stool-pigeoning on their fellow workers in order to get the fat $150–$200-a-week checks that come from working fifty, sixty, and seventy hours. Meanwhile those inside the plant become ever more removed from those outside.

The philosophy of "Workers of the World Unite" is also in rags and tatters. The AFL-CIO has official connections with organized labor in other countries and periodically sends a token sum to support a strike. But American organized labor's attitude to the workers of the world is essentially the same as its attitude to the outsiders at home. They should be thrown a bone now and then, but if they were to make any real progress it would be a threat to the insiders. Thus, organized labor is as opposed to imports from foreign countries and as anxious about America's future in relation to the European Common Market as the most reactionary employer. It is as opposed as the American government to the independent development of the economy of the underdeveloped countries and as ready to act as a counterrevolutionary force against all revolutions in the underdeveloped countries.

What about the union militants? Every few months around any auto shop, groups of workers are getting together to discuss how to "bring the union back to the shop." The union is already there, officially. It is recognized by the company; a contract exists between the company and the international governing that particular plant. Yet these workers are constantly getting together with the expressed purpose of "bringing the union back." For them "bringing the union back" means bringing back the atmosphere that existed in the late 1930s and the early 1940s—when they would shut down the plant over a production dispute and settle the issue then and there; when they could talk back to the supervisor without being penalized; when they could go to the toilet whenever they needed to; when they could get a day off to attend someone's funeral without begging the foreman, as they have to do nowadays.

These are very natural and human rights, rights the workers themselves know they have lost. Yet these groups attract very little support. In fact, the more militant they are the less support they get. Instead, the groups who more or less follow the union machine usually win majority support, easily coming out on top in union elections without even making any promises to the workers except to support the policies of the international.

The militants who are always meeting and discussing and devising ways and means of "bringing back the union" are generally the most advanced workers in the sense that they are ready to struggle for better working conditions. Yet when you tell these militants that they are never going to bring the union back to where it was because the union that they are thinking about and hoping for has already outlived its usefulness, and that the workers are never again going to struggle for and through this kind of organization, they can't understand why. They have become so accustomed to what used to happen in the early days of the union, when large numbers of workers were very militant, that they still believe that there are plenty of militant workers left in the shop and that all they have to do is get together and organize them. They cannot face the changes that have taken place in production since the 1930s. They cannot get it into their heads that these old workers who used to be so militant are now a vanishing herd who know that they are a vanishing herd, who know that, because of automation, the days of workers like themselves in manufacturing are numbered, and who have therefore decided that all they can do now is fight to protect their pensions and seniority and hope that the company will need them to work until they are old enough to retire or die, whichever comes first.

You would think that in this restless group of militants who have fought so hard for progress there would be some who could see the handwriting on the wall and realize that work as they have known it and the mobilization of people in the struggle over working conditions have become obsolete. But it is in this group of militants that you find the greatest reluctance to accept the inevitability of the workless society. In this refusal to face reality, these militants who are so advanced are really behind the average worker who has reconciled himself to eventual oblivion. Why?

It is precisely because these workers are more advanced, in the sense of wanting to struggle for progress, that they cling to the idea of organizing the struggle through work. The fact is that it is through the struggle over work that social reforms have been won over the last hundred years, especially in this country from the mid-1930s to the mid-1940s. The struggle around working conditions has been the most progressive factor in American society, educating and organizing people to fight for human rights as nothing else in this society has been able to do. These militants know this because they have lived through it. Most of them, without ever having read a word of Marx, have experienced in life what Marx analyzed in theory. They cannot give up an idea or a method on which they have depended for progress until they can see another one, and they have not yet seen or figured out another way to fight for human needs and human rights.

There are a lot of people outside the shop, not only radicals but liberals also, who have much the same idea as these union militants. Only it is not as obvious in their case because they are not in the shop and therefore do not have the opportunity to organize themselves into little groups so easily. But these liberals and radicals are also hoping and waiting on the workers to struggle. Even those who attack Marx most viciously still think like Marx, because what Marx thought was so true until only a few short years ago when the new age of nuclear energy, automation, and cybernation began.

Actually these union militants will go down fighting for things like a shorter work week (thirty-for-forty), or two months' paid vacation, or six months' paid furlough, or the four-hour day—all of which are within the framework of keeping the workforce intact. Even when there is no longer any reason, because of the development of automation and cybernation, to keep the workforce intact, they will still fight to keep it intact. Therefore it is hopeless to look to them as the ones to lead the fight for a workless society. The workless society is something that can only be brought about by actions and forces outside the work process.

Government officials, labor officials, and the university professors whom they both hire to help them beat their brains are working overtime, trying to find some scheme to create full employment. But whatever schemes they come up with, whether the thirty-five-hour week, new training programs, bigger and badder war contracts, or bigger and better public works projects, they are playing a losing game. America is headed toward full unemployment, not full employment.

In 1962 I visited the West Coast where a large percentage of the country's war work is concentrated and the newspapers rejoice every time a new war contract is awarded to the area. Yet, talking to guys who work in the plant like myself, I found that their main worry is what to do about automation and the people it is throwing out of work. A friend of mine told me about a Mexican American who works in the plant with him and who describes automation as a beast of the world that is moving in on people and nobody knows what to do about "it." This worker has come to the conclusion that the only sensible solution is for the company to put in new machines as fast as it can, while every guy who is displaced by these new machines continues to receive his weekly paycheck. His idea is that the sooner the machines become fully employed and the people become fully unemployed, the better.

My friend has put some thought into how this would work and has decided that if the old philosophy that man has to go to work must be retained, then the displaced workers could continue to go to the plant and just sit around and watch the machines. He was quite sure that if this happened the workers would be continually putting forward new suggestions as to how to redesign the machines to make them more efficient and displace more men, instead of doing what they are now doing, constantly trying to think up new ways to fight the machine so as to keep their jobs. We both agreed that there is nothing more agonizing than holding back the ideas that every worker is constantly getting as to how to increase productivity.

I told him that I could foresee a time when machines would be so perfected that there would be no need for the great majority of people to go into the plant except occasionally and that I was quite sure that, once released from the necessity to work, men and women would come up with new ideas for increasing productivity that would astonish the world. Fishermen just fishing for fun would come up with new ideas for fishing, guys puttering around their lawns would think up new ways to grow grass, people with nothing to do but sit around and observe would be constantly producing new ideas and bursting to share them with others. It is only the necessity to work, *forced labor,* that has created in man the need to fight new modes of production and to keep new ideas about increasing production to himself.

One immediate step out of the dilemma would be to employ the seniority system in reverse. As new machines are brought in, those who have been working longest, instead of being kept on the job, should be eased out of work. Every company, even if it has to get subsidies from the government to do so, should put in the most modern equipment available, and as this is done those workers with the highest seniority should be laid off with continued full pay equal to that of those still working.

This would be very far from being a solution, however, since it does not take into consideration the million and a half young people who are entering the adult world every year plus the millions like them who, being unemployed, have no claim on any company. It is in connection with this group of outsiders that those who hope for full employment are really caught in a dilemma. These millions can never become part of any workforce in the sense that we know it. There is no Siberia to which they can be sent, and even if there were they wouldn't go. They have seen too much of what is possible in this society; they also know that there are enough of them around to be a threat. Already the big question in cities like Detroit is whether a way can be found for these outsiders to live before they kill off those of us who are still working. How long can we leave them hanging out in the streets ready to knock the brains out of those still working in order to get a little spending money?

Obviously it would be far better to give these outsiders a weekly check also rather than leave them with no alternative but to look for guns and knives to use against the insiders. But giving them a check is not enough. There has to be some way in which to develop their creative abilities and sense of responsibility, because without this they can become completely empty creatures. What makes it so easy to propose a weekly paycheck for those who have worked all their lives is that they have already acquired some discipline and sense of responsibility from their work. But those who have never worked and will never get a chance to in this society will have to find some other way to develop their creative abilities before these are destroyed by forced idleness.

This is one of the great challenges facing our society today. Another is the question of peace and war, to which we now turn.

Chapter 5
Peace and War

When the A-Bomb was exploded by the United States over Hiroshima, the vast majority of Americans rejoiced. To them the bomb simply meant the end of the war and the return home of brothers, sons, fathers. Few Americans realized the potential threat that the bomb represented to all mankind. In fact, not until much later was it learned that key scientists who had actually been involved in the creation of the bomb had argued against its military use, pointing out that it would be only a few years before other countries would have the same weapon. Einstein, without whose theories the A-Bomb could never have been created, said later that if he had known the use to which his ideas would be put, he would have become a plumber.

Outside the United States today what comes to many people's minds when the bomb is mentioned is the fact that it was first dropped on a nation of colored people and not on the Germans who were also the enemy in World War II. Inside the United States this fact is rarely mentioned.

For four years after the end of the Second World War the A-Bomb was to the United States what the British navy had been to Western Civilization prior to the First World War. It made the United States "boss," and the Americans didn't let anybody forget it. But it was obvious that the United States could not long retain its monopoly of the bomb. In fact, in the era of scientific technology symbolized by the bomb, the United States could only lose the military supremacy it had previously enjoyed on the basis of mass armaments production. It was difficult, therefore, for people outside the United States to take seriously the American offer to put the bomb into mothballs if no other power would try to produce one.

Then in 1949 two things happened that brought about a radical change in world politics. First, the largest country in the world, China, was taken over by the Communists. And second, Russia exploded an A-Bomb.

The mere thought that the United States would now have to justify its position as a world power in more or less equal competition with the Russians produced panic in every section of American official society. It was this panic that created the environment in which McCarthy ran wild. In rapid succession a list of subversive organizations was issued by the attorney general and laws were passed to screen and bar from the United States anyone suspected of radical connections. Noncitizens were denied the formal democratic rights of free speech, free belief, and free association, of arrest only with warrant, and of the right to judicial appeal over administrative decree. Naturalized citizens, some of them residents of this country since infancy, became subject to denaturalization and deportation by administrative action if suspected of radical politics at any time in their lives. The heads of government began accusing their predecessors of treason, like murderers and cutthroats at bay in a basement. New Deal liberals were hunted with the ferocity of a pack of bloodthirsty wolves; scientists, newspapermen, and artists were hounded into becoming informers or else giving up their professions. People hid their books, destroyed records by Paul Robeson, and canceled their subscriptions to liberal newspapers and magazines, lest by these signs of intellectual activity they invite investigation on suspicion of subversion.

In foreign policy the United States began its brink-to-brink improvisation; the hasty gathering up of allies like Franco and Chiang Kai-shek, completely discredited in their own countries and abroad; the wooing of Tito; the arming of Germany; and finally the reckless development and testing of bigger and better bombs and guided missiles, competing with Russia like two football teams competing for an international championship.

During this time the Marxist organizations in the United States persistently pointed out the horrors of the bomb, but primarily in the spirit of propaganda, against capitalism and some against Russian communism, and in general for socialism. Meanwhile they went their merry or unmerry way, as if the bomb were just another stage in imperialist warfare, saying little about it as long as the workers were quiet about it. With the history of past antiwar groupings in mind, and particularly comparing their own "realism" with the idealism of the pacifists, they were content to rest their hopes on the workers' eventually making a revolution, taking control of society, and putting an end to imperialist war. Actually, what they failed to realize is that just as automation represents a revolution in the process of production, so the A-Bomb, H-Bomb, and intercontinental missiles represent a revolution in the process of warfare. Mankind has now reached the stage of push-button war and mass suicide.

Up to now it had been possible to speculate about what attitude the workers or the masses of the population might or ought to adopt toward a war once it had been declared or started, e.g., organize a general strike or rise in protest and bring it to an end. It had been possible to predict that the shattering effects of a prolonged war fought with modern weapons would set the stage for revolutions, after which the workers could begin the herculean task of reconstructing society.

The new reality today, however, is that the bomb does not recognize any distinctions between race, class, or nation. When it falls, it will fall on everybody, regardless. When it falls, it will leave no class behind to reconstruct society—not even the workers. A nuclear war would leave no time for anyone to debate or argue about policy or organize a general strike. If there is going to be any movement that will stop the bomb and create the conditions for revolution, it will have to come *before* the bomb is dropped—not afterward. If there is going to be a revolution over the question of nuclear war, it will have to be *before* the nuclear war starts—not afterward.

With the launching of Sputnik and its beep-beep-beep overhead, the world suddenly became aware that an H-Bomb could be launched in the same way. The Atlantic and Pacific oceans, which had made so many generations of Americans feel so secure, no longer appeared as a protection. Americans began to feel the dread and horror with which Europeans for years had been responding to the brinkmanship of Dulles.

But the years of cold war had made war a way of life for the government and all its military and paramilitary departments. It had become a way of life for half of America's major industries. It had become a way of life for America's workers. It had become a way of life for the trade unions. It had become a way of life for the professional crusaders against communism and the elements in the population whom they represent. It had become a way of life even for most of America's churches.

Significantly, the only people who had begun a serious questioning of war as a way of life were those most directly and intimately involved in the revolution that had taken place in modern warfare: the atomic scientists themselves. Even before the explosion of the first bomb over Japan, a task force of scientists, headed by Dr. James Franck, had set itself up as a "Committee on Social and Political Implications" and submitted a report to the government arguing against the direct military use of the bomb. In 1945, after the bomb had been dropped, a group of scientists under the leadership of Eugene Rabinovitch, a Chicago chemist, began publishing the *Bulletin of the Atomic Scientists* as a forum where scientists could point out the perils of nuclear warfare and examine roads to disarmament. So intense have been the debate and discussion among scientists that it is possible to speak of two unofficial "parties" in the American scientific community: the "humanitarian party," which calls in varying degrees for a ban on the bomb, and the "government" party, which supports and lends authority to the government's policy. The humanitarian party, emphasizing the cooperative, non-national, and in fact international character of science, has been responsible for holding international conferences with their colleagues from behind the iron curtain. These conferences have become known as the Pugwash Conferences, since the first three of them (1957–59) were held on the Pugwash, Nova Scotia, estate of American industrialist Cyrus Eaton, after permission to enter the United States was denied by American authorities to communist scientists.

However, the humanitarian party among the scientists has remained isolated from the American public. The loudest voice heard in public has been that of Dr. Edward Teller, chiefly responsible for the creation of the H-Bomb and leading exponent of government policy. When Nobel Laureate Linus Pauling was called before a congressional committee in 1960 and asked to inform on those who had helped him get up a 1958 ban-the-bomb petition to the UN (this petition had been signed by 11,021 scientists from 49 countries, including 104 from the United States), it caused scarcely a ripple in this country.

In the summer of 1961 this situation began to change. After a three-year moratorium on testing by the two powers and at the height of the Berlin crisis, the Russians resumed nuclear testing at a rapid rate. By this time the American people could no longer comfort themselves by doubting the technological capacities of the Russians. Gagarin and Titov put an end to that.

In Britain where the country had been caught between East and West and where it was obvious that the whole island could be destroyed by one bomb, the ban-the-bomb movement had been growing for years and reached a peak in 1960–61. The Africans declared their opposition to any nuclear testing on their soil. But in the United States antibomb demonstrations could rarely rally more than a few hundred supporters, mainly longtime pacifists.

Following the Russian tests, however, the movement began to take on mass momentum. On November 1, on the initiative of a few women in Washington, D.C., a series of demonstrations took place in sixty cities from coast to coast. In all, about fifty thousand women took part. In New York and Los Angeles there were several thousand women in the demonstrations. In the Boston area hundreds of students and university faculty members marched on the Federal Arsenal at Watertown. With the entry onto the scene of the women, the students, and the professors, the ban-the-bomb movement began to take on a broad social character. Since November 1, 1961, Women Strike for Peace committees in various cities have remained more or less intact, in order to organize periodic demonstrations at the UN, before federal buildings, to march on Washington, to send delegations to city councils and state legislatures, etc. Across the country over four thousand professors added their names to an open letter to President Kennedy, protesting the futility of civil defense in this age of nuclear war. Students from all over the country organized a march on Washington on February 16, 1962.

It is quite obvious that these demonstrations have begun to take on the character of a social movement, confronting the warfare state and implying a challenge to it despite the announced (and no doubt genuine) intentions of the participants simply to implement the "peace race" proposals of the president. In turn, the growth of the ban-the-bomb movement has given and will give further impetus to the counterrevolutionary super-patriots, led by the Birchites, the militant ex-generals, the Dixiecrats, and the China Lobby, and gain support among the veterans and middle-class layers who live on the past glories of the all-American state. Up to now the organized labor movement has given only token support to the peace movement. Obviously fearful that widespread agitation against the bomb will upset the warfare economy and increase dissatisfaction among workers already living in dread of unemployment, it has carefully refrained from calling upon workers to participate in the ban-the-bomb movement.

The new peace groupings, particularly the scientists and women, have already passed one test that other organizations in the United States have failed since the cold war and McCarthy era began. They have been able to meet and overcome the label of "pro-communism." This was the great victory won by the Women Strike for Peace at the House Un-American Activities Committee hearings in late 1962. Up to then, every grouping that had been labeled in this way by patriotic organizations or by any of the various governmental committees and agencies had been fatally weakened. But so great is the fear of nuclear annihilation among the scientists and women that it has enabled them to overcome the fear of communism. Communism at worst could only mean a change in the political system. The bomb would mean no existence and therefore no system at all. In that sense these peace groupings have gone beyond the "Better Red than Dead" smear, and this in itself is a great victory.

But the United States is so full of other social and economic contradictions that even though the new peace movement has been able to surmount the kind of official and unofficial attack that heretofore has crippled other organizations that began to tackle the warfare state, this has not been enough. In October 1962 the Cuban crisis came along, and although many of the members of the peace movement found themselves in protest picket lines, the heart of the peace movement has practically stopped beating since that time. The fact is that for the peace movement really to have contested the president's actions in Cuba, it would have had to call upon the missile workers in *this* country not to produce missiles and for the sailors of *this* country not to man the ships. In other words, it would have had to face the reality that as long as the United States has missiles and rockets, every other country has the right to have missiles and rockets, even one only ninety miles off the shores of the United States and regardless of whether such missiles are offensive or defensive.

Up to the time of the Cuban crisis the peace movement in this country only had to grapple with the question of bombs and missiles in the hands of the two great powers—the United States and the USSR. But in the Cuban crisis it was confronted with the question of missiles and bombs in the hands of a country that is part of the world revolutionary and anticolonial struggle. This is the question the peace movement is going to have to face increasingly as the months and years pass.

In the Cuban crisis the peace movement was confronted with the question of the ex-colonial countries and their rights, just as in the course of its development inside this country, it has already been confronted with the question of its relation to the Negro struggle. The reason is that the question of peace is much greater than the question of simply stopping bomb tests. All the factors that go into deciding whether a nation should have to depend upon the bomb or not are shaped by the world revolutionary struggle and also by the struggle between the already developed nations and developing nations. Climaxing it all is the question of China and who will be able to talk to the Chinese. What peace group in the United States would even be allowed to send someone to China? How would they even know the road to China, considering the colossal ignorance that exists in this country on the question of China? What will they have to offer the Chinese? And why should the Chinese even listen to any of these Americans when the Chinese have already been read out of the human race by Americans, in the same way that Negroes have been read out of the human race by Americans for three hundred years? It is quite clear that the Chinese are not caught in the same predicament that the Negroes have been caught in for so long. The Negroes were trapped inside this country, but the Chinese have their own country and they are not asking to be integrated into this country. In fact, they are not even asking to be integrated into the world society. They existed long before other modern societies came on the scene, and they are not begging anyone to recognize their independence. They achieved it themselves through a revolution in 1949.

Will the peace movement fight for the recognition of Red China simply from the standpoint of fear, or is it going to fight for the recognition of Red China from the standpoint of the plain humanity of the Chinese? The peace movement cannot save humanity as long as it refuses to face the inhumanity that exists inside this country toward other racial and national groupings and that exists in the relations of this country to other races and nations. Nor can it ever get a peacetime economy in this country until it clashes with the war economy and the reasons why such a war economy exists. Because the same people who are for war in this country are those who are for discrimination against races and nations. They are the ones who are for the continuation of American superiority over other nations and other areas of the world. They are the ones who want the workers to continue to work in order to live, even if the work they are doing is nothing but war work in order to kill. And they are the same ones who are for taxing the war workers in order to get the money to keep on making war materials. There will be no peace until there is war against these Americans.

Chapter 6
The Decline of the United States Empire

History has known many empires—the Sumerian Empire, the Assyrian Empire, the Chaldean Empire, the Egyptian Empire, the Roman Empire, the Holy Roman Empire, the British Empire, to name only a few. All these empires came to an end, usually as a result of a combination of military defeat and internal revolt. Now it is the turn of the United States Empire.

For over a century, under the cover of the Monroe Doctrine, the United States has ruled its Latin American domain as Chicago gangsters rule a certain territory, warning all others to keep out.* Long before the word "satellite" was used to describe the relationship of the Eastern European countries to Russia, it was obvious that the economic and political life of Latin America revolved around the Yankee sun. What the Asian and African colonies were to the European powers and what Eastern Europe has been to Russia, the Latin American republics have been to the United States. Although independent in name, their economies have been completely at the mercy of Big Brother to the north, and therefore their politics have been as well. They have been kept in the status of countries with one-crop economies, supplying sugar, bananas, coffee, tin, copper, etc., chiefly to the United States, which could therefore control them by manipulating commodity prices and quotas. At the same time the United States has been the largest supplier of Latin American imports of manufactured goods and of investment capital. In fact, 80 percent of foreign capital invested in Latin America, public and private, comes from the United States. When manipulation and control by economic means have fallen short, the United States has hesitated only a moment before using money and arms directly to prevent and foment, divert and steer revolutions and counterrevolutions, to make and unmake governments. The chief function of the U.S. government has been to protect the right of firms like United Fruit to exploit the cheap labor and rich resources of Latin America; to maintain in power anti-communist and pro–United States dictators like Batista in Cuba and Trujillo in the Dominican Republic; and to protect the landowners of gigantic estates from revolt by peasant laborers.

All this time few people in the United States knew anything about this vast continent just below the Gulf of Mexico and the Rio Grande. Those who thought about it at all did so in terms that the movies have made familiar, as the land of bananas and

---

* I am not implying that Latin America constitutes the entire U.S. empire. But together with Canada, Latin America does constitute the heart and core of the empire, and both its problems and its fate can best be studied there.

tropical splendor where North Americans can go live it up in the midst of poverty and misery, where Yankee adventurers decide to sell or not to sell guns to rebel generals according to their love or hate for beautiful damsels. Then in 1958 Vice President Nixon was sent on a goodwill tour to reassure the South Americans that, despite the billions of dollars of aid sent only to Europe, their Good Neighbor to the north had not forgotten them. When the vice president was spat on and stoned by mobs in Peru and Venezuela, the government and the people of the United States began to realize how overdue was an agonizing reappraisal of their relations with Latin America. It was clear that the Good Neighbors to the south were getting out of hand and that the winds of change were blowing in Latin America, stirring up revolutions of the masses that were quite different from those of rival factions the United States had found so easy to control.

The winds of change became a hurricane in the Cuban Revolution. What started out in Cuba as opposition to Batista inevitably became a head-on conflict with Yankee imperialism. All upheavals that had fallen short of social revolution had fallen back into dependence on Yankee imperialism; Venezuela is a good example. Large-scale private property in Cuba, which was in fact primarily U.S. private property, had to be confiscated before Cuba could be truly politically independent. Going deeper into social revolution meant deepening the conflict with Yankee imperialism and vice versa. This was the path Castro had to follow whether he wanted to or not.

But Yankee imperialism could not afford to let Cuba set an example in social revolution for the rest of Latin America. Before the Second World War Mexico could get away with the expropriation of foreign oil properties because there was no real danger then that the example would spread. But in 1960, the survival of the Cuban Revolution meant its certain imitation by the rest of Latin America. On the other hand, to have a social revolution in Cuba is practically like trying to have one in one of our fifty states. The Cuban one-crop sugar economy was almost as closely tied to the U.S. economy as the one-crop auto economy of Detroit is. To reorganize and diversify this one-crop economy required not only confiscation of large-scale United States property. It also required an enormous amount of technical and economic aid. Under the circumstances of U.S. hostility, this aid could come only from countries that not only recognized the validity of Cuba's struggles for independence but had reason to welcome them.

In Africa, thousands of miles away from the cold war powers, it is not too difficult to be neutral. But Cuba, only ninety miles away from Florida, began by being as much an economic, military, and political satellite of the United States as Hungary and the other Eastern European countries are of Russia. Therefore, to break away, it had to have the political and economic aid which, for example, Yugoslavia got from the United States after it broke with Russia in 1948. But Cuba's problem was even more critical. Yugoslavia did not have to confiscate Russian property, and it continued to claim membership in the "socialist camp." Cuba not only had to confiscate U.S. property. It had to denounce capitalism altogether.

Revolutionaries in the United States hailed the Cuban Revolution as the first socialist revolution in the Americas. The communist world also hailed it as such. The revolutionaries living under U.S. capitalism had particular reason to rejoice. U.S. capitalism, against which they had been fighting all these years and which is the greatest capitalist power of this century, had been challenged. But revolutionaries have many different and conflicting ideas as to what does and what does not constitute a socialist revolution. To some it is a matter of material gains; to others it is the nationalization of property; to others it is the political freedom and organization that the masses achieve and/or the arming of the masses; to others it is the formation of workers' councils to control production; to others it is joining the "socialist camp"; and to still others it is remaining entirely neutral of any bloc. The standards and the procedure used in determining the degree of support and rejoicing are much the same as those the various revolutionary groupings have been employing for over forty years with regard to the Russian Revolution.

What these groupings rarely take into consideration is the fact that the world has moved in these forty years far beyond where it was at the time of the Russian Revolution and that it is today divided into three blocs: the Western bloc, the Eastern bloc, and the neutralist bloc, with the last bloc lacking economic power but wielding great moral power. But moral power is a long-range thing. When a country within either the Western or the Eastern bloc breaks away from that bloc, it must *immediately* face the question of getting aid from the other bloc in order to survive. This reality has to be faced, not from the point of view of North American revolutionaries and *their* desires, hopes, standards, and morale but from the standpoint of the country that is making the revolution. In Hungary the revolution was crushed before anyone but the Hungarians had to face the fact that the other Eastern European countries and the Russian people had not come to the support of the Hungarian Revolution and that therefore the Hungarian Revolution could survive only if it received aid from the Western bloc.

Revolutionaries in the United States are going to be faced with a similar reality time and again in the period ahead as the Latin American revolution spreads. They have no right to use these revolutions to bolster their own morale or to test their own theories about what is socialism. First and foremost, they must take the position that they are *for* these revolutions and that it is the right of all these countries to break away from the power that has dominated them for so long and to govern themselves. They must be *for* all the Latin American countries freeing themselves from U.S. domination. And they must be *for* the people in these countries whenever the latter, feeling that their government is not running the country in the best interests of the people, throw that government out by whatever means they choose to take. The only time when they can legitimately take a position contrary to this is if the revolution takes the form of discrimination against a race or nationality, as for example against the Negroes in the United States or the Jews in Germany. They cannot start with the question, "Where is the revolution going to end?" Any genuine revolution today is going to have to go in a leftward-forward direction because the expectations of the masses everywhere can be satisfied only by permanent revolution in a leftward-forward direction. Except episodically, the direction is not going to be backward because the moment that the revolution goes backward, there is going to be another revolution. Having clarified their minds on this fundamental position, radicals in the United States will no longer have to spend endless hours trying to justify these revolutions as socialist, trying to decide whether they should hold elections or not, whether the people are ready for parliamentary democracy or not.

It is quite obvious that the breakaway of the Latin American satellites will deprive North American capitalists of their main source of super-profit, and there is no reason to doubt that they will try to make their own people pay for these losses. The people of the United States will have to begin facing the fact that their luxurious standard of living has been won, in part, at the expense of the peasants and workers of Latin America. It is unlikely that U.S. capitalism will be able to arouse the people sufficiently to support an open, large-scale invasion of Cuba for counterrevolutionary purposes. Its strategy is rather to seek to isolate the Cuban Revolution through such measures as the Alliance for Progress. But the Cuban Revolution is not an artificial imported revolution, and the ingredients that set it off exist in all the Latin American countries. This means that, in addition to the Alliance for Progress, which has already become a joke, the United States will be carrying out all kinds of maneuvers and gangster tactics—diplomatic, military, and economic—from the use of warships to the blackmail use of economic aid, as it has been doing in the Dominican Republic and at the conferences of the Organization of American States.

It would be unrealistic to expect the people of the United States to come directly to the aid of the Latin American revolutions on any large scale. The grievances and issues that underlie these revolutions and propel them to success are in Latin America itself. But there are going to be many, many shameful episodes similar to that of the attempted invasion of Cuba in 1961 that will shake up the people of the United States, make them squirm, and force them to question themselves and their government. The spread of the Latin American revolutions means that before the people of the United States there lies a painful period of decline in prestige and in confidence, both in themselves and in their governments, similar to that which the British have been experiencing with the decline of their empire. All this will help deepen the general revolutionary crisis in this country.

Chapter 7
Rebels with a Cause

When people talk about how many Russians were killed behind the iron curtain in the concentration camps, it doesn't move American Negroes at all. The reason is very simple. The same thing happened to them in this country. White American workers didn't have to go through what the Russian workers went through under Stalin because the Negroes went through it for them on the cotton plantations of the South. Every immigrant who walked off the gangplank to make his way in the land of opportunity was climbing onto the Negroes' backs. For the United States is not like any other country that has built itself up on the basis of slavery. This country committed the most unpardonable crime of all. After freeing the slaves, it then segregated them off on the basis of color as inferior to the rest of the population, both in law and in fact. For this crime the United States will occupy a position in the annals of history comparable only to that occupied by Hitler Germany for the crimes it committed against the Jews. But Hitler lasted only twelve years, during which he killed six million Jews. The crime of the United States has lasted over a century.

To this day, the American nation celebrates the Civil War and records it as a war to free the slaves. But in the eyes of Negroes the Civil War was the war that made it possible for the United States to be industrialized, the war that resulted in the Bargain of 1877 between northern capital and southern landed aristocracy, which left the former slaves living and working under a caste system as brutal as that of slavery itself.

Following the Civil War and a brief period of Reconstruction during which Negroes enjoyed their newly won freedoms, the North made its infamous deal with the South. According to this deal, the South could go its way, using the Negroes as sharecroppers on the cotton plantations. In return, the North got from King Cotton much of the capital it needed for industrialization, both through export of cotton to England and from its own textile mills. This Bargain of 1877 was never recorded, but it ranks with the other more famous compromises on principle that have distinguished the United States in its relation to slavery.

The Negro question in the United States has therefore never been purely a question of race, nor is it purely a question of race today. Class, race, and nation are all involved. The American nation has become the giant of industry that it is today on the backs of the Negroes. The working class has from the very beginning been divided. The white workers were an aristocracy that benefited first and always from the exploitation of the Negroes and in between by the exploitation of each new wave of immigrants.

What has made the problem of the socialist revolution in the United States so complicated and difficult for American Marxists is the fact that there has been no mass party of labor in this country as in the industrialized countries of Western Europe. What American Marxists have failed to understand is that in Western Europe the mass parties of labor were formed and were able to endure not only because of the working-class struggle against capital but also because the workers struggled against the landed aristocracy. During this same period no mass party of labor arose here because the workers, as long as they could go their way settling on the free lands of the West and working as free labor in the new industries of the East, were ready to allow the landed aristocracy of the South to exploit the Negroes. Thus the concept of "Black and White, Unite and Fight" has never had any basis in fact in this country: the blacks and whites were never struggling for the same things nor were they united in the same cause even when they were fighting side by side.

When the Civil War ended with the Negroes being returned to serfdom, it was the first major defeat of the class struggle in the United States. From that time on, Americans, including the radicals among them, have regarded the Negro question as a race question. Before the Civil War, Negro struggles were called rebellions and revolts. But after the Civil War and the formal emancipation of the Negroes, any violent action by Negroes was just called a "race riot" even when these actions were based on economic grounds, such as jobs, housing, or prices.

So long have the American people lived with this contradiction that it has become a way of life for them. That is why the question of what the Negro struggle really represents, what should be done about it, what is right and what is wrong, is shaking the United States more than any other issue. Why should America fight to free the world when America is itself not free? Why did America fight the last war for democracy when America itself does not have democracy? How can Americans really be for the freedom of Africa when they are not for freedom inside the United States? How can Americans be for freedom and equality the world over when they do not practice freedom and equality at home? How can Americans say they are for parliamentary democracy and free elections abroad when they do not have parliamentary democracy and free elections at home? How can America give advice to countries all over the whole world on how to solve their problems when it cannot solve its own problems? Why does America claim to want to give so much economic progress to everybody else when it finds it so hard to give economic progress to its own colored citizens? How can Americans say they have a free society when the question of where to eat and where not to eat, where to ride and where not to ride on buses, streetcars, and trains in order to avoid the Negro haunts the average American white before he even leaves his house in the morning?

Thus what began as a class issue and was made into a race issue by the simple act of separating off the Negroes on the basis of color has now in fact become a national issue, the great, the pervasive, the all-American question that is shaking up every organization, every institution, and every individual inside America and affecting the relationships of all these to the rest of the world: labor, the professions, the church, the courts, the armed forces, industry, employment, transportation, the family, marriage, schools, hospitals, neighborhoods, cities, suburbs, government on all levels, police, firemen, social welfare, political parties, press, TV, radio, movies, sports. The list is endless.

In the period following the Bargain of 1877, the Negro question remained dormant. Although this period was characterized by the most brutal and shameful beatings, lynchings, and rape (worse than before the Civil War because now things were supposed to be different), Americans found it possible to look the other way. All that the abolitionists had talked about and exposed in the prewar period was drowned out in the thunderous expansion of American industry and the shifting of the class struggle to the railroads and new industries created as a result of the war.

The first serious eruption of violence between whites and Negroes came in the big riot of 1908 in Springfield, Illinois. This in turn led to the birth of the NAACP, an organization formed by Negro intellectuals to defend Negro rights. The First World War and the crisis of American capitalism propelled into the urban centers and the U.S. Army many Negroes who brought with them all the questions and grievances that up to then had been silenced by the police state in the South. It was at this juncture that Negroes began to discover the many "ifs" and "buts" of American democracy. Up to this point they had been considering "up North" a haven, revering Abe Lincoln and the Republican Party as their benefactors, putting the Yankee on a pedestal as the fighter for their freedom. Their disillusionment with northern democracy continues to smolder in every Negro who has settled up North after knowing life in the South.

The clash between their expectations and the harsh realities of life in the North, plus the blow that they sensed had been dealt to Western Civilization by the First World War and the Russian Revolution, created the mass basis for the Garvey movement, which at its height is estimated to have attracted anywhere from one to six million Negroes and forced the people of the United States for the first time since the Civil War to face the reality of the Negroes as a force. This reality was never to leave them completely again.

After the First World War the northern ghettos began to swell as Negroes in the South who could eke out enough money to make the trip continued to migrate to the North. In 1931, simultaneously with the depression, the Scottsboro Case, involving the legal lynching by the southern courts of nine young Negro boys, raised the Negro question once again to the status of a major issue not only in the United States but throughout the world. But Negroes were still on the defensive. During the depression more thousands of Negroes, displaced by the mechanization of the farms, flocked into the cities both north and south. Here they took every advantage of the social reforms of the New Deal.

During the 1930s the CIO erupted, and the pattern that had been created by American capitalism in the Civil War repeated itself. To save the Union, Lincoln had freed the slaves. Now to save the union, Negroes were admitted into it, lest the capitalists use them as strikebreakers and scabs. But this was not too difficult for the unions to do. There were not too many Negroes in industry anyway, except at Ford (which was not unionized until 1941) and in steel where the Negroes did the heaviest and most menial work out of which the immigrants had been upgraded. The bulk of the Negroes were unemployed and on relief.

With the coming of the Second World War, Negroes up North made use of the opportunity created by the weakness of American capitalism to organize the March on Washington movement. Out of this movement came Executive Order 8802, opening up jobs in defense industries to Negroes. Negroes did not give credit for this order to Roosevelt and the American government. Far from it. Recognizing that America and its allies had their backs to the wall in their struggle with Hitler and Tojo, Negroes said that Hitler and Tojo, by creating the war that made the Americans give them jobs in industry, had done more for them in four years than Uncle Sam had done in three hundred years.

Working in industry, fighting inside the armed forces, the Negroes now began to seize upon all the weaknesses of American capitalism. This led to a series of riots in army camps and major cities in the North that reached their peak at the height of the war in the year 1943. Only when the official records of the armed services are made public will Americans know how many hundreds of revolts took place among the Negro soldiers and sailors during the Second World War.

Inside the plants of the war industries the newly employed Negro workers carried on an offensive battle against both management and the white workers, forcing the white workers to face up to the idiocies of their prejudices and making them admit for the first time that Negroes could perform or learn all the operations of American production the world had been led to believe could only be done by the superior whites. On the union floor, Negro workers raised problems the white workers and the union had never before had to face, often causing splits inside the union and among the workers on the issues of human rights and human behavior.

When the war was over, the Negroes did not return to the farms as they had done in large numbers after the First World War. They had established themselves in industry and in northern communities, and in many plants they had built up seniority while white workers were losing it by moving from plant to plant.

In the South the whites started again the old intimidation that had been launched after the First World War. The Klan was reborn and a series of bombings and lynchings erupted from Florida to Mississippi in a campaign to put back in his place this Negro who, having seen another world in the army and in industry, was determined never to be tied down again. In 1948 President Truman, recognizing the growing political strength of the Negroes in the northern cities, fought and won the election on a program of civil rights, despite the split-away of the Dixiecrats in Mississippi, Louisiana, South Carolina, and Alabama. By now the national government was on the defensive, both in the world and at home. The cold war was under way and the familiar American pattern was repeating itself. "To save the free world from communism" the United States was now ready to yield some rights to its Negro citizens.

In 1954 the Supreme Court handed down its famous decision regarding school desegregation, repudiating the old ruling that separate schools could be equal. The Court expected the desegregation to take place only "with all deliberate speed." Instead, Negro parents in the South began to organize and mobilize to send their children to formerly all-white schools, even in the face of hostile mobs bent upon upholding the familiar ways of American life and ready to spit and jeer at little children to do so. Then fourteen-year-old Emmett Till from Chicago was brutally lynched in Mississippi and his kidnapers and murderers were let off scot-free in the courts. The flood tide of Negro revolt that had been dammed up for so long began to burst. For the first time Negroes were ready for an offensive against white society. Hitherto their actions had been defensive. Now there would come a series of offensive actions with staggering momentum, one right after the other. Going from the defensive to the offensive, the Negroes now constituted a revolutionary force completely different from that of the immigrant workers, each group of which had been assimilated into the "American way of life."

In 1955–56 the Montgomery bus boycott became an international issue as an entire community organized itself to boycott public transportation until the buses were desegregated according to federal law. In the border states of Kentucky, Tennessee, Arkansas, Missouri, and Oklahoma, and in Washington, D.C., Negro parents were determined not to be put off by white mobs, and Eisenhower had to send federal troops to Little Rock to uphold the Supreme Court decision.

Meanwhile, as the sleeping giant of Africa began to waken, the Negro people, who up to that time had been somewhat ashamed of their ancestry, instead began to feel ashamed that, living in the most advanced country in the world, they were so far behind their African brothers in achieving freedom. For the first time the Negroes began to appreciate that although they are a minority in the United States they are a majority in the world, and that what in the United States is portrayed as a race question is on a world scale the question of the rights of the majority of the human race.

In 1960 the Negro offensive took a new step forward. The sit-in movement started, astonishing Negroes who had migrated North in the belief that southern Negroes would never rise up and fight for their rights. The student sit-in movement aimed at taking and enforcing equal rights in restaurants, stores, libraries, movies, beaches, parks, and all other public places in the South. Unlike any previous Negro movement, it aimed at creating the issue, provoking it. The Negro students were not just in the courts arguing the law, as the NAACP had been doing for so many years. They were making and enforcing it themselves, on the spot.

These Negro students were the sons and daughters of Negroes who fought and worked during the war, taught their children what their own parents had not taught them—that they were inferior to no one and had the same rights as any American—and now sent them to college to prepare for their equality. Their movement created pandemonium in the whole apparatus of the southern courts—local courts, appeals courts, federal courts contradicted each other right and left, often in the presence of hundreds of Negroes who jammed the courtrooms. As the movement enlisted support and participation from thousands of white students on southern and northern campuses, pandemonium also began to be created between these youths and their parents. In 1961 the movement took on national scope with mixed groups of Freedom Riders converging on Deep South cities from both North and South.

Negro youth employed the nonviolent tactics that had been evolved by Martin Luther King in the Montgomery boycott. These tactics were extremely effective insofar as they enabled the youth to take the initiative in a disciplined manner, achieve cooperation between white and Negro youth, and dramatize the realities of southern justice. But the white mobs in the South responded with violence, and it was these mobs who were upheld by the southern authorities as they restored order by hosing the students, throwing tear gas at them, arresting and jailing them, convicting them of breaking the law, and fining or imprisoning them.

Meanwhile another road was being worked out by Negro workers, both in the North and in the South. In Monroe, North Carolina, the Negro community, under the leadership of Robert F. Williams, an ex-Marine and former auto worker, armed itself to meet Ku Klux Klan violence with violence. In the big cities of the North—Chicago, Detroit, Harlem, Los Angeles—the black Muslims began to consolidate and multiply, attracting to their ranks hundreds of thousands of the lowest layers of Negro workers—domestic servants, the unemployed made expendable by automation, and outcasts from society in the prisons and hospitals. Through the militant black nationalist philosophy of the Muslims, these Negroes are now being rehabilitated and their social personalities liberated, *but not for integration into this society.* The black Muslims, whose membership consists only of Afro-Americans, emphasize the need for American Negroes to follow the example of the Africans. According to their philosophy, white society is·doomed and the only hope for the black man is to cut himself off entirely from this doomed society, develop a citizenship of his own, taking for himself the "40 acres" promised but never given him after the Civil War, and preparing himself to defend his people against all white injustice and aggression.

With the growth of the black Muslim movement and the emergence of the new

Negroes in the South represented by the students and the Monroe community, the old Negro organizations like the NAACP have become a joke. NAACP, as Dick Gregory says, means Negroes who *A*re not *A*cting like *C*olored *P*eople. Whites who protest "But I belong to the NAACP" are laughed at for deluding themselves that they have thereby bought insurance against the coming explosions. Like the union, the NAACP at this stage of the struggle has been bypassed by harsh realities.

Antagonisms among Negroes themselves have grown as debate and disagreement have sharpened over methods of struggle; Negroes have begun to realize that they will also have to fight Negroes before they win their freedom. Not only that. Inside the CIO, which built its reputation on the solidarity of the workers, there has sprung up a new organization of Negro workers who have made it clear that when the Negro masses explode, the labor organizations cannot expect Negro unionists to defend labor against the Negroes, for labor itself has proved to be too much a part of the "American way of life" that has to be uprooted. Thus, at this point in American history when the labor movement is on the decline, the Negro movement is on the upsurge. The fact has to be faced that since 1955 the development and momentum of the Negro struggle have made the Negroes the one revolutionary force dominating the American scene. Today the whole nation and the world are aware of their striking force, from boycotts to sit-ins to wade-ins to Freedom Rides. Inside the United States there is widespread fear of the growing strength of the black Muslims, described by Martin Luther King as the "extremist elements lurking in the wings." In the last half-dozen years hundreds of organizations for Negro struggle have sprung up around specific issues, disbanding as speedily as they were formed when their objectives are achieved and organizing anew when new problems require action. Among these, and growing in significance every day, are the parents' organizations in northern cities which, through the issue of school redistricting, are challenging the whole social pattern of city and suburb and of government of the black central city areas by white "absentee landlords" that has grown up since the war.

All this poses very fundamental questions not only for American society as a whole but for American revolutionaries. The old slogan "Black and White, Unite and Fight" has been proved false and obsolete, and the same is now happening to the assumption that Negroes can achieve their rights inside *this* society or without shaking up and revolutionizing the whole social structure. What is involved is not only the likelihood of open and armed revolt of the Negroes against the state power in the South. The Negroes are now posing before all the institutions of American society, particularly those that are supposedly on their side (the labor organizations, the liberals, the old Negro organizations, and the Marxists), the same questions that have been posed by the Algerian Revolution to all of French society, with the difference that Algeria is outside France while the Negroes are right here inside America. But in the same way that, during the course of the Algerian Revolution, Algerians fought Frenchmen, and Algerians fought Algerians, and Frenchmen representing the national government eventually had to fight Frenchmen in Algeria, and the Algerians had to take over political power and now have to expropriate the property of Frenchmen, so in the United States the Negro revolt will lead to armed struggle between Negroes and whites, Negroes and Negroes, and federal troops and armed civilians, and will have to move to political power and economic power. Already clashes between federal troops and white civilians have been narrowly averted. The counterrevolution in the South may not yet be as well organized as the Secret Army Organization was in Algeria and France, but the attitudes, actions, and atrocities perpetrated by white civilians against Negroes are no different.

American Marxists have tended to fall into the trap of thinking of the Negroes as Negroes, i.e., in race terms, when in fact the Negroes have been and are today the most oppressed and submerged sections of the workers, on whom has fallen most sharply the burden of unemployment due to automation. The Negroes have more economic grievances than any other section of American society. But in a country with the material abundance of the United States, economic grievances alone could not impart to their struggles all their revolutionary impact. The strength of the Negro cause and its power to shake up the social structure of the nation come from the fact that in the Negro struggle all the questions of human rights and human relationships are posed. At the same time the American Negroes are most conscious of, and best able to time their actions in relation to, the crises and weaknesses of American capitalism, both at home and abroad.

American Marxists have also allowed themselves to fall into the trap of treating the question of violence and nonviolence in the Negro struggle in a way that they would never dream of in relation to the class struggle. That is, they have toyed with the idea that the Negroes are a minority who might be massacred if they used other than nonviolent methods. This is because American Marxists have always thought of the working class as white and have themselves discriminated against Negroes by hesitating to recognize them as workers.

Now they must face the fact that the Negro struggle in the United States is not just a race struggle. It is not something apart from and long antedating the final struggle for a classless society that is supposed to take place at some future time when American capitalist society is in total crisis.

The goal of the classless society is precisely what has been and is today at the heart of the Negro struggle. It is the Negroes who represent the revolutionary struggle for a classless society—not indeed the classless society of American folklore in which every individual is supposed to be able to climb to the top in order to exploit newcomers at the bottom. Every other section of the working class has been to one extent or another assimilated into this "American way of life." Only the Negroes have been excluded from it and continue to be excluded from it, despite the frantic efforts of Kennedy & Co. to incorporate a chosen few Negroes at the top. It is this exclusion that has given the Negro struggle for a classless society its distinctive revolutionary character. For when the Negroes struggle for a classless society, they struggle that all men may be equal, in production, in consumption, in the community, in the courts, in the schools, in the universities, in transportation, in social activity, in government, and indeed in every sphere of American life.

American Marxists have never been able to grasp this because they have always thought that the social revolution in America must be led by white workers. They have also been afraid that if Negroes started violent revolutionary action, they would find the white workers lined up against them. Even when the Marxists have verbally repudiated the theory of "Black and White, Unite and Fight" this theory and these fears about Negro revolt have remained with them. But the crisis in the United States today and the corresponding momentum of the Negro struggle are such that it is obvious that Negroes are not going to consult whites, workers or not workers, before taking action. They will go their way, doing what they think they must do, taking what actions they feel they must take, and forcing the whites to make up their minds whether, when, and if they are coming along.

The chief need for all Americans is to recognize these facts and to be ready to take bold action along with Negroes, recognizing that the Negroes are the growing revolutionary force in the country and that just as capitalist production has created new methods of production and new layers of workers, it has also produced new Negroes.

Many, including some Negroes, will say that they do not understand just what the Negroes are fighting for in this period. That is primarily because the Negro struggle, as an offensive social struggle, is only about eight years old. In those eight years the Negroes have been evolving their own strategy and tactics, not trying to fit into any preconceived pattern, using each and every method, nonviolent resistance, violent resistance, moral suasion, economic boycotts, sit-ins, stand-ins, etc., sometimes confusing but more often clarifying the nature of the coming showdown.

Today, as a result of all these struggles, they are learning that their chief weakness is the lack of political power. They do not control one sheriff in the United States, north or south. They have no say about federal troops, National Guards, city police, FBI, Interstate Commerce Commission, post office authorities, school boards, voting registration, or employment commissions. Yet in every issue and in every sphere, and whatever methods they have used, they have found themselves directly up against the corrupt powers that be.

Up to now it has been unnatural for the Negroes to think in terms of black political power. Instead they have thought in terms of investing white politicians with power and then putting pressure on them to deal out justice to the Negroes. Now, to Negroes in the South, it is becoming clearly a question of investing blacks with power, and nobody knows this better than the whites who openly admit their fears that this is the inevitable result of Negro voting.

The struggle for black political power is a revolutionary struggle because, unlike the struggle for white power, it is the climax of a ceaseless struggle on the part of Negroes for human rights. Moreover, it comes in a period in the United States when the struggle for human relations rather than for material goods has become the chief task of human beings. The tragedy is that all Americans cannot recognize this and join in this struggle. But the very fact that most white Americans do not recognize it and are in fact opposed to it is what makes it a revolutionary struggle. Because it takes two sides to struggle, the revolution and the counterrevolution.

Chapter 8
The American Revolution

Any social movement starts with the aim of achieving some rights heretofore denied. Sometimes a portion of these rights is achieved without a change in the social structure of the country. When this happens, the movement is not revolutionary, even though it has brought about social change. Such a movement was the CIO. At other times a movement is unable to achieve the rights it seeks without taking power from the existing government and creating a totally new order. When this happens, it is a revolution.

Very few revolutions start with a conscious attempt to take power. No revolution has ever started with everyone in the country agreeing with the goal of the revolutionary movement. It is clashes, both ideological and physical, among segments of the population and usually the whip of the counterrevolution that give the revolution its momentum. Sometimes the revolution is violent, sometimes it is nonviolent, but always it is the revolution. Sometimes those in the revolution are conscious of the consequences of their actions, sometimes they are not, but always there is action.

Who will and who will not start a full-scale revolution cannot be foretold. The basis for a revolution is created when the organic structure and conditions within a given country have aroused mass concern. Sometimes the revolution is started by its opponents, who by some act arouse the masses to anger and action. Sometimes a very marked improvement in living conditions inculcates in the masses a belief that there is no limit to what they should or can have. Sometimes it is just seeing one segment of the population living so much better than the rest.

No one has ever been able to predict which class or race would start a revolution or how many people would be required to do it. The only certainty is that the success of a revolution depends on the joining in of the working people who make up the bulk of the population.

Marx's theory of revolution was developed in relation to the advanced capitalist countries. The United States is the most advanced capitalist country in the world. Not only that. It is the citadel of world capitalism without which the other capitalist countries could not survive. Therefore, any revolutionary who evades facing the specific conditions and realities of American capitalism is like the British workers in Marx's day who were so preoccupied with keeping the Irish workers down that they couldn't fight for their own advancement, or all the American socialists who have been so preoccupied with Stalinism, either pro or con, that they have not sought or been able to find the basis of the revolution that is here, right in front of their eyes, in the most advanced capitalist country in the world. American socialists have never been able to understand why there should be a revolution in the United States when there is such an abundance of commodities in this country. Rather than face this question squarely, they have become refugees in theory, if not in physical fact, from the American Revolution.

Preoccupied, while still living in America, with how revolutionary regimes live up to or fall short of their socialist ideals, American revolutionaries have failed to understand the problems actually faced by these regimes after they come to power. They have not understood the nature of the problem of accumulating capital enough for industrialization and that the burden of this accumulation must be placed on the backs of the workers—just as it was in all capitalist countries, and especially on the backs of Negro workers in the United States—unless they can get the needed capital from already developed countries like the United States. But the United States will share its resources with the underdeveloped countries only if there is a social revolution in the United States. Which brings us right back to the question of the American Revolution.

The American Revolution does not necessarily have to start from economic grievances. Nor does it have to start with the American working class in the lead. The development of capitalism in the United States has generated more than enough contradictions to pose the question of the total social reorganization of the country. Some of these contradictions relate to sheer poverty and the workers' life in production. Others are just as important and have even wider bearing on the quality of social existence. Man is imaginative and creative. His needs go far beyond the realm of the material.

What is man's greatest human need in the United States today? It is to stop shirking responsibility and start assuming responsibility. When Americans stop doing the one and start doing the other, they will begin to travel the revolutionary road. But to do this they must use as much creative imagination in politics as up to now they have used in production. The fact is that the more imaginative Americans have been in creating new techniques of production, the less imaginative they have been in creating new relations between people. Americans today are like a bunch of ants who have been struggling all summer long to accumulate a harvest and then can't decide how to distribute it and therefore fight among themselves and destroy each other to get at the accumulation.

The greatest obstacle in the way of the American people beginning to behave like human beings rather than like animals is the great American illusion of freedom.

Stop an American and begin to make some serious criticisms of our society, and nine times out of ten his final defense will be: "But this is the freest and finest country in the world." When you probe into what he means by this, it turns out that what he is really talking about is the material goods that he can acquire in exchange for his birthright of political freedom. That is, he is free to have an automobile, a TV, a hi-fi, and all kinds of food, clothing, and drink as long as he doesn't offend anybody he works for or anybody in an official capacity, and as long as he doesn't challenge the accepted pattern of racial, economic, and political relations inside the country or its foreign policy outside. On these questions most Americans absolve themselves from any responsibility by saying that all that is "politics" and "I am not interested in politics." What they really mean is that they are afraid to assume political responsibility because it would mean jeopardizing their economic and social status. No people in the world have more to say about the lack of free speech in Russia, China, Cuba, and Ghana. The reason is that as long as they have these other places to talk about, they can evade facing the silent police state that has grown up inside America. If you casually mention the police state to an American, the first thing that comes to his mind is some other country. He doesn't see his own police state.

That is because in the United States, more than in any other country in the world, every man is a policeman over himself, a prisoner of his own fears. He is afraid to think because he is afraid of what his neighbors might think of what he thinks if they found out what he was thinking, or what his boss might think, or what the police might think, or the FBI, or the CIA. And all because he thinks he has a lot to lose. He thinks he has to choose between material goods and political freedom. And when the two are counterposed, Americans today will choose material goods. Believing they have much to lose, Americans find excuses where there are no excuses, evade issues before the issues arise, shun situations and conversations that could lead to conflict, leave politics and political decisions to the politicians. They will not regain their membership in the human race until they recognize that their greatest need is no longer to make material goods but to make politics.

But politics today in the United States is not just ordinary politics made by ordinary politicians. Not since the 1930s and the era of Franklin D. Roosevelt has there been political statesmanship in the United States. Roosevelt's problems and therefore his responsibilities, as he made very clear in his First Inaugural Address, were extraordinary. But Roosevelt's problems were largely domestic. Today, in contrast, every issue, no matter how local or domestic it may seem, has international repercussions inherent in it from the very beginning.

In President Eisenhower's Farewell Address, he warned the people of the growing power of the "military-industrial complex" inside the country. Ike was speaking mainly of the actual military power and personnel. He did not go into the way this apparatus has been intertwined with those who control the economic processes of the country and with the various investigating agencies that at every level control the thought processes of the population. All together, these now constitute a military-economic-police bloc that was not elected by the people and cannot be held responsible to the people but makes all the decisions controlling the life of the people.

This bloc has its present power because the United States actually does have its back to the wall both domestically and internationally. Domestically, it is dependent upon the war economy for economic survival as a capitalist country, and has been so dependent since the Great Depression of the 1930s. Internationally, it is dependent upon the military for protection against the world revolutionary movement that is arising among the have-not peoples of the world, and has been so dependent since the 1949 revolution in China and the Korean War. The United States has lost all the spiritual power that underlies political power of a peaceful kind.

It is the refusal of the American people to face this situation openly and to assume responsibility for tackling it uncompromisingly that gives the military-economic-police bloc its strength. If the secret police were not so secret and silent, it would be much easier to fight. An open enemy is the best enemy. But the fear of the American people of clashing openly with this bloc adds strength to it.

Most secret of all is the CIA, which even members of Congress do not dare question. Yet the CIA has the power to go into a country, organize a war or a revolution or a counterrevolution, and recruit among the American people for its schemes; it has the funds and the staff at its disposal to fight an underground war not only against the Russians but against every country in the world.

The FBI is the secret police force closest to the lives of the people. Unlike the FBI of the 1930s, which used to be hailed as the great protector of the people against the criminal elements, the FBI today functions chiefly as a political police to pry into the private lives and thoughts of every American.

What the FBI does in complete secrecy, the House Un-American Activities Committee does in semisecrecy, having the power to drag before it any individual or group that actively challenges the status quo in this country. In this way it dangles over all whom it queries the kind of public suspicion and silent condemnation from which there is only one way for the individual to escape—to prove his or her loyalty to the police state by becoming an informer for it.

If the leap that the American people have to take in order to meet the problems of this new age of abundance were not so great, the powers of the secret police would likewise not be so great. In the 1930s the problems were relatively simple. All that was required was that the poor struggle against the rich, who were the capitalists and whose failure was clear and obvious.

Today in the 1960s, the struggle is much more difficult. What it requires is that people in every stratum of the population clash not only with the agents of the silent police state but with their own prejudices, their own outmoded ideas, their own fears that keep them from grappling with the new realities of our age. The American people must find a way to insist upon their own right and responsibility to make political decisions and to determine policy in all spheres of social existence—whether it is foreign policy, the work process, education, race relations, or community life. The coming struggle is a political struggle to take political power out of the hands of the few and put it into the hands of the many. But in order to get this power into the hands of the many, it will be necessary for the many not only to fight the powerful few but to fight and clash among themselves as well.

PART III

BLACK POWER
PROMISE, PITFALLS, AND LEGACIES

Introduction to Part III

The writings in this section document James Boggs's engagement with the Black Power movement and its legacy. From the movement's emergence in the mid-1960s to its dissipation a decade later, he was a consistent presence in the Black Power struggle both as an activist working to build the movement through various initiatives and organizations and as an intellectual articulating ideas and analyzing the movement's advance. Spanning the years 1963–79, these selections chart Boggs's thinking from the years immediately preceding the emergence of the Black Power movement, through the movement's rise and fall, and into its immediate aftermath. He published essays in some of the most prominent Black Power–era publications, such as the anthologies *Black Fire* and *The Black Seventies* and the journals *Liberator, The Black Scholar,* and *Review of Black Political Economy* (including the inaugural issues of the latter two).[1] His work also appeared in a range of other publications including *Ebony, Monthly Review,* and the *New York Times.* Equally important, Boggs's intellectual engagement also consistently assumed nonpublishing and more grassroots forms, such as the many speeches he delivered across the country as well as the pamphlets he wrote and distributed.

Accordingly, this is a somewhat disparate group of writings that together point to the multiplicity of venues, formats, and audiences that Boggs engaged. Among them are published essays, speeches, self-published pamphlets, and an op-ed. The topics vary as well, ranging, for example, from a pamphlet theorizing the black revolutionary party to essays on urban governance to a speech on education. Some but not all of the selections directly tackle the concept of Black Power; others engage it indirectly, while a few make no reference to the movement at all. Still, the Black Power movement or its immediate aftermath provided the context in which all of these pieces were written, and Boggs intended each one as a distinct intervention into the thinking and activism of the period. What binds these pieces, then, is Boggs's consistent concern with clarifying the meaning of Black Power (including its limits, failures, and legacies) and charting a course of black struggle and social transformation during and after the movement.

Boggs's relationship to the Black Power movement, both as an activist and a thinker, grew primarily and organically from what he experienced and observed in Detroit. The Motor City was one of the earliest and most active centers of Black Power politics. During the early 1960s, the Group on Advanced Leadership (GOAL), UHURU, and the Rev. Albert Cleage spearheaded a militant protest community that challenged civil rights orthodoxy and advanced a nationalist (and internationalist) sentiment.[2] Boggs collaborated with all three of them (and also mentored some of the young activists in UHURU), and he was a central figure in this community. Among the highlights of their efforts were the Grassroots

Leadership Conference (of which Boggs served as chairperson) in November 1963 and the organization of the Freedom Now Party the next year. When the Black Power slogan emerged as a national phenomenon in the summer of 1966, ideas that proved central to the new movement—rejection of nonviolence and embracing self-defense, rejection of integration, independent political action, strident calls for racial unity and cultural autonomy, international solidarity—were already shaping protest activity in Detroit, and the city quickly became a hotbed of Black Power activity. Indeed, by 1966 Boggs had cofounded two organizations, the Organization for Black Power and the Inner City Organizing Committee, which grappled with these ideas in an effort to develop both a theoretical framework and a grassroots program for this new stage of struggle emerging in the mid-1960s. These years also saw in Detroit a burgeoning of artistic activity, cultural activism, and institution building (such as Dudley Randall's Broadside Press), all of which was of a piece with the increasingly militant political protest in the city and which made Detroit a national focal point of the Black Arts movement.[3]

Black Power activity in the city intensified in the wake of the 1967 Detroit rebellion,[4] making the Motor City a major tributary of the national movement. By the late 1960s Detroit was home to a wide range of Black Power formations, including the League of Revolutionary Black Workers, Rev. Cleage's Black Christian Nationalism, the Republic of New Africa, and a local chapter of the Black Panther Party. Each of these was a particular expression of Black Power politics, representing divergent (and at times competing) ideological tendencies and political trajectories. This reflected the specific dynamics of the Detroit Black Power movement, but it was also part of a larger picture of distinctions and divisions across the country—some already in evidence, others soon to emerge—as the rise of the Black Panther Party, the spread of urban rebellions, and other developments spurred tremendous growth in the Black Power movement at the end of the 1960s. James Boggs sought in his writings and speeches to make sense of this growth and of the tensions in ideology and program that it produced. As both participant and observer (and with a keen recognition of the interplay between local and national movement developments), he devoted considerable effort to critically assessing the movement's many expressions, assaying their respective shortcomings and pitfalls, and charting a way forward for the movement.

The underlying focus and objective of his thinking on Black Power, as in every stage of his political activity and intellectual work, was to help theorize and bring about a social revolution in the United States. During the preceding two decades the labor movement, the organized left, and especially Marxism had structured his thinking about revolutionary change. The African American struggle had also been central to his thinking, but with the growth of the civil rights movement (and a simultaneous rise of nationalist sentiment outside it) during the early 1960s, the coordinates of his vision for revolutionary politics shifted. By the time the Black Power movement began, Boggs had rejected the Marxist scenario of revolution and had begun articulating the idea that African Americans, not the American working class, had the potential to forge a revolution in the United States. As the writings presented here demonstrate, Boggs moved away from Marxism in this period as he sought to develop the theoretical and practical framework for Black Power to become a revolutionary movement. While he clearly turned away from Marxism in this period, Boggs's writings on and during the Black Power movement reflect a continuing engagement (or perhaps confrontation) with Marxism in the sense that the Marxist view of revolution frequently serves as the starting point for his theorizing about the revolutionary process and his projection of the black struggle as a potentially revolutionary force. Many of these writings critique Marxists for their inability to think creatively and update their theories based on contemporary political developments; at the same time we see an element of Marxism or the influence of Marxist thought in Boggs's analysis, namely his calls for a Leninist vanguard party (which will be discussed below) to provide leadership to the movement and for socialist revolution as the ultimate goal of revolutionary Black Power.

The emergence of Black Power then served as both context and impetus for his continued theorization of the black struggle and his evolving concept of revolution. From the beginning of the movement he saw Black Power not only as a new stage in the black movement but also as a potential vehicle for creating the next American revolution; he envisioned the ultimate task of Black Power as not just combating and eliminating racism, and thus improving black people's place in society, but of fundamentally transforming society for the benefit of everyone. As he wrote in 1970,

The Black Power movement must recognize that if society is ever going to be changed to meet the needs of black people, then Black Power will have to resolve the problems of the society as a whole and not just those of black people. In other words, Black Power cannot evade tackling all the problems of this society, because at the root of all the problems of black people is the same structure and the same system that is at the root of all the problems of all the people.[5]

The writings collected here reveal how he arrived at and articulated this position. By charting the structure and evolution of his thinking before, during, and after the movement, they give us a picture of the movement's development along with various entry points for interpreting its history. They also locate Boggs as a significant figure in the history of Black Power. To grasp and evaluate his contribution to an understanding of Black Power, it will be useful to outline key dimensions of his thinking on the movement.

Boggs first sought to clarify the meaning of Black Power. He had begun projecting the significance of black political power in his writings in the early 1960s, when few observers anticipated or took seriously the prospect of the civil rights struggle transforming into a struggle for Black Power. In "Liberalism, Marxism, and Black Political Power," a review essay of black journalist Louis Lomax's 1962 book *The Negro Revolt,* Boggs noted that in some quarters of black opinion and politics there was a rising nationalist sentiment, rejection of integration, and desire for black political power, all of which he saw as pointing to the next stage of the black revolt. He chided Lomax for begin "a Negro who still thinks in terms of white power as naturally as he thinks of eating when he's hungry. His mind simply has not stretched beyond the idea of whites ruling and giving Negroes a greater share in this rule."[6] The essay ends with a prediction that within months would begin to be realized in Detroit by the successful formation of the Freedom Now Party and within three years would be dramatically proved accurate with the rise of the Black Power movement. "The struggle of the Negroes in the very near future," he wrote, "will be the struggle for black political power, and by black political power is meant, not the power of Negroes to put white men in office, to whom they can go and ask for things, but rather their own power to dispose over things."[7] He again argued for the timeliness and necessity of obtaining black political power in "The City Is the Black Man's Land," an essay coauthored with Grace Lee Boggs and published in April 1966, just two months before the Black Power slogan took flight. The following year, as the nation engaged in a heated debate over the very definition and meaning of Black Power, Boggs published "Black Power: A Scientific Concept Whose Time Has Come." He argued that Black Power had "nothing to do with any special moral virtue in being black" but grew out of black people's place in American society and the evolution of their struggle beyond civil rights. The essay principally takes on Marxists but also extends the critique to "most of those writing for and against Black Power" because they "would rather keep the concept vague than grapple with the systematic analysis of American capitalism out of which the concept of Black Power has developed."[8]

As the movement grew and multiple articulations of the concept of Black Power emerged, Boggs critically assessed them and their attendant lines of political action (or inaction). For example, early in the movement he looked critically at the ways in which segments of the movement deployed culture, African heritage, and notions of black unity. In the essay "Culture and Black Power" published in 1967, he warned against allowing identification with Africa or celebrations of black cultural heritage to serve as an evasion or mystification of the struggle at hand. "Of what profit," he asked, "is our history and our culture unless it is used in a vision of our future?"[9] In many of these pieces—such as his 1972 *New York Times* opinion piece "Beyond Rebellion" and the speech "Think Dialectically, Not Biologically" (1974)—a consistent theme is the idea that Black Power must be seen as a new stage in the black struggle. This meant understanding Black Power in relation to the previous stage (the struggle for civil rights) and to the historical development of the country as a whole. "Most of those who call themselves black power advocates," he wrote in "Beyond Rebellion," "are trying to find a solution for blacks separate from a solution for the contradictions of the entire United States. Actually, this is impossible. Therefore, many black nationalists are going off into all kinds of fantasies and dreams about what black power means—like heading for Africa, or isolating themselves in a few states, or whites just vanishing into thin air and leaving this country to blacks."[10]

Boggs was relatively unique in his ability to thoughtfully analyze the movement as it unfolded and consistently offer insights into its development. Throughout the period he received invitations to lecture and speak on the movement, and he showed a keen ability not only to make sense of dramatic and rapid developments but also to submit them to critical reflection. His speech "The Myth and Irrationality of Black Capitalism" is an example. He prepared it as one of the keynote speeches to the National Black Economic Development Conference in April 1969, a gathering of various forces in the Black Power movement held in Detroit. The conference reflected the increasing attention on the economic dimensions of racial oppression and discussions within the movement of black economic strategies, including a debate over the meaning and desirability of "black capitalism." Boggs used his speech to reject the very notion of black capitalism as distinct from capitalism in general and to challenge the idea that any capitalist enterprise or program could be a viable path to a nonracist future. Boggs identified the relationship between capitalism and racism in the United States as the source of African Americans' underdevelopment, argued for an alternative vision of economic organization, and proposed specific "fundamental guidelines for any programs aimed at developing black communities."[11] Boggs's speech, along with most of the conference proceedings, was overshadowed by James Forman's presentation of the "Black Manifesto" calling for $500,000,000 in reparations. But the fact that he was selected to give one of the keynote speeches and the substance of his analysis speak to his standing as an astute analyst of Black Power.

His reputation grew in 1970 with the publication of his second book, *Racism and Class Struggle: Further Pages from a Black Worker's Notebook,* a collection of essays and speeches from 1963 to the end of the decade (several of which are among the writings presented in this section). As the title suggests, the book was something of a follow-up to his first. In this new volume he developed further his ideas about black political power and the revolutionary potential of the black movement, but now with greater analytical and rhetorical vigor as he commented on and analyzed the development of the Black Power movement through the mid- and late 1960s.

The volume's final essay, "The American Revolution: Putting Politics in Command," which is the only essay written specifically for the book, is one of Boggs's most thorough statements on the Black Power movement. It traces the steps leading to the movement's emergence, assesses the type of leadership that the movement requires, and details the divisions in the movement. In the process the essay provides a picture of key points in the movement's development, such as when SNCC, which had been central in birthing the movement, "was unable to provide the revolutionary leadership and organization needed in the struggle for Black Power, [and] a vacuum was created in the black movement which was soon to be filled by the Black Panther Party."[12] Indeed, the essay is particularly noteworthy for its careful and astute analysis of the Black Panther Party (BPP). Formed in 1966 in Oakland, California, as an early local organizational manifestation of Black Power and then exploding across the country in 1967 and especially after Martin Luther King's assassination in April 1968, the BPP came to be perhaps the most visible expression of the movement. Boggs believed that the BPP's growth reflected "the mushrooming revolutionary force of black school and street youth seeking a political identity, national leadership, and militant action."[13] He said, further, that the group's significance lay in being "the first major attempt by a section of the black movement to form a revolutionary vanguard party based on this growing revolutionary social force."[14] Boggs then spends several pages analyzing the Panthers, because "careful study and evaluation [of the BPP] can teach the movement many important lessons for the future. To evaluate the Black Panther Party," he asserted, "is not to question the sincerity and revolutionary dedication of its members, about which there can be no question. But the party is a political party, and it must therefore be judged politically in terms of whether or not it adequately meets the requirements of a revolutionary vanguard party."[15]

The role of a vanguard party—a disciplined cadre organization committed to providing revolutionary leadership—came to occupy a central place in Boggs's thinking about the Black Power movement. In the 1950s, Boggs was a member of a Marxist organization, Correspondence, which had rejected the vanguard party idea and instead proclaimed the capacity of the masses or ordinary people to assume leadership. This view celebrated spontaneity and self-activity as forces of revolutionary movement, blurring the distinction between mass action and political leadership. During the 1960s, however, as the Black Power movement escalated, and especially after the urban rebellions, Boggs saw limits to this theory. The urban rebellions had been spontaneous mass eruptions that successfully brought the struggle to the stage of *rebellion*, he said, but to move it to the stage of *revolution* required an organization to provide clear and committed leadership. In the face of growing opportunism and adventurism, such an organization must be a cadre organization of people ready to accept discipline and the responsibility of giving principled leadership. Moreover, he said that the revolutionary party must be able to organize and project a strategy of action to mobilize the masses around concrete goals. Boggs tried to build such an organization throughout the Black Power period, beginning with the Organization for Black Power, which he and Grace Lee Boggs helped found in 1965. Many of his writings during this period discuss the role of a black revolutionary party.

The concept received its fullest articulation in his 1969 pamphlet *Manifesto for a Black Revolutionary Party*. Here Boggs set out three roles for such a party. First, it should constantly clarify the goals of the Black Power movement, attending in particular to the specific and unique characteristics of the African American struggle (distinguishing it from historical examples of revolutionary change, such as the Russian Revolution, as well as contemporary examples in the third world). The second function of the party was to provide an organizational vehicle for the revolutionary energies among the masses. It was to be organized to avoid the limitations of the many ad hoc groups that had recently been formed in the cauldron of Black Power militancy. Such groups, Boggs explained, were formed around particular issues in the course of struggle, and they successfully aroused the emotions of the masses. As such they were capable of fostering rebellion but not leading a revolution. In contrast, the revolutionary party must be a "cadre-type organization" of politically conscious individuals who are completely committed to the struggle and to building the party. The core of such an organization would be "cold, sober revolutionaries who are bound together by a body of ideas" and "recognize the vital importance of disciplined organization and strong leadership to revolutionary struggle."[16] The final role of the black revolutionary party was to conceive and project a strategy for revolutionary social transformation. This strategy, Boggs wrote, should "give the masses of black people a sense of their growing power to improve their conditions of life through struggle."[17] A fundamental objective of such a strategy was to enable people to create "parallel power structures," meaning community control of urban institutions such as schools, health care, welfare, housing, and police.

It should be emphasized that Boggs's notion here of community control differed from the more popular use of that idea during the Black Power movement. Most advocates of community control meant local control of institutions, that is, black people exercising economic and political control over their own communities. In contrast, Boggs envisioned parallel power structures as "liberated areas" serving as "steps on the road to black revolutionary power."[18] That is, the standard idea of community control called for black people to control their communities *within cities*, where Boggs envisioned black leadership of the city as a whole, or black control *of cities*. In this sense, the task of the black revolutionary party was to give leadership, first to black people but ultimately to the entire society. The *Manifesto* included a section on "how Black Power will revolutionize America"[19] that gives an extended discussion of the revolutionary social agenda that was first outlined in "The City Is the Black Man's Land." The analysis proceeds from Boggs's belief that the nation had reached extremely high levels of economic development and productive capacity but its politically underdeveloped citizenry was not up to the task of making socially responsible choices about its economic and technological capabilities. Thus, Black Power was coming at a time when "the productive forces are already sufficiently developed to establish a material basis for communism, i.e., a society in which each has according to his needs and contributes according to his abilities." Therefore, "the urgent need today," he wrote, "is to increase the political power, participation, and understanding of the great masses of people in order to develop their capacity to become socially responsible and creative human beings."[20]

This reflects two ideas that James Boggs began articulating during the early 1960s and that he and Grace Lee Boggs would continue to develop through the end of the Black Power movement and into the final decades of the twentieth century. The first is that those who seek revolutionary change must confront the central contradiction in the late twentieth-century United States: the fact that the country was economically and technologically advanced but politically underdeveloped, meaning that the vast majority of people avoid participating in the political struggles needed to arrive at important political decisions. Thus, in 1970, the Boggses wrote that "the fundamental goal of a revolution in this country" was to "to create a society of politically conscious, socially responsible individuals able to use technology for the purpose of liberating and developing humanity."[21] The second idea follows the first: revolutionary transformation in the economically advanced but politically backward United States required "two-sided transformation," that is, as people work to transform the institutions and structures of society, they must also struggle to transform themselves into more socially responsible human beings.

With the collapse of the Black Power movement in the mid-1970s, Boggs sought to account for its end and to clarify its implications for revolutionary struggle in the United States. As early as 1972 he began formulating an analysis of the movement's demise, the central theme of which was the emergence of nationalism as a stage in the movement that both advanced and stymied the movement. "The chief weakness of the black movement in the United States at this stage," he said in a speech titled "Beyond Nationalism," "arises from the fact that most black militants view nationalism as an end in and of itself. They cannot face the fact that nationalism only puts you into the position where you can clarify to the masses the uniqueness of their oppression." Speaking at a moment still rife with nationalist sentiment, he asserted that "Nationalism is not a revolutionary ideology; it does not provide you with a revolutionary solution to the contradictions of your society. It is only a means to an end, a stage in the development of revolutionary struggle—just as rebellion and insurrection are stages in the development of revolutionary struggle."[22]

Boggs continued to make this analysis to audiences across the country throughout the 1970s. He spoke to organizations such as the Congress of African People as well as numerous universities, in speeches such as "Correcting Mistaken Ideas about the Third World," "Class Consciousness and Revolution," "Relevant Philosophy for the Late 20th Century," and "What Is Black Liberation?" In a 1978 speech titled "Liberation or Revolution?" he argued that the failure to move beyond nationalism produced two results. Some in the movement splintered into "a bunch of little sects, spouting slogans such as liberation, affirmative action, Pan-Africanism, etc., slogans they have picked up from revolutionary struggles in other parts of the world and have no meaning in our country because they are not based on *our* reality and *our* history as Americans."[23] The other result was incorporation into the system. "Millions of blacks today have been incorporated into the electoral machinery of bourgeois politics, into the universities and into the administration of the welfare state at every level."[24] Having failed to move the protest politics of Black Power into a struggle to fully transform society, these blacks embraced "the individualistic and materialistic goals of white middle-class Americans and became part of the "big pacification package at the Democratic Convention in 1976." For Boggs, this was a telltale sign that "the black movement no longer exists"[25] and African Americans had entered a new period in their relationship to the nation: "Each group, labor, blacks, women, liberals and conservatives, smelling victory for the Democratic Party, was able to submerge differences long enough to get Carter elected. As a result, blacks have become just another self-interest group like labor, concerned only with what benefits them and the hell with everybody else."[26]

The need to recognize the emergent challenges and contradictions—"new and more complex questions"[27]—confronting the nation and African Americans in particular in the wake of Black Power constituted another central theme of these speeches. Boggs called on blacks to recognize the extent to which they, by becoming integrated into the system and participating more fully in society, had also been corrupted by the values of the larger culture. For example, in a 1979 speech titled "The Challenge Facing Afro-Americans in the 1980s," he said that the black community until recently had been "very critical of the individualistic and materialistic values of white Americans" and "prided itself on the trust and respect that blacks had for one another, contrasting it with the way that whites would do anything for a buck." But now, "since the barriers of racism have been lifted to let blacks into the system," they have adopted the "individualistic and materialistic values that were always at the heart of the American Dream."[28] "Thus, the black movement—which started out to resolve one contradiction, racism—has ended up creating new contradictions not only for blacks but for everyone else in American society."[29] Moving into the 1980s, he said that racism still existed but was no longer, as it had been just a decade ago, "the principal contradiction of our society."

pal contradiction of our society."[30] He challenged his audience to recognize that the very success of the black movement created a new situation requiring new thinking and new questions to produce new visions of struggle that go beyond the struggles for rights and self-interest valiantly waged in the preceding decades.

The twentieth century in which the main line was the color line is coming to an end. This does not mean that racism has ceased to exist; it still exists in many forms. But the struggle for the twenty-first century is the struggle for new relationships not only between the races but between ourselves and Nature, between the advanced countries and the third world, between men and women. The struggle for the twenty-first century is the struggle to create new relationships in all these areas on the basis of new principles of mutual responsibility, respect, and cooperation.[31]

Boggs's assessment of the political choices to be made in the wake of Black Power led him to make observations on American culture which, though made in the 1970s, are remarkably resonant now, in the second decade of the twenty-first century. For example, his discussion of the corrupting influence of rampant individualism and materialism in "The Challenge Facing Afro-Americans in the 1980s" includes this passage:

Because as Americans we have not replaced the American Dream of becoming as rich as Rockefeller with another vision of how human beings should live, we are now at the mercy of these multinational corporations and their commercials. Most Americans now have no other purpose in life but the unlimited accumulation of consumer goods and the unlimited pursuit of immediate pleasures. Even though all around us our institutions, our families, our communities, our schools, our economy, and our government are falling apart, all we can think of is what we are going to buy next, or what we are going to wear to the newest disco joint, or who we are going to make a killing in the lottery or at the racetrack or on Beat the Clock. Most people, whether they are middle class or poor, live by credit cards, owing as much money as they earn. In every walk of life, in every ethnic group, beating the system by becoming part of it has become the driving force that keeps Americans going from one day to the next.[32]

Boggs made similarly prescient remarks in "The Next Development in Education" and "Toward a New Concept of Citizenship," speeches which, unlike the other writings in this section, did not focus in any direct way on the black movement but nonetheless present Boggs's thinking on concepts he thought essential to a renewed vision of political and civic responsibility and revolutionary action in the final quarter of the twentieth century. These speeches, then, can be read as Boggs's search for antidotes to the corrupting values cited above. For example, in "Toward a New Concept of Citizenship," delivered just days after the 1976 presidential election of Jimmy Carter, Boggs decried the damage to society done by the pursuit of economic interests and the narrow emphasis on modern technology to the exclusion of the public good: "Instead of being people, we have become masses, that is, individuals who believe that consumption and possession are what life is all about. . . . Meanwhile, as the quality of life continues to decline and the dangers to our planet increase, the only solutions that we can think of are in the form of more technology."[33] He urged his audience of students not to evade questions of social responsibility, recognizing that active citizenship requires us to face "the choices that we as human beings have to make as to what kind of society we want to live in and how much we are ready to struggle to bring that kind of society into being."[34] Similarly, in "The Next Development in Education" (1977) he argues that the concept of education is in crisis: "for so long we have gone on believing that education is the road to economic success that we have not even begun to evaluate what happens to a people who treasure economic benefits and economic development more than they treasure human relations and human benefits." He called for a reconceptualization of education "from the concept of education for earning, to the concept of education for the purpose of governing." Electoral politics, he hastened to explain, was not what he meant by governing: "We have all kinds of mayors and state senators who are not prepared for governing, and we have all kinds of electors whose only concept of governing is the mechanical one of going to the polls every few years to elect somebody else to look out for their interests." By contrast, he was referring to "the activity of governing," by which he meant

the continuing exercise of our distinctly human capacity to make meaningful choices that human beings can make: between policies that will benefit our communities and our posterity and those that serve only our immediate self-interest. In other words, I am talking about preparing ourselves to use that all-around capacity that only human beings have: to think about the society we live in, determine what will advance our society, and then join with others to make the politically conscious and socially responsible decisions that will help mold and shape our society in the direction that we believe it should go.[35]

"Liberalism, Marxism, and Black Political Power" was originally published as "Black Political Power" in the March 1963 issue of *Monthly Review* and was included in James Boggs's book *Racism and the Class Struggle: Further Pages from a Black Worker's Notebook.*

Liberalism, Marxism, and Black Political Power

In *The Negro Revolt,*[*] Louis Lomax gives a moving historical account of the step-by-step movement of American Negroes into American life: first, their arrival as imported slaves; next, their rise as free men during Reconstruction; and then, as a result of political manipulations both in the national Congress and in the southern states, the rapid decline of their short-lived freedom until finally, by the end of the nineteenth century, they were not even being treated as well as during the period of slavery. Lomax also points out something that few other writers have bothered to say: that long before 1619 a number of Negroes had come to America, not as slaves with only their naked backs but as part of the early force of adventurers, playing a role in the settling of the western hemisphere and bringing with them some of their own culture.

Then, very rapidly, Lomax traces the futile attempts made by Negroes to establish themselves in business with the aim of setting up a black economy. The failure of this effort left them with no alternative but to become wage earners in white industries. Next, as Lomax describes the different organizations that have been formed over the years as weapons for Negro liberation, the book really picks up momentum and one begins to feel the pull of the Negro mass. Not only does Lomax deal seriously with the rise of these organizations and the role that they have played; he also makes a penetrating analysis of why today most of these organizations face the loss of support by Negroes. For either what they seek to achieve is no longer what the Negroes want or the pace of their achievement is too slow for the impatient demands and the pent-up emotions of black men in revolt. If for no other reason than to understand the shifts in the Negroes' support of various organizations and the contradictions and conflicts now faced by Negro leaders as they try to find out where the Negro masses are, this book is worth its price.

It is when Lomax tries to do what Negro leaders themselves have not been able to do—that is to say, tries to plot a direction for the Negro struggle and make proposals as to the Negroes' allies in this struggle—that he gets into serious trouble.

The NAACP began as an organization to *defend* Negroes in the period when they couldn't defend themselves, relying mainly upon white courts to give favorable decisions to black men, under laws written and interpreted by white legislators, white

---

[*] Louis Lomax, *The Negro Revolt* (New York: Harper and Row, 1962).

judges, and white juries. It began to falter when it could not meet the new challenge of Negroes wanting to go over to the *offensive.* The new organizations, like the Congress of Racial Equality (CORE), the Student Nonviolent Coordinating Committee (SNCC), and Martin Luther King's Southern Christian Leadership Conference (SCLC), have been mainly direct-action groups. They take the law out of the courtroom and begin to implement or test it in action, in the streets and in the marketplace. This is the stage the Negro struggle has already reached and from which it cannot retreat.

There is only one apparent exception to this generalization, and it is a most important one: the black Muslim movement, which the author too lightly dismisses as just a group of fanatics. It would be much closer to the truth to say that the Muslims are in fact planting the ideological seed for the next stage of revolt. The black Muslims are doing something no other Negro organization has attempted: rehabilitating Negroes spiritually and morally to the point where they feel that they are men in every sense of the word and the salt of the earth; what they want is *not* integration with whites but separation and independence from white society because they reject white society and all its ways and values. This idea, which Mr. Lomax feels is mumbo jumbo, is the heart of the Negro question and the American revolution today. It is through this that we can begin to comprehend the Negro revolt in its present stage in the United States.

The United States was built up on an economy of slavery. That in itself was no crime. Many societies and countries have been based on slavery. The crime of the United States is that it is the first and only country which, having freed its slaves legally, by proclamation, by law and in the courts, then continued to enslave them and deny them equal rights on the basis of their color. The unique character of the Negro question in the United States stems from the infamous raw deal of 1877 that permitted the southerners to keep the Negroes in servitude as long as the northern industrialists could industrialize the country and accumulate capital and the white workers could have homesteads in the West to provide the foodstuffs needed for an industrialized East. It is this deal that has given the Negro struggle both its *class* and its *race* character.

In most countries the struggle of the oppressed has been of a class character only. But in the United States the Negroes have not only been at the bottom of the economy, they have been kept there on a race basis. Therefore, it is not just the economic system against which the Negro struggles, as many Marxists would like to have it. And it is not just a question of persuading and reeducating some southern Bourbons and reactionaries, as the liberals would like to believe. The Negro is kept at the bottom of the economic ladder by another *race* that keeps him there because of *his race* and benefits from keeping him there. Therefore, all those people above the Negro—i.e., all the whites—become responsible for the Negro's position, either actively or passively. It is not just big business or management or the rulers of the economic system who are allied against the Negroes. It is the white *people.* This is what gives the Negro struggle its peculiar duality: it is both a class struggle of the bottom revolting against the very structure of the American system, and also a race struggle because it is directed against the American white people who have kept Negroes at the bottom of their society. The rebellion of the Negroes today, like the slave revolts of the pre—Civil War days, is therefore a revolt and not just some sort of a "race riot," as the white politicians from right to left continue to think of it.

Lomax ends his book by giving reasons why Negroes should stick with the liberals. Behind his reasoning is the assumption that Negroes want exactly what whites have. Lomax never faces the truth behind the common saying among Negroes that all the white man has is his "white." This "white" is exactly what the Negro despises and doesn't want any part of, because it is nothing but racial superiority. So that when a Negro says that the whites have better opportunities, what he means is that these better opportunities exist only in relation to an opportunity that Negroes are denied. Or to put it the other way, when a Negro says that what he means is that he wants *a system of equality* or a way of life in which there is no advantage to anyone on the basis of race. Under these conditions, what the whites now have will no longer exist. Only if Negroes wanted to be superior or to look down on another race would they want to be like whites.

Lomax thinks Negroes need the support of white liberals because he envisages the Negro being gradually elevated into white society. He can only see Negroes as a minority who must depend upon these liberal forces. This is a position similar to that held by most Marxists on the Negro question, except that the Marxists substitute the working class for the liberals as the ally that the Negroes need. Neither does Lomax, purporting to speak for the working class, face the fact that great revolutions have never depended upon sheer numbers but rather upon the relationship of forces in the existing political arena. Today, when the existing political arena is a world arena, the Negro's relationship is to the world. The more revolutionary he and the world become, the more clearly he sees this relationship between himself and the world as part of the revolution that is taking place in the world. As he knows, and as all white America knows, "the whole world is watching."

Marxists are still thinking of Negroes in terms of their prewar role as sharecroppers in the countryside. They have not grappled with the new reality of the agricultural revolution in America and of the Negroes' migration to the big cities and their concentration in the center of these cities.

Both liberals and Marxists are imprisoned in thought patterns that have now become outmoded by the industrial and social development of the past generation. They are still thinking in categories of the democratic revolution at a period when Negroes have become the hub of the industrial centers of the country, and when what Negroes are fighting for is part of the world revolution and therefore against the whole structure of American society. They are looking so hard at the Negroes' color that they can't see the Negroes' social, economic, and world role in relation to the accumulation of capital, to the development of automation, and to the world revolution of the have-nots.

Theoretically, the Marxists are worse than the liberals. The Marxists recognize that a revolution is involved in the Negro struggle but still they want the Negroes to depend upon the white worker being with them. The Negro worker who works in the shop knows that if he is going to depend on the white worker he will never get anywhere. The average white worker isn't joining any liberal organizations or radical organizations. If he is joining anything, he is joining racist organizations like the home improvement (i.e., keep the Negroes out) associations, the Ku Klux Klan, and the White Citizens Councils. The white worker is becoming more of an enemy every day. Labor unions, which were supposed to be the most advanced part of America, are to this day practicing and fostering discrimination in the same manner as every other segment of American society. Only recently, at the Chrysler Jefferson plant where I work, when it was rumored that management was going to promote a few Negroes into skill trades, it was the steward who rushed to the men to arouse them to protest against Negroes coming into the department. It was not the company's fault, as Marxists would have the Negroes believe. It was the fault of plain American workers. For when the Negro fights, he fights not "in the last analysis"—i.e., not according to the thought patterns of Marxists—but *in reality*. His enemy is not just a class. His enemy is people, and the people are American whites of all classes, including workers.

The liberals are basing their whole case upon the assumption that Negroes want to integrate into white society and be equal within the present mess. We have to be very clear about this. America has never been based upon equality for all. It has always been based upon equality for a few, with the others trying to climb up on each other's backs so that they could be equal to those at the top and above those at the bottom. Most Negroes in the United States not only know this, they also know that their greatest progress has come when disaster has struck American society rather than when America was flourishing or because of the goodness of the American people. The first real upsurge came with World War I, when thousands and thousands of Negroes flocked to the North. The second upsurge came with World War II, when Negroes were able to work in industry en masse for the first time because of Hitler and Tojo, a fact that leads many Negroes to say today that Hitler and Tojo did more to advance the Negro cause in four years than Americans have done in four hundred. It is by facing this fact that one can begin to grasp that the Negro struggle is in no sense either a struggle to salvage American society or purely an American struggle; rather it is a struggle of an exactly opposite nature.

What is fundamentally wrong with Lomax's book is that it is written by a Negro who still thinks in terms of white power as naturally as he thinks of eating when he's hungry. His mind simply has not stretched beyond the idea of whites ruling and giving Negroes a greater share in this rule. He doesn't visualize that it could be the other way around, that it is in fact time for Negro political power to manifest itself. In the South today the one thing that both Negroes and whites are clear about is that when Negroes think of voting they are thinking of voting for Negroes to replace whites because they know that only when they do that will they get their rights. That is why whites are so determined to keep Negroes from voting. But up North where Negroes have been voting for decades, they still don't know what they are voting for. This is particularly true in the urban centers where Negroes have simply not grappled with what is implicit in the fact that who is mayor and who is police commissioner is decided by where the Negro vote goes. In no major city have the Negroes yet elected a mayor. Nor has any Negro writer yet realized that a Negro mayor of a big city like Detroit or Chicago or Philadelphia would be as natural as an Irish mayor once was in Boston or a white mayor now is in Minneapolis or Las Vegas or some small little town in Maine where the whites are the overwhelming majority.

It is only when Lomax can break clear of the image of the Negro always asking the whites for something and can begin thinking of Negroes ruling that his mind will be able to move to where the Negro nationalist organizations have moved. The struggle of the Negroes in the very near future will be the struggle for black political power, and by black political power is meant not the power of Negroes to put white men in office, to whom they can then go and ask for things, but rather their own power to dispose over things.

"The City Is the Black Man's Land" first appeared in the April 1966 issue of *Monthly Review* and was also included in James Boggs's *Racism and the Class Struggle: Further Pages from a Black Worker's Notebook.* Grace Lee Boggs coauthored this essay.

The City Is the Black Man's Land

Population experts predict that by 1970 Afro-Americans will constitute the majority in fifty of the nation's largest cities. In Washington, D.C., and Newark, New Jersey, Afro-Americans are already a majority. In Detroit, Baltimore, Cleveland, and St. Louis they are one-third or more of the population and in a number of others—Chicago, Philadelphia, Cincinnati, Indianapolis, Oakland—they constitute well over one-fourth. There are more Afro-Americans in New York City than in the entire state of Mississippi. Even where they are not yet a majority, as in Detroit, their schoolchildren are now well over 50 percent of the school population.

In accordance with the general philosophy of majority rule and the specific American tradition of ethnic groupings (Irish, Polish, Italian) migrating en masse to the big cities and then taking over the leadership of municipal government, black Americans are next in line. Each previous ethnic grouping achieved first-class citizenship chiefly because its leaders became the cities' leaders, but racism is so deeply imbedded in the American psyche from top to bottom, and from right to left, that it cannot even entertain the idea of black political power in the cities. The white power structure, which includes organized labor, resorts to every conceivable strategy to keep itself in power and the black man out: urban renewal or Negro removal; reorganization of local government on a metropolitan area basis; population (birth) control. Meanwhile, since their "taxation without representation" is so flagrant, safe Negroes are appointed to administrative posts or handpicked to run for elective office. In Hitler-occupied Europe such safe members of the native population were called collaborators or Quislings.

All these schemes may indefinitely delay or even permanently exclude the black majority from taking over the reins of city government. There is no automatic guarantee that justice will prevail. But those who invent or support such schemes must also reckon with the inevitable consequences: that the accumulated problems of the inner city will become increasingly insoluble and that the city itself will remain the dangerous society, a breeding place of seemingly senseless violence by increasing numbers of black youth, rendered socially unnecessary by the technological revolution of automation and cybernation, policed by a growing occupation army that has been mobilized and empowered to resort to any means considered necessary to safeguard the interests of the absentee landlords, merchants, politicians, and administrators, to whom the city belongs by law but who do not belong in the city and who themselves are afraid to walk its streets.

America has already become the dangerous society. The nation's major cities are becoming police states. There are only two roads open to it: *either* wholesale extermination of the black population through mass massacres or forced mass migrations onto reservations as with the Indians (white America is apparently not yet ready for this, although the slaughter of thirty-two blacks in Watts by the armed forces of the state demonstrates that this alternative is far from remote); *or* self-government of the major cities by the black majority mobilized behind leaders and organizations of its own creation and prepared to reorganize the structure of city government and city life from top to bottom.

This is the dilemma northern liberals have been evading since May 1963, when the Birmingham city masses (Birmingham is over 40 percent black) took the center of the stage away from Dr. Martin Luther King and precipitated a long hot summer of demonstrations, followed by a long hot summer of uprisings in Harlem, Philadelphia, Rochester, New York, and New Jersey in 1964. The McCone Commission has warned that the 1965 revolt in Watts may be only a curtain-raiser to future violence in the nation's ghettos unless the public adopts a "revolutionary attitude" toward racial problems in America; and Vice-President Humphrey proclaims that the "biggest battle we're fighting today is not in South Vietnam; the toughest battle is in our cities." But the war is not only *in* America's cities; it is *for* these cities. It is a civil war between black power and white power whose first major battle was fought last August in Southern California between eighteen thousand soldiers and the black people of Watts.

A revolution involves the conquest of state power by oppressed strata of the population. It begins to loom upon the horizon when the oppressed—viewing the authority of those in power as alien, arbitrary, and/or exclusive—begin to challenge this authority. But these challenges may result only in social reform and not in the conquest of power unless there is a fundamental problem involved that can be solved only by the political power of the oppressed.

It is because labor is becoming more and more socially unnecessary in the United States and another form of socially necessary activity must be put in its place that a revolution is the only solution. And it is because Afro-Americans are the ones who have been made most expendable by the technological revolution that the revolution must be a black revolution.

If the black liberation movement had erupted in the 1930s in the period when industry was in urgent need of unskilled and semiskilled labor, it is barely possible (although unlikely in view of the profound racism of the American working class and the accepted American pattern of mobility up the economic and social ladder on the backs of others) that Afro-Americans might have been integrated into the industrial structure on an equal basis. But the stark truth of the matter is that today, after centuries of systematic segregation and discrimination and only enough education to fit them for the most menial tasks abandoned or considered beneath their dignity by whites, the great majority of black Americans now concentrated in the cities cannot be integrated into the advanced industrial structure of America except on the most minimal token basis. Instead, what expanding employment there has been for Afro-Americans has been in the fields of education and social and public service (teaching, hospitals, sanitation, transportation, public health, recreation, social welfare). It is precisely these areas that are the responsibility of city government, and it is also precisely these areas of activity that are socially most necessary in the cyber-cultural era. But because the American racist tradition demands the emasculation of blacks not only on the economic and sexual but also on the political level, the perspective of black self-government in the cities cannot be posed openly and frankly as a profession and perspective toward which black youth should aspire and for which they should begin preparing themselves from childhood. Instead, at every juncture, even when concessions are being made, white America makes clear that the power to make concessions remains in white hands. The result is increasing hopelessness and desperation on the part of black youth, evidenced in the rising rate of school dropouts, dope addiction, and indiscriminate violence. Born into the age of abundance and technological miracles, these youths have little respect for their parents who continue to slave for "the man" and none for the social workers, teachers, and officials who harangue them about educating themselves for antediluvian jobs.

The fundamental problem of the transformation of human activity in advanced America is as deeply rooted as the problem of land reform in countries that have been kept in a state of underdevelopment by colonialism. Like the colored peoples of the underdeveloped (i.e., super-exploited) countries, Afro-Americans have been kept in a state of underemployment, doing tasks that are already technologically outmoded. But where 75 to 80 percent of the population in a country like China or Vietnam lives in the countryside, a comparable proportion of Afro-Americans now lives in the city side. And whereas countries like China or Vietnam still have to make the industrial revolution (i.e., mechanize agriculture and industry), North America has already completed this revolution and is on the eve of the cyber-cultural revolution. Socially necessary activity for the majority in an underdeveloped country is essentially industrial labor; education for the majority is vocational education. The peasantry has to be educated to the need to abandon outmoded farming methods, prepare itself for technological change, and meanwhile be mobilized to work to provide the necessary capital for modern machinery. It can be educated and mobilized for this gigantic change only through its own government. In an advanced country like the United States, on the other hand, the black population, concentrated in the cities, has to be educated and mobilized to abandon outmoded methods of labor and prepare itself for the socially necessary activities of political and community organization, social services, education, and other forms of establishing human relations between man and man. As in the case of the underdeveloped countries, this can be achieved only under its own political leadership. Hence the futility of the War on Poverty program, which is essentially a program to keep the poor out of the *political* arena where the controlling decisions are made and to train them for industrial tasks that are fast becoming as obsolete in advanced North America as farming with a stick already is in Asia, Africa, and Latin America.

Marcus Garvey and Elijah Muhammad, the only two leaders who ever built mass organizations among urban blacks, both recognized the need for self-government if the Afro-American was ever to become a whole man. Both of them seemed to understand intuitively Aristotle's dictum that "man is a political animal." Garvey created a political apparatus and proposed a "Back to Africa" program, which to many seemed fantastic. It was difficult for him to do otherwise in the period after World War I when Negroes were making their first mass migration to the big cities from the agricultural hinterland but had not yet reached sufficient numbers or development for him to envisage their political leadership of the cities. Muhammad's strength has also been in northern cities. His most pronounced achievement, the rehabilitation of black men and women, was based on his philosophy that the so-called Negro would inevitably rule his own land and his creation of an organizational framework (the Nation of Islam) that approximates the structure of government, including leaders, followers, taxation, discipline, and enforcement agencies. Muhammad's weakness was his failure to recognize the significance of technological development in an advanced country; hence his concentration on landownership and small businesses. Also, as so often happens with those who build a powerful organization, he became preoccupied with the protection of the organization from destruction by a determined enemy. As a result, when the northern movement erupted in 1963, he did not take the offensive which, consciously or unconsciously, large numbers of non-Muslim blacks (the so-called 80 percent Muslims) had been hoping he would take. It was this failure to take the offensive that led to Malcolm X's split from the organization. That such a split was inevitable was already portended in Malcolm's now famous speech to the Northern Negro Grassroots Leadership Conference in Detroit on November 10, 1963, in which he analyzed the black revolution as requiring a conquest of power in the tradition of the French Revolution and the Russian Revolution. Malcolm was assassinated before he could organize a cadre based on his advanced political ideas, but in one of his last speeches he made very clear his conviction that "Harlem is ours! All the Harlems are ours!"

It was in 1965 that black militants began to discuss Black Power seriously. Before 1965 the movement had been so dominated by the concept of integration, or the belief that the "revolution" would be accomplished if American Negroes could win equal opportunities to get jobs, housing, and education, that even black militants who were profoundly opposed to the American way of life devoted a major part of their time and energies to the civil rights struggle. What, up until 1965, few black militants had grappled with is the fact that *jobs* and *positions* are what *boys* ask to be *given,* but *power* is something that *men* have to take and the taking of power requires the development of a revolutionary organization, a revolutionary program for the reorganization of society, and a revolutionary strategy for the conquest of power.

As early as August 1963, at the March on Washington, the idea of Black Power had been anticipated in John Lewis's speech threatening to create some source of power and in the announcement of the formation of a Freedom Now Party by William Worthy. In 1964 the Freedom Now Party won a place on the ballot in the state of Michigan and conducted a statewide campaign, running candidates for every statewide office and stressing the need for independent black political action. The party did not win many votes, but it contributed to establishing the idea of independent black political power inside the northern freedom movement. In early 1965 a Federation for Independent Political Action was created in New York by militant black leaders from all over the country who went back into their communities to link the idea of black power with the concrete struggles. On May 1, 1965, a national Organization for Black Power was formed in Detroit.

The first task the Organization for Black Power set itself was to establish a scientific basis for the perspective of black political power in the historical development of the United States. Thus, the following statement was adopted at the founding conference.

At this juncture in history the system itself cannot, will not, resolve the problems that have been created by centuries of exploitation of black people. It remains for the Negro struggle not only to change the system but to arrive at the kind of social system fitting to our time and in relation to the development of this country.

That Negroes constitute this revolutionary social force, imbued with these issues and grievances that go to the heart of the system, is not by accident but a result of the way in which America developed. The Negroes today play the role that the agricultural workers played in bringing about social reform in agriculture and the role that the workers played in the 1930s in bringing about social reform in industry.

Today the Negro masses in the city are outside of the political, economic, and social structure, but they constitute a large force inside the city and are particularly concentrated in the black ghettos.

The city itself cannot resolve the problems of the ghetto and/or the problems of the city. The traditional historical process by which other ethnic groupings were assimilated into the economic and political structure has terminated with the arrival of the Negroes en masse (1) because of the traditional racism of this country that excludes Negroes from taking municipal power as other ethnic groupings have done and (2) because of the technological revolution that has now made the unskilled labor of the Negroes socially unnecessary. The civil rights movement that originated in the South cannot address itself to the problems of the northern ghetto, which are based not upon legal (de jure) contradictions but upon systematic (de facto) contradictions. It remains therefore for the movement in the North to carry the struggle to the enemy in fact, i.e., toward the system rather than just de jure toward new legislation.

At this conference we arrived at the recognition that the prop, the force, that keeps the system going is the police, which is an occupation force of absentee landlords, merchants, politicians, and managers, located in the city, and particularly in the black ghetto, to contain us.

Negroes are the major source of the pay that goes to police, judges, mayors, common councilmen, and all city government employees, taxed through traffic tickets, assessments, etc. Yet in every major city Negroes have little or no representation in city government. WE PAY FOR THESE OFFICIALS. WE SHOULD RUN THEM.

The city is the base we must organize as the factories were organized in the 1930s. We must struggle to control, to govern the cities, as workers struggled to control and govern the factories of the 1930s.

To do this we must be clear that power means a program to come to power by all the means through which new social forces have come to power in the past.

1. We must organize a cadre who will function in the cities as the labor organizers of the 1930s functioned in and around the factories.

2. We must choose our own issues around which to mobilize the mass and immobilize the enemy.

3. We must prepare ourselves to be ready for what the masses themselves do spontaneously as they explode against the enemy—in most cases, the police—and be ready to take political power wherever possible.

4. We must find a way to finance our movement ourselves.

Since the founding conference, and particularly since the Watts revolt and the deepening crisis from the U.S. occupation of Vietnam, black revolutionaries all over the country have been working out the theory and practice of building a black revolutionary organization.

1. They are clarifying what black political power would mean in real terms, that is to say, the program that black government in the cities would institute. Thus, for example, black political power would institute a crash program to utilize the most advanced technology to free people from all forms of manual labor. It would also take immediate steps to transform the concept of welfare to one of human dignity or of well-faring and well-being. The idea of people faring well of the fruits of advanced

technology and the labors of past generations without the necessity to work for a living must become as normal as the idea of organized labor has become. There should be no illusion that this can be accomplished without expropriating those now owning and controlling our economy. It could not therefore be accomplished simply on a citywide basis, i.e., without defeating the national power structure. However, by establishing beachheads in one or more major cities, black revolutionary governments would be in the most strategic position to contend with and eventually defeat this national power structure.

In elaborating its program, the black revolutionary organization, conscious that the present Constitution was written nearly two centuries ago in an agricultural era when the states had the most rights because they had the most power, also aims to formulate a new Constitution that establishes a new relationship of government to people and to property, as well as new relationships between the national government, the states, and the cities, and new relationships between nation-states. Such a Constitution can be the basis for the call to a Constitution Convention and also serve to mobilize national and world support for the black government or governments in the cities where they establish beachheads and where they will have to defend themselves against the counterrevolutionary forces of the national power structure.

2. They are concentrating on the development of the paramilitary cadres ready to defend black militants and the black community from counterrevolutionary attacks. The power these cadres develop for defense of the community can in turn bring financial support from the community as well as sanctuary, when needed, in the community.

3. The most difficult and challenging task is the organizing of struggle around the concrete grievances of the masses, which will not only improve the welfare of the black community but also educate the masses out of their democratic illusions and make them conscious that every administrative and law-enforcing agency in this country is a white power. It is white power that decides whether to shoot to kill (as in Watts) or not to shoot at all (as in Oxford, Mississippi, against white mobs); to arrest or not to arrest; to break up picket lines or not break up picket lines; to investigate brutality and murder or to allow these to go uninvestigated; to decide who goes to what schools and who does not go; who has transportation and who doesn't; who has garbage collected and who doesn't; what streets are lighted and have good sidewalks and what streets have neither lights nor sidewalks; what neighborhoods are torn down for urban renewal and who and what are to go back into these neighborhoods. It is white power that decides which people are drafted into the army to fight and which countries this army is to fight at what moment. It is white power that has brought the United States to the point where it is counterrevolutionary to, and increasingly despised by, the majority of the world's peoples. All these powers are in the political arena, which is the key

arena that the black revolutionary movement must take over if there is to be serious black power.

It is extremely important that concrete struggles and marches, picket lines and demonstrations, be focused on the seats of power so that when spontaneous eruptions take place the masses will naturally form committees to take over these institutions rather than concentrate their energies on the places where consumer goods are distributed. Political campaigns to elect black militants to office play a useful role in educating the masses about the importance of political power and the role of government in today's world. They are also a means of creating area organizations. But it should be absolutely clear that no revolution was ever won through the parliamentary process and that as the threat to white power grows, even through the parliamentary process, it will resort to all the naked force at its disposal. At that point, the revolution becomes a total conflict of force against force.

4. The most immediate as well as profound issue affecting the whole black community and particularly black youth is the war in Vietnam. The black revolutionary organization will make it clear in theory and practice that the Vietcong and the Black Power movement in the United States are part of the same worldwide social revolution against the same enemy and that, as this enemy is being defeated abroad, its self-confidence and initiative to act and react are breaking down at home. This is the revolutionary task Malcolm was undertaking and the reason why he was assassinated. Like the black youth of Watts, the black revolutionary organization will make it clear that black youth have no business fighting in the Ku Klux Klan army that is slaughtering black people in Vietnam. Their job is to defend and better their lives and the lives of their women and children right here. Moreover, speaking from a power base in the big cities even before there is national revolutionary government, black city governments are the only ones that could seriously talk with the governments of the new nations without resorting to the power that comes out of the barrel of a gun, as the United States must do today.

One final word, particularly addressed to those Afro-Americans who have been brainwashed into accepting white America's characterization of the struggle for black political power as racist. The three forms of struggle in which modern man has engaged are the struggle between nations, the struggle between classes, and the struggle between races. Of these three struggles, the struggle of the colored races against the white race is the one that includes the progressive aspects of the first two and at the same time penetrates most deeply into the essence of the human race or world mankind. The class struggle for economic gains can be, has been, incorporated within the national struggle. Organized labor is among the strongest supporters of the Vietnam War. The struggle of the colored races cannot be blunted in such ways. It transcends the boundaries between nations because historically the colored peoples all over the world constitute a black underclass that has been exploited by the white nations to the benefit of both rich and poor at home.*

In the struggle of the colored peoples of the world for the power to govern themselves, the meaning of man is at stake. Do people of some races exist to be exploited and manipulated by others? Or are all men equal regardless of race? White power was built on the basis of exploiting the colored races of the world for the benefit of the white races. At the heart of this exploitation was the conviction that people of color were not men but subhuman, not self-governing citizens but "natives." White power not only exploited colored peoples economically; it sought systematically to destroy their culture and their personalities and anything else that would compel white people to face the fact that colored peoples were also men. When Western powers fought each other, they fought as men. But when they fought colored peoples, they killed them as natives and as slaves. That is what Western barbarism is doing in Vietnam today. Now the black revolution and the struggle for black power are emerging when all people are clamoring for manhood. Thereby they are destroying forever the idea on which white power has built itself: that some men (whites) are more equal or more capable of self-government (citizenship) than others (colored).

---

* Because Afro-Americans were the first people in this country to pose the perspective of revolutionary power to destroy racism, I have been using the word "black" as a *political* designation to refer not only to Afro-Americans but to people of color who are engaged in revolutionary struggle in the United States and all over the world. It should not be taken to mean the domination of Afro-Americans or the exclusion of other people of color from black revolutionary organizations.

"Black Power: A Scientific Concept Whose Time Has Come" first appeared in the April and May 1967 issues of *Liberator* and was included in *Racism and the Class Struggle: Further Pages from a Black Worker's Notebook*.

Black Power: A Scientific Concept Whose Time Has Come

Black Power. Black Power. This is what is being written about and talked about in all strata of the population of the United States of America. Not since the specter of communism first began to haunt Europe over one hundred years ago has an idea put forward by so few people frightened so many in so short a time. Liberals and radicals, Negro civil rights leaders and politicians, reporters and editorial writers—it is amazing to what degree all of them are fascinated and appalled by Black Power.

The fact that these words were first shouted out by the little-known Willie Ricks and then by Stokely Carmichael to a crowd of blacks during a march to Jackson, Mississippi, in the spring of 1966 has heightened the tension surrounding the phrase. For earlier in the year the Student Nonviolent Coordinating Committee (SNCC), which Carmichael heads and of which Ricks is an organizer, had issued a public statement on American foreign policy condemning the war in Vietnam as a racist war and connecting the black movement in this country with the anti-imperialist movement in Asia. In that same period, SNCC had begun to analyze the role white liberals and radicals could play in the movement, aptly characterizing it as one of supporting rather than decision making. Coming after these statements, the cry of Black Power was seen by most people as deepening the gulf between the pro-integrationists and nationalists. Whether or not Carmichael had intended this cannot really be determined since the phrase had scarcely left his lips before the press and every so-called spokesman for the movement were making their own interpretations to fit their own prejudices or programs.

When Malcolm X was assassinated in February 1965, every radical in the country and every group in the movement began to seize on some slogan Malcolm had raised or some speech he had made or some facet of his personality in order to identify themselves with him or to establish support for some plank in their own program. The same process of attempted identification is now taking place with Black Power. The difference, however, is that Black Power is not just a personality or a speech or a slogan, as most radicals, liberals, and Negro leaders would like to regard it. The immediate and instinctive reaction of the average white American and the white extremist or fascist is far sounder than that of the liberal, radical, or civil rights leader. For these average whites reacted to the call for Black Power simply and honestly by reaffirming "white power." Their concern is not civil rights (which are, after all, only the common rights that should be guaranteed to everyone by the state and its laws). They are concerned with power, and they recognize instinctively that once the issue of power is raised it means one set of people who are powerless replacing another set of people who have the power. Just as Marx's concept of workers' power did not mean workers becoming a part of or integrating themselves into capitalist power, so Black Power does not mean black people becoming a part of or integrating themselves into white power. Power is not something that a state or those in power bestow upon or guarantee those who have been without power because of morality or a change of heart. It is something that you must make or take from those in power.

It is significant that practically nobody in the United States has tried to seek out the extensive theoretical work that has been done on the concept of Black Power. Actually, most of those writing for and against Black Power don't want to investigate further. They would rather keep the concept vague than grapple with the systematic analysis of American capitalism out of which the concept of Black Power has developed. In *The American Revolution: Pages from a Negro Worker's Notebook,* I stated my belief that if Marx were living today he would have no problem facing the contradictions that have developed since his original analysis because his method of analysis was itself historical. I said further that I considered it the responsibility of any serious Marxist to advance Marx's theory to meet today's historical situation, in which the underdeveloped— i.e., the super-exploited—nations of the world, which are in fact a world underclass, confront the highly developed capitalist countries in which the working classes for the most part have been incorporated or integrated into pillars of support for the capitalist system. Yet such an analysis has not been seriously attempted by either European or American Marxists. European Marxists have not seriously grappled with (1) the fact that Marx specifically chose England (at the time the most advanced country industrially in the world) as the basis of his analysis of the class struggle in terms of the process of production or (2) the fact that at the same time that the European workers were beginning to struggle as a class against the capitalist enemy at home, this same class enemy was expanding its colonial exploitation of Africa, Asia, and Latin America and thereby acquiring the means with which to make concessions to and integrate the working class into the system at home. Therefore, the working classes in the advanced countries were to a significant degree achieving their class progress at home at the expense of the underclass of the world. It was Lenin who dealt with this question most seriously when the European workers supported their capitalist governments in the first imperialist world war, and it was Lenin who, finding it necessary to deal seriously with the anti-colonialist revolutionary struggle after the Russian Revolution, recognized the nationalist and anti-colonialist character of the black struggle in the United States. Yet today, nearly a half century after the Russian Revolution and after two generations of European workers have shown themselves just as opposed to independence for the peoples of Africa and Asia as their capitalist oppressors, European Marxists are still using the slogan "workers of the world, unite" and evading the scientific question of which workers they are calling on.

Who is to unite? And with whom? The underclass of Africa, Asia, and Latin America that makes up the colonized, ex-colonized, and semicolonized nations? Or the workers of highly developed Europe and America whose improved conditions and higher standard of living have been made possible by colonial exploitation of the world underclass? Isn't it obvious that the working classes of Europe and America are like the petty bourgeoisie of Marx's time and that they collaborate with the power structure and support the system because their high standard of living depends upon the continuation of this power structure and this system?

The United States has been no exception to this process of advanced nations advancing through exploitation of an underclass excluded from the nation. The only difference has been that its underclass was inside the country, not outside. Black men were brought into this country by a people dedicated to the concept that all blacks were inferior, subhuman savages and natives to be used as tools in the same way that machines are used today. The phrase "all men" defined in the Constitution as "created equal" did not include black men. By definition, blacks were not men but some kind of colored beings. It took 335 years, from 1619 to 1954, before an effort was made to extend the definition of manhood to blacks. Yet American radicals have sought to propagate the concept of "black and white, unite and fight" as if black and white had common issues and grievances, systematically evading the fact that every immigrant who walked off the gangplank into this country did so on the backs of the indigenous blacks and had the opportunity to advance precisely because the indigenous blacks were being systematically deprived of the opportunity to advance by both capitalists and workers.

The United States has a history of racism longer than that of any other nation on earth. Fascism, or the naked oppression of a minority race not only by the state but by the ordinary citizens of the master majority race, is the normal, natural way of life in this country. The confusion and bewilderment of old radicals in the face of the Black Power concept is therefore quite natural. U.S. and European radicals accept white power as so natural that they do not even see its color. They find it perfectly natural to exhort blacks to integrate into white society and the white structure but cannot conceive of its being the other way around. Integration has been an umbrella under which American radicals have been able to preach class collaboration without appearing to do so. Under the guise of combating the racism of whites, they have actually been trying to bring about collaboration between the oppressed race and the oppressing race, thus sabotaging the revolutionary struggle against oppression which, by virtue of the historical development of the United States, requires a mobilization of the oppressed blacks for struggle against the oppressing whites.

There is no historical basis for the promise, constantly made to blacks by American radicals, that the white workers will join with them against the capitalist enemy. After the Civil War the white workers went homesteading the West while the southern planters were being given a free hand by northern capitalists to re-enslave the blacks systematically. White workers supported this re-enslavement just as the German working class supported Hitler in his systematic slaughter of the Jews. The gulf between blacks and white workers in the United States is just as great as that between the Jews and the German workers under Hitler. The difference is that Hitler lasted only a few years while systematic oppression and unceasing threat of death at the hands of ordinary whites have been the lot of blacks in the United States for nearly four hundred years. The present so-called white backlash is just white people acting like white people and just as naturally blaming their white hate and white anger not on themselves but on the blacks wanting too much too soon.

Despite their slavish allegiance to the concept of "black and white, unite and fight," most radicals and liberals are well aware that they do not constitute a serious social force in the United States. Few, if any, of them would dare go into a white working-class neighborhood and advocate that slogan. They would be about as safe doing it there as they would be in South Africa. That they go so easily into the black community with the slogan but steer clear of white communities is just another example of how naturally they think white. For whether they admit it to themselves or not, if anyone wanted to build a quick mass organization in a white working-class neighborhood today, his best bet would be to go in as a Ku Klux Klan or White Citizens Council organizer to mobilize white workers to unite and fight against blacks. Out of self-mobilization white workers have already come up with the slogan: "Fight for what is white and right!"

Revolutionaries must face the fact that the black revolt is now under way and is not waiting for that "someday" when the white workers will have changed their minds about blacks. Like it or not, they must face the fact that the historical and dialectical development of the United States in particular has made the blacks the chief social force for the revolt against American capitalism and that the course of this black revolt itself will decide which side the white worker will be on. The more powerful the black revolt, the more blacks move toward black power, the greater the chances of the white workers' accepting revolutionary change. On the other hand, the more the black revolt is weakened, diluted, and deluded by class collaboration (e.g., "black and white, unite and fight" and "integration"), the more chance there is of the white workers remaining counterrevolutionary.

Black Power in the United States raises the same question that Stalin could not tolerate from Mao: Would the revolution in China come from the urban workers or from the peasantry? Mao pursued his theory, based upon the specific conditions in China, and was proven right by the revolution itself. In the United States today, the question is whether the blacks (over 75 percent of whom are now concentrated in the heart of the nation's largest cities) will lead the revolution or whether they must wait for the white workers. In the twentieth century the United States has advanced rapidly from a semi-urban, semirural society into an overwhelmingly urban society. The farms that at the beginning of the century still employed nearly half the working population have now become so mechanized that the great majority of those who formerly worked on the land have had to move into the cities. Their land is now the city streets. Meanwhile, industry itself has been automated, with the result that black labor, which over the centuries has been systematically deprived of the opportunity to become skilled, has become economically and socially unnecessary. Unemployed or underemployed, the now expendable blacks are a constant threat to the system. Not only must they be fed in order to cool off the chances of their rebelling, but they occupy the choicest and most socially critical land in the heart of the nation's cities from which the racist white population has fled in order to remain lily white. Moreover, since blacks have become a majority in the inner-city population, they are now in line to assume the political leadership of the cities in accordance with the historical tradition whereby the largest ethnic minorities have successively run the cities. The city is now the black man's land, and the city is also the place where the nation's most critical problems are concentrated.

Confronted with this dilemma, the power structure, from its highest echelons to the middle classes, is seeking to incorporate or integrate a few elite Negroes into the system and thereby behead the black movement of its leadership. At the same time the power structure has devised ingenious methods for mass "Negro removal." Under the pretext of "urban renewal," it condemns and breaks up entire black communities, bulldozes homes, and scatters the black residents to other black communities, which in turn are judged to need "urban renewal." Meanwhile, under the auspices of white draft boards black youths are sent as cannon fodder to die in the counterrevolutionary wars the United States is carrying on all over the world as it replaces the old European colonial powers. Today the sun never sets on an American empire that maintains bases in at least fifty-five different worldwide locations. The war in Vietnam is a war of sections of the world underclass fighting one another, for it is the poor, uneducated, and unemployed who are drafted and the privileged (mainly white) who are deferred. This U.S. counterrevolution all over the world has the support not only of the general population but of organized labor. A peace demonstration in any white working-class or middle-class neighborhood brings out a hostile mob, which is sure to come even when the peace demonstrators are allegedly guarded by police.

Those progressives who are honestly confused by the concept of Black Power are in this state of confusion because they have not scientifically evaluated the present stage of historical development in relation to the stage of historical development when Marx projected the concept of workers' power vs. capitalist power. Yesterday the concept of workers' power expressed the revolutionary social force of the working class organized inside the process of capitalist production. Today the concept of Black Power expresses the new revolutionary social force of the black population concentrated in the black belt of the South and in the urban ghettos of the North—a revolutionary social force that must struggle not only against the capitalists but against the workers and middle classes who benefit from and support the system that has oppressed and exploited blacks. To expect the Black Power struggle to embrace white workers inside the black struggle is in fact to expect the revolution to welcome the enemy into its camp. To speak of the common responsibility of all Americans, white and black, to fight for black liberation is to sponsor class collaboration.

The uniqueness of Black Power stems from the specific historical development of the United States. It has nothing to do with any special moral virtue in being black, as some black nationalists seem to think. Nor does it have to do with the special cultural virtues of the African heritage. Identification with the African past is useful insofar as it enables black Americans to develop a sense of identity independent of the Western civilization that has robbed them of their humanity by robbing them of any history. But no past culture ever created a revolution. Every revolution creates a new culture out of the process of revolutionary struggle against the old values and culture that an oppressing society has sought to impose upon the oppressed.

The chief virtue in being black at this juncture in history stems from the fact that the vast majority of the people in the world who have been deprived of the right of self-government and self-determination are people of color. Today these people of color are not only the wretched of the earth but people in revolutionary ferment, having arrived at the decisive recognition that their undevelopment is not the result of ethnic backwardness but of their systematic confinement to backwardness by the colonial powers. The struggle against this systematic deprivation is what has transformed them into a social force or an underclass.

The clarion call "black people of the world, unite and fight" is only serious if it is also a call to black people to organize. The call for Black Power in the United States at this juncture in the development of the movement has gone beyond the struggle for civil rights to a call for black people to replace white people in power. Black people must organize the fight for power. They have nothing to lose but their condition as the wretched of the earth.

The call for Black Power is creating—had to create—splits within the movement. These splits are of two main kinds. The first is between the Black Power advocates and the civil rights advocates. The civil rights advocates, sponsored, supported, and dependent upon the white power structure, are committed to integrate blacks into the white structure without any serious changes in that structure. In essence, they are simply asking to be given the same rights whites have had and blacks have been denied. By equality they mean just that and no more: being equal to white Americans.

This is based on the assumption that the American way of life (and American democracy) is itself a human way of life, an ideal worth striving for. Specifically and concretely and to a large extent consciously, the civil rights advocates evade the fact that the American way of life is a way of life that has been achieved through systematic exploitation of others (chiefly the black people inside this country and the Latin Americans) and is now being maintained and defended by counterrevolutionary force against blacks everywhere, particularly in Asia and Africa.

Inside the Black Power movement there is another growing split between the idealists or romanticists and the realists. The romanticists continue to talk and hope to arouse the masses of black people through self-agitation, deluding themselves and creating the illusion that one set of people can replace another set of people in power without building an organization to take active steps toward power, while at the same time agitating and mobilizing the masses. Masses and mass support come only when masses of people not only glimpse the desirability and possibility of serious improvement in their condition but can see the force and power able to bring this about.

The realists in the movement for Black Power base themselves first and foremost on a scientific evaluation of the American system and of revolution, knowing that Black Power cannot come from the masses doing what they do when they feel like doing it but must come from the painstaking, systematic building of an organization to lead the masses to power. The differentiation now taking place inside the Black Power movement between idealists and realists is comparable to the classic differentiation that took place inside the Russian revolutionary movement between the Mensheviks, who were opposed to building disciplined organization, and the Bolsheviks, who insisted upon it.

The organization for Black Power must concentrate on the issue of political power and refuse to redefine and explain away Black Power as "black everything except black political power." The development of technology in the United States has made it impossible for blacks to achieve economic power by the old means of capitalist development. The ability of capitalists today to produce in abundance not only makes competition with them on an economic capitalist basis absurd but has already brought the United States technologically to the threshold of a society where each can have according to his needs. Thus black political power, coming at this juncture in the economically advanced United States, is the key not only to black liberation but to the introduction of a new society to emancipate economically the masses of the people in general. For black political power will have to decide on the kind of economy and the aims and direction of the economy for the people.

"The City Is the Black Man's Land" laid the basis for the development of the type of organization that would be in tune with the struggle for Black Power. Such an organization must be clearly distinguished not only from the traditional civil rights organizations that have been organized and financed by whites to integrate blacks into the system, and thereby save it, but also from the ad hoc organizations that have sprung up in the course of the struggle, arousing the masses emotionally around a particular issue and relying primarily on the enthusiasm and good will of their members and supporters for their continuing activity. By contrast, an organization for Black Power must be a cadre-type organization whose members have a clear understanding of, allegiance to, and dedication to the organization's perspectives and objectives and who have no illusions about the necessities of a struggle for power.

A cadre organization cannot be made up of just enthusiastic and aroused people. Its essential core must be cold, sober individuals who are ready to accept discipline and who recognize the absolute necessity of a strong leadership that can organize and project a strategy of action to mobilize the conscious and not-so-conscious masses around their issues and grievances for a life-and-death struggle against those in power. Such a cadre must be able to continue the revolutionary struggle despite the inevitable setbacks because they believe that only through the revolution will their own future be assured.

At the same time that it recognizes the inevitability of setbacks, such an organization must build itself consciously upon a perspective of victory. This is particularly necessary in the United States, where the idea of the defeat of the black man has been so systematically instilled into the black people themselves that a tendency toward self-destruction or martyrdom will lurk unconsciously within the organization unless it is systematically rooted out of every member, leader, and supporter. The movement for Black Power cannot afford to lose other Malcolms, other Emmett Tills, other Medgar Everses, and it must build the kind of organization that has the strength and discipline to ensure that there will be no more of these.

Nor can such an organization build itself on the counterrevolution's mistakes or abuses of the masses as the civil rights movement has done. Rather, it must seriously plot every step of the course—when to act, when to retreat, when to seize upon an issue or a mistake by the ruling power and when not to.

Within such a cadre there must be units able to match every type of unit that the counterrevolution has at its disposal, able not only to pit themselves against these but to defend them. Colonialism, whether in Asia, Africa, Latin America, or inside the United States, was established by the gun and is maintained by the gun. But it has also been able to hold itself together because it had skilled, disciplined colonizers and administrators well versed in the art of ruling and able to make the decisions inseparable from rule.

There will be many fundamental questions and problems facing such an organization as it moves toward power. How will it create new national and international ties with other people within the country and without? What will it do about industry when its takeover is imminent and those in power resist? What will it do about the armed forces and how will it win them over? In what cities or localities should a base first be built? What will it do when confronted by those in power as they respond to the threat of replacement? What segments of the old apparatus can be useful and which should be destroyed? And most important, how can it expose its alleged friends as the real enemies they are? These are all questions of strategy and tactics that no serious organization for power would write too much about.

As I said in *The American Revolution,* the tragedy is that so few see the urgency of facing up to this reality. But as I also said, that is what makes a revolution: two sides—the revolution and the counterrevolution—and the people on both sides.

"Culture and Black Power" first appeared under the title "Power! Black Power!" in the January 1967 issue of *Liberator* and was included in James Boggs's book *Racism and the Class Struggle: Further Pages from a Black Worker's Notebook*.

Culture and Black Power

Recently I attended a conference on black culture. As I sat there looking at all the beautiful black faces, I could see in them the drive, the desire, the compassion, and the hope that in that meeting and out of that meeting they could find the unity to take them down Freedom Road. And yet inside myself I could feel only a seething. A seething because there were so many things that I wanted to say, things I wanted to tell my people, things that I thought they should know and would understand if only I could put them in a form that would show them where they had come from and where they were going. I wanted to stand up before them and say, "Look at me, look at my face. Am I not black just like you? Look at the lines in my face. Could I not have been Emmett Till's uncle standing in that doorway in Mississippi when the two white men came? Can't you just hear me saying, 'Don't take the boy, boss; please don't take the boy. He's just a little old boy from Chicago. He don't know no better. Boss, don't take the boy; don't hurt the boy.' Yes, I could have been Emmett Till's uncle. And the little girls in Birmingham. Couldn't I have been a cousin or a brother to one of them? Can't you just see me standing there sobbing over their little bodies that have been bombed into oblivion? Or couldn't I have been a relative of that African rebel who, long, long years ago, dived into the sea rather than allow himself to be brought in chains to this continent? Could I not have been any one of these? Look at my face. What do you see in it?

But that wasn't all that I wanted to say. I wanted to say to them, "You speak of all the miracles and the grandeur and the splendor of our ancestors in the yesteryears of Africa. But don't you know that we are living today in an age of new miracles? Two years from now a man will be walking on the moon, and what only a few years ago was to most people mainly a beautiful symbol of love and of the unknown will be a walking place for men. And the first men to land on the moon and set up a colony there will be initiating a phenomenon that will dominate world history for the next five hundred years—that is, if by that time we have not all been blown out of world history by that power man has today because Marco Polo brought gunpowder back from China several hundred years ago.

"All that knowledge is in me, too. Can't you see it in my face? And all of it is in you as well. And we have to remember that today we are in a different age and that now when we think of our culture, we have to think not only of where we were at one time in history but where we are today and where we are going. For what good is all that culture if we cannot use it as a stepping stone to take us into the last quarter of the twentieth century?"

And as they talked of African kings and princes and the deeds and miracles that these performed and of which they are so proud, I wanted to tell them, "Yes, all of that is us. But the miracles of today are ours as well. When Thomas Edison created a light-bulb, he created a miracle greater than those of Jesus of Nazareth because he gave us light by which to walk the streets at night. For at the time of Jesus of Nazareth, it was often impossible to walk the roads because of thugs who waylaid men along the way." I wanted to tell them that when our mothers were giving birth to us, this light made it possible for the doctors to perform the miracles that enabled mothers and babies to survive, just as the invention of the freezer has made it possible to keep medicine in the sterile form needed by these doctors. And I wanted to tell them, "If you don't believe me, just ask some of our young black chemists. We have many of them now who will verify what I have told you, and they are just as much a part of our future as you are. And like me, they know that the foods we eat and which you are particular not to eat are no longer harmful. They know, as I do, that in every age, in every country, men have eaten particular types of food because these were suited to the climate and to the surroundings of the particular country. If they lived near the sea, they ate fish; if they lived inland, they ate other foods, particularly grains from agriculture. But today if any food (no matter where it might have been grown) is clean and refrigerated so that it won't spoil, it is not harmful. These are some of the miracles that modern man has brought about in the age of industrialization, miracles that are ours whether black men invented them or not."

But more than that, I wanted to tell them that we are already living in an age of power and that the power of America, which is reflected every time and everywhere it breathes in the world, comes from the fact that it has brought together the cultures and peoples of so many continents. I wanted to tell them that the African culture of which they spoke so proudly and lovingly should chiefly be the basis for our feeling the need to wrest some of this power from these American giants so that they will not be able to control what happens to the Africa from whence we came. And when some said that they wanted to go back to Africa, I wanted to scream at them, "How do you expect to go back? In the first place, who will let you get on the plane or the boat? Might not the man say that you can't go, that you are only going back to start trouble? And even if you were lucky enough to get away on the boat or plane, isn't it possible that a torpedo or missile could hit it just a few miles away from the African shores (to be reported afterward as just a terrible shipwreck or disintegration of the plane in the air)? All that is power. And even if you then escaped from the sinking boat or the crashed plane, might not some black African be standing there as you arrive, ready to bash out your brains with the barrel of a gun because the white bwana had told him these Negroes had only come to start trouble? This is what is happening in Africa today. And what country in Africa could you go to and be away from the man, who has prolonged your agony for so many centuries in the United States? What country could you go to, if you please? What country is there in Africa that has no neocolonial boss telling the Africans what they can do, when they can do it, and how they have to do it?

"We can't escape our destiny. Our destiny is right in this country. It is here in this country because it has been on our backs that all the immigrants who have come to this continent and helped it grow and of whom Americans speak so proudly have walked as they came off the gangplank. It has been on our backs that they walked off. Out of *our* blood, sweat, and toil have come the riches that have made America great, and it is we whose struggle can change America from a land in which men walk up the ladder on the backs of others into a land where each man walks in the sun equal to everyone else."

And there was still more that I wanted to tell them. I wanted to tell them that the question of why we are as we are is nothing that was decided on a majority/minority basis. In every country, including even our beloved Africa, it has always been a minority that ruled. And this minority has ruled because it has had power. Take the United States, for example. If the twenty largest industrialists who control the industrial heart of this country were to decide tomorrow that they want every black man to be able to walk the streets as free as he pleased, not one white person in this country would dare to say no (provided that each of them knew in advance that if they said no they would lose their jobs). It's not the president who has this power, mind you, and he was presumably elected by the majority, but just these twenty largest industrialists who are a very small minority and who were never elected by any majority but who still have this power to throw people out of work. This is what I wanted to tell them. I wanted to remind them that it is the minority that rules. All they have to do is look at South Africa, where a small minority can tell the African majority where they can walk, where they can't walk, where they can sleep, and where they can work. And the same is true in practically every country. A minority rules because it has the power to rule. That is what I mean when I say that blacks must have power.

Take, for example, the police. When I talk about the police, I don't mean getting a few more blacks on the police force to make it look like the police force is hiring blacks in proportion to their numbers. No, what I am talking about is the power to be police commissioner, so that when I lay down the rules it makes no difference who is on that force, black or white. They obey the rules I lay down or they lose their jobs. The police commissioner in every city in the United States right now—in Chicago, New York, Cleveland—could fire every white on the force and hire blacks to take their places. And in the morning he could tell those blacks to go out on the streets and whip some black folks, and they would do it because he had this power to tell them what to do. Likewise, a black police commissioner could lay off every black policeman on the force and bring in whites in their places, and they would have to follow their orders. That is what I am talking about when I speak about power.

It is the same with education. He who controls the board of education, the super-intendent of schools, and the finances of education is the one who decides what kind of education our children get. It doesn't mean that all the whites have to be taken out. But it does mean blacks having the power to tell the principals and teachers, no matter what their color, what they should teach and how they should teach it—because it is black children who are suffering most under the present system of education. And that is what we mean when we say that it is necessary to move into the arena of power and take power by whatever means necessary.

People talk about housing. Is it a question of a few more black people getting into some housing projects or into some homes in the outer city from which whites are flee-ing? Or does it mean blacks at the head of the housing commission deciding what kind of housing, when it is going to be built, and where it is going to be built because it is the black people who are the ones in most desperate need of decent hosing? This doesn't mean that architects, contractors, plumbers, and brick masons of all colors won't be needed to build houses. But it does mean who will have the power to decide what kind of housing, when, where, and how.

Seek ye first the political kingdom and all things will be added unto you.

That role is not easy. But we know, and need to admit to ourselves for once, that a lot of our ancestors came here because some tribal chiefs who were just as black in hue as they were went out and kidnaped them and sold them into bondage for a rifle or a barrel of rum. These African chiefs had the *power* of life and death over other Africans. We also know that immigrants who were supposed to have come in freedom from other countries practically came in bondage because in the countries from which they came, some people had the power to say that they must leave the country or lose their lives.

Oh, there were so many things I wanted to tell them so that they would have a vi-sion of the possibilities of the future. I wanted to remind them that we are not going back to the farm or each to his garden, that the farms have been outmoded and that in a few short years the Kingdom of the Sea may produce far more of the food the world needs than even the richest farmlands of this country, that there will be ships and fleets of ships bringing countless riches in minerals and foods back from the bottom of the sea, and at the same time people in laboratories now working on the land. That is the kind of future we must be preparing for.

I wanted to tell them about the future that lies ahead of us in education, where in-stead of blackboards we will have TV screens, where by a turn of a switch we can bring to people the accumulated wealth of science, literature, history, mathematics. And not only will grading be done by computers, but even the classrooms will be swept clean by centrally controlled machines.

This is the age of miracles in which our children's minds are growing up. It is an age where in cold climates all the houses can be heated by the sun and in the hot climate the houses can be cooled by air-conditioning. It is an age where we will soon be able to turn on our faucets and draw from them milk and other beverages piped into our homes as water is today. I wanted to remind them, too, that many of them had come to that conference in jet planes that had whisked them in two or four hours further than Columbus could travel in as many weeks.

Of what profit, then, is our history and our culture unless it is used in a vision of our future? For if our ancestors were kings and sat on golden thrones, of what avail were those thrones against the gunpowder Marco Polo introduced to Western civilization? It was this same gunpowder that gave Europe the power to go into Africa and wrest it away from our ancestors. Had they not Balkanized our Africa, would kings still be sitting on their thrones, or would Africa today be one of the most developed continents in the world? Who knows, and who can say that it would not have been? But for us who have lived in twentieth-century society, there is one thing we should be sure of, and that is that the road is not back but ahead to power.

Some of you laugh and scoff when you read in the American press that Mao Tse-Tung says that power comes out of the barrel of a gun. But nobody in the world should know that better than he. Because he knows that all the culture in China could not stand up against Western civilization once the civilization had mastered the gunpowder it took from China. He knows this because this power was used against him. And because the United States has this gunpowder, it has bases all around the world, in Asia, in Africa, in South America, and it is able to keep these bases not because Asians and Africans and Latins are inferior but because the United States has so much power—power not only to control the markets and the commodity prices of the world but firepower to destroy anyone who threatens this control.

The Chinese have a great deal of culture, as all the world knows. But Mao Tse-Tung, cultured as he was, did not sit around and talk about the virtues of being yellow and boast about his yellow ancestors. No. He said, "Because we have been so we shall be." And today the Chinese are spending their time trying to build the most powerful country in the world and developing their lands and minerals and training their people in mind and body so that they can step forward into the twentieth and twenty-first centuries with power. Gird up your armor. Face up to reality. For whether we get beat up in the alley by a cop, whether our kids go without an education and end up in Vietnam, whether they work or eat, whether they sleep in a decent house or in a rat-infested shack, whether they are tossed into a river with irons around their necks or whether they sit in the halls of Congress or in the White House or in a general's seat at military headquarters is a question of power. And we shall have power, or we shall perish in the streets.

"The Myth and Irrationality of Black Capitalism" was first published in James Boggs's book *Racism and the Class Struggle: Further Pages from a Black Worker's Notebook.* It is the text of a speech delivered at the Black Economic Development Conference, a national gathering of black activists convened on the campus of Wayne State University in Detroit on April 25–27, 1969. The conference proceedings were dominated by the "Black Manifesto," a document calling for white religious institutions to pay $500 million in reparations to African Americans. Activist James Forman presented the "Black Manifesto" during his keynote address, and the conferees adopted it as the official conference statement.

The Myth and Irrationality of Black Capitalism

I cannot account for why many of us are here, but the fact that we *are* here indicates to me that the black movement has now reached the stage where it compels us to confront the question: What kind of economic system do black people need at this stage in history? What kind of economic system do we envisage, not as a question for abstract discussion but as the foundation on which we can mobilize the black masses to struggle, understanding that their future is at stake.

It is now fifteen years since the black movement started out to achieve civil rights through integration into the system. Year after year the movement has gained momentum until today millions of black people in all strata of life consider themselves part of the movement. At no other time in our four hundred years on this continent have black people sustained such a long period of activity. We have had rebellions and revolts of short duration, but it is quite apparent that what we are now engaged in is not just a revolt, not just a rebellion, but a full-fledged movement driving toward full growth and maturity and therefore requiring a serious examination of the fundamental nature of the system that we are attacking and the system that we are trying to build.

It is also now quite clear that black people, who have been the chief victims of the system that is under attack, are the ones who have to make this examination; because for us it is a very concrete and not just an abstract question. We have evaded this question because in reality we recognized that to tamper with the system is to tamper with the whole society and all its institutions.

Now we cannot evade the question any longer.

When we talk about the system, we are talking about capitalism. I repeat: When we talk about the system, we are talking about capitalism. Let us not be afraid to say it. And when we talk about capitalism, we are talking about the system that has created the situation that blacks are in today! Let us be clear about that, too. Black underdevelopment is a product of capitalist development. Black America is underdeveloped today because of capitalist semicolonialism, just as Africa, Asia, and Latin America are underdeveloped today because of capitalist colonialism. We cannot look at the underdevelopment of the black community separately from capitalism any more than we can look at the development of racism separately from capitalism.

The illusion that we could resolve racism without talking about the economic system came to an end when we arrived at the point of talking about power to control and develop our communities. Now we are forced to face the question of what system to reject and what system to adopt. This has forced us to face squarely the relationship of racism to capitalism.

Capitalism in the United States is unique because, unlike capitalism elsewhere—which first exploited its indigenous people and then fanned out through colonialism to exploit other races in other countries—it started out by dispossessing one set of people (the Indians) and then importing another set of people (the Africans) to do the work on the land. This method of enslavement not only made blacks the first working class in the country to be exploited for their *labor* but made blacks the foundation of the capital necessary for early industrialization.

As I pointed out in the *Manifesto for a Black Revolutionary Party:*

Black people were not immigrants to this country but captives, brought here for the purpose of developing the economy of British America. The traffic in slaves across the Atlantic stimulated northern shipping. The slave and sugar trade in the West Indies nourished northern distilleries. Cotton grown on southern plantations vitalized northern textile industries. So slavery was not only indispensable to the southern economy; it was indispensable to the entire national economy.

At the same time the land on which American southern plantations and northern farms were developed was taken from the Indians. Thus Indian dispossession and African slavery are the twin foundations of white economic advancement in North America. No section of the country was not party to the defrauding of the red man or the enslavement of the black.

What white people had achieved by force and for the purpose of economic exploitation in the beginning, they then sanctified by ideology. People of color, they rationalized, are by nature inferior; therefore, every person of color should be subordinated to every white person in every sphere, even where economic profit is not involved. The economic exploitation of man required by capitalism, wheresoever situated, having assumed in this country the historical form of the economic exploitation of the black and red man, this historical form was now given the authority of an eternal truth. Racism acquired a dynamic of its own, and armed with this ideology white Americans from all strata of life proceeded to structure all their institutions for the systematic subordination and oppression of blacks. . . .

The early struggles to abolish the relatively superficial manifestations of racism in public accommodations have now developed into struggles challenging the racism structured into every American institution and posing the need to reorganize these institutions from their very foundations. Housing, factories, schools, and universities; labor unions, churches, prisons, and the armed services; sports, entertainment, the mass media, and fraternal organizations; health, welfare, hospitals, and cemeteries; domestic and foreign politics and government at all levels;

industry, transportation, and communications; the professions, the police, and the courts; organized and unorganized crime; even a partial listing of the institutions now being challenged suggests the magnitude of the social revolution that is involved.

In the course of its escalating struggles, the black movement has steadily and irreversibly deprived all these institutions of their legitimacy and their supposed immunity.

I said earlier that black underdevelopment is the result of capitalist development. At the bottom of every ladder in American society is a black man. His place there is a direct result of capitalism supporting racism and racism supporting capitalism.

Today, in an effort to protect this capitalist system, the white power structure is seeking once again to re-enslave black people by offering them black capitalism. Now, scientifically speaking, there is no such thing as a black capitalism that is different from white capitalism or capitalism of any other color. Capitalism, regardless of its color, is a system of exploitation of one set of people by another set of people. The very laws of capitalism require that some forces have to be exploited.

This effort on the part of the power structure has already caused certain members of the black race, including some who have been active in the movement, to believe that self-determination can be achieved by coexistence with capitalism—that is, integration into the system. In reality, black capitalism is a dream and a delusion. Blacks have no one underneath them to exploit. So black capitalism would have to exploit a black labor force that is already at the bottom of the ladder and is in no mood to change from one exploiter to another just because he is of the same color.

Nevertheless, as residents and indigenous members of the black community we recognize its need for development. Our question, therefore, is how *can* it be developed? How *should* it be developed? To answer these questions, we must clarify the nature of its underdevelopment.

The physical structure and environment of the black community is underdeveloped not because it has never been at a stage of high industrial development but because it has been devastated by the wear and tear of constant use in the course of the industrial development of this country. Scientifically speaking, the physical undevelopment of the black community is decay. Black communities are used communities, the end result and the aftermath of rapid economic development. The undevelopment of black communities, like that of the colonies in Africa, Asia, and Latin America, is a product of capitalist development. At the same time there is an important difference between the economic undevelopment of a colony in Africa, Asia, or Latin America and the economic undevelopment of the black community inside an advanced country like the United States.

The economic undevelopment of a colony is the result of the fact that the colony's natural and historical process of development was interrupted and destroyed by colonialism, so that large sections of the country have been forced to become or remain pre-industrial or agricultural. For example, many of these societies once had their own handicraft industries, which were destroyed by Western economic penetration. Most were turned into one-crop countries to supply raw materials or agricultural produce to the Western imperialists. In struggling for independence from imperialism, these societies are fighting for the opportunity to develop themselves industrially.

On the other hand, the physical structure of the black communities inside the United States is the direct result of industrial development, which has turned these communities into wastelands, abandoned by an industry that has undergone technological revolutions. The physical structure of black communities is like that of the abandoned mining communities in Appalachia whose original reason for existence has been destroyed by the discovery of new forms of energy or whose coal veins were exhausted by decades of mining. It would be sheer folly and naiveté to propose reopening these mines and starting the process of getting energy from their coal all over again. When one form of production has been rendered obsolete and a community devastated by an earlier form of capitalist exploitation, it would be supporting a superstition to propose its rehabilitation by a repetition of the past. You don't hear any proposals for white capitalism in Appalachia, do you?

Second, the black community is not technologically backward in the same way as the majority of communities in undeveloped nations in Asia, Africa, or Latin America are. In these countries the vast majority of people still live on the land and, until recently, had had experience in using only the most elementary agricultural tools, such as the hoe or the plow. In these countries a revolution in agriculture must accompany the industrial revolution. By contrast, the mechanization of agriculture has already taken place in the United States, forcing the black people (who were this country's first working class on the land) to move to the cities. The great majority of blacks have now lived in the city for the last generation and have been exposed to the most modern appliances and machinery. In the use or production of these appliances and machines, the blacks are no less developed than the great majority of white workers.

The undevelopment of blacks is primarily in two areas.

1. They have been systematically excluded from the supervisory, planning, and decision-making roles that would have given them practical experience and skills in organizing, planning, and administration.

2. They have been systematically excluded from the higher education that would have given them the abstract and conceptual tools necessary for research and technological innovation at this stage of economic development, when productivity is more dependent on imagination, knowledge, and the concepts of systems—on mental processes—than it is on manual labor.

From the preceding analysis we can propose certain fundamental guidelines for any programs aimed at developing black communities.

1. Black communities are today capitalist communities, communities that have been developed by capitalist methods. Their present stage of decay, decline, and dilapidation—their present stage of undevelopment—is a product of capitalist exploitation. They have been used and reused to produce profit by every form of capitalist: landlords, construction industries, merchants, insurance brokers, bankers, finance companies, racketeers, and manufacturers of cars, appliances, steel, and every other kind of industrial commodity. Development for the black community means getting rid of these exploiters, not replacing white exploiters with black ones.

2. Any future development of the black community must start from the bottom up, not from the top down. The people at the very bottom of the black community, the chief victims of capitalist exploitation, cannot be delivered from their bottom position by black capitalist exploitation. They are the ones in the most pressing need of rapid development. They are also the fastest-growing section of the black community. They are the black street force, the ADC mothers, welfare recipients, domestic servants, unskilled laborers, etc. These—not the relatively small black middle class—are the people who must be given an opportunity to exercise initiative, to make important decisions, and to get a higher education if the black community is to be developed. The creation of a middle class of black capitalists would make the distribution of income inside the black community less equal, not more equal. It would be the source of greater chaos and disorder inside the black community, not more order and stability, because the layer at the bottom of the black community, far from seeing these black capitalists as models and symbols to be admired and imitated, would be hostile to and strike out at them.

3. Struggle should be built into any program of black community development in order to stimulate crisis learning and escalate and expand the sense of civic rights and responsibilities. The struggles should be on issues related to the concrete grievances most deeply felt by the lowest layer of the black community—on issues of education, welfare, health, housing, police brutality—and should be aimed at mobilizing this layer for control of these institutions inside the black community as the only means to reverse the manifest failure of these institutions to meet the needs of black people. It is only through struggle over such grievances that the largest and most important section of the black community can be involved in decision making. The most important obstacle to the development of the black community is the lack of power on the part of blacks, and particularly on the part of this section of the black community, and therefore the lack of conviction that anything they do can be meaningful. It is only through struggles for control of these institutions that they

can achieve a degree of power and an increasing awareness of their importance and their responsibilities. Only through struggle can a community be developed out of individuals and the leadership necessary to any community be created.

4. Any program for the development of the black community must provide for and encourage development at an extremely rapid, crash program pace and not an evolutionary or gradual pace. Otherwise, in view of the rapid growth of the black population, and particularly of its most oppressed sector, deterioration will proceed more rapidly than development. For example, in a community where there is a pressing need for at least ten thousand low-cost housing units, the building of a couple hundred units here and there in the course of a year does not begin to fill the need for the original ten thousand units—while at the same time another thousand or more units have deteriorated far below livable level. The same principle applies to medical and health care. To set up a program for a few hundred addicts a year is ridiculous when there are hundreds of new addicts being created every week.

5. The black community cannot possibly be developed by introducing into it the trivial skills and the outmoded technology of yesteryear. Proposals for funding small businesses that can only use sweatshop methods or machinery that is already or will soon become obsolete means funding businesses that are bound to fail, thereby increasing the decay in the black community. Proposals for vocational training or employment of the hard core in black or white businesses (on the theory that what black people need most to develop in the black community is the discipline of work and money in their pockets) are simply proposals for pacification and for maintaining the black community in its present stage of undevelopment. There is absolutely no point in training blacks for dead-end jobs such as assembly work, clerical bank work, court reporting, elevator operating, drafting, clerking, meter reading, mail clerking, oil field or packinghouse working, painting, railroad maintenance, service station attending, steel mill or textile working. There is little point in training blacks for status quo jobs such as accountant, auto mechanic, bank teller, bricklayer, truck driver, TV and appliance repairman, sheet metal worker. There is great demand for these jobs now, but new methods and new processes will make these jobs obsolete within the next decade. The jobs for which blacks should be educated are the jobs of the future, such as aerospace engineers, recreation directors, dentists, computer programmers, mass media production workers, communication equipment experts, medical technicians, operations researchers, teachers, quality control experts. There can be no economic development of the black community unless black people are developed for these jobs with a bright future.

At the same time the preparation of blacks for these bright-future jobs must not be confined to simply giving them skills. In the modern world, productivity depends upon continued innovation, which in turn depends upon research and the

overall concepts needed for consciously organized change. The only practical education for black people, therefore, is an education that increases their eagerness to
learn by not only giving them a knowledge of what is known but challenging them
to explore what is still unknown, and to interpret, project, and imagine. The only
practical enterprises to develop the black community are those that are not producing for today but include research and development and the continuing education
of their employees as an integral part of the present ongoing program.

Black youth, born during the space age, are particularly aware not only of the
racism that has always confined blacks to dead-end jobs but of the revolutionary
changes that are a routine part of modern industry. Any attempt to interest them
in dead-end jobs or in education for dead-end jobs will only increase the decay and
disorder in the black community because rather than accept these jobs or this education, black youth will take to the streets. Any programs for developing the black
community must have built into them the greatest challenge to the imagination,
ingenuity, and potential of black youth. What youth, and particularly black youth,
find hard to do are the "little things." What can mobilize their energies is "the impossible."

6. Any program for the development of the black community must be based on large-
scale social ownership rather than on private individual enterprise. In this period
of large-scale production and distribution, private individual enterprises (or small
businesses) can only remain marginal and dependent, adding to the sense of hopelessness and powerlessness inside the black community.

The social needs of the community, consciously determined by the community,
not the needs or interests of particular individual entrepreneurs must be the determining factor in the allocation of resources. The philosophy that automatic progress
will result for the community if enterprising individuals are allowed to pursue their
private interests must be consciously rejected. Equally illusory is the idea that development of the black community can take place through the operation of "blind"
or "unseen" economic forces. The black community can only be developed through
community control of the public institutions, public funds, and other community
resources, including land inside the black community, all of which are in fact the
public property of the black community.

Massive educational programs, including programs of struggle, must be insti-
tuted inside the black community to establish clearly in the minds of black people
the fact that the institutions that most directly affect the lives of the deepest layer
of the black community (schools, hospitals, law-enforcement agencies, welfare
agencies) are the property of the black community, paid for by our taxes, and that
therefore the black community has the right to control the funds that go into the
operation and administration of these institutions. This right is reinforced and made

more urgent by the fact that these institutions have completely failed to meet black needs while under white control.

All over the country today the police are organizing themselves into independent political organizations, outside the control of elected civilian officials, and challenging the right of civilian administrations and the public, whom they are allegedly employed to protect, to control them. Community control of the police is no longer just a slogan or an abstract concept. It is a concrete necessity in order to overcome the increasing danger of lawlessness and disorder that is inherent in the swelling movement toward independent bodies of armed men wearing the badges of law and order but acting as a rallying point for militant white extremists.

In these campaigns special emphasis should also be placed on the question of land reform and acquisition. Over the last thirty years, the federal government has changed land tenure and agricultural technology through massive subsidies involving the plowing-under of vast areas of land, rural electrification, agricultural research, etc., but all this has been for the benefit of whites who have become millionaire farmers and landowners at the expense of blacks who have been driven off the land altogether or have been retained as farm laborers, averaging less than $5 a day, or $800 a year, in wages.

In the South the black community must undertake a massive land reform movement to force the federal government to turn these plowed-under lands over to the millions of blacks still in the South for black community organizations to develop. Black community development of these areas in the South should include not only the organization of producers' and distributors' cooperatives but also the organization of agricultural research institutes, funded by the federal government, where blacks working on the land can combine production and management with continuing education, research, and innovation. The responsibility of the government for funding research in relation to agricultural development is well established. Nobody has a greater right to these funds than the blacks now in the South and other blacks who will be drawn back to the South to assist in community development of agricultural lands.

In order that the black people in these agricultural areas do not fall behind their brothers and sisters in the cities, land in these communities should also be set aside for recreation, medical facilities, and advanced community centers.

A similar campaign for land reform and acquisition should be organized in the urban areas of the North where the great majority of blacks are now concentrated. The concept of "eminent domain," or the acquisition of private property for public use, has already been well established in the urban renewal program. However, up to now "eminent domain" has been exercised only in the interest of white developers and residents, and against the interests of black homeowners and the black community. Federal subsidies have been used to expel blacks from their homes, businesses, and churches, and then to improve the areas, which have then been turned over to private developers to build homes for middle-class and wealthy whites.

The principle of "eminent domain" must now be employed to acquire land for the purposes of the black community. Vacant land, land owned by whites that has been allowed to deteriorate, etc., must be acquired and turned over to black communities to plan and develop under black control and with black labor for the purpose of creating communities that will meet the many-sided needs of black people for housing, health, education, recreation, shopping facilities, etc., and will be a source of participation, pride, and inspiration to the black community and particularly to black youth.

The black community cannot be developed unless black youth, in particular, are given real and not just rhetorical opportunities to participate in the actual planning and development of the black community. The feeling black youth have now is that the streets of the black community belong to them. But without a positive and concrete program to involve them in the planning and construction of the black community, they can only wander these streets angrily and aimlessly, each one a potential victim of white-controlled dope rings.

The application of the concept of social ownership and control by the black community is essential to the involvement of the black street force in the development of the black community. These "untouchables" have no property they can call their own and absolutely no reason to believe that they will ever acquire any. The only future before them is in the prisons, the military, or the streets. They are the ones who have sparked the urban rebellions. Yet, up to now, after each rebellion they have been excluded from participation, while middle-class blacks have presumed to speak for them and to extract petty concessions that have uplifted these blacks but have left the "untouchables" out in the cold. The "untouchables" have not been organized into decision-making bodies with issues and grievances and aspirations and rights to development. Instead, middle-class blacks have been used to pacify them. But the fact is that these street forces will not just disappear. They are growing by leaps and bounds, threatening not only the system but also those who stand between them and the system, including those blacks who presume to speak for them.

7. Since pacification of these rebellious forces has been the chief purpose of all so-called development programs, it is no accident that most of these programs have been single-action, one-year, or "one hot summer" programs without any fundamental perspective for developing new social institutions or for resolving the basic issues and grievances that affect the largest section of the black community.

On the other hand, it is obvious that any serious programs for the development of the black community must be based on comprehensive planning for at least a five-year period. Piecemeal, single-action, one-year, or "one hot summer" programs are worse than no programs at all. They constitute tokenism in the economic sphere and produce the same result as tokenism in any sphere: the increased discontent of the masses of the community.

The purpose of these five-year comprehensive programs must be the reconstruction and reorganization of all the social institutions inside the black community that have manifestly failed to meet the needs of the black community. Any programs for the development of the black community worth funding at all must be programs that are not just for the curing of defects. Rather they must be for the purpose of creating new types of social institutions through the mobilization of the social creativity of black youth, ADC mothers, welfare recipients, and all those in the black community who are the main victims of the systematic degradation and exploitation of American racism. Development for the black community at this stage in history means social ownership, social change, social pioneering, and social reconstruction.

Manifesto for a Black Revolutionary Party was published in 1969 and went through several printings. The fifth printing of this self-published pamphlet, issued in 1976, carried a new introduction, which is included here.

Manifesto for a Black Revolutionary Party

We do not at all regard the theory of Marx as something complete and inviolable; we are convinced to the contrary that it has laid the cornerstone of that science which socialists must further advance in all directions if they do not wish to lag behind life. We think it is particularly necessary for socialists independently to analyze the theory of Marx, for this theory provides only general guiding projections which must be applied differently in England from France, in France from Germany, in Germany from Russia according to the particular circumstances.
—V. Lenin

Contents

Introduction to the Fifth Printing   196

Preamble   200

1. Racism and Revolution   202

2. Who Will Make the Revolution?   204

3. How Black Power Will Revolutionize America   212

4. The Black Revolutionary Party   220

Conclusion   228

Introduction to the Fifth Printing

As we go to press with this fifth printing of the *Manifesto for a Black Revolutionary Party,* we are more than ever convinced that the most important task before the movement in the United States remains the building of a vanguard party to lead not only blacks but all progressive Americans in creating a new nation wherein no one will be alienated from anyone else because of race, class, sex, age, creed, or national origin.

This fifth printing provides us with the opportunity to explain why the manifesto was originally issued in 1969 and to indicate some of the advances in our own thinking as a result of developments in the movement and our own unceasing theoretical and practical struggles to build a vanguard organization along the lines set forth in the manifesto.

To understand the historic significance of the manifesto, it is necessary to recall the fervor and ferment of the late 1960s. In 1966 Stokely Carmichael, on the march through Mississippi, had raised the slogan of "Black Power." The slogan caught on almost immediately with black youth in the northern cities who had become frustrated by the failure of the civil rights movement to grapple with the real problems of their daily lives and were striking out aimlessly and erratically in rebellions all across the country. Now, inspired and united by the slogan "Black Power," black youth exploded in mass uprisings in Newark and Detroit in the summer of 1967 and in more than a hundred cities following the assassination of Dr. Martin Luther King Jr. in the spring of 1968. The idea of "Black Power" was also greeted enthusiastically by militant white middle-class youth who had committed themselves to the struggle against racism and the Vietnam War but had never raised the question of power for themselves.

It was at this point that a few people—who were active in the black movement and who had behind them the experience of the labor movement of the 1930s (which never raised the question of power)—assumed responsibility for issuing the *Manifesto for a Black Revolutionary Party.* Proceeding from the recognition that this country had entered a revolutionary period with the raising of the question of power by those who had been most oppressed, the manifesto stated that this nation now faced three alternatives: "(1) continue rotting away as it is today; (2) naked counterrevolution; or (3) black revolutionary power." It was necessary for blacks to build a vanguard party that would give revolutionary direction and keep before the movement an enlarged vision of the goals of revolutionary struggle. Without such a party and such a vision, a movement based upon spontaneous rebellions could only end up in opportunism or sectarianism. Black Power would turn into its opposite: black powerlessness.

The soundness of this analysis has been abundantly demonstrated by the collapse of both the black and white movements over the last seven years. Today most of the militant and charismatic black leaders, who thought revolutionary leadership consisted of articulating the grievances of the masses, have become incorporated into the system through the many pacification programs hurriedly set up by educational, church, and governmental agencies to stave off further rebellions. Some are trying to make black capitalism or black bourgeois politics work while others, caught up in the various nationalistic tendencies, have fantasies of going back to Africa or taking over a few southern states. Others are dead or in prison because they interpreted revolution to mean unending confrontation with the armed forces of the state.

The white militants of the 1960s have followed a parallel course. Many went back to the university and are now doctors, lawyers, or social workers who make their living off the miseries of the masses. Some have returned to the bourgeois politics of the Democratic Party, while others have adopted the sectarian politics of old and new Marxist groupings. Still others have been caught up in the terrorism of groups like the Weatherman or the SLA [Symbionese Liberation Army].

Meanwhile, without revolutionary leadership, the black street youth, whom the manifesto projected as the main social force to make a revolution in the United States, have degenerated into a mob of individualists, preying on one another and on other members of the community. The result is that our cities, and especially black neighborhoods within our cities, have become a wasteland of alienated individuals who are more afraid of one another than our ancestors used to be of wild beasts.

At the same time, those at the other end of our society who are responsible for political, economic, and social leadership of the nation stumble from crisis to crisis. Confronted with the mass unemployment and inflation of modern capitalism, with the "standing up" of the third world, with the growing alienation and rebellion of young people, and with crime in the streets and pollution in the atmosphere they promote social disorder and demoralization by expanding multinational corporations, by increased military spending, and by the desperate scrambling of ambitious politicians for office (which reached a peak in Watergate).

For a brief period it seemed to some people that the Black Panther Party might become the kind of party that could keep the street forces from degenerating into lumpen. But the young people who organized the Black Panther Party did not take the time to develop the revolutionary ideology necessary to lead an American revolution. Nor did they develop the kind of process necessary to weed out those attracted to the party as a gun-toting, hell-bent-for-leather organization. Although many saw the need for a vanguard party, few were ready to commit themselves to the protracted process of internal political development, digging deep roots inside their communities, and carrying on the continuing dialogue with the masses—which is necessary to gain confidence and change the consciousness of masses whose only political experience has been of spontaneous rebellions over immediate grievances. Hence, even though the

Black Panther Party had originally conceived of itself as an organization to defend the community, it soon found itself frantically calling upon the community to defend the party and to free an unending list of its leaders and members from prison.

Nevertheless, the Black Panther Party was important because it was the first attempt by a section of the black movement to form a vanguard party and project the need for socialist revolution in the United States based upon a social force in continuing ferment. Because it was the first, but by no means the last, the movement can learn many important lessons by careful study and evaluation of its mistakes.

The collapse of the Black Panther Party and the deepening social crisis helped us arrive at a more profound understanding of the distinction between a revolution and a rebellion—which is a basic theme of the manifesto—and thereby realize that in the United States there cannot be a black revolution but only an American revolution.

"A revolution is not just for the sake of correcting past injustices. A revolution involves a projection of man/woman into the future. It begins with projecting the notion of a more human being, i.e., a human being who is more advanced in the specific qualities which only human beings have—creativity, consciousness and self-consciousness, and a sense of political and social responsibility."

On the other hand, "rebellion is a stage in the development of revolution but it is not revolution. It is an important stage because it represents the 'standing up,' the assertion of their humanity on the part of the oppressed. Rebellions inform both the oppressed and everybody else that a situation has become intolerable. They establish a form of communication among the oppressed themselves and at the same time open the eyes and ears of people who have been blind and deaf to the fate of their fellow citizens. Rebellions break the threads that have been holding the system together and throw into question the legitimacy and the supposed permanence of existing institutions. They shake up old values so that relations between individuals and between groups within the society are unlikely ever to be the same again. The inertia of the society has been interrupted.

"Only by understanding what a rebellion accomplishes can we see its limitations. A rebellion disrupts the society, but it does not provide what is necessary to establish a new social order.

"In a rebellion the oppressed are reacting to what has been done to them. Therefore rebellions are issue-oriented. They tend to be negative, to denounce and expose the enemy without providing a positive vision of a new future. They also tend to be limited to a particular locality or to a particular group—workers, blacks, women, Chicanos. For all these reasons the time span of a rebellion tends to be limited—usually to a few days or a few weeks.

"When those in rebellion talk about power, they are employing the rhetoric of revolution without substance. In fact, they are simply protesting their condition. They see themselves and call on others to see them as victims and the other side as villains. They do not yet see themselves as responsible for reorganizing the society, which is what revolutionary social forces must do in a revolutionary period. Hence a rebellion begins with the feeling by the oppressed that 'we can change the way things are,' but it usually ends up by saying 'they ought to do this and 'they ought to do that.' So that while a rebellion generally begins with the rebels believing in their right to determine their own destiny, it usually ends up with the rebels feeling that their destiny is, in fact, determined by others."*

Witnessing the destructive effects of this "victim mentality" upon the black street force over the past period, we have begun to understand how deeply rooted this kind of thinking is in the dynamics of American capitalism at its present stage of welfare statism. Because of its tremendous productivity and its determination to keep producing for profit, American capitalism not only keeps its victims alive but even encourages them to consume at an expanding rate in order to provide a market for its expanding production. At the same time, by constantly producing more victims of the system, it also provides jobs for the new middle class of social workers, defense lawyers, court clerks, prison guards, mental health workers, etc., etc., all of whom, black and white, constitute a mushrooming social basis for American liberalism.

Under these circumstances, it is not enough for a vanguard party only to "raise" the consciousness of those who have been most victimized by the system. If the vanguard party is to transform the oppressed into a revolutionary social force, it must struggle to "change" their consciousness—*from* the consciousness only of self-interest *to* the consciousness that comes from commitment to the struggles necessary to change things from the way they are to the way they should be. Otherwise the more conscious the oppressed become of the evils of the system, the more they tend to see themselves as determined or shaped by the system, and the more they struggle only to get "more" of what the system has to offer.

The chief weakness of all Marxist groupings in this country is that they spend most of their time exposing the evils of capitalism and racism and agitating the oppressed to militant struggles to get "more" for themselves. They do not understand that, insofar as they do not challenge the masses to begin taking responsibility for changing the system, they are in fact reinforcing the "slave" or "victim mentality" of the masses.

The vanguard party must give priority to transforming blacks from rebels into revolutionists, able and willing to give revolutionary leadership to all the American people and possessing a profound vision of the new, more human men and women who are the only people able to lead an American revolution to victory. At the same time, it must be consciously developing whites and members of the many ethnic groups who

---

* James Boggs and Grace Lee Boggs, *Revolution and Evolution in the Twentieth Century* (New York: Monthly Review Press, 1974), 16–19. —Ed.

make up this country so that they can also give leadership in the protracted and many-sided struggles necessary to revolutionize this country.

Blacks are potentially the most revolutionary social force in the United States. But as long as they see themselves only as victims of racism and capitalism, American society will continue to degenerate. Blacks, therefore, are pivotal to the advance—or decline—of American society. Moreover, unless blacks are an integral part of the leadership of an American revolution, the chances are that after a revolution, they will end up at the bottom, where they are today.

It is only because we began by committing ourselves to the theoretical and practical struggles projected in the *Manifesto for a Black Revolutionary Party* that we have been able to expand our vision of the kind of revolution that can resolve the unique contradictions of a country as technologically advanced and politically backward as the United States.

Today many white youth and a few black youth are forming groups to study the writings of Marx, Lenin, and Mao in the mistaken belief that they can find in these documents—written at a completely different time and under completely different circumstances—the revolutionary ideology on which to build a vanguard party in the United States. Because they have not recognized that capitalism in the United States has advanced far beyond anything that Marx could possibly have envisaged, they cannot struggle against their own liberalism or the "slave mentality" of the oppressed. The best they will ever be able to do is to agitate the masses to rebel against their grievances, as was done in the 1960s.

On the other hand, we have tried to draw the maximum lessons from the rich social practice of the 1960s and are continuously learning from our own struggles and the rapid, many-sided changes that take place in a revolutionary period. We are therefore constantly expanding our vision of the new nation that an American revolution will create and will, we are confident, lift all humankind to a new plateau.

[April 4, 1976]

Preamble

In the last fifteen years, before the eyes of the entire world, the black movement in the United States has moved steadily, and apparently irresistibly, from a struggle for rights to a struggle for power, from hope in reform to a realization of the need for revolution. Year after year, as the movement has expanded its geographical arena, from south to north and from coast to coast, it has also broadened its appeal from top to bottom of the black community until, today, literally millions of black men, women, and youth consider themselves comrades in arms in the black revolution.

In every city dozens of organizations have sprung up to offer leadership and direction to these brothers and sisters. Some of these organizations have come into being out of spontaneous eruption. Others are simply hangovers from the reform stage of the movement. Some are based upon ideas once held by only a few so-called fanatics but are now gaining wider support as a result of the growing ferment and search by black people for extreme solutions. A goodly number exist for no better reason than that the white power structure needs them as channels of communication into the black movement.

Whatever their origins and however varied and often conflicting their programs, all these organizations claim to be part of the "Black Revolution." The result is that the concept of revolution is being deprived of any scientific meaning and the black movement in the United States is losing all sense of direction precisely at the moment when the counterrevolution of the United States is gaining in strength and purposefulness, not only at home but abroad.

Especially since the murder of Dr. Martin Luther King Jr. in April 1968, and with it the final shattering of the illusion that moral appeals could resolve the fate of black people inside America, the black movement has been floundering, uncertain and divided on its goals and methods. Meanwhile, the mass base of the militant counterrevolution, feeding itself on the fears and deep-seated racism of white Americans, is growing by leaps and bounds. In the wings fascist leaders wait, confident that as the cries for laws and order become more strident, their turn will come as surely as did Hitler's in Germany.

There is only one way out of this crisis that affects the survival not only of black Americans but of all men on earth. *The time has come to organize a black revolutionary party in the United States,* a party that will, in the face of skepticism or opposition from whatever quarter, black or white,

(1) make clear that black liberation cannot be achieved except through a black revolution, and that the goal of the black revolution in the United States (like the goal of every revolution, regardless of its color) is to take power for the purpose of bringing about a fundamental change in the social, economic, and political institutions of the society;

(2) establish and keep before the movement and society as a whole the revolutionary humanist objectives of the black revolution in this country, a country that is both the technologically most advanced and the politically and socially most counterrevolutionary in the world; and

(3) develop a revolutionary strategy and a revolutionary leadership to achieve these objectives, building on the struggles, sacrifices, and achievements of the past and learning from previous mistakes and shortcomings how to struggle more effectively toward victory in the future.

[Detroit, Michigan
February 21, 1969]

Chapter 1
Racism and Revolution

The history of the two races in the United States is a history of the exploitation of blacks for the benefit of whites. Black people were not immigrants to this country but captives, brought here for the purpose of developing the economy of British America. The traffic in slaves across the Atlantic stimulated northern shipping. The slave and sugar trade in the West Indies nourished northern distilleries. Cotton grown on southern plantations vitalized northern textile industries. So slavery was not only indispensable to the southern economy; it was indispensable to the *entire* national economy.

At the same time the land on which American southern plantations and northern farms were developed was taken from the Indians. Thus Indian dispossession and African slavery are the twin foundations of white economic advancement in North America. No section of the country was not party to the defrauding of the red man or the enslavement of the black.

What white people had achieved by force and for the purpose of economic exploitation in the beginning they then sanctified by ideology. People of color, they rationalized, are by nature inferior; therefore, *every* person of color should be subordinated to *every* white person in *every* sphere, even where economic profit is not involved. The economic exploitation of man required by capitalism, wheresoever situated, having assumed in this country the historical form of the economic exploitation of the black and red man, this historical form was now given the authority of an eternal truth. Racism acquired a dynamic of its own, and armed with this ideology white Americans from all strata of life proceeded to structure *all* their institutions for the systematic subordination and oppression of blacks.

Beginning with the first shipload of slaves uprooted from their homes in Africa and continuing down through the centuries, black people in America have never ceased to struggle against overwhelming odds to try to liberate themselves from this degradation, individually and collectively, violently and nonviolently. But only in the last two decades have they been able to impart to their struggles the revolutionary dynamics of a self-developing movement.

The black movement of our time is distinguished from the black struggles of all previous periods because year after year, from its inception in Montgomery, Alabama, in 1955, it has increasingly drawn ever larger numbers of black people into ever-expanding and ever-deepening struggles over the issue of racism in the United States. As a result, every American today, in every section of the country, of every class and every color, on both sides, for and against black liberation, now faces the questions posed by the black movement in the very concrete and intimate terms of his daily life.

Precisely because the hopes of so many were raised by the initial efforts of the movement to abolish racism through reform measures, the movement has been impelled to develop increasingly more revolutionary positions as these hopes were disappointed. The early struggles to abolish the relatively superficial manifestations of racism in public accommodations have now developed into struggles challenging the racism structured into *every* American institution and posing the need to reorganize these institutions from their very foundations. Housing, factories, schools, and universities; labor unions, churches, prisons, and the armed services; sports, entertainment, the mass media, and fraternal organizations; health, welfare, hospitals, and cemeteries; domestic and foreign politics and government at all levels; industry, transportation, and communications; the professions, the police, and the courts; organized and unorganized crime; even a partial listing of the institutions now being challenged suggests the magnitude of the social revolution that is involved.

In the course of its escalating struggles, the black movement has steadily and irreversibly deprived all these institutions of their legitimacy and their supposed immunity. As layer after layer of racism has been unveiled in each institution, the hypocrisy and corruption of all those who control and benefit from the racist structure have been exposed. The liberal critic of racial prejudice has been revealed to be an accomplice in maintaining the system that creates it. As the contradiction between the humane pretensions of this society and its actual antihuman practices in regard to blacks has become more glaring, its barbarism toward other people and in other spheres has also become more unbearable. All the evils of the society begin to hang together: racism at home and genocidal destruction of whole nations abroad; the prostitution of its intellectuals and its educational institutions to the military-industrial complex; its transformation of active human beings into passive consumers in order to keep its gigantic productive apparatus in continuous operation.

The result is that today, from one end of the world to the other, the United States is hated and dishonored. A tiny nation in Southeast Asia is able to challenge and render impotent its most advanced and ingenious weaponry. In every country its emissaries and embassies barricade themselves against demonstrators protesting the crimes of U.S. imperialism. At home, alienation, frustration and hopelessness, anger, fear, and desperation pervade every section of the population as all about them they experience the crumbling of old beliefs and the uncertainty and confusion among those who presume to rule.

Formerly accepted values no longer command assent. Old-established customs no longer govern the daily relations between the races, the sexes, the classes, or the generations. Each person is thrown back on his own resources to determine the course of action he should pursue in what were once routine situations. No longer sure of what they should do or where they belong, great masses of people search for radical solutions. In turn, government at all levels, lacking the moral authority that comes from popular, unreflecting acceptance of its purposes and procedures, increasingly resorts to arbitrary decision and physical force in order to maintain law and order.

Thus, what only fifteen years ago appeared as a simple struggle by a minority of the population to achieve the rights already enjoyed by everyone else in the society has burgeoned into a total crisis of the whole nation.

Chapter 2

Who Will Make the Revolution?

In every pre-revolutionary situation the critical question becomes which social stratum or strata can provide the social force necessary to put an end to the old disorder and create a new order in which new social disciplines have been born out of a new faith in the potentialities of man. In an advanced capitalist country like the United States, this social force is usually expected to be the working class, while in an undeveloped country it is the peasantry.

The United States, however, is unique because its industrialization has taken place by a specific historical process in which various ethnic groupings have been successively exploited and integrated into the system, each climbing up the social and economic ladder on the backs of the ethnic groups directly beneath it, and all the white ethnic groupings climbing up on the backs of the blacks.

The result of this specific historical development is that the working class in the United States is today enjoying the fruits and defending the benefits not only of U.S. imperialist exploitation of the peoples of Latin America, Africa, and Asia but also of the centuries-old racist exploitation of blacks inside the country itself.

In the 1930s the American working class led a great social movement to humanize relations in production. But the movement did not develop into a revolutionary struggle for political power, and the capitalist class was therefore able to incorporate the labor movement into the capitalist system through the concession of economic and fringe benefits. As a result, the white workers in the United States today enjoy the standard of living and have the political attitudes of a middle class while their organizations are among the staunchest defenders of the status quo at home and abroad.

Blacks, on the other hand, are the ones who have been least integrated into the American way of life. They have benefited least from its material progress and been corrupted least by its abundance. They are therefore in the best position to question its mode of operation and reject its fundamental values. Against a society that has made such spectacular material progress through the most ruthless exploitation of human and natural resources, black Americans possess the greatest revolutionary potential for overthrowing the present system and replacing it with a new one in which human values take precedence over material values.

Blacks distinguish themselves from other strata of the population not only because of their aspirations to revolutionary change but because of their very concrete grievances that enable the largest section of the community to be involved and to learn through concrete struggle where the revolution has to go. They are an exceptional force inside this highly advanced capitalist society because they are antagonized not only by what this society has imposed upon *them* but by what it has imposed and continues to impose upon the four-fifths of mankind who are struggling to liberate themselves from racism, colonialism, and neocolonialism. Although millions of whites are also exploited, frustrated, and angry, they cannot at this historic juncture identify both racism and capitalism as the enemy that has to be destroyed. For blacks, on the other hand, the dehumanizing exploitation of racism is inseparable from that of capitalism.

Black people in the United States are the most advanced and determined section of all the exploited. They do not share in the misconception that there are natural laws that require the social relations existing in the United States, a misconception pervading the thinking of most white Americans because they have benefited by the past values of this society. Black people also do not share the white American's sense of racial, cultural, and political superiority over the rest of the world. The United States, for them, is not the best of all possible worlds; they have no reason to be anti-socialist or anti-communist.

The black struggle in the United States has the combined force and drive of a *national* revolution and a *social* revolution.

After centuries of the most ruthless exploitation on the land, first as chattel slaves and then as sharecroppers, blacks have now been driven by the mechanization of agriculture into the major cities of the North. There they are herded into rigidly segregated ghettos, living in the slums that surround the financial and commercial centers of the city, trying to make homes out of dilapidated dwellings that have been worn out by successive generations of white workers, attending schools and churches that have been abandoned by whites as they fled to the suburbs to escape the expanding black population, scavenging the dirtiest jobs that white workers feel are beneath their dignity and skills.

Employed or unemployed, young or old, born and educated in the North or a recent immigrant from the South, unskilled worker or professional, on welfare or making a comfortable living, *every* black man, woman, and child in these ghettos is fleeced and supervised by a huge network of white absentee entrepreneurs and administrators. This network includes landlords, merchants and usurers, bankers, plant owners and managers, realtors, racketeers and politicians, union leaders, licensing and inspection bureaucrats, university and school administrators, doctors, lawyers, and policemen. Most of these live in the outlying sections of the city or in the suburbs that surround the city like a white noose. In the morning they drive into the city to rule the "natives." At night they leave behind their police army of occupation and drive back on publicly subsidized freeways to their own neighborhoods to enjoy the profits and salaries that are their reward for ruling these "natives." Their entire way of life depends upon blacks remaining so weak, poor, and ignorant that they offer no threat to white authority.

Against these exploiters and overseers, the black community is now struggling for its self-determination like a colony against an imperialist power, conscious that any serious improvement of the condition of black people depends upon their ridding themselves of this whole parasitical white structure. Hence, the black movement has the revolutionary dynamic of a revolution for national liberation. This dynamic is expressed in the mounting struggles for community control of schools, of health and welfare institutions, of housing and police, and of the commercial and industrial enterprises located inside the black community. These institutions and enterprises, now occupied by the white oppressor, must be liberated.

At the same time blacks in the United States are an underclass inside the most highly advanced capitalist society in the world. In total numbers far exceeding the organized working class in the United States and the population of most nations, they are concentrated in the heart of the major cities, experiencing every day the contradiction between the spectacular material development of this country and its extreme backwardness in human relations, between the actual misery and degradation of their daily lives and a constantly beckoning world of abundance and ease. This contradiction drives the black movement toward social revolution.

What the affluent white majority conceives abstractly as a statistical gap between enormous national resources and the human misery of millions, the entire black community experiences concretely not only as a racial insult and oppression but as intolerable social injustice. To black youth in the ghetto especially, the situation is a source of unending fury and agitation. Why should people be tied down to a job (a "slave") when machines could produce all that is needed? Why should the operations of welfare be made so humiliating when more goods are produced than can even be sold? Why can't a society that produces upward of nine million cars a year produce an efficient system of rapid mass transit? Why should a society that can send men to the moon be unable to build decent homes for people on earth? Why should black people fight to destroy the Vietnamese in the name of a democracy that we don't enjoy?

These questions go to the very heart of the urban *and* the international crises of the United States, twin crises that embody the failure of the American way of life. The solution to these questions entails much more than the substitution of black faces for white in positions of authority. It entails a social revolution that will establish a new society based upon human needs rather than on the exploitation of human beings for economic profit and technological progress.

The combined dynamics of a national struggle for self-determination and a social struggle to resolve the contradictions of an advanced capitalist society have steadily driven the black movement from a struggle for reforms to a struggle for Black Power and are now driving the movement from black cultural nationalism to black revolutionary nationalism.

The black movement began in the South under the leadership of Dr. Martin Luther King Jr. as a struggle for civil rights or a struggle to achieve for black people what every other group in this country already has. The social base of King's movement was chiefly the older generation of churchgoers, black people who still had to be convinced that they were as good as whites.

King's great contribution to the movement was the clarity with which he stated his goal and the consistency with which he pursued his strategy. His goal was *integration* but his strategy was *confrontation,* and in the actual struggle the first was turned into its opposite by the second. The strategy of confrontation, or disciplined demonstrations in search of reforms, systematically exposed both the pitiful inadequacy of the reforms and the bestiality of the white society into which the demonstrators were struggling to integrate. Thus, while King's professed aim was civil rights legislation and integration, the means of confrontation taught black people that all the civil rights legislation in the world could not solve their real grievances and led them to question whether, after all, whites were good enough to integrate with or whether it was worth fighting to get into a "burning house."

King did not draw the dialectical conclusion of his movement. This was the historical contribution of the young blacks in the Student Nonviolent Coordinating Committee who pursued his strategy in every state of the South. Thus, in 1966, the black movement arrived in practice, before the eyes of the whole nation, at the concept of the struggle for Black Power that Malcolm X had been developing before black audiences in the North since his break with the Muslims in 1963.

In the spring of 1963, following the confrontation between black youth and white police in the streets of Birmingham, Alabama (the "Pittsburgh of the South"), the black struggle had moved to the North. Here the ghetto masses were concerned not with legal or democratic rights but with very concrete grievances in the arena of jobs, housing, schools, and police. Between 1964 and 1968, growing desperation over these grievances drove these masses to a series of violent and escalating rebellions. Each of these rebellions created hundreds of thousands of new adherents to Malcolm's concept of "black liberation by all means necessary."

These urban rebellions heralded the emergence of a new social force inside the black community itself: the street force of black youth. This force is made up of the new generation of young blacks who in the past would have been integrated into the American economy in the traditional black role of unskilled and menial labor. Now they have been rendered obsolete by the technological revolutions of automation and cybernation and driven into the military, the prisons, and the streets. Outcasts, castaways, and castoffs, they are without any future except that which Black Power can create for them.

Automation and cybernation have made these blacks expendable to the economy, but they have also liberated blacks for the first time in their history on this continent from the necessity to work on behalf of white development. After the Civil War blacks were legally free, but they could be re-enslaved because they were still economically necessary as agricultural, domestic, and industrial servants in the tasks disdained by whites. In the present period, however, legal recognition of the civil rights of blacks has coincided with the separation of blacks from their traditional relationship to the economy. Rejected by the economic system, today's "field hands" have also been freed to reject the system. Pushed out of the system by the system itself, they have become outlaws, at war with all the values and legalities of white America.

It is this rejection of the values and legalities of white America, objectively rooted in the separation of these black youth from the economic system, which invests the slogan of "Black Power" with such revolutionary potential. When black youth run through ghetto streets, flinging Molotov cocktails and yelling "Black Power," they defy and declare themselves outside the present and future jurisdiction of white economic, political, and social values. When in Afro haircut and dashiki they raise their fists in the Black Power salute to affirm black pride and black consciousness, they proclaim that, after four hundred years of the most dehumanizing oppression, the essential humanity of blacks is being mobilized to destroy this system and create a new one. When they celebrate Malcolm X as their hero, they celebrate the capacity within even the most depraved street hustler to transform himself into a dedicated fighter for black liberation.

These black youth infuse the slogan of Black Power with a revolutionary political content very different from the chiefly cultural content cultivated by an earlier generation of black nationalists. Their political orientation is determined by the objective fact that they are doomed to extinction unless blacks get real power and replace labor as the socially necessary activity of the society. Hence the terror that the slogan of Black

Power now strikes in the hearts of all who benefit from and support the present system.

In an effort to protect the American way of life against this revolutionary threat, the white power structure is desperately seeking to give the black middle class a stake in the system that it will, hopefully, be ready to protect against this black street force. The methods employed are varied: support for black economic development (black capitalism) and for black politicians; increasing the number of visible blacks in private industry, on television, and in the proliferating pacification agencies funded by government at various levels, private foundations, and the church hierarchy. The objective is unvarying: to develop a sector inside the black community that will interpret "Black Power" to mean blacks becoming like whites in everything except pigmentation.

These efforts by the white power structure have found a certain response among black preachers, politicians, professionals, and businessmen who would like to believe that black self-determination can be achieved through peaceful coexistence with white capitalists, i.e., integration into their *system*. Hence their fascination with black capitalism.

In reality, capitalism for black people is a dream and a delusion. Black underdevelopment is a product of white economic development. The system of exploitation that created the problem in the first place can hardly be expected to solve it. As we have pointed out, white capitalism was built upon the systematic exploitation over many years of the black man and the red man, from whose labors and land the original capital of America was accumulated. Blacks have no one underneath them to exploit. So black capitalism would have to exploit a black labor force that is in no mood to substitute black exploiters for white ones.

Equally important, black capitalism could never rival or compete with white capitalism. Trying to catch up, it could only remain far behind, marginal and dependent, in permanent neocolonist subjection to the enormous capital resources American whites control and with which they can manipulate interest rates, commodity prices, and wages and thereby destroy or sustain large and small enterprises at home and abroad. American capitalism today is the citadel of international capitalism, controlling two-thirds of the whole world's resources. It has been able to reach this point of predominance only by subjecting other state powers to its will (imperialism). American capital decides, in an afternoon, whether to protect or to undermine another government by giving or withholding loans of millions of dollars. Its control of the cocoa market of Ghana enabled it to engineer the overthrow of Nkrumah's government. By continuing investment in the South African economy, it keeps the South African government and its racism intact.

No less naïve is the dream of black liberation through the election of black politicians. Black politicians continue to delude themselves that they are revolutionaries infiltrating the American political parties. In fact, these parties are, like every other American institution, the embodiment of institutionalized racism. That is why the specific American tradition by which various ethnic groups have successively taken over municipal government has come to a stop with black people. No other ethnic group has ever constituted such a substantial minority in the major cities. But white people control the entire process of voting. They make the rules and they also change them as they go along. When threatened with blacks voting themselves into power in any area, they simply change the political boundaries (gerrymandering) or superimpose regional or county government upon city government.

The U.S. Congress has given dramatic evidence of how it is organized to maintain the racist structure of this society by summarily expelling the one black congressman who after two decades had acquired an important committee chairmanship. After over a century of emancipation, black congressmen constitute less than 2 percent of the congressional membership and can only beg for crumbs at the congressional table. Out of 550,000 elected officials in the United States, only 800 (less than one-half of 1 percent) are black. No wonder that every economic, social, and legislative concession won by blacks in this country has been the result of independent black struggle outside the electoral arena. Whenever black people, from the days of Reconstruction to the modern practice of supporting the Kennedys, Johnson, and Humphrey, have sought liberation through integration into the existing political system, they have weakened their own position and strengthened the control of American racist institutions over their lives.

In the final analysis, all these pacification programs are doomed to failure because all depend upon the quiescent acquiescence of the black street force, a force that is anything but quiescent or acquiescent. These black youth do not allow anyone in this society to forget their existence, and especially not the other members of the black community in whose midst they live and operate.

From the time they reach their teens, and while they are still in school, these youth know that they have no future within this system. What form a new system will assume they are not sure, but they know instinctively that for their own survival they must fight this one at every turn. Where once they were visible mainly during the summer rebellions, now they make their presence forcibly felt, year in and year out, at all hours of the day and night, in and out of school.

As denizens of the streets, they perpetually challenge the police for the right to rule these streets. Hired into the old industrial plants as part of the pacification program of private industry, they drift in and out of the plant, meanwhile carrying on an unceasing agitation against the dead-end assembly jobs and the racism of the unions with which older blacks have learned to live. Push outs or dropouts, with plenty of time on their hands, they invade public buildings and private businesses, schools and offices, demanding and taking, challenging and defying, deepening the sense of crisis and insecurity inside the black community. No longer needed by the capitalist system as producers in the labor process but still exploited as consumers, many of them prey on each other and on other members of the community, especially those who are trying to make it inside the system by running small businesses or saving a few dollars.

Thus these young blacks are not only a challenge to white authority. They are also a challenge to all those inside the black community, including their parents, who still have their little jobs and dream of peaceful coexistence with white America. With their black pride, their rejection of white values, *and* their expendability to the economy, these youth represent the future of black people—*one way or the other.* If their revolutionary potential is systematically encouraged and developed, they can become the most dedicated fighters for black liberation. If, on the other hand, older blacks join with white America in calling for their repression and extermination as troublemakers and criminals, the white power structure will be glad to oblige. But after they are gone, of what use will the black middle classes be to white America?

The black street force thus compels every member of the black community, on pain of extinction, to face up to the failure of all institutions in modern America: the economic system, the schools, the welfare system, the hospitals, the police, the political system, i.e., the entire American way of life, and to develop a perspective and strategy for the total revolutionizing of America.

Without such a perspective and a strategy to take power in order to realize it, you have rebels but not revolutionists, rebellions but not revolutions.

◉ ◉ ◉

In the past few years the growing crisis in American society has brought into the arena of struggle another potentially revolutionary force: white university youth. This section of the population is constantly growing in numbers as the university increasingly becomes a factor to turn out highly trained technicians and administrators for the U.S. industrial war machine at home and abroad. But growing numbers also have been the students resisting integration into a system whose basic inhumanity has been exposed by the black movement and the Vietnam War and who see no hope for themselves as human beings without a complete transformation of the system.

The demonstration of university youth against the Vietnam War and against racism, particularly on college campuses, has played an important role in accelerating the disintegration of U.S. institutions and thus deepening the general social crisis. While the black movement has been tearing up American society at its base, the student movement has been tearing it apart in its middle and upper echelons, attacking and undermining its most cherished values. Precisely because these students are the beneficiaries of the established order, their attacks on it have caught it off balance. Like a Trojan horse inside the enemy's camp, they have created the kind of confusion, division, and demoralization that are invaluable assets in winning a revolutionary war.

The weakness of this movement among white university youth is its lack of a mass base in any community with which the students can interact in the course of struggles over concrete grievances and thereby develop a sustained revolutionary perspective. They cannot organize inside the black community because of the national character of the black movement. They are not welcome in the white working class, which is at this juncture among the staunchest defenders of the status quo.

Chapter 3
How Black Power Will Revolutionize America

Black Power is not any more difficult to understand than workers' power. It is the state power to destroy the existing system and replace it with a new one that will benefit not only blacks but all the people in this country and throughout the world.

This means, first and foremost, that Black Power will use its political supremacy to take power from those who now hold it. There must be no illusion that this can be done without expropriating all those who now own and control the means of production, distribution, and communications.

Black Power will then redistribute these national resources to local communities. By no other means will it be possible to transfer political power into the hands of the people. For what is political power but the power of people to determine the organized structure of the society in which they live and function from day to day? And how can people have the power to determine the structure of their society unless they have the actual control over resources that are sizable enough to make a real difference? Up to now the crucial decisions of this society have been made by the capitalist power structure which, in the process of controlling the people, has not only reduced the people to a dehumanized mass but has itself become so dehumanized that it threatens the destruction of the whole world.

Black Power is coming at the stage of the development of the productive forces when it is no longer necessary to concentrate the social forces of the society on the goal of increasing production. The productive forces are already sufficiently developed to establish a material basis for communism, i.e., a society in which each has according to his needs and contributes according to his abilities. The urgent need today is to increase the political power, participation, and understanding of the great masses of people in order to develop their capacity to become socially responsible and creative human beings.

Since the ability to produce goods in the amounts needed to fulfill the material needs of people already exists, the first step will be to declare everyone, black or white, North or South, young or old, entitled to the material goods they need to live in dignity, regardless of whether or not they have been involved in the process of labor. Naturally, in the early stages following such a declaration, there will be grabbing and hoarding because the masses of people who have been in want will still be imbued with the old capitalist conception that the measure of a man's worth is the amount of his material possessions. But, in the process of discovering that plenty is available to everyone without the need to grab and hoard and at the same time be involved in making the decisions as to what should be produced and how the community should be organized, people will soon recognize that mere possession is not the height of human value.

In the course of deciding what goods should be produced, people will be confronted with the fact that today there is enormous duplication in the production of every commodity on the mass market from toothpaste to TVs, from aspirin to cars. This will lead them into the determination not only of the quality of goods but of the variety and quantity necessary to produce of particular goods. For example, what are the relations of auto production to the crisis of the cities, rapidly being turned into asphalt jungles of parking lots and freeways because living space for cars has become more profitable than living space for people? Human decisions on the function of the auto in this society cannot be made until, first, the auto manufacturers have been expropriated and, second, the workers making autos have been guaranteed their right to live without having to worry about their jobs.

In making these decisions about autos as they relate to human needs and the crisis of our cities, questions of transportation by other means will have to be resolved. For example, should highways, parking lots, and cars continue to displace people, or can a form of mass transportation be devised to take people from where they are to where they want to go? There is, in addition, the very simple human question of the extent to which transportation by mechanical means is virtually destroying the human ability to use our feet. The ability to walk upright and to be related to our environment and to other people in a walking position at a walking pace is one of the great physiological and psychological achievements of man. Yet we are permitting this achievement to be eroded today by automobiles, which are creating barriers between individuals and between people and their environment.

Black Power will make public transportation a free public service, with the community deciding what kind of transportation best fits its needs. There is no question that if technological progress can be used to send human beings to the moon, it can be used to design fully automated subways that will leave the ground free for people to walk on.

Only by making everyone entitled to the goods they need to live in dignity, regardless of whether or not they are working, can society resolve the problem of the growing number of second-class citizens who are looked down upon today because they are on various forms of welfare. Today there are millions not working and without any possibility of ever working. Yet those who control our institutions and our economy insist that people are less than human if they don't work. The U.S. Constitution guarantees all citizens the right to pursue happiness. In effect, this means that citizens are judged by how hard they pursue money. By removing the social distinction between the working and the not-working, Black Power will guarantee those not working absolute equality in their right to social involvement and decision making.

With advancing technology, capitalism has created the politically dispossessed classes of the young, the aged, and mothers with dependent children. All three of these groups are today looked down on by the rest of society precisely at the time when they are growing in numbers and have the maximum time to be involved in political and social decision making. Black Power will not only guarantee economic independence to these sections of the population. It will specifically encourage and value their participation in all the issues facing our society. Mothers with dependent children will be encouraged to play a maximum role in developing the children of the community to become fully human beings through their participation not only in community centers for infants and preschool children but in every sphere of community decision making.

Young people in their teens will be encouraged and valued for their participation in deciding what goods should be produced, what services are necessary in a community, what courses should be included in schools and factories. Teenagers will thus be given scope for their energies, imagination, and dedication precisely at the time in their lives when they are most in need of developing their capacity for social responsibility. By no other means can the generation gap be bridged and the talents of young people mobilized for the building of society rather than for tearing it down.

The specific contribution of the aged, namely, the ability to convey a sense of continuity and transition, will also be encouraged and cherished.

By all these means welfare will be transformed from a degraded status to a status of well-faring. Who knows what creative talents will mushroom when society is organized to encourage such involvement?

There is relatively little use in entitling everybody to a living unless society is at the same time making life enjoyable and healthful. Even though today in the United States the best medical care is available, many poor people, especially blacks, are denied proper and necessary health care. A few years ago the president of the American Medical Association voiced an opinion shared by many capitalistically minded physicians: that medical care is a privilege and not a right.

Black Power will guarantee everybody the right to full and free medical care from birth, as distinguished from the present practice of entitling people to medical care that they can afford only as they approach the grave. Such a guarantee will not only assure everybody of medical care but will create the need for large numbers of people, young and old, men and women, to develop a greater understanding of medical science at all levels. This will make it possible to eliminate both the massive waste in useless drugs that now flood the market and the sense of impotence that dominates those who are ill or ailing.

Medical research will be freed from the competitive market and the search for profits. The skills of those involved in medical science can then be applied to finding the cures for cancer, bad teeth, arthritis, mental disorder, and the other common and growing ills of an urban society. Who knows how many lives could be saved, altered, or made more enjoyable if medical research and practice were devoted to human development rather than to profit? Health, like transportation, is a human right. Instead of the private drug chain and the profit-making pharmaceutical laboratory, we will have community clinics and health centers under the control of the local community where everyone will be automatically entitled to care. Preventive medicine, in which this country lags far behind other industrially advanced countries, will then be possible.

Not since the Indians built their wigwams or the early European settlers their log cabins has shelter been built for human needs in the United States. From the cotton-patch shacks in the South to the industrial tenements in the North, housing in this country has been built to meet the needs of capitalism for labor to work on the farms in the mines, mills, factories, and offices. Homes have not been built to meet the need of human beings to live together, interact with one another, young and old, intellectual and non-intellectual, of varying backgrounds and interests.

In the cities the vast majority of the people have lived in slum houses and tenements progressively abandoned by ethnic groups as they were assimilated into the higher economic brackets of the society. In this hand-me-down process blacks have been the final scavengers, inheriting and paying the highest rents for housing that has become unfit for human habitation, just as they have inherited the old jobs, the old schools, and the old churches discarded by whites. Today, over half the dwellings in this country are dilapidated primarily because houses continue to be built and marketed to meet the needs of land speculators, landlords, and the building industry rather than the needs of people.

Broken homes are not just homes that lack two parents. Broken homes for great numbers, and particularly for blacks, are broken-down shacks, like those in the South, without running water, windows, toilets, and often even without roofs. Broken homes in the North are those filled with the stench of generations of excrement, infested with rats and roaches, with broken windows, plumbing, and plaster, and rooms that have been divided and subdivided to enrich the landlords and deprive the residents of the space and amenities that would enable them to live like human beings. Today these slum houses are being wiped out by urban renewal, only to make room for the white middle class to reoccupy the prized areas near the center city that they originally abandoned to escape the nearness of blacks. Meanwhile new ghettos are being created as masses of displaced blacks are crowded into neighboring and underserviced areas, thus rendering them candidates for more urban renewal or "Negro removal." The land from which blacks have been removed is then put at the disposal of land speculators and the construction industry, which means that new housing cannot possibly be within the reach of the displaced blacks to purchase or rent.

To talk about a guaranteed living for everyone without taking radical measures to resolve this question would be to evade the elementary need of people for an environment in which they are not only sheltered from the elements but encouraged to develop their humanity.

Black Power will institute a national crash housing program on the scale of a war program to provide land, labor, and materials to build new temporary housing for the millions. Such a program would have to be on the scale of a war because for millions of the poor, the blacks, and the aged, there is now a war going on for a place to live. At the same time Black Power will make clear that there has to be overall long-range planning by the people themselves in order to make cities into human places to live and grow, where people will have privacy and at the same time the open social spaces to interact and cooperate, where provisions can be made to produce and transport goods and services without destroying the opportunities for human mobility and interaction, where centers for education, recreation, and all forms of human enrichment can be developed. The creation of such communities must involve whole communities in their planning, with the understanding that they are building not just for today but for tomorrow, not just for themselves but for generations to come.

Capitalist production has forced the worker to work in order to live. It has also reduced the worker to a fragment of a man, dominated by the means of production, constantly threatened with loss of work by revolutions in technology, crippled by lifelong repetition of the same trivial operations. Today work is hated and avoided by many not because they are lazy but because they refuse to accept the indignities to which the average worker is subjected on the job.

Black Power will, first of all, remove the forced character of work and the stigma on those not working by guaranteeing everyone a living. Second, in order to create humane conditions of production, it will give control over production to those on the job. Workers can then make their place of work a place not only for the production of goods but for developing their mastery over technology and for releasing their creativity in the productive arena. People will thus be liberated to enjoy the human aspects of work.

To implement their control over production, workers will hold meetings on the plant floor to discuss and make decisions about their work and about the plant, to select work organizers and plant managers, and to elect representatives to other plants and to the community. They will be encouraged to make their place of work an arena of continuing education not only for themselves but for young people, both in technology and in the process of decision making relative to production and technology.

By no other means can society reverse the present disastrous trend toward the creation of technological and political elites who make all the decisions to be carried out by the technologically and politically powerless. The chief objective of workers' control of production thus becomes the creation of socially conscious and technologically creative men, women, and youth who, instead of seeking their own individual self-interest, can develop themselves as human beings doing socially necessary production and carrying on technical education of themselves and others for the good of society. Workers will be the rulers of technology rather than its slaves, masters of the factory rather than its prisoners.

In the field of education, Black Power will make it clear, first of all, that the obvious and indisputable failure of the present system of education is deeply rooted in the racist-capitalist character of this society. Through its centuries-old glorification of the white race, of Western culture and of America's "Manifest Destiny," and the corresponding denial of historical and cultural existence to other peoples and particularly to blacks, American education has not only robbed blacks of self-knowledge. It has also dehumanized whites to the point where today millions are ready for the "final solution" of exterminating the black street force because of the threat it offers to the system. In addition to this dehumanization by racism, American whites have been systematically dehumanized by an education system dedicated to producing a technical and administrative elite for the perpetuation of the capitalist system.

Black Power will reverse this trend by making clear that the fundamental purpose of education in the modern world is to produce socially responsible human beings, conscious of their responsibility for creating a social environment in which people can live and interact with one another as human beings, ready to struggle against all who stand in the way of such a humane society and constantly seeking to rid society and their own selves of any tendencies toward elitism and individualism.

Toward this end Black Power will turn over control of schools to local communities so that, together, parents, students, and teachers can transform the schools into real centers for the building of the community. Education can then become what it should be, not just the teaching of the three Rs but the development together by all sections of the community of the values and skills required to build a truly human society.

One of the most important acts of Black Power will be to initiate steps to change the relations of the United States with the rest of the world.

The U.S. government has today become the chief obstacle to four-fifths of mankind struggling to rid themselves of colonial and neocolonial exploitation and to build societies in which their people can live and develop as free human beings. Through intrigue, propaganda, CIA agents, economic and military aid, Peace Corps workers, and direct destruction with the power that comes out of the barrel of a gun, the United States today subverts revolutionary movements toward liberation.

Black Power is the only U.S. power that can be trusted by this four-fifths of the world to establish the kind of relations that will aid rather than impede their development.

First, Black Power will recognize the right and duty of all nations to establish the kind of society they deem suitable to their needs. In this connection, it will recognize particularly the rights of the people in Latin America, Asia, Africa, and the Middle East who have been systematically exploited by Western imperialism to whatever economic aid they themselves decide is necessary to assist in their development. Where there is a conflict of opinion in these countries, Black Power will unequivocally aid the social and political forces inside these countries that represent the greatest mobilization and deepening of the revolutionary consciousness of the masses in these countries.

Black Power will immediately withdraw all military forces and bases in other nations. It will also abolish all travel restrictions to this nation based on the alleged or real communist and/or socialist ideas and activities of individuals or groups of individuals.

It is impossible to give a completely detailed program of what Black Power will do, but the above is sufficient to establish certain guidelines and to make clear the fundamental principles underlying Black Power. Black Power aims to turn over or overturn ("fan shen") this society and human beings, liberating both society and man from the barbarism and the subjugation to inhuman forces into which they have been plunged by capitalism and racism. It aims to create new socially responsible, socially creative human beings.

In seeking to do this, Black Power does not base itself upon ideas that have been invented or discovered by well-intentioned liberal reformers or idealists. We have attempted to show how the antihuman work relations that have governed this country since the rise of capitalism and racism have now been made obsolete by the revolution in technology. We have also attempted to show how liberation from work will liberate people for meaningful human activity.

To those who are concerned that man will have nothing to do with his free time, we point out the innumerable things to be done that are not being done now. Millions of mothers and fathers have no time to take care of their homes or their children, to play with them, to work with them in the yard or in the house, to cook, to sew, and to build things; in other words, to make family life or the relations between the generations more meaningful. Other mothers don't have to do all these things because they have servants to do them. When everybody has a guaranteed income, working or not, they won't be able to get these servants and will have to discover how to do these things themselves. People will have time to fix their cars, fix machinery around the house, rediscover and retransmit to the younger generation some of the skills that the householder used to have and of which the youth of today have barely any inkling. People will have time to participate in controlling their communities, time to develop the background to make social decisions on such questions as production, transportation, schools, health, and recreation. They will have time to travel, to tour this country and other countries, to establish relationships between themselves and other communities and peoples. For the first time in human history great masses of people will be free to explore and reflect, to question and to create, to learn and to teach, unhampered by the fear of where the next meal is coming from.

To argue against all this seems to us as ridiculous as arguing against social security, old-age assistance, and Medicare, or as insisting that we must go back to the idea of rugged individualism in an age when everyone and everything is related and it is impossible to evaluate social questions in terms of personal weaknesses or strengths.

However, the first practical, that is to say, realistic, question is the need to struggle to take the power away from those who now have it. In the 1930s a great social upheaval was necessary to bring about the social reforms of social security, collective bargaining, unemployment compensation, and aid to dependent children. It must be clearly understood that an even greater upheaval will be necessary to bring about the drastic changes that are now on the historical agenda. What is now at issue are not just greater economic benefits but the complete abolition of the exploitative economic system itself. What is now at stake is not just bargaining power; it is state power.

A generation ago, following the Great Depression, American capitalism was only able to absorb the blacks who had been displaced by the mechanization of agriculture because of World War II. At the time blacks were primarily concerned about the opportunity to work at any kind of job. Today the most rebellious layer of blacks is not concerned chiefly with jobs. It is concerned with achieving the power necessary to transform the institutions that have been organized to exploit and dehumanize blacks. Those who now hold that power are not going to yield it without a struggle.

To the question whether black revolutionary power is possible, the answer is yes. Concretely American society faces only three real alternatives: (1) to continue rotting away as it is today; (2) naked counterrevolution; or (3) black revolutionary power. The fact that these are the only concrete alternatives makes black revolutionary power as realistic a possibility as the other two.

The key to the whole question is that the United States cannot go home again.

First, the black community is rapidly approaching the point where it cannot survive unless the present system based upon the exploitation of human labor is abolished and a new society based upon the development of socially responsible human beings is established. The momentum of the black struggle to establish such a society is already well under way and cannot be reversed except by naked counterrevolution.

Second, the black struggle for liberation, coinciding with the struggle of the world black revolution, has already created such turmoil and crisis in the entire society that great masses of people are searching for political leadership to restore to the country a sense of purpose and direction.

Third, inside the white community we can expect increasing conflict, division, and splits between a substantial minority demanding the counterrevolutionary crushing of the black movement, a small minority who are ready to accept black revolutionary power, and the overwhelming majority in the middle who will be immobilized, not because they want Black Power but because they are afraid that resistance to it will reinforce the naked counterrevolutionary repression that, once unleashed, cannot possibly stop with the black community.

Finally, and never to be forgotten, the struggle for black revolutionary power in the United States is developing in the context of international conflict between the world black revolution and the white counterrevolution of American imperialism, a conflict the United States cannot possibly win.

This conjuncture of historical circumstances makes black revolutionary power possible. It does not make it inevitable. To bring it into being will require a long, sustained, and carefully organized struggle. To ensure the success of this struggle, *the most important task now before the black movement is the building of a black revolutionary party.*

Chapter 4

The Black Revolutionary Party

A black revolutionary party is necessary to achieve black revolutionary power for the same reason that a Workers Revolutionary Party is necessary to achieve workers' revolutionary power in a country where the workers are the chief revolutionary social force.

The role of the black revolutionary party is, *first,* to develop and keep before the movement, the nation, and the world the real meaning and objectives of the life-and-death struggle in which the black community is now engaged; *second,* to bring together in a disciplined national organization the revolutionary individuals who are being constantly thrown up by spontaneous eruption and the experience of struggle; and *third,* to devise and project, in constant interaction with the masses in struggle, a long-range strategy for achieving black revolutionary power in the United States.

Constant clarification of the goals of the black revolution in the United States is especially necessary because there are no historical models for a revolution in a country as technologically advanced and as politically backward as the United States. Never before in human history has a minority people been faced with such an enormous responsibility. Never before in human history has the counterrevolution had at its disposal so many resources to confuse, corrupt, and divert the revolutionary forces. Without a strong revolutionary party to establish and maintain the perspectives and overall strategy of the revolutionary struggle, the inevitable differences between various tendencies inside the black movement can be used to divide and demoralize the masses of the black community.

The black revolutionary party must be distinguished clearly not only from the traditional civil rights organizations that have been organized to integrate blacks into and thereby save the system but also from the ad hoc organizations that have sprung up in the course of struggle, arousing the masses emotionally around a particular issue and relying primarily on the enthusiasm and goodwill of their members and supporters for their continuing activity. By contrast, the black revolutionary party must be a cadre-type organization of politically conscious individuals, totally committed to the struggle for black revolutionary power and the building of the black revolutionary party as the only solution to the problems of black people.

A revolutionary party cannot be made up of just enthusiastic and emotionally aroused individuals. Its essential core must be cold, sober revolutionaries who are bound together by a body of ideas, recognize the vital importance of disciplined organization and strong leadership to revolutionary struggle, and are convinced that their own future and that of black people can be assured only through black revolutionary power. Only such a cadre will be able to continue to revolutionary struggle and resist the temptation to withdraw into separatist fantasies in the wake of inevitable setbacks.

No revolution has ever been successful without exposing and defeating the tendency toward opportunism, or the tendency to compromise with the power structure, or the tendency toward adventurism, or the tendency to engage in futile confrontations. But in no country are the dangers from these tendencies greater than in the United States.

Year after year, as the threat from the black movement has grown, the white power structure has been consciously and purposefully trying to co-opt black leaders and potential leaders through bribery and corruption, through pacification appointments, and through cultivation in the mass media. After years of exclusion from the system, it has not been easy for many blacks, particularly middle-class blacks, to resist this co-optation.

Year after year, also, as the repression of blacks has become more brutal, there are those who begin to believe that responding to these provocations by engaging the enemy in violent confrontations is the only way to prove black manhood and revolutionary dedication. This tendency is particularly powerful inside the United States because of the popular folklore that the gunfighter is the maker of history. Black youth, recognizing their expendability to American capitalism, can most easily be provoked to fight the battle on the enemy's grounds because they see no alternative to headlong confrontation.

To combat these tendencies toward opportunism and adventurism, the black revolutionary party must keep before the movement the perspective of victory, systematically rooting out the idea of defeat as well as any tendencies to martyrdom. The basic principle of war is to increase one's own strength and weaken the enemy's. The black movement cannot afford the loss of more Malcolms, Emmett Tills, Medgar Everses, and Martin Luther Kings, and it must build the organization that has the strength and discipline to ensure that there will be no more of these.

The black revolutionary party must also combat the individualism that is rampant in the United States and expose the tendency to confuse individual acts of rebellion or promotion with revolutionary struggle by masses of people. Black liberation is not advanced by headlong confrontation with enemy forces, such as the police, the FBI, or the CIA, any more than it is by accepting appointment into the establishment on the theory that the higher the position the greater the service a black leader can render to his people. It can only be advanced by revolutionary struggles in which masses of black people increase their control over their real conditions of life.

The revolutionist can only win the confidence of the masses and provide them with leadership if they can see that the revolutionist himself is the embodiment of revolutionary humanist values. They must be able to witness in the revolutionist his or her continuous personal development and transformation into a more conscious, more human, more socially responsible man or woman, without personal ambition, ready to sacrifice personal self-interest, prepared to tackle the most difficult tasks if these will help improve the condition and heighten the political consciousness of the masses, constantly educating himself so that he can educate others. This unceasing self-humanizing process by the revolutionist is especially necessary in the United States, a country that is so inhuman that it can even drive those in rebellion against it to inhuman acts that only demoralize the masses by confirming their suspicion that you can't beat the system.

The black revolutionary party will pay special attention to the development of the political consciousness and revolutionary dedication of black street youth. These youth have no place in the existing society except as mercenaries, preying on people of color in the far-flung imperialist armies of the United States or on their own people in the streets of the ghetto. On the other hand, under the leadership of the black revolutionary party and imbued with the consciousness of the new society that black revolutionary power will create, they are the best guarantee of the success of the black revolution.

The black revolutionary party will repudiate any tendency to black male chauvinism or the tendency to relegate black women to an inferior position in the struggle in order to compensate for the emasculation black men have suffered in white America. The extraordinary fortitude black women have brought to the struggle for survival of black people in America is one of the greatest sources of strength for the black revolutionary party.

A black revolutionary party cannot come into being ready-made. It has to be molded and shaped by hard work and the criticism and self-criticism that ceaselessly transform and develop the revolutionist and the revolutionary organization. The American racist-capitalist system has caused much backwardness, ignorance, selfishness, suspicion, deception, and competition among black people and has thereby kept them disorganized, divided, and politically unaware. The alteration that is necessary to man on a mass scale can only take place through revolution. Meanwhile, in the black revolutionary party, this alteration of revolutionary cadres can take place through the constant learning and teaching that are inseparable from conscious interaction with masses in revolutionary struggle.

The most difficult and challenging task is the organizing of struggles around the concrete grievances of the masses, which will not only improve the welfare of the black community but also educate the masses out of their democratic illusions and increase their consciousness that every administrative and law-enforcing agency in this country is a white power. It is white power that decides whether to shoot to kill (as in every urban rebellion) or not to shoot at all (as in Oxford, Mississippi, against white mobs); to arrest or not to arrest; to break up picket lines or not to break up picket lines; to investigate and punish brutality and murder or to allow these to go uninvestigated and unpunished. It is white power that decides who eats and who goes on welfare when out of work and who does not eat and does not go on welfare; who gets medical care and who doesn't; how schools are run and how they fail to run in the black community; who has transportation and who hasn't; who has garbage collected and who doesn't; what streets have neither lights nor sidewalks; what neighborhoods are torn down for urban renewal and what and who are to go back into these neighborhoods. It is white power that decides what people are drafted into the army to fight and which countries this army is to fight at which moment. It is white power that has brought the United States to the point where it is counterrevolutionary to and increasingly despised by the majority of the world's peoples. All these powers are in the political arena, which is the key arena that must be taken over by the black revolutionary party if there is to be serious Black Power.

The black revolutionary party must devise strategies that give the masses of black people a sense of their growing power to improve their conditions of life through struggle and enable them to create dual or *parallel power structures* out of struggle. Struggle, therefore, must be on issues and terrains that enable the black community to create a form of *liberated area* out of what are at present *occupied areas*. It is for this reason that struggles for community control of such urban institutions as schools, health, welfare, housing, land, and police are such powerful steps on the road to black revolutionary power.

In these arenas the characteristics of a classical revolutionary or pre-revolutionary situation already exist: the failure of those in power; the division of opinion among them as to what should be the next step; the constant worsening of the conditions of the masses; and the increasing activity among these masses.

For example, the failure of the educational system has created turmoil and confusion in every major city, from top to bottom, not only inside the individual classroom but at the center of the huge school bureaucracy. Those who have had the control over billions of dollars over the last few years are completely bankrupt, morally and financially, constantly begging for more money to shore up a system that has already collapsed, reduced to calling in police and police dogs in an attempt to control black children who, as the chief victims of this failure, are in a state of unceasing rebellion.

This crisis has compelled the entire black community to come to grips with the issue of how long it is going to allow education to remain in the hands of a racist power structure which, having crippled the minds of our children, now wants to use armed force against them. Control by the black community over education would not only give black people their unquestionable right to control the minds of black children and therefore the destiny of black people. It would give the black community the control over enormous financial resources and the actual physical area of the schools. Thus, through the struggle for community control of education, it is possible for the black movement to acquire the counterpart of a liberated area in an urban setting.

Similar, if not quite so dramatic, crises exist in the spheres of health, welfare, and housing, where the poorest and neediest sections of the black community have for years suffered humiliation and degradation at the hands of the white power structure. In these spheres there are similar opportunities for the creation of liberated areas and a dual power structure through increasing struggle and mobilization of the black community. At stake are not only the improvement of conditions and the saving of black lives but also the development of new skills, the control of resources, a substantial increase in responsibilities, and an escalating vision of the social services and social interaction possible in this day of technological miracles.

Because all these struggles are for control and power, implicit within them and growing increasing explicit as the struggles intensify is also the drive to redefine the goals and methods of the institutions whose failure can no longer be questioned. Thus, even if black parents join the struggle for community control of schools with the aim of raising the reading achievement level of their children to that of white children, they are led in the course of their struggle to challenge the fundamental philosophy and methods of contemporary American education. Black college students, fighting for autonomous black studies departments and for unrestricted admission of third world students, are not only challenging the racism structured into American higher education. They are exposing the defense of the status quo and the vested interests of an intellectual elite that hides behind the professed objectivity and academic standards of the liberal intellectual. Thereby they are laying the groundwork for a new concept of intellectual integrity based upon the integration of theory and practice and on the relevance of learning to the needs of the most oppressed section of our society.

Young black workers, struggling against racist managements and racist unions and refusing to adjust to dead-end assembly jobs, begin to pose questions as to how factories might be reorganized under workers' control to become places where young people can master technology and develop their creative energies. Black welfare recipients and black social workers, insisting on increased allotments and demanding community control of welfare institutions, are raising questions as to how today's material abundance can be used to free people rather than to increase their dependence upon material necessities.

In the course of fighting city housing and planning commissions for control over model cities construction, black homeowners are faced not only with the question of how to build the millions of homes required to meet the elementary needs of shelter in this country but with the fundamental role of the city itself in the last quarter of the twentieth century. How can the community organize the various elements that make up the physical environment of a city—homes, schools, streets, shopping centers, promenades, factories, cultural centers—in order to meet the human needs of the community and make possible creative interactions between human beings in the various phases of their development from infancy to old age? Or how can man build cities that will bring technology into line with human purpose rather than vice versa?

Thus, in the course of struggling to create liberated areas, the black movement has the opportunity to liberate increasing numbers of people from the illusion that the conditions under which they now live are worth protecting in view of the conditions under which they could live.

It is obvious that a genuinely liberated area cannot exist until the only armed forces in the area are the armed forces protecting the improved conditions and power of the black community against all attempts to restore the former situation. Armed struggle can only be effective when the revolutionary social forces have been convinced by political education and political struggles that they have no other recourse to defend their own lives and the power they have won to control their lives.

Spontaneous eruptions are inevitable in the present period of police occupation and provocation of the black street force. Every such eruption throws up more rebels seeking political perspective and a political organization that will give effective meaning in their struggles and without which they can be reduced to individualistic acts of desperation. The task of the black revolutionary party is to develop these rebels into revolutionists on the principle that the best revolutionary fighter is the politically educated revolutionary fighter.

The black revolutionary party must replace the illusion of "instant revolution" (which is as American as apple pie) with the concept of a long-range strategy to mobilize the masses in revolutionary struggle. Bearing in mind always the need to shape the enemy rather than to be shaped by it, it should not hesitate to retreat in order to increase its strength or to draw the enemy forces into conflict on terrain that is geographically and politically more favorable to the revolutionary forces. The counterrevolution, feeding itself on the fears, ignorance, and deep-seated racism of the white workers and middle classes, and with millions of dollars at its disposal, can come to power almost overnight. The revolution needs time and patience to escalate the struggle and vision of the revolutionary forces to the point of no return.

By concentrating on issues that affect the broadest section of the black community, the black revolutionary party is able to develop a united front of all the classes inside the black community while never hiding from the masses the danger that as the struggle develops there will also develop a tendency to compromise in the more privileged sections of the black community. The aim of the black revolutionary party is at all times to draw the maximum number of people from the black community into the momentum of the struggle, creating unity whenever possible, neutralizing those who can be neutralized, and attacking or isolating only those who must be isolated or attacked.

Because of the nationalist character of the black revolutionary struggle, the black revolutionary party must be all-black in its membership, but like all revolutionary parties the black revolutionary party is by no means opposed to other sections of the population organizing for revolutionary struggles. The black revolutionary party will encourage white revolutionaries to organize their own communities in order to create splits among whites over fundamental issues of racism, imperialist war, and the urban crisis, to educate the population as to the advantages that will accrue to the entire society from black revolutionary power, and, in particular, to liberate the minds of white children and youth.

Finally, the black revolutionary party must at all times keep before the movement the need to support the national liberation struggles in Asia, Latin America, and Africa and the need for international support for the revolution inside the United States. No revolution was ever successful without international support. This truth, which was demonstrated in the first American Revolution, is even more relevant today because of the basic unity the black revolution in the United States has with the world black revolution, because of the minority position of blacks inside the United States, and because of the world character of the American counterrevolution.

The black revolution in the United States is an integral part of the world revolution against American imperialism. Racism, like imperialism, is a totalitarian system for the dehumanization of one people by another, in all ways possible and by all means necessary, economically, politically, militarily, culturally, ideologically, and biologically. In order to dehumanize the oppressed people or nation, the oppressor has created a total system of dehumanization. The revolution against racism and/or imperialism, therefore, is not only to free the oppressed people or nation from the physical presence of their oppressors but to destroy the institutions of total dehumanization and to create in their place totally new relations between people, totally new relations between people and their institutions, and totally new institutions.

In the struggle of the black peoples of the world for the power to govern themselves, the very meaning of man is at stake. Do people of other races exist to be exploited and manipulated by others? Or are all men equal regardless of race? White power was built on the foundation of exploiting the colored races of the world for the benefit of the white race. At the heart of this exploitation was the conviction that people of color are not men but subhuman, not self-governing citizens but natives. White power did not only exploit colored people economically. It sought systematically to destroy their culture and their personalities and anything else that would compel white people to face the fact that colored people are also men and women. When Western powers fought each other, they fought as men. But when they fought colored peoples, they killed them as natives and as slaves. That is what Western barbarism is doing in Vietnam today.

Faced with the most powerful weapons that an advanced technology could invent, the peoples of Vietnam, China, Cuba, and the liberated areas of Africa have had to pit human power. To defeat the weapons of dehumanization, they have had to develop the weapons of rehumanization. In the face of an enemy constantly expanding its unprincipled power through the permanent revolution in technology, they have had to create a principled social force based upon a permanent revolution in human beings.

In the course of so doing, they have at one and the same time exposed the essential inhumanity and historical obsolescence of U.S. economic, political, and social institutions and begun a new historical epoch of revolutionary humanism based upon the permanent release of creative political energies in masses of people.

If mankind still lives a thousand years from today, the chief contribution of this historic epoch to human progress and the advance of civilization will be recognized to have been *not* the flight to the moon nor the conquest of outer space but the discovery in Vietnam, China, Cuba, the Middle East, and the liberated areas of Africa of the revolutionary process by which great masses of technologically undeveloped peoples are transforming themselves into the politically most advanced human beings the world has ever known. With the conscious mass creation of these new men, women, and youth in the second half of the twentieth century, the history of humanity really begins.

We do not mean by this to minimize the scientific achievement that is embodied in spaceships and flights to the moon. But, in the first place, such accomplishments have long been implicit in the scientific method and technical organization that have produced steam, hydroelectric, and nuclear energy and invented the telegraph, telephone, and television. The perfection of the complex technical organization that would make space flight possible was only a matter of time. Even more important, as Hiroshima, Nagasaki, and Vietnam have shown, these culminations of the constant revolutionizing of technology can be used against humanity as well as on its behalf. Hence the big question mark that hangs over the existence of mankind one thousand years hence.

On the other hand, in Vietnam, China, Cuba, the Middle East, and Africa, masses of people are discovering and perfecting the secret of how to develop the new type of human being who can be trusted to use these technological marvels for the advancement of mankind rather than for its destruction.

This is the world black revolution of the majority of the world's people of which the black revolution in the United States is an integral part.

Conclusion

The history of all past revolutions teaches us that a victorious revolution is impossible without a revolutionary party of the masses based on the scientific analysis of the historical reality it seeks to transform, free from opportunism and uncompromising in its attitude toward all forces that stand in the way of its struggle for power. Without such a party the masses are without revolutionary leadership, and without revolutionary leadership there is no successful revolution.

The history of all past revolutions further teaches us that the parties of parliamentary democracy, such as the Republican Party, the Democratic Party, and all other parties that talk of social reform but dread and oppose social revolution, cannot possibly be transformed into revolutionary parties.

A black revolutionary party in the United States can only be built from the ground up, scrupulously and perseveringly, by black revolutionists. Up to now the black movement has relied upon the spontaneous struggles of the masses to drive it forward. The need now is to shape these struggles by giving them a clear purpose and direction. This can only be done by a black revolutionary party.

"The American Revolution: Putting Politics in Command" first appeared as the final chapter of *Racism and the Class Struggle: Further Pages from a Black Worker's Notebook* (1970).

The American Revolution: Putting Politics in Command

In 1963 I concluded my first book with these words:

If the leap that the American people have to take in order to meet the problems of this new age of abundance were not so great, the powers of the secret police would likewise not be so great. In the 1930s the problems were relatively simple. All that was required was that the poor struggle against the rich, who were the capitalists and whose failure was clear and obvious.

Today in the 1960s, the struggle is much more difficult. What it requires is that people in every stratum of the population clash not only with the agents of the silent police state but with their own prejudices, their own outmoded ideas, their own fears that keep them from grappling with the new realities of our age. The American people must find a way to insist upon their own right and responsibility to make political decisions and to determine policy in all spheres of social existence—whether it is foreign policy, the work process, education, race relations, or community life. The coming struggle is a political struggle to take political power out of the hands of the few and put it into the hands of the many. But in order to get this power into the hands of the many, it will be necessary for the many not only to fight the powerful few but to fight and clash among themselves as well.

Today, as we begin a new decade, the conflict between the social forces needed to drive the revolution forward has advanced far beyond our wildest expectations. Seven years ago the idea of a twentieth-century American revolution was so remote that most people assumed that the title of my book, *The American Revolution,* referred to events two hundred years ago. Now, side by side with the growth of irreconcilable social forces, the headaches of daily life in America have become so intolerable that the question is no longer whether there will be an American revolution but rather what it means, when and if it will be over, and what kind of new society it will produce.

Every problem that confronted the United States in the early 1960s has become not only infinitely more complex but infinitely more demanding of solution and decision by the American people.

The war in Southeast Asia is not just a military war. It is an international political struggle in which the traditional and systematic use by the United States of its advanced technology to determine the economic, social, and political destinies of the world's peoples is being contested and defeated. Moreover, each setback to the counterrevolutionary policies of this country (in China, Korea, Cuba, and Vietnam) has only served to accelerate the growth of a *new international* of developing nations, representing a revolutionary humanist social force of billions, a force the United States cannot destroy short of atomic warfare powerful enough to destroy the entire planet. Faced with this reality, the American people must decide whether, in order to preserve their own system, they are now prepared to accept a state of permanent war against the majority of the world's peoples (mostly colored) and the garrisoning of American troops in over fifty countries of the world as an integral part of the American "way of life," in the same way and for many of the same reasons that a hundred years ago they accepted racism as an integral part of the American way of life.

Labor, once the most important means to expand production and consumption, has become increasingly expendable as the profits derived from its exploitation have been reinvested in advancing technology. This technology in turn has made the remaining labor so monotonous and fragmented that it is more worthy of robots than of human beings. The result is that a growing number of people, both in and out of work, are beginning to question the purpose of labor and the validity of the prevailing philosophy that man should live only by the sweat of his brow.

In American schools and universities, amid turmoil and growing tensions, it is becoming increasingly clear that the American system of education, dedicated to the increase of earning power and representing an investment of many billions of dollars and the full-time occupation of some fifty million people, is a failure and that the basic purpose of education itself must be redetermined.

With a big question mark over the value of both labor and education, courts, jails, and prisons all over the country have now become so crowded with those charged with antisocial activities that none of these institutions can any longer claim to be deterrents to crime, let alone agencies of rehabilitation. Instead, the courts, the jails, and the prisons are now generally acknowledged to be key links in a system by which youthful delinquents are transformed into hardened criminals. Instead of protecting society from the criminal, these institutions have become fertilizers for the crimes that most threaten society.

In every city and across the country the very environment that has made possible man's progress and survival for thousands of years is being polluted so rapidly by the waste and residue of today's unlimited mass production that ecologists are seriously discussing the possibility of life disappearing on this planet before the end of the twentieth century. Closely related to the destruction of the natural and social environment by industrial and consumer waste is its steady demolition to serve the needs of private transportation. With rapid public transportation disappearing because the jobs and profits of the auto industry require the encouragement of private transportation, parking and driving space for private chariots has been given unquestioned priority over living and breathing space for human beings. The result is that the earth is being turned into an asphalt jungle and the atmosphere into smog.

Overwhelmed by the problems created by industrial technology, society will soon be faced with the even more complex issues arising out of biotechnology, which brings with it the power of a few to create masses of superhuman or subhuman beings.

Frustrated by their inability to cope with problems that have become insoluble on an individual basis but still hoping for an individual solution, millions of people seek escape in all sorts of drugs—from tranquilizers to heroin—pushed at them from all directions: on the TV screen, in the poolroom, and on the street corner. At the head of this legal and illegal drug traffic are both organized crime and an equally unscrupulous drug industry which, in the interests of profit, has helped transform the world's wealthiest nation into one of its unhealthiest. Increasing drug addiction has brought in its wake increasing crime to feed drug habits, until no street, day or night, is safe for the ordinary pedestrian. Thus America has also become one of the world's most dangerous societies.

Meanwhile, the contradiction between the humane pretensions of this society and its actual antihuman practices, particularly to blacks inside the country and to billions of colored people outside, has become increasingly intolerable not only to blacks but to young whites, leading to increasing revolt, increasing rebellion, and increasingly violent talk and action in the streets and on the campuses.

The result is that alienation, confusion, uncertainty, frustration, hopelessness, anger, fear, and desperation pervade every section of the population as it feels its traditional beliefs crumbling and as it witnesses the assassination, in full public view, of one after another of those who promise leadership out of the wilderness of demoralization and powerlessness. Not even the landing of men on the moon last July—the greatest technical achievement in the history of humankind—could restore this country's confidence in itself. Even before the first giant step had been taken on the moon, the debate as to the value and purpose of the exploit had begun to rage on earth, not only on the airwaves where all could hear but in the privacy of each man's doubts.

Faced with division inside the country, all levels of a government that formerly claimed to referee the conflicting interests of different sections of the population now increasingly resort to physical force and open psychological manipulation to mobilize their supporters against their critics. The police forces, from J. Edgar Hoover's on down, take on the functions of political organizations, openly dedicated to the preservation of white supremacy and the American way of life, more concerned with protecting the status quo from radical ideas and organizations than with protecting society from organized crime. By its deliberate efforts to muddy up the fundamental distinction between political activity and crime, the federal government itself is fostering disrespect for the judicial process, inciting riot and murder, and unleashing the most reactionary forces in the nation. With every passing day its illegitimacy becomes more transparent.

In this crisis more and more people are beginning to feel that only a revolution can bring them release from their fears and anxieties. It is not difficult to feel. The difficulty comes in attempting to make the feeling concrete. This is not surprising since when we talk about a revolution in the United States we are talking about a revolution for which there is no historical precedent. History has nothing to tell us about a revolution in a country where so large a proportion of the population has materially benefited from the system even while being exploited by it and therefore feels that its own interest is bound up with the active defense of the system.

When people talk about a revolution, the first model that usually comes to mind is the Russian Revolution. Remembering only the period from February to October 1917, most people think of the Russian Revolution as a hurricane that moved rapidly from the collapse of the old regime in the face of military defeat to the seizure of power by the Bolsheviks, all within an eight-month period.

Another model that comes to the popular mind is that of the Cuban Revolution. In this case, most people think of the landing of the *Gramma* in 1956 followed by three relatively short years of guerilla fighting by a small armed force in the mountains and then the victorious march on Havana in 1959.

Finally, there are the models of the Chinese and Vietnamese revolutions, involving long years of protracted struggle through which the great masses of people were transformed into new kinds of socially conscious, socially responsible human beings, their will to struggle and their vision escalated through escalating conflicts over issues affecting their daily lives.

Whatever their differences, all these revolutions had in common the fact that they took place in economically undeveloped countries. In each of these countries the consciousness of economic backwardness compared to that of the Western nations and the consciousness of the urgent need for economic development pervaded the entire population and was a crucial factor in unifying the majority of people behind the revolution and driving it forward despite innumerable setbacks.

When we come to the United States, however, there is no urgency about economic development, either to meet the material needs of the people or to compete with other nations. The United States excels in the economic arena. It is not a feudal or semideveloped colonized land; nor is it threatened by military defeat at home or by an alien power from abroad.

The first question that has to be answered, therefore, is whether there is any arena in which the United States urgently needs revolutionary—that is to say, rapid and fundamental—development and reorganization. The answer is unequivocally yes. But, unlike the nations of Africa, Asia, and Latin America, the arena in which this country needs revolutionary change is not the *economic* but the *political,* not the material but the *social.* The essential, the key, contradiction in the United States that must be resolved if this country is to survive is the contradiction between economic overdevelopment and political underdevelopment.

The urgent, crying need of the American people is to undergo a fundamental transformation from the individualists and materialists they are today into a new breed of socially and politically conscious and responsible human beings. Instead of being concerned only with their own material advancement and satisfied with the political decisions of the military-industrial-academic complex as long as these expand production and consumption, the American people must be dragged, pulled, and pushed into situations where they are compelled to make socially responsible decisions—until the energy, the skill, and the will to make such decisions have become second nature.

Such a radical transformation in hundreds of millions of persons, difficult under any circumstance, seems almost impossible in a country that was founded on the extermination of one race of people, the Indian, and the enslavement of another, the African. From the very beginning of this nation, the behavior pattern of subordinating human to economic values has been systematically inculcated into the people by precept and by practice. After the Civil War it was not difficult for whites, from the highest to the lowest, to accept the virtual re-enslavement of blacks, despite constitutional measures guaranteeing their freedom, since this guaranteed a labor supply for the dirty work on the southern cotton plantations that nourished the northern textile industry and at the same time made jobs in expanding industry available to immigrant whites.

Economic development has been the reason for the super-exploitation of blacks at every stage, and the super-exploitation of blacks has in turn accelerated economic development. Thus, the American way of life has been created, a life of expanding comfort and social mobility for whites, based upon servitude and lack of freedom for blacks. This in turn has encouraged everyone to look upon everyone else as a stepping-stone to personal advancement.

In the course of creating this system the country has become the technologically most advanced country in the world, but it has also become a nation so dedicated to technological advancement that its citizens systematically evade any political decisions that might interfere with their personal economic interest. Thus the United States has become a nation that is as backward in political and social decision making as most new nations are in technological decision making. The American people have been going along with whatever advanced their own immediate material interests for so long that they have no interest or practice in evaluating and deciding political issues. Except for the unions that functioned briefly in the 1930s as mass social and political assemblies for the working class, Americans have created no structure, no apparatus within which they can fight over the issues and grievances of their daily lives or those of their communities and their country, coming to decisions for which they can be held responsible.

The essence of the American way of life has been and continues to be the organization of all institutions to achieve the most rapid economic development, and this in turn is expected to solve all the problems of the society. Now, however, it is clear that economic development has created as many problems as it has solved. The United States is a society in which there is an increasing investment in highly advanced technology and an increasing concentration of economic and political power in the hands of a few individuals and corporations that control this vast technological apparatus. But accompanying this rapid technological development and the concentration of skills and power at one pole has been a systematic and continuous decline in skills, responsibility, and participation at the other pole, particularly at the very bottom of the ladder among the blacks, Mexican Americans, Puerto Ricans, Indians, etc. At the same time, because of the reliance on economic development to solve all social problems, no institutions or procedures exist to bring about the rapid political development needed to cope with rapid technological and social change.

Thus we have arrived—not because of the malice of any particular individual or group but as the climax of the natural development of the system—at the present dangerous situation where the American people, with the techniques to destroy or advance mankind at their disposal, do not have the political will or consciousness to choose one rather than the other.

The American system has been able to arrive at its present stage because the majority of the population (white) accepted the philosophy of economic development as the key to social progress. They did not question it because, on the whole, they have benefited from it. The chief victims have been blacks, who stayed at the bottom scavenging white leavings, until recently too convinced of their own inferiority to rebel.

As long as blacks did not dream of reaching the middle or top rungs of the American economic and social ladder, they were no threat to the system. But sixteen years ago, precisely at the time when the number of positions on the middle and lower rungs of the ladder was declining because of automation and cybernation, blacks began to feel and believe in their right to equality. Competing with whites for higher positions, they have aroused the fury of whites for disturbing what whites have wanted to believe was a perfect society. Actually, by making themselves visible blacks have only been exposing the bankruptcy of a system that has put economics in command of politics and has failed to develop the politics that can command economics.

In disrupting the smooth operations of the system, blacks are also revealing to themselves the inseparable and antagonistic relation between their own undevelopment and lack of freedom and the system's freedom to develop. It is impossible for blacks to free or develop themselves without turning over every institution of this society, each of which has been structured with blacks' insoluble contradictions in a system that has developed freely through the enforced underdevelopment of one group of people. Today 35 to 50 percent of black young people are unemployed and roaming the streets, their only future a prison cell or a rice paddy in Southeast Asia. Automation and cybernation have made the unskilled, undeveloped labor of your young men and women increasingly expendable. Displaced from the land and concentrated in the slums of the nation's cities, we are no longer needed as producers. Yet we are constantly urged by the mass media to become consumers in order to keep the mass production lines of America operating at full capacity, even if we can only get the wherewithal for such consumption by one or another form of hustling. Hence at the end of the road for millions of our people looms only a prison cell.

It is only from this realistic appraisal of the organic interrelationship between our role as black people and the economic system that a perspective for revolutionary struggle can be developed. No longer needed in a structure that has been created to meet the needs of rapid economic development even at the cost of exterminating human beings, we face extermination unless we can revolutionize the ends and means of the entire society.

Blacks, and particularly young blacks, are the revolutionary social force inside this country, the only social force in irreversible motion. Yet blacks have not faced the need for the revolutionary political theory and political organization that they must develop in order to give political leadership to the task of revolutionizing the entire society. This is because blacks are also part and product of the country's political undevelopment. They are reluctant to tackle the responsibilities of revolutionary politics because they, too, share in the American tendency to evade reality, hoping to find simple solutions for very complex problems.

In the last sixteen years the black movement has tested and explored many different solutions to the problem of black people in this country, from mass demonstration to mass rebellion, from voting black to buying black. In the course of many activities, the movement has produced a tremendous social force of millions of black people, formerly apathetic and apathetic and apolitical but now anxious to act. At the same time the movement has rid itself of a number of illusions: the illusion that integration in and of itself is the solution; or that nonviolence or violence in itself is the solution; or that spontaneous eruptions in and of themselves are the solution; or that militant rhetoric is the solution; or that the unity of sheer numbers is the solution. It is now clear that the problems of black people cannot be solved by the most charismatic or most militant spokesmen for black grievances, or by economic aid from city, state, or federal governments, or by massive programs for hiring the hard-core unemployed.

Faced with these realities, the black movement is now painfully evaluating its past actions and seeking a program for the future. In the meantime the revolutionary momentum of the black movement has brought into the social arena a white counter-revolutionary force that feels certain that its entire way of life is threatened and that it must wipe out the black movement before it acquires any more momentum. Unlike the black revolutionary forces, the counterforces do not have to search for an ideology before they can plot their actions. Their ideology is that of the existing society: materialism, individualism, opportunism. Even if, as white workers and middle classes, they do not reap all the benefits from this system, even if they are powerless to affect its major decisions about what to produce or when to go to war, they still believe that it is the best system in the world because it is the system that has enabled them as whites to climb up and over any blacks. It has therefore become for them a system of privilege worth defending at all costs.

The present cry for "law and order" and the prevailing police terror in black communities are not just some conspiracy dreamed up by a few right-wing policemen and Minutemen and then foisted upon the masses of whites. They are a reflection of what most whites expect and demand from their police force in order to preserve the American way of life.

It is because blacks can see this growing counterrevolutionary force all around them that so many tendencies have developed inside the black movement during the past few years. Most of these tendencies are attempts to escape the cold realities of the American economic system and the protracted struggle necessary to revolutionize America that are the price of black freedom. Among the various solutions to the dilemma of black people in America that are offered or advocated at the present time are: (1) return to Africa; (2) set up separate states; (3) black control of black communities, leaving the task of changing the "mother country" to whites; (4) black cultural separation; and (5) black capitalism. There are even large numbers of blacks who still believe that they can be assimilated into this society as the old immigrant groups were if only they can elect some more black politicians. Most of these tendencies are led by and reflect the interests of various sections of the black middle classes—the professionals, artists, preachers, businessmen, and politicians. All of these consider themselves part of the Black Power movement that has dominated the black revolt in the wake of the Watts, Newark, and Detroit rebellions; and each, with its particular goal, has some support within the black community. Each believes that if the black masses would support its particular solution, the black problem would be solved and the black revolution would have succeeded. Black militants, and particularly black youth, drift restlessly between these organizations, attracted "wherever the action is," not particularly concerned about the practicality of any particular goal. Meanwhile, large numbers of older blacks still maintain a lingering hope for integration, despite the fact that the manifest failure of integration was what originally gave birth to the mass rebellions and the Black Power movement.

Whatever may be the present shortcomings of the black movement, it has created the largest concentration of revolutionary social forces that this country has ever known. It has also created an unprecedented level of mass political development and of mass effort to find the correct solution to real social problems. Within this unprecedented political force there exists the potential for mass political consciousness and for revolutionary struggle on a level never before achieved in this country.

The revolutionary leadership of black people inside this country is presently at the black nationalist stage; the conception of Black Power is still within the black nationalist framework. Black people have recognized that there is uniqueness about their history and about their present condition that sets them apart from the rest of the people inside the United States. They have also recognized that this, the basis of their oppression, is also a source of strength. Such a sense of nationalism could only have been achieved as a result of a long process of continuing struggle that has forced blacks to give up certain myths: that they can ever become like white people, or that it would be desirable to become like white people, or that they will ever be free as long as they are ruled by white power. The protracted struggle of the last sixteen years, with its minor victories and its many failures and setbacks, has not only swelled the ranks of the black movement; it has given blacks a sense of their uniqueness and their identity as a nation of people.

Black nationalism is and has been progressive because it has bound black people together and given them strength, but black nationalism in and of itself is not a sufficient answer to the problems of black people. Black people will have to go beyond the stage of black nationalism into the stage of black revolutionary nationalism if they are going to resolve the very real problems of black people. Only black revolutionary nationalism will enable them to attack the real causes of their problems. Black nationalism has created a united black consciousness, but a black consciousness that does not develop into a real and realistic attack on the causes of black oppression can only become a false consciousness, a breeding ground for the cultism, adventurism, and opportunism that are rampant in the movement. Black revolutionary nationalism involves real and realistic programs of struggle not only against those who control the very real institutions of this society but also to reorganize these institutions to make them serve human needs rather than the need of the economic system for profit and technological development.

The first step in the development of nationalism inside a colony in Africa, Asia, or Latin America is usually very simple: it is to oust the colonial oppressor. The second step is much more difficult because it requires a rapid political development of the people, enabling them to bring about a drastic reorganization of the economic and political system. If this rapid political development does not take place simultaneously with the struggle for national independence—or immediately thereafter—the new nation will soon sink back into neocolonialism. This is what has happened with most of the African colonies. This is what Sékou Touré in Guinea and Amílcar Cabral in Guinea-Bissau are striving to avoid by concentrating on the political transformation of their people side by side with the struggle against the colonial oppressor.

In the United States the problem for blacks is much more complex because our lives and our condition are so bound up with those of the oppressor. On the one hand, we have lived a separate and distinct life. On the other, we have been an organic—an indispensable and intrinsic—part of the development of the most highly industrialized country in the world. Even while we have been systematically denied all the benefits of rapid industrialization, we have first been the direct source of the profits by which the country could industrialize itself rapidly and then been made superfluous by the results of this rapid industrialization. It is thus impossible to separate the development of our conditions of life as blacks in this country from the development of the system itself. Nor is it possible for blacks to free themselves without turning over every institution of this society.

The Black Power movement must recognize that if this society is ever going to be changed to meet the needs of black people, then Black Power will have to resolve the problems of the society as a whole and not just those of black people. In other words, Black Power cannot evade tackling all the problems of this society because at the root of all the problems of black people is the same structure and the same system that is at the root of all the problems of all the people.

Even though blacks in the United States have many of the characteristics of a colonial people (super-exploited, undeveloped, powerless, segregated), there is no point in anyone, black or white, dealing or not dealing with the black movement as if blacks were in Asia or Africa. It is true that blacks must get themselves together before they can give leadership to whites. But even while they are getting themselves together, blacks cannot evade the questions that make revolution in the United States essential. Nor can the white movement evade the fact that blacks constitute the vanguard for revolutionary struggle in this country and try to go its own way, just because whites are not accepted into black organizations. The fact that blacks are inside the United States, not in Africa or Asia or Latin America, is the specific historical condition of the American revolution that black *and* white revolutionaries must face. Revolutionary-minded whites who try to evade this real historical condition are tempted to actions that provide an outlet chiefly for their psychological need to be "revolutionary." Revolutionary blacks who insist on ignoring the existence of whites in this society begin to build a fantasy realm in which all blacks can be judged to be brothers on the basis of color rather than on the basis of politics.

It is difficult for the Black Power movement to face this fact because, unlike the King movement, which was trying to reform the total society and provide leadership for both black and white, the Black Power movement, developing in reaction to the failure of integration and of the King movement, has confined itself to seeking a solution only for blacks, deliberately closing its eyes to the fact that the black condition is the result of a system whose influence and domination blacks cannot escape as long as the system continues to exist.

Confronted with such questions, the first declaration of most black groups today is: "We are not concerned about whites." The question is not whether blacks ought to be concerned about whites; it is whether blacks *can* solve their own problems without solving those of the total society and therefore those of whites.

King's fundamental mistake was not his willingness to give leadership to whites as well as blacks. It was his illusion that whites could be reformed by moral appeals and that the American way of life can be reformed when it must be totally revolutionized—which can only be done by taking power away from whites. The growing problems of both the black and the white movements cannot be resolved until Black Power assumes the responsibility of leadership of the American revolution as a whole.

This is not to propose interracial organization and activity, such as during the period of the integration movement. But if and when the Black Power movement accepts the awesome responsibility for revolutionizing this whole country, it will not have to spend so much of its time evading the question of what will happen to white people under Black Power. It will be able to put behind it the present psychosocial preoccupation with black-white relationships and recognize that sooner or later it will have to assume the responsibility for giving political direction to white revolutionaries who remain an auxiliary force because they lack a community with which to interact and develop in struggle. Most important, the movement will be able to devote its time and energy to the task whose time has come: the task of developing a black revolutionary leadership with the ideology, the perspective, the vision, and the program to win the Black Power necessary to revolutionize America.[*]

The first task of the developing revolution in the United States is to benefit black people who have the greatest need and the greatest concentration of social forces for this revolution; but the changes that this revolution will bring will benefit all but the small minority—as indeed every revolution must do. The peasants and workers in China were the ones with the most urgent need for revolution; hence it was from their needs and their mobilization that the fundamental perspective and program of the revolution were determined. But the Chinese revolutionary leaders did not spend their time worrying about whether or not other sections of Chinese society might also benefit from the revolution or whether they should utilize other sections of the population in the revolutionary struggle. They assumed, as every revolutionary leader must, that the entire society would benefit. They were concerned, as every revolutionary leader must be, to use every possible section of the society for the purpose of defeating the existing regime and building a new society.

---

[*] See James Boggs and Grace Boggs, "The Role of the Vanguard Party," *Monthly Review* 21, no. 11 (1970): 9–24.

The essence of revolutionary leadership is the ability to give to the social forces with the most urgent need for fundamental social change a vision of a new society in which they will be in a position to make the changes so vital to their needs. Mere awareness of their oppression and exploitation is not enough; they must be convinced that their present condition is unnecessary (hence that the present system is illegitimate) and that revolutionary struggles will enable them to solve a wide variety of the ills and grievances that make their lives so intolerable. The inability to project such a vision has been one of the chief weaknesses of white radicals in most advanced countries. Confronted with a ruling class that has been able to give workers an increasingly higher standard of living, white radicals have been unable to give workers any vision of a new kind of society that will better meet their concrete material, human, and social needs. Without such a vision, those who are psychologically bent on "revolution for the sake of revolution" begin to dominate the movement, implying that anyone who hesitates to go along with the "baddest" schemes is a "fraidy cat" and that any attempt to develop a revolutionary perspective, program, and organization is a manifestation of "liberalism."

The present division in the black movement over goals is healthy in the sense that it reflects a growing search for fundamental perspectives and solutions. But the goals projected still reflect the American tendency to "instant revolution." Until the present movement gained its momentum, white power in this country had always been able to keep blacks from serious political struggle over fundamental issues, either by repression or corruption or co-optation of their leaders. Today, the black movement has advanced beyond the stage where it can be indefinitely diverted from serious consideration of what a black revolution in this country must mean.

To solve the immediate and urgent problems of black people, and particularly of black young people, Black Power must revolutionize every institution in modern America: industry, education, health, housing, welfare, transportation. In the next period the black movement will continue to confront the total society with struggles over these issues, no matter how violently white society reacts. In this way the vision of both black and white will be escalated to recognize the general need for revolutionizing these institutions under popular control. Out of this conflict there will begin to emerge the vision of the new society that is now possible in America if politics is put in command of economics.

As long as the black movement does not realize that the solutions to the fundamental ills of this entire society are contained in its struggles, as long as it continues to seek to solve the problems of black people without facing their causes in the society as a whole, it can only dissipate its energies in opportunism, adventurism, and a multiplicity of diverse tendencies and cults. It is true that blacks did not create the problems of this society, but neither did Vietnamese or Cuban peasants create the problems of

Vietnam or Cuba. Blacks will have to assume the leadership to resolve the problems of this society just as the most oppressed people in every country have had to assume this leadership in every modern revolution. No oppressor ever resolved the problems of the oppressed; nor have the oppressed ever been able to deliver themselves from the yoke of oppression until they took upon themselves the responsibility for acquiring the power to do so.

The problem of black people is not just white people. The problem of black people is a structure, a network of institutions created by white people, which has left black people powerless, undeveloped, unfree. That is why the project of Black Power as the solution to the problems of black people changed the entire character of the movement. Black people were forced to deal with and explore the root cause of their oppression and to define the meaning of Black Power. From that point onward it was necessary to reevaluate the past and to plot a new course. As long as the movement was just talking of rights, it was leaving the responsibility for power in the hands of whites. Once the movement began to think in terms of power, the question of what blacks must do with power has been on the agenda.

The launching of the Black Power slogan by SNCC chairman Stokely Carmichael in 1966 also launched the black movement on a road for which it was totally unprepared theoretically and organizationally. In the course of its struggles to reform the system by actions that challenged the system, SNCC had discovered that black people were powerless and that, being powerless, they could not reform the system. It was an important political discovery coming out of the harsh experiences of real struggles that had made masses of black people and militant activists ready to accept radical concepts.

However, the black movement had not yet established any revolutionary goals for Black Power. SNCC in particular had not done the political analysis of what Black Power meant or of how SNCC itself would have to reorganize if it were to give leadership to the struggle for Black Power. True, three years earlier, at the Grassroots Conference in 1963, Malcolm X had stated that the black revolution, as distinguished from the Negro revolution, had to have a base (land) and had to be achieved by all means necessary, including violence. But this was still a long way from an analysis of revolutionary goals or from a revolutionary program.

As long as the vast majority of black people and black activists were primarily concerned with reforming the system, what had been required from black leaders was chiefly the agitation of the masses by increasing their consciousness of the injustice of the system. The leadership that had emerged during the stage of reform was eminently suited to this task of arousing mass consciousness of grievances.

Black Power requires a different kind of leadership, a leadership that is able to develop the strategy and tactics necessary to organize the masses first to take facets of power and eventually to take total power away from the enemy. To develop such a strategy and tactics a clear concept of goals is required, because it is only when you have a concept of your goals that you can program a series of struggles toward achieving those goals and measure your progress. At the time of the launching of the Black Power slogan the black movement had not even begun to create this kind of leadership. The result was that the interpretation of Black Power was left entirely to individual spokesmen, the most articulate and charismatic of whom the mass media projected and interpreted to the point that the concept of Black Power was actually being shaped by the tremendous power of the media.

It is easy to blame white power for this takeover of the slogan of Black Power, but it is much more important to understand that it was the movement's unpreparedness that made this takeover possible. Having neglected to make the necessary analysis, the easiest thing for black militants to do was to use Black Power as a slogan to keep the masses in a high state of excitement and expectation. This concept of keeping the masses in a high state of agitation is itself based on the erroneous belief that the masses in themselves are revolutionists and that if they are constantly urged on by revolutionary rhetoric, they will be able to lead the revolutionary struggle to success. The readiness to believe in the revolutionary spontaneity of the masses was reinforced by the mass urban rebellions that spread throughout the North from 1964 to 1968. These seemed to make the building of a revolutionary organization or the development of revolutionary strategy and tactics superfluous. All that was apparently necessary was a charismatic leader or leaders who could move around the country as mass spokesmen for the long pent-up grievances and the growing black pride and rebellion of the black masses.

With practically every militant black leader seeking to capitalize on this growing black pride and black rebellion, and with the mass media exploiting these militants' hunger for exposure in order to feed its own and the general masses' hunger for star personalities, the organizations that had played the most militant roles in the period of reform began to fall apart. This was particularly true of SNCC, from which most was expected because it had already given so much.

As long as SNCC had been engaged in struggle in the South, it had needed some kind of organization. Without an organization, it would have been unable to struggle for a moment since the black masses in the South have few if any democratic illusions, spontaneous struggles by blacks are practically unknown, and no individual spokesmen could long survive the tight conspiracy between the law and the white mob. There are some who say that if SNCC had remained in the South (for example, in Lowndes County), actual political and social conditions would have forced it to develop an organization with the ideology and cadres necessary to lead the struggle for Black Power. This is sheer speculation. Historically, SNCC's major contribution was from 1960 to 1966 in the struggles to translate what had been laid down by law into concrete reality and in the conclusion drawn from these struggles that integration and democracy in the United States are myths. SNCC came to this conclusion from its experiences in the South at the point when the black masses in the North had begun to rebel spontaneously. It moved immediately to give leadership to these masses without realizing that spontaneous rebellion is not revolution but rather represents the highest stage of the frustration of the masses seeking a way out from intolerable oppression.

SNCC was by no means the only black organization to capitalize on the spontaneous rebellion of the masses. All over the country individual leaders and groups emerged to make demands on the power structure, threatening it with continuing mass rebellion unless it acceded to certain demands and claiming to have the power to turn this rebellion on or off. The result has been increasing corruption and growing opportunism in the black movement as individual militants compete with each other as the "real" spokesmen for the black community in order to obtain grants and positions for themselves and their associates. Thus the rebellion of the masses has been exploited to advance individuals.

When SNCC was unable to provide the revolutionary leadership and organization needed in the struggle for Black Power, a vacuum was created in the black movement that was soon to be filled by the Black Panther Party. Particularly after the murder of Dr. King in April 1968, the Black Panther Party began to reflect the mushrooming revolutionary force of black school and street youth seeking a political identity, national leadership, and militant action. This social force had already been growing by leaps and bounds in the wake of the urban rebellions. The King murder shook up every black organization, every black grouping, every section of the black community, but its greatest impact was on these youth, particularly those of junior and senior high school age. As of April 4, 1968, every administration, every white institution, had lost its legitimacy, its validity, and its authority in the eyes of these youth. They were now "ready for anything."

Black street youth have certain political characteristics that reveal the high stage of revolutionary consciousness that has already been achieved by America's "rebels with a cause."

1. Unlike the black middle classes who dream of building black economic and political power with the support and encouragement of the white power structure, these youth see themselves as engaged in continuing confrontation and irreconcilable struggle with the police, the school system, industry, the unions, the housing authorities, health and welfare administrators—indeed, with every institution inside the black community.

2. Their consciousness springs from very concrete grievances, the everyday abuses and hardships suffered by the great bulk of the black community on the job, in the

streets, in the schools, at the welfare office, in the hospitals, grievances with which their elders have learned to live but which these young people refuse to tolerate any longer. Their refusal to accommodate themselves to oppression has, in turn, made them the victims of even more open and vicious oppression than that suffered by their elders.

3. They also recognize that although a particular confrontation may be precipitated by an individual incident, their struggle is not against just one or another individual but against a whole power structure comprising a complex network of politicians, university and school administrators, landlords, merchants, usurers, realtors, insurance personnel, contractors, union leaders, licensing and inspection bureaucrats, racketeers, lawyers, and especially policemen—the overwhelming majority of whom are both white and absentee, and who exploit the black ghetto in much the same way that Western powers exploit the colonies and neocolonies in Africa, Asia, and Latin America.

4. They are for the most part anticapitalist, generally believing that the profit system is at the root of black oppression and that as long as capitalism exists black people will become increasingly expendable.

5. They are also consciously anti-imperialist, identifying with the world black revolution, opposed to U.S. exploitation of the colored peoples of Africa, Asia, and Latin America, and determined not to die abroad for a democracy denied them at home.

6. They are consciously antiliberal. Having assimilated the experiences of the civil rights movement, they recognize the futility of reform legislation and are ready to pursue the struggle by all means necessary, by which they usually mean armed struggle. To an extent difficult for most whites to understand, their fundamental attitudes to life and struggle have been shaped by their own daily battles to survive on the city streets and, more recently, by the violent deaths of Malcolm, Martin Luther King Jr., and more than two dozen Black Panthers.

These attitudes, taken as a whole, amount to a repudiation not only of the American racist-capitalist system and American politics but also of the vehement anti-communism or anti-egalitarianism that is deeply rooted in white Americans. The average white American's profound antagonism to communism stems essentially from the benefits from the American way of life as a system of social mobility for the individual and for successive ethnic groups. For the average black street youth, this concept of America as a land of opportunity and peaceful progress is not only a fraud but an insult. The final proof that the American Dream was dead was the vicious murder of the man who had tried hardest to make it live: Dr. Martin Luther King Jr.

The Black Panther Party represents the first major attempt by a section of the black movement to form a revolutionary vanguard party based on this growing revolutionary social force. But it is by no means the last. Because it was the first, it has inevitably made some mistakes, and careful study and evaluation can teach the movement many important lessons for the future. To evaluate the Black Panther Party is not to question the sincerity and revolutionary dedication of its members, about which there can be no question. But the party is a political party, and it must therefore be judged politically in terms of whether or not it adequately meets the requirements of a revolutionary vanguard party.

In the first place, the fanfare with which the party announced its existence and intentions reveals democratic illusions about the rights a revolutionary party seriously contending for power can expect to enjoy in this country. Second, the original name of the party, the Black Panther Party for Self-Defense, shows that its central focus is confrontation with, reaction to, and defense against white oppression, particularly in the form of the police occupation army, rather than an offensive strategy leading to the conquest of power. Its Ten-Point Program, which is supposed to contain such a strategy, is more a statement of grievances and concessions demanded from the white power structure than it is a program to mobilize black people in escalating struggles for control and power.

In developing a program to mobilize black people in revolutionary struggles to gain control and power, three things must be borne in mind.

1. The struggle is a struggle to defeat those in power and to gain power for one's own forces. It is a power struggle to get rid of one power and replace it with another. Such a goal cannot be achieved overnight or by instant revolution. The struggle must be a protracted one, taking advantage of the enemy's internal contradictions and finding ways to use his strength against him rather than confronting him head-on.

2. The people who are striving for power must themselves be transformed into new people in the course of the struggle. Their will to struggle, their vision of what they are struggling for, their social consciousness and responsibility, and their capacity to govern must all be systematically increased. The struggle must therefore be an escalating one, focused on problems the people can learn from. It cannot be hit-and-miss or in reaction to what the enemy does but must be based on a strategy that has been mapped out in advance and permits the organization to take advantage of the enemy's predictable actions or mistakes. Indispensable to victory is the strategic employment of time as a dimension of struggle within which contradictions are deepened, conflicts escalate, and there is an accelerated growth of the revolutionary social forces not only in numbers and understanding but in organization and

sense of community. In the wake of the spontaneous mass rebellions from 1964 to 1968, each of the erupting communities experienced temporarily that sense of community and mutual responsibility characteristic of most southern black communities but has been subverted by the dog-eat-dog existence of the cities. Spontaneous rebellions alone cannot give this sense of community and underlying social structure that city dwellers so urgently need. This can only come from developing struggles.

3. All struggles must take place over very concrete issues and institutions whose resolution and control the people feel are vital to their existence.

The black community has all the necessary ingredients for such programs of struggle in every institution inside the black community. Black people already know that these institutions have failed them and that they have a right to take over their control. By giving leadership to programs of struggle to achieve control over each of these institutions, a black revolutionary party can develop united front organizations within each institution, which would be de facto parallel power structures. The more these institutions inside the black community become liberated from white control and reorganized to meet the needs of black people, the more they become *bases* for expanded struggle, since the community would be prepared to defend them by all means necessary. Thus, the black movement can expand from programs of struggle for control of the black community into programs of struggle to control the cities, and thence to national struggles.

Lacking such programs of struggle to develop the urban equivalent of liberated areas, the Black Panther Party has resorted to social service programs, such as the Free Breakfast and Free Health programs. Instead of mobilizing the black community to compel the city, state, or federal government to provide such services under community control, the party has taken over the responsibility for their funding and administration.

Still caught up in the illusion that the masses are revolutionary in themselves, the Black Panther Party has grown at the rate of a small mass party rather than that of a revolutionary vanguard party. A vanguard party recruits into membership *only* those who have previously undergone rigorous orientation training and tests to determine fitness for membership. A small mass party, on the other hand, tends to recruit into membership those who are followers—those who are sympathetic to its aims and attracted by its image but who have not met strict standards of membership. As a result, the small mass party finds itself being led by those who should be following.

The Black Panther Party has developed other weaknesses. In reacting against the nonviolent philosophy and opportunism of many black organizations, it has been easy to veer over into a philosophy of violence and an adventurism which, despite its aggressive appearance, actually keeps the organization tied up in legal defense actions. Critical of the lack of ideology in such organizations as SNCC and CORE, the Panthers borrowed intact the *Little Red Book* without distinguishing between what is appropriate to China, or a post-revolutionary situation, and what is appropriate to the United States, or a pre-revolutionary situation. Repelled by the intellectualism of most SNCC members, the party's appeal has been almost exclusively to black street youth who, in the absence of a highly developed political leadership and programming, naturally tend to impatience and a militaristic viewpoint. Forced on the defensive by the "search and destroy" operations of the police, the party has been led, step by step, into increased reliance upon the financial and legal help of white radicals, as well as into variations on their outmoded ideas of class struggle and "black and white, unite and fight."

Despite these mistakes and weaknesses, the Black Panther Party is historically important because it has demonstrated conclusively the tremendous potential among black street youth in this country for the discipline and self-sacrifice necessary to overthrow racism and capitalism and the tremendous hunger for a total ideology that will invest their lives with social and historical meaning and direct their explosive energies into revolutionary political channels. It is this potential and this hunger—far more than any immediate danger from actual actions or rhetoric—that have provoked the counterattack from the police. In turn, the ruthlessness of the counterattack has clarified for many black adults the manner in which racism in this country operates to deprive black youth of the right to live and learn from experience. The rallying of the entire black community to the defense of the Black Panthers is an indication of the essential unity that exists among blacks of all ages and generations in the face of white oppression, a source of strength whose implications have yet to be fully developed.

"What we need is leadership." This is and has long been the cry of black people searching for a road out from their oppression in white America. When blacks speak of leaders, they are usually thinking of a man like Martin Luther King, who articulated their dreams, or Malcolm, who had the unique ability to challenge and chide black people at the same time, or Stokely, who made blacks glow with black pride, or H. Rap Brown, who made clear the readiness of black youth to make their extermination too expensive for the white man even to contemplate.

Each of these leaders has made a major contribution to the developing momentum of the black revolution. Each both expressed and helped create a certain stage of the movement. Each was a public figure, attacking the enemy openly and frontally. Malcolm was murdered on a public platform as he was making clear his intention to organize ties between the black revolutions at home and abroad. King was murdered after he began to take an active part in the anti-Vietnam movement, threatening to meddle in the arena of foreign policy that white power considers its own preserve and in which it felt on very shaky ground. Now Fred Hampton, who was emerging as a black street youth leader, has been ambushed in his bed.

These murders should give the black movement much food for thought. The question is not that death is to be feared but rather whether a movement that has reached the stage of contending for power has the right to organize itself in such a way that its leadership is so much in front. Lenin went into hiding many times—without announcing that he was about to do so. Ho Chi Minh changed his identity so often that there was frequent speculation as to whether he was still alive. One cannot imagine a Vietcong fighter marching into Saigon with "Guerrilla Fighter" or "Minister of Defense" inscribed on his jacket. Yet so pervasive is the theatrical model of revolution that those supposedly struggling for power have been publicly playing the roles and assuming the posts of those who have already achieved the power to defend themselves.

As long as the black movement and black people were seeking primarily to reform the system, what was required from leadership was relatively simple. It was the outspoken, unrelenting condemnation of the system, arousing the black masses to a heightened sense of their grievances. This is something that black leaders have always done well. The chief difference has been that in this period they have had organizations behind them and have been part of an ongoing national movement. When the movement changed from being essentially an attempt to reform the system into a struggle for power, a new phase began. This new phase requires a different kind of organization with a different, more scientific ideology: different, more disciplined members; a different, more functional structure; a different, more strategically developed program of struggle; and a different, less flamboyant leadership.

What has bogged the movement down during the last few yeas is that it has wanted to change direction without changing the tasks, the structure, and the activities of leadership. The old leaders, accustomed to the limelight, have wanted to keep their image public. They have been unable to adapt themselves to the new need for the painstaking and often unglamorous tasks of building cadres dedicated to working in the community, carrying out and developing programs of struggle that will lead to the conquest of power, and projecting political solutions and perspectives of power to which the masses may not immediately subscribe but which they can begin to understand through a process of escalating struggle. Considering how the movement actually developed (i.e., empirically), it is natural that the black masses continue to look for charismatic leaders who can articulate their grievances and put up a tough public image and that leaders continue to come forward to play this role. But those who have recognized the seriousness of the struggle for power and the kind of strategy and tactics, leadership and organization, required for such a struggle have no right to confuse what the masses *want* with what the movement *needs*. If they have any doubt, they have only to reflect for a moment on how little we know about the counterrevolution, its leaders, its cadres, even its numbers. Yet it is common knowledge that its forces are far better organized, better disciplined, and better equipped than those of the black movement.

As long as the black movement does not set itself the task of creating the kind of leadership necessary for a serious struggle for power, it will betray the fact that it is still expecting white power to resolve the problems of black people. Blacks will still be evading the struggle for power and the responsibilities that go with such a struggle.

When the perspective of blacks revolutionizing and ruling America is projected as the only solution to the total crisis of this society, the first response from black and white is usually negative. This stems, first of all, from the acceptance of the myth of "majority rule"—as if this country were not ruled by a minority of individuals and cor-porations. Also, both black and white are still stuck in the statistical picture of blacks as a small minority, when in politics what matters is not numbers as such but rather the strategic position of your forces. Even from the point of view of numbers, colored people constitute approximately 25 percent of the American population when you take into consideration the third world peoples inside United States, all of whom have suf-fered a similar exploitation under the American racist-capitalist system.

The chief objection whites have to black revolutionary power is basically racist: they simply cannot conceive of blacks ever having the political intelligence or skill to govern. Even the few whites who accept Black Power in theory are fearful that the deep racial animosity that exists in the average white American would mean such un-ceasing and bloody white resistance that blacks would never have a chance to rule.

Blacks also still lack confidence in their capacity to rule. Moreover, having expe-rienced the barbarism of white racism for so many centuries and conscious of being outnumbered, they can't even imagine a situation in which they are ruling whites. Hence, when they talk about Black Power or the black revolution, they are usually envisaging complete geographical separation from whites; *or* control of only the black community, leaving revolution in the "mother country" to whites; *or* eventually being the junior partner in a revolutionary coalition led by whites.

What all these objections and hesitations show is a lack of understanding of the nature of all revolutions and of the specific character of the American revolution. In any revolution the new ruling power derives its legitimacy not only from the benefits it brings to the specific social forces it represents but from the fact that it replaces the old system with a new one that benefits all the people in the country. The great need of the total community in the United States is a rapid development in all the people of a social consciousness, a sense of social responsibility, and a control over economic and social institutions, all of which are necessary for self-government. This is the revolutionary humanist essence of the revolutions now taking place in Asia, Latin America, and the liberated areas of Africa. It is also the essence of the black revolution in America.

Blacks are the social force with the greatest need to struggle for control over the economic and social institutions that dominate their daily lives because they are the ones these institutions have most manifestly failed. In the course of the protracted struggles necessary to achieve this control, blacks will be the ones who can most rapidly develop the parallel power structures and the skills to govern these institutions on new foundations. They are the ones with the greatest need to redefine the goals and methods of these institutions to make them relevant to human rather than economic needs.

A new revolutionary power also derives its legitimacy from the fact that it is the only social force that can put an end to the prevailing disorder and create a new order in which new social disciplines have been born out of a new faith in the potentialities of man. Today the accumulation of social problems and of violence and counterviolence in the United States is reaching the point where there appears to be no possibility of peaceful coexistence between the races, the nations, the sexes, and the generations. Human life itself is beginning to seem less valuable than that of animals. As I wrote in the *Manifesto for a Black Revolutionary Party:* "Concretely, American society faces only three real alternatives: (1) to continue rotting away as it is today; (2) naked counter-revolution; or (3) black revolutionary power. The fact that these are the only concrete alternatives makes black revolutionary power as realistic a possibility as the other two."

As we enter the 1970s, time is running out on the first alternative. The second alternative, fascism or the "new order" that enforces adherence to the *old* values by violence and intimidation, is coming closer every day. Experience shows that fascism cannot be stopped short of a total revolution that establishes a new social order based on new values. The struggle *by blacks* to establish this new social order and *between whites* to determine how far they are ready to go to support or crush this new social order will dominate the 1970s.

"Beyond Rebellion" was published as an op-ed in the *New York Times* on September 23, 1972.

Beyond Rebellion

The black movement has gone through a number of stages in the last fifteen years. First, there was the civil rights movement, which reached a critical stage with the Birmingham confrontations of 1963 and finally collapsed with the assassination of the Rev. Martin Luther King Jr. in 1968. Then, there has been the Black Power movement, which began to rise with Malcolm in 1963–64 and mushroomed into a national movement following the Watts uprising of 1965 and the Newark and Detroit rebellions of 1967.

Today we are still in the stage of trying to clarify what Black Power means. At the present time most "movement" people are still in the purely nationalist stage of Black Power. That is to say, most of those who call themselves Black Power advocates are trying to find a solution for blacks separate from a solution for the contradictions of the entire United States. Actually, this is impossible. Therefore, many black nationalists are going off into all kinds of fantasies and dreams about what Black Power means— like heading for Africa, or isolating themselves in a few states, or whites just vanishing into thin air and leaving this country to blacks.

We have yet to come face to face with our contradiction that just as it has been on the backs of the black masses that this country has advanced economically, so it is only under the revolutionary political leadership of black people that this country will be able to get out of its contradictions. We are hesitant to face up to this truth because it is too challenging. We have the fear that always haunts the revolutionary social forces, the fear of not knowing whether they can win, the lack of confidence in themselves and in their ability to create a better society.

This is not a fear that is unique to blacks. All revolutionary social forces have this fear as they come face to face with their real conditions of life and the growing realization that they must assume the revolutionary responsibility of changing the whole society, so that their lives as well as those of others in the society can be fundamentally changed. Because the task is so great, it becomes much easier to evade the tremendous challenge of and responsibility for disciplined scientific thinking and disciplined political organization that are necessary to lead revolutionary struggle.

Confronted with this political choice, many of those who have been frustrated by the failure of the civil rights movement and the succeeding rebellions to solve all our problems have begun to put forward all kinds of fantastic ideas as to what we should now do. Some say we should separate and return to Africa. Some say we should separate but should remain here and try to build a new black capitalist economy from scratch inside the most advanced and powerful capitalist economy in the world! Some say we should join the Pan-African movement of the African peoples in Africa and build a military base in Africa from which we will eventually be able to attack the United States.

Others say we should just struggle for survival from day to day, doing whatever has to be done for survival. And finally, others have just given up struggling for anything at all and have turned to astrology or drugs or religion in the old-time belief that some metaphysical force out there in the twilight zone will rescue us from our dilemma.

We have to examine all these theories realistically and scientifically—whatever their origin and whosoever is proposing them—whether they are our friends or our relatives; whether or not they are old comrades with whom we have demonstrated and gone to jail in the past; whether or not we admire them for their past deeds or for their charismatic personalities or because they make us feel good when we hear them rapping against "the man." All these personal considerations are irrelevant when measured against the real miseries of our present conditions in this country and the real future we must create for ourselves and our posterity in this country. We live in this country, our labors have laid the foundation for the growth of this country. Our contradictions are rooted in this country's unique development and can only be resolved by struggles under our leadership to eliminate the roots of these contradictions in this country.

As we look at our communities, looking more and more each day like wastelands and fortresses, as we look at our younger brothers and sisters scrambling and nodding on the streets of our communities, as we think of the children whom we will be bringing into this world—we cannot just grab onto any ideas of liberation just because they are being pushed by old friends of ours or because they give us an emotional shot in the arm.

We can start by categorically rejecting astrology, drugs, religion, black capitalism, separatism, and all those messianic complexes that someone else or we ourselves are going to become "the leader" whom the black masses are waiting for, to lead them out of the wilderness of their oppression. In other words, we can start by turning our backs on all the various escape routes by which many people are still traveling, in the vain hope that somehow they can evade grappling with the real contradictions of this country, this society.

"Beyond Nationalism" is a speech that was delivered to a forum sponsored by the Ethiopian Students Union of North America (ESUNA) held at Teachers College, Columbia University, on May 18, 1973. It is followed by a condensed version of the question-and-answer session that followed the speech. The text of the speech was published in the January 1974 issue of *Monthly Review*.

Beyond Nationalism

Good evening. It is good to be in New York. Good to have the opportunity to speak to a group that has taken on the responsibility of reflecting upon the state of Ethiopian society in the last half of the twentieth century. All too often it has been my experience to meet African students who embody a conflict of loyalties. That is, they are torn between two roads, between two directions. On the one hand, they feel that they should devote their energies to trying to find a way to mobilize the forces at home to make revolutionary changes in their lives. On the other hand, having tasted the inducements of the West, they are tempted to devote their energies to enhancing their own selfish interests, even though they know that this usually means abandoning their homeland. So they rationalize by insisting that the conditions at home are natural and inevitable at this stage of the historical development.

From the literature I have read of the ESUNA group that is sponsoring this meeting, I get the distinct and very gratifying impression that you have chosen the road of responsibility for developing a revolutionary ideology and organization that can involve the masses in struggle for a new way of life in a section of Africa still dominated by a way of life already repudiated nearly two hundred years ago in the French Revolution.

I do not know what the position of this audience is in regard to Ethiopia. But let me make clear what my position is, in order to remove any suspicion that I think in any biological or racialist way. By this I mean that I am not going to allow my thinking about the fate of mankind to be decided by my color or by the color of people, be they white or black, yellow or red or brown. All too often today, people tend to excuse or rationalize or support actions by individuals on the basis of their ethnic background. In the course of so doing, they lose all sense of principle in human behavior and historical development. So their minds degenerate. I call this kind of biological thinking "racialism." "Racialism" is the kind of thinking in terms of color or biological origin that an individual chooses and therefore the kind of thinking an individual can also repudiate. It is not the same as "racism," which is a social system based on economic and political power.

Ethiopia plays a very special role in the thinking of Afro-Americans. Because Ethiopia has a long recorded history and is referred to in the Bible, and also because of the attack on Ethiopia by Mussolini in the 1930s, there has been a broad strand of sympathy here for Ethiopia. This sympathy has been—as sympathy often is—an obstacle to the kind of distinctions and the kind of critical thinking we have been willing to apply to other nations at a like stage of development.

What we have to acknowledge is that feudalism—just like tribalism, which came before feudalism—was a stage in the development of man that is now outmoded. Today, wherever feudalism exists, whether it is in Asia or Africa or South America, it is a fetter upon the further development of men and women. It is backward in the sense of going backward. It is against the continuing evolution of mankind, and it is therefore counterrevolutionary or anti-mankind.

Those who hail Haile Selassie, whatever their rationale may be, are in essence sanctifying the forces in society who are determined to keep men and women in a state of bondage in order to maintain their own class privileges and their class domination over the material, political, and social development of others. Naturally we must realize that feudalism does not exist anywhere today in its original forms. The forms of its appearance have been modified by the tentacles of capitalism, either in the form of imperialism or colonialism or neocolonialism or multinational capitalism. Today the feudal landlords act as agents of world capitalism and are a comprador class or a class of collaborators. But in this form they are even more counterrevolutionary because they have added to their own reactionary interests, the interests and the power of world imperialism.

But I did not come here to speak about Africa or Asia or Europe. I have very definite views about different sections of the world and particularly about Africa. But I do not aspire to concentrate (and therefore I do not want to give the impression that I have concentrated) my political thinking and activities on Africa. It is my view that the indigenous peoples of Africa have the responsibility for making the revolutions in Africa, just as the Asians, the Europeans, and the Latin Americans have the responsibility for making the revolution in their sections of the world.

What we must all be aware of is that we have been living in a different world since the end of World War II—which was a life-and-death struggle between the old imperialist powers. Since that time, new social forces have emerged who have begun not only to question the realities of their existence but to struggle to develop the theory and practice for how to change the present reality from what it is, to a new reality based upon the conviction that there is another way that men and women can and should live.

Often their thoughts have been confused or too superficial. Sometimes upon reflection they have been able to recognize their mistakes by examining their social practice. One factor that usually takes some time, and real practice, for anyone involved in revolutionary struggle to realize and internalize is that every country has its own unique and specific historical process of development. The process by which any country becomes a nation is unique to that country. Therefore, the scenario of the revolution in any country is unique and cannot be borrowed or applied dogmatically from the revolutionary scenario of any other country.

As a matter of political decision, I have chosen to concentrate my thoughts and efforts on the development of the revolutionary social forces in the United States. I am very much aware of the fact that the many tentacles of U.S. capitalism extend to other continents, but I am also aware that the United States is the last stronghold of world capitalism. Therefore, when and if the people of the United States move to the level of making a revolution, the forces for advancing all mankind will be released on a level never before experienced by mankind in our many thousands and thousands of years of searching and striving to become more profoundly human.

There is a very direct relationship between the struggles of people in the rest of the world and the struggles of "we all too few" here in the United States. However, the people in the rest of the world have to fight wherever they are against the tentacles of capitalism, be these naked imperialism or colonialism or multinational capitalism. It is my revolutionary duty to struggle here, in the citadel of capitalism itself. Therefore, I support the forces who represent the future in countries fighting to rid themselves of the stranglehold of imperialism. And I oppose the forces in power within these countries who have chosen to ally themselves with capitalism: the compradors and the collaborators. In taking these positions, I make clear which side I am on and at the same time clarify my own politics in relation to mankind on a global scale. I support the revolutionary struggle the world over, but in particular I accept the duty and responsibility for making the revolution in the United States.

The capitalist system, which is so technologically advanced today in the United States, was built upon the backs of my ancestors who came from Africa. They were the ones who endured the oppression of the slave masters and thereby built the infrastructure in agriculture that was a necessary foundation for the rapid development of industrial capitalism. I have a duty to them, my ancestors, to struggle so that all their hardships and sufferings shall not have been in vain. Equally important, I too have lived through the history of this country in my own lifetime and in my own life, from agriculture to industry, to automation and cybernation. So I am a product of this country in its many manifestations.

Therefore, I have the responsibility as well as the right to confront every section of this society, every ethnic group within this society, and challenge them to discover a new and higher form to express their humanity at this stage of technological and historical development.

Earlier I referred to the first turning point at which ordinary people first began to believe that they could change society, first became citizens rather than subjects. This occurred less than two hundred years ago, at the time of the French Revolution. That great social upheaval signaled the end of feudalism in Europe and the birth of mercantile capitalism.

More than a hundred years later, the whole world, wherever ordinary people suffered and labored, was thrilled and challenged by the Russian Revolution, the first revolution that began with the clear and conscious intent of going beyond capitalism and creating a socialist system. For many years, regardless of the stories circulated by the bourgeoisie and the renegades who fled from the Russian Revolution—some true and some false—the historic event of the Russian Revolution remained an inspiration to millions of people the world over. That was the second turning point.

The third turning point was 1945. With the British, French, and Dutch empires in shambles and the whole of Europe near collapse, ordinary people all over the world unleashed a powerful struggle to rid themselves of the yoke of imperialism and colonialism, taking advantage of the weaknesses now clearly visible in the old powers, often using the strength of the now powerful Russian nation to reinforce their country's struggle for independence; their nation's struggle for liberation; and their people's struggle for revolution.

As we now know, quite a number of countries have achieved their independence. They have become nations. But most of these nations still have to struggle for liberation from neocolonialism. Only a very few—China, Cuba, North Vietnam, North Korea, and Albania—have made their own socialist revolutions and therefore achieved *both* independence and liberation.

After World War II, here in the United States—a country that during the period of the French Revolution achieved its independence from British colonialism and thus was able to develop as a nation—black people who had been brought in chains from Africa also began to question the realities of their existence, thus creating the civil rights movement.

Like practically all struggles that may eventually end in revolution, the black struggle began as a reform movement. Like most reform movements, it was led by the section of society that felt the greatest frustration because of its exclusion from the society, since it believed it had the ability to share in all that the present system was making available to everybody else. Year after year, from 1954 until the middle of the 1960s, this movement moved ahead steadily, knocking down all the *legal* barriers that had been systematically designed to keep blacks out of or at the bottom of every institution of the society.

What made this movement different from previous reform struggles by blacks was that it became a self-developing movement. That is to say, each year the movement kept developing momentum as every gain brought ever-widening forces of people into the struggle. However, as with any self-developing movement that begins to gain ground, there comes a point when the great masses of people are rebelling outside the confines of the movement because they feel that the amount of progress that has been made is inadequate to the amount of progress that should be made.

Thus, in the late 1960s, wave after wave of mass rebellion swept the country, in city after city, from coast to coast. Out of these rebellions came a mounting fervor of nationalism.

Nationalism in the black movement in the United States, as elsewhere in the world, is usually the second stage of a movement on the road to revolution. It is the stage when the oppressed social forces, recognizing that they are not going to be readily accepted into the system, begin to feel that there is something unique about their oppression that makes it necessary for them to look only to themselves and think only of themselves. The nationalists usually include all classes of people—those who are economically most oppressed as well as those who are very well-off. At a certain stage in the movement, nationalism provides an encasement within which all classes are temporarily united, whether they are doctors or lawyers, small businessmen or workers. It is at this stage that they all recognize that the question is no longer one of rights but that it has become a question of political power to determine economic and social relations.

The unique strengths and weakness of the nationalist stage of revolutionary struggle have to be analyzed in the light of the unique development of the United States.

In the United States racism has been a twin prong to the rapid development of capitalism. It has been an integral part of capitalist development in this country, making possible the rapid development of the economy as a whole and the upward mobility of every other ethnic group except blacks. Every other ethnic group has been able to advance upward in this society because blacks have been an underclass, kept at the bottom. This upward mobility has been the distinct and unique feature of U.S. capitalism.

At the civil rights stage of the movement, those involved in the struggle and those leading the struggle thought they could separate the struggle against racism from the struggle against capitalism. As long as they limited the struggle in this way, there was no need for them to think about a struggle for power.

However, when the nationalist stage of the movement erupted, the opportunity was created to raise the question of changing the system, in other words, posing the perspective of blacks taking power in order to change the system, i.e., to make a socialist revolution. But very few of the nationalists were ready to face the awesome responsibilities that are involved in making a socialist revolution. Therefore, they began doing what nationalists who do not go beyond nationalism to socialist revolution usually tend to do.

Some began to drop out completely and just try to make it for themselves, as doctors or lawyers or businessmen or as directors of various pacification projects. Others became African scholars, both in the universities and in the streets, going back thousands of years to prove that Africans had also had kings and queens (as if black kings and queens didn't have subjects just like white kings and queens).* Some began to think in purely ethnic terms, dreaming of going back to Africa. Others began to scheme

---

* Using the African past as a justification, some are even doing the same thing to women that we used to find so ridiculous in the southern whites—keeping them pregnant and making them walk a few steps behind on the streets.

about getting a piece of this country—three states or five states. Still others began to live by the stars. For many Black Power began to mean the pure symbolism of long hair (the longer the better) or doing the same kind of dances that blacks have always done in this country but now in African garb! And for a whole lot of people, Black Power has come to mean just "doing my own thing" regardless of the consequences to anybody else.

The chief weakness of the black movement in the United States at this stage arises from the fact that most black militants view nationalism as an end in and of itself. They cannot face the fact that nationalism only puts you into the position where you can clarify to the masses the uniqueness of their oppression and the historical reasons why they should struggle for a new society. Nationalism is not a revolutionary ideology: it does not provide you with a revolutionary solution to the contradictions of your society. It is only a means to an end, a stage in the development of revolutionary struggle—just as rebellion and insurrection are stages in the development of revolutionary struggle.

In developing a revolutionary ideology for the United States, it is necessary to be very scientific about the difference between the role that black people have played in the development of this country and the role that colonial people play in the development of the imperialist country that exploits them. In relation to U.S. capitalism, blacks have played a role that is both like and unlike that of colonial peoples. They have been super-exploited like all colonial peoples, but they have also played an integral part in the internal development of this country from its very beginning. This country has no history separate and apart from the history of black people inside it. By the same token the history of black Americans cannot be separated from their history in the development of this country.

Therefore, nationalism in this country cannot possibly have the same meaning as nationalism in countries like Kenya or Ethiopia or Ghana. These countries have been trying to rid themselves of an oppressor who has invaded them from outside. Therefore, they can fight first for independence, for self-rule, to get the imperialists to leave, and then for liberation—to rid their economies of control by neocolonialism.

In the United States there are no colonial settlers or colonial administrators to leave. Everyone in the United States, whether they came as settlers or immigrants, as indentured servants or as slaves, has been an integral part of the developing of this country. Whether they came by choice or in chains, whether their ancestors are in Africa or in Asia or in Europe or in Latin America, their culture, their history is now a part of this country's history and not with their ancestors on other continents.

Because they are reluctant to face the revolutionary responsibilities that flow from this historical truth, many black Americans continue to call themselves Pan-Africanists, thus encouraging greater confusion and disarray in the black movement. Many

Pan-Africanists in the old days lacked deep roots either in this country or in any country. Most of them were West Indian intellectuals, often very gifted individuals, who left their homelands many years ago because the little islands on which they were born offered no basis for individual advancement. Today's Pan-Africanists have been influenced by Marcus Garvey, the Jamaican who formed the Back-to-Africa Movement after World War I at a historic juncture when it appeared that the European powers had been so thoroughly weakened by the war and by the Russian Revolution that black Americans could retake Africa from them. For that period, this was an extraordinarily bold conception.

But Pan-Africanism in the United States today is mainly a confession of revolutionary frustration and failure by people who were, first, in the civil rights movement, then were lifted to revolutionary enthusiasm by the rebellions and the Black Power movement, but are now evading the awesome responsibility for leading a revolution in the United States. This would require them to grapple with the real contradictions of this entire society because a revolutionist aims to change the political, social, and economic relations of everybody and for everybody in the particular society. Because of this evasion, the black movement today is in a state of complete disarray—with people going in all directions—to the stars, to Africa, to three states, to five states. The result is that at this point when the system is in one of its gravest crises, there is no revolutionary movement of any consequence in the United States, neither black nor white.

So, as I have already explained, I support Pan-Africanism for Africans, i.e., as an objective for African liberation from the yoke of colonialism and imperialism, but I am not a Pan-Africanist. Even Pan-Africanism as a necessary part of the struggle for African liberation does not necessarily mean a socialist United States of Africa. Already we have witnessed how many of those African nations that have achieved independence are governed by Africans who have no intention of mobilizing the masses to struggle for socialism. All too many of them are content with being instruments of neocolonialism, no different from the old feudal compradors or collaborators. We here in the United States have had a very instructive experience of how independence does not necessarily lead to socialism. The first American Revolution freed the American people from British colonialism so that they could build this country into the most powerful capitalism ever developed by man—and the chief architect today of world counterrevolution.

The black movement in the United States will not become a revolutionary movement until more of those who call themselves black revolutionaries are ready to accept the historical reality that, although our ancestors came from Africa, our future, like our past, is deeply rooted in the history of this country. If we attempt to evade this historical reality and the responsibilities that flow from it, we are no better than the

African students who abandon their historic roots and their people in Africa for the fleshpots of the West. Those who evade historical reality begin by being idealists and end up by becoming vulgar materialists, interested only in their own comforts.

Now I did not come here to say what many of you might like to hear from me or what would just be pleasing to your ears. Too many of our political meetings these days have just turned into entertainment, and too many of our so-called leaders are little better than entertainers.

I came here to challenge you to begin using your minds, that is, to set into motion the processes of creative and scientific thinking that each of you, as a human being, is capable of; to urge each of you (1) to reflect upon the experiences of the past (especially those of the last period since the end of World War II); (2) to take a courageous self-critical look at the present deterioration that has taken place in our communities and the degeneration that has set in among the American people, black and white alike; and (3) to wonder about the kind of future we must create in order to advance all man/womankind—which is the fundamental purpose of any revolution. Let there be no doubt about this: any movement that does not have as its aim to advance the human race as a whole is not a revolution. It is just a protest movement, a long list of complaints about what other people have done to you—in order to win the sympathy and help of liberals.

I come before you as a revolutionist dedicated to the creation of a revolutionary ideology and a revolutionary vanguard organization of political cadres, ready and able to act as transmission belts to take ideas from and to the masses in order to heighten their political consciousness and help them grasp the most advanced ideas so that these ideas can become a material force capable of transforming themselves and society.

I am very conscious—and we must all be very conscious—of the fact that the United States is a very developed country technologically but that its people are politically very undeveloped. It is a country where, historically, principles have been sacrificed and political choices have been evaded for the sake of economic benefit. In an economically undeveloped country, it is clear that the socialist revolution must have as one of its main aims to develop the country and the people technologically. But we have yet to discover precisely what is the purpose of a socialist revolution in an advanced country like the United States where material abundance and technological advancement already exist, where more is stolen in the ghettos everyday than is produced in most African countries during an entire year, and where many of the most oppressed have a higher standard of living than the middle classes in most countries.

There are some historical lessons we should have already learned.

History teaches us that the leaders who undertook struggles for liberation but did not develop a vanguard party to give continuing structure and momentum and re-evaluation and self-criticism to the struggles of their peoples were unable to keep their people in continuing progressive struggles after independence—and were therefore either overthrown or themselves degenerated.

History also teaches us that no revolution ever succeeded simply by relying on the spontaneity of the masses or without an organization that was constantly advancing its theory in accordance with social practice and its practice in accordance with its theory.

Finally, history teaches us that in order for there to be success in revolution, there must be revolutionary leadership that recognizes that progress never takes place in a straight line and does not encourage its masses to act like victims but rather has the courage to challenge the masses, confident that through protracted and prolonged struggle we will win—because history is on our side and not on the side of the oppressor. People who are always calling upon others to free them from prison or from their miseries—people who have a victim mentality—don't make revolutions. They make liberals. Revolutionists make revolution.

The United States presents the greatest challenge to revolutionary-minded men and women of any country in the history of mankind. It is my revolutionary duty to take that challenge to every strata of this country, to every ethnic group, every social layer, beginning with the most oppressed, confident that, despite the fact that the United States today is the most racist, the most counterrevolutionary, the most dehumanized country in the world, nevertheless it is possible to discover those individuals who are ready and able to develop themselves so that they can give revolutionary leadership to the great masses of the American people in every stratum of this society.

Socialists thought begins with the idea of advancing the society in which you have your roots so that all will benefit from the advance. Bourgeois thought begins with the idea of advancing some men and women at the expense of others. I take my stand with the advance of all men and women.

Questions and Answers (condensed)

Q: What is your program for the American Revolution?

A: I am not going to try to outline for anyone in five minutes a program for the American Revolution. It would be an insult to your intelligence. What I have been trying to make clear is that this is the period when people ought to begin finding out who is ready to take responsibility for making an American Revolution and for thinking about what must go into making the American Revolution and especially the uniqueness of what is involved in making a revolution in an advanced country like the United States. How do you advance an advanced country—since revolutions certainly are not made to lead a country backward? Until we have struggled over these questions, there is no point talking about program. How can I discuss program with people I have just met, whose views I don't know but who I *do* know have all kinds of differing views, going in all kinds of different directions, to all kinds of different places, with whom I have had no relationship and may never meet again.

Q: Why didn't you have anything to say about the national unemployed and welfare rights organization that was recently founded and is such an important step to the American Revolution?

A: I received an invitation to speak to a similar organization but I did not accept because I would have had to tell them some things that most of them didn't want to hear. The radical groups have been pushing welfare rights and confusing the struggle for rights with making a revolution. People on welfare are not automatically revolutionary; in fact, the more welfare they get, the more they begin to act like subjects. Subjects don't make revolution. Revolutionists make revolution. In their dogmatic application of nineteenth-century Marxism to twentieth-century America, the radicals are also doing a disservice to the workers. They idealize the workers as being revolutionary; they don't confront the workers with their internal contradictions because they don't even have an idea of these contradictions in workers. When workers strike, they are not striking for the interests of the whole society; they are striking for their own interests. And the more they strike and the more they win by striking, the less revolutionary they become and the more of a special interest group they become. Lenin, seventy years ago, made clear that economic struggles by workers do not mean political or socialist class consciousness. Today's radicals in the United States haven't even gotten as far as Lenin. Socialist class consciousness means being concerned with the interests of the whole society. I have been in most of these radical groups and I also worked for twenty-eight years in the plant. I have seen how remote the radicals are from the reality of the workers, how trapped the workers are in their contradictions, and how necessary it is to challenge them to face these contradictions (which we will be doing soon in a pamphlet) to face their tendency to narrow self-interest and to becoming an interest group.

Q: Who is the vanguard of the world revolution?

A: If you are still talking about "the vanguard for the world revolution" you didn't understand anything that I was saying. My main point is that people in every country have to make their own revolution. In that sense there is no "world revolution." Revolutions are made by people in specific countries. The Chinese are not going to make our revolution. I am not going to make the Chinese revolution. Nor am I going to make an African revolution. Africans will make the African revolution.

Q: What about the Black Panther Party?

A: The question of the Black Panther Party is a very important question because the

Black Panther Party at least confronted everybody on the American revolution-ary political scene with the need to build a vanguard party, and they also showed every serious person how not to build a vanguard party. The Black Panthers started out as a defense organization (Black Panther Party for Self-Defense) and with a symbolic demonstration at the California state capitol. So every cat who felt like talking tough and was anxious to put on a beret and leather jacket joined the party. Thus the party began recruiting into itself individuals who should have been followers rather than cadres; they were trapped in the concept of the "small mass party" (which every revolutionary organization must struggle against and overcome before it can really advance). A revolutionary party must begin with a revolutionary ideology, i.e., it must have developed and must be able to project a vision of where it proposes to lead the entire country. The Panthers didn't do this. Although they started out with the idea of "Serve the People," before long they had recruited so many corrupt and adventuristic elements that they had to call upon the people to "Serve the Party." The further they got away from Oak-land, the more corrupt the party became until by the time it got to New York it was little more than a gang.

"Think Dialectically, Not Biologically" is a speech delivered in the Department of Political Science at Atlanta University on February 17, 1974. It was part of a weekly seminar for graduate students and faculty during which invited guests—activists, scholars, politicians, and others—addressed issues facing black people in the United States and globally. During the year preceding Boggs's visit, guests included Julian Bond, Samora Machel, Archie Singham, Maynard Jackson, and Max Stanford.

Think Dialectically, Not Biologically

This is the first opportunity I have had to speak to an audience in Atlanta, a city that in the last few years has become the center for many tendencies in intellectual and political thinking by blacks. Many black groups from all over the country have held conferences here, and in this process you have had an opportunity to evaluate the movement of the black indigenous forces that erupted in the 1960s and within a few years brought this whole country into its present state of social upheaval.

Here in the South, which gave birth to the movement all over the country, we should be especially able to see the difference between the present movement and past movements. For although there have been many revolts and rebellions in other sections of the United States—revolts and rebellions that have led to some social and economic reforms—the present movement that started out in the South was unique. It was unique because at its inception it raised the human question in its most fundamental form. What is the appropriate relationship between human beings, between one man and another? The movement began as a quest for a higher form of human relationships between people, relations not yet shared and not even believed in by most people, but which those who launched the movement believed could or should be shared by people in the United States.

In raising the question of human relations so fundamentally, this movement touched every person in the United States, North and South, and for a period of time it seemed that the country—despite the obvious divisions and opposition of many—would be lifted to a new level of human relationships. Instead, today, nearly twenty years after the movement began in the 1950s, we are experiencing the most dehumanized, blackmailing relationships between blacks and whites, and between blacks and blacks. In terms of material conditions, most blacks are much better-off than they were twenty years ago at the beginning of the black movement. But in terms of relations among ourselves as human beings, we are all worse-off. This is the reality we must be willing to face squarely.

I shall not attempt to review the many struggles and confrontations that created the movement. You know and have experienced these either directly or indirectly. What I want to emphasize instead is that this kind of struggle could only have been unleashed in the South. This is not just because the South was more racist or more impoverished—which it surely was. Rather it is because in the South the tradition of viewing blacks as inferior had been rationalized and given legitimacy by a philosophy. All over the country, the philosophy that one set of human beings is inferior to another on the basis of race was practiced. But in the South this philosophy was not only practiced; it was preached. Therefore the movement that was organized to struggle against racism in the South also had to develop a philosophy as the basis for struggle: the philosophy of the essential dignity of every human being, regardless of race, sex, or national origin. That is why the movement began to draw everybody into it—either pro or con—because it put forward a philosophy with which everybody, regardless of race, color, or sex, had to grapple.

In our lifetime we have also witnessed how no social upheaval in any one part of this country can be isolated indefinitely from social upheaval in the rest of this country. Therefore, what started out in the South as a movement whose aim was chiefly to reform the South quickly spread all over the country. Everybody, oppressed and oppressor, was drawn into the confrontation.

But when everyone is drawn into a conflict that is as deeply rooted in the history of a society as racism is rooted in this society, there is no telling how far the struggle will have to go. You begin to open up contradictions that most people in the society have been evading or tolerating—for various reasons. Some because they benefit from them—as many do—others because they believe these are beyond their power to challenge or negate—as blacks used to think—and still others because they think that to confront these contradictions will create too much antagonism and upheaval.

Once the struggle began to extend out of the South, it became clear that every institution of this country—economic, social, political, cultural—was based upon keeping blacks at the bottom. The whole development of this country had been based upon treating blacks as scavengers, to take the leavings of whatever whites considered beneath them—whether these were jobs or houses, churches or whole neighborhoods. In this process of treating blacks as scavengers, U.S. capitalism had been able to develop more rapidly than any other country in the world because it has had the wherewithal to exploit on a double basis. Not only was it able to exploit wage labor in production and the consumer in the market, as every capitalist society does. But when factories and machinery became obsolete for the exploitation of whites, capitalism could always use them for the exploitation of blacks. Used plants, used houses, used churches, used clothing, used anything and everything could be recycled. After being discarded by whites, they could always be used or reused to exploit blacks both in production and consumption. Thus all whites in this country could get to the top faster because blacks were kept at the bottom.

In providing this opportunity for rapid upward mobility to whites, the system of American capitalism has developed very differently from other capitalisms. First of all, this country, from the very beginning, had to import labor, either by force or by promises. Second, every ethnic group that came to this country voluntarily came in order to get to the top as quickly as it could. Therefore, these groups closed their eyes to the obvious fact that they were able to rise as rapidly only because the indigenous labor force of the blacks was being excluded from the same opportunities. In this way the system of American racism—or the institutionalized exclusion of blacks from equal opportunity—was inseparably interconnected with American capitalism—or the system of upward mobility for special ethnic and special interest groups at the expense of others. Whites could not see this because they were the beneficiaries of the system. The eruption of the black movement exposed the historical connection between racism and capitalism in the United States and made it clear that it is not possible to get rid of racism in this country without getting rid of American capitalism any more than it was possible to carry on a struggle to reform the South without carrying on a struggle to change this entire nation. How is it possible to get rid of racism without getting rid of the method of thinking that has become ingrained in the American people as a result of the special historical development of this country, namely, that special groups should advance at the expense of others?

There is a very important dialectical principle here that every student of political science needs to understand. A struggle may start out with the aim of resolving one contradiction. But in the course of the struggle, if the contradiction it sets out to negate is fundamental enough, the main contradiction may change; it may become enlarged or expanded. Struggle is social practice and when you engage in social practice, you gain new insights. You find out that there was much more involved than you had originally perceived to be the case when you began your struggle. Therefore, you are faced with the need to raise your level of understanding, your level of conceptual knowledge. If you do not raise your level of understanding as the struggle expands and develops, then what began as a progressive struggle can turn into its opposite.

When the struggle that began in the South exploded all over the country, the question of racism became no longer just a regional but a national question—a question of transforming this whole nation. It has been a national question ever since: national in the sense that it involves this whole country and national in the sense that it embraces all the aspects of this nation. We now face the question of the second reconstruction of the United States. What kind of nation should the United States be? What kind of society should we build in the United States? On what kind of philosophy concerning the relations between people should we base ourselves—because no movement can ever develop momentum without a philosophy.

Note that I used the word "we." I mean "we." The strength of the movement that began in the South stemmed from the fact that those who led and participated in it understood that blacks had to change this society—this country. They had many illusions about the possibilities of reforming this society, but at least they did not have the romantic and escapist notions about leaving this country to make the revolution in Africa that nationalists of today have. However, once the movement came north and the tremendous complexity of the struggle that would be necessary to transform this whole society began to dawn on blacks, all kinds of romantic and escapist notions began to develop within the black movement. These romantic and escapist notions are now crippling the minds of many of our black young people.

All kinds of black militants call themselves black revolutionists these days. But few of them have yet been willing to come face to face with the contradiction that just as it has been on the backs of the black masses that this society has advanced economically at such tremendous speed, so it is only under the revolutionary political leadership of black people that this country will be able to get out of its contradictions. We are hesitant to face up to this truth because it is too challenging. We have the fears that always haunt the revolutionary social forces: the fear of not knowing whether we can win; the fear that if we set our sights too high we may provoke the enemy to counterattack; the lack of confidence in ourselves and in our ability to struggle to create a better society.

This is not a fear that is unique to blacks. All revolutionary social forces have this fear as they come face to face with their real conditions of life and the growing realization that they must assume revolutionary responsibility for changing the whole society so that their lives as well as those of others in this society can be fundamentally changed. Because the fear is so great, it becomes much easier to evade the tremendous challenge and responsibility for disciplined scientific thinking and disciplined political organization that are necessary to lead revolutionary struggles.

Confronted with this political challenge, many of those who have been frustrated by the failure of the civil rights movement and the succeeding rebellions to solve all our problems have begun to put forward all kinds of fantastic ideas as to what we should now do. Some say we should separate and return to Africa. Some say we should separate but remain here and try to build a new black capitalist economy from scratch inside the most advanced and powerful capitalist economy in the world. Some say we should join the Pan-African movement of the African people in Africa and build a military base there from which we will eventually be able to attack the United States.

Others say we should just struggle for survival from day to today, doing whatever has to be done for survival. They have just given up struggling for anything at all and have turned to astrology or drugs or religion—in the old-time belief that some metaphysical force out there in the twilight zone will rescue us from our dilemma.

And finally, most black militants of the 1960s, even while they are still talking their nationalist rhetoric, have today just become a part of the system. They are doing their best to get to the top in one form or another, regardless of whom they have to step on to get there, just as every other ethnic group has always done in this country.

The American System: Incorporation of Ethnic Groups

Those who have given a great deal to a particular struggle in the past always find it hard to realize that what began as a struggle for equal justice, equal representation, or equal rights can, precisely because it gains momentum, become just another factor in the development of the system. A system doesn't have any color. It is a way of social functioning that not only has institutions and structure but also has an ideology and the tendency to perpetuate itself. In the United States the capitalist system functions not only by exploitation of different groups but also by incorporation of successive ethnic groups into the system. This is the way that it has historically transformed what might become antagonistic social forces into non-antagonistic social forces. Already we have seen how American labor has been incorporated into the system in the wake of the militant labor struggles of the 1930s. Instead of being a threat to the system as it used to be, labor now helps the system to function. Labor keeps demanding more for itself in the way of more wages, pensions, and other benefits and doesn't give a damn if this "more" is extracted out of the super-exploitation of people in other parts of the world or passed on to the consumer. In this way the labor organizations that came out of the great social struggles of the 1930s and 1940s are today just mainstays of capitalism itself. They not only act as obstacles to its overthrow; they actively keep the system going.

The black movement is now running a parallel course. Gradually blacks are being incorporated into the structure, the institutions, and the ideology of U.S. capitalism. This is happening because in the wake of the black rebellions of the 1960s, the black movement has made no serious effort to repudiate the bourgeois method of thought on which U.S. capitalism is based, which involves each individual or group just getting more for itself. It has made no serious effort to create a movement based on a more advanced method of thinking and that aims to transform the whole of society for the benefit of the majority of the population.

It would be childish to blame U.S. capitalism for incorporating blacks into the system. In doing this, the system is only doing what it is supposed to do in order to maintain itself. In this respect U.S. capitalism is doing and has done very well. From the time of the Johnson administration tens of thousands of black militants, who might have become revolutionists, have been incorporated into various pacification programs. Scholarships were made available on a mass basis to blacks so that they could go to college and become part of that huge apparatus of social workers and teachers that keeps the system going. Now we have blacks in every sphere of capitalist society—junior executives of corporations, local and national politicians, mayors and judges, sheriffs and policemen. Blacks have acquired the same entourage of officials that every other ethnic group has. In this sense blacks have risen in the sliding scale of upward mobility just as the Kerner Commission proposed. They have not supplanted or replaced whites.

But as whites have been elevated upward, blacks have replaced them on the levels they have vacated. Hence today blacks are taking over the cities in the traditional pattern of other ethnic groups. In the past, as we pointed out in "The City Is the Black Man's Land," this upward mobility in the politics of the city had always stopped at blacks. But after the rebellions U.S. capitalism was ready to make this concession. Just as it incorporated labor after the class struggles of the 1930s, it has now incorporated blacks in the wake of the racial struggles of the 1960s.

Today blacks are inheriting the old cities which are more poverty-stricken and crime-ridden than they have ever been. Technology has made it possible for capitalism not to depend on the city anymore as the main base for its production facilities. So industry is abandoning the cities for the rural areas with the same ease that in the nineteenth century it abandoned the rural areas for the cities. It is in the rural areas that U.S. capitalism is developing the new technical industries, leaving behind the cities to be fought over by petty-bourgeois careerists, whites and blacks. These blacks and whites can't do anything to restore the cities, which have become little more than urban reservations. All that is happening is that thousands of careerist blacks are getting plush jobs for themselves and living high on the hog. But the cities continue to deteriorate.

The Struggle between Two Roads

In *The American Revolution* I pointed out there are two sides to every question—but only one side is right. There are many ways that we can look at what is happening in this country today. But in the end we are going to have to recognize that we now have only the choice between two roads for the movement—only two directions of thought and action.

Will the United States continue to be a society based on the bourgeois system of upward mobility, with each rebellious group becoming incorporated into the system through its careerist or opportunist members while the mass at the bottom sinks deeper into despair? Or can we build a society in this country based upon social responsibility between individuals and between groups in which everyone tries to make decisions based on the interests of the whole rather than on the special interest of his or her ethnic group?

The black movement started out in the belief that racism was the only contradiction in this society and that if it could only win equal opportunity for blacks to advance in the system, blacks and whites would end up equal. In the course of two decades of struggle, i.e., in the course of social practice, it has become clear that racism is not the sole contradiction and that it is inseparable from the capitalist contradictions that arise from each group advancing at the expense of others and individuals within each group using the group to advance themselves.

The more nationalist the black movement has become, the easier it has been for U.S. capitalism to incorporate blacks into the system. Not only has it been easy for the system to identify the individuals to be incorporated. But the more nationalistic blacks became, the more they began to fool themselves and allow themselves to be fooled by black opportunist leaders into believing that everything black is beautiful and everything non-black is ugly or worthless or a threat to blacks. More and more blacks began to think and insist that "all we care about are blacks—and to hell with everybody else." Thus step by step they have taken on the dehumanized ideology of U.S. capitalism.

Thus, in the course of only twenty years, both the integrationists, who only wanted to reform the system so that blacks could be included in capitalist exploitation, and the nationalists, who claimed to be against the system, have each gradually been brought into the system and are assuming responsibility for it and the chaos that has been created as a result of the system.

The nationalists ended up by going into the system because they made the mistake of thinking that nationalism in and of itself is a revolutionary ideology, when in fact nationalism is only a stage in the development of a struggle by an oppressed people. It is the stage when all layers of an oppressed group—the petty bourgeoisie, workers, peasants, farmers—come to the conclusion that they have shared a common oppression and have a common history.

In the United States nationalism was an inevitable stage in the development of black struggle because throughout the history of this country, blacks have been kept at the bottom of this society as blacks, i.e., on a racial basis. But ever since the Black Power movement erupted in the late 1960s, the question facing the black movement has been not the past but the future. The question has become "What are we going to do about the future of this country, this society? What kind of society must we create here in this country for our children and our children's children?"

In other words, from the time that the nationalist or Black Power stage erupted in this country, the need has been for blacks to develop a revolutionary ideology for this country. But instead of doing this, black militants began to look toward Africa and toward the past, in other words, to a world that they really couldn't do anything about. Instead of grappling with the tremendous challenge of transforming the conditions and relations in this country, they began to idealize the past. Instead of examining the changes that would have to be made in this country—which would inevitably benefit not only blacks but everybody else in this country—they began to think of themselves as living in some metaphysical space totally separate and apart from everybody else and what was happening in this country. They began to insist that blacks in this country are third world people. They refused to face the reality that black GIs were raping and massacring the people of Vietnam just like white GIs. Or that blacks are an integral part of the 5 percent of the world's population living in the United States and using up

40 percent of the world's energy resources for their big cars and their new appliances, just as whites are doing.

Unwilling to face their actual conditions of life inside this country and the challenge of bringing about fundamental changes in this country, blacks have drifted steadily into bourgeois methods of thinking and bourgeois practices. The result is that today blacks are no different from whites in seeking individual advancement based upon the capitalist principle that every individual can "make it" in the system if only they are ready to use others to get there, exploiting even those closest to them in the most degrading ways, from the pimp on the street to the politician seeking office. Meanwhile, instead of confronting this growing criminal mentality among black people, black militants have been making excuses for it—thus helping this criminal mentality to become even more widespread among black children and youth.

Today, in the year 1974, blacks all over the country are bragging about how many black mayors have been elected, while practically every black who can get together a few hundred dollars is running for one office or another. In terms of numbers this looks like progress for black people. But in terms of grappling with the fundamental issues that confront this country and everyone inside it, including blacks (crime, the energy crisis, the corruption at all levels of government), this rush of black politicians only means that more blacks are now caught up in the system of bourgeois politics. Just like white politicians, they cannot raise any of the real questions that confront this country and force the American people and those who might elect them to office, i.e., their own constituents, to discuss and clarify their positions on them. If they did this, they might not get elected to office, which is their main aim. So black politicians are now making deals to please the most voters—just as white politicians have been doing for the last hundred years. Thus the elevation of blacks into the system has weakened the black movement and the overall struggle for real change in this country—even though on the surface it may seem to have strengthened it. In this sense, even if we took the process to the logical conclusion of electing a black president and vice president, all it would mean would be trapping more blacks in the position of defending and projecting the practices and ideology of the system.

Learning from Social Practice

There is no use wondering what might have happened differently. Now we must try to learn from what has happened. There is a good side to this. Now that blacks have been incorporated into the bourgeois practices of this country, the fundamental issue facing blacks is much clearer than it could possibly have been twenty years ago. It is easier for young people to see now that blacks, like everybody else in this country, now only have the choice between two roads.

Either you can join the blacks who are now rushing in to defend and expand a system based upon the exploitation of many for the benefit of a few. Or you can take the socialist direction, which has as its aim to create a society based on advancing the many and all mankind above the interests of a few.

In making this choice, those who are ready to take responsibility for changing society in the direction of a socialist society can't start by taking a poll of the masses. Nor can they just wait for the masses to rebel and then rush in to become their spokesmen, which is what most of the black militants of the 1960s did. Like all masses the black masses are full of internal contradictions. They can only acquire the strength to fight against the external enemy by first struggling against their own internal contradictions and limitations. No potential revolutionary social force has ever become an actual revolutionary social force except through struggle to overcome its limitations and weaknesses.

Through past struggles blacks have rid themselves of physical fears standing in the way of struggles against oppression. This is the first obstacle any oppressed group has to overcome—an obstacle that is usually overcome through mass rebellions. Now the great need is for blacks to rid themselves of the fear of theoretical and political struggles against their own limitations. This requires a different kind of courage and boldness. It also requires discipline and patience and a readiness to struggle to acquire an appreciation of the dialectical process by which development takes place.

Our first need now is to look critically at the past of the black movement of the 1950s and 1960s, not in order to blame black leaders for what they did not do or to dream about what might have been if somebody had done differently but to prepare for the next stage of struggle.

Black intellectuals especially must be ready to look very critically at how quick they were to accept the idea that there is such a thing as "black thought," i.e., that thought is based on color or biology rather than on the creative use of the mind to analyze historical and social developments and to project new direction for an actual society. By accepting the idea that biology is the basis for thinking, black intellectuals have not only crippled their own minds but also the minds of millions of young people—until today few blacks knew how to think historically or to make social judgments based on anything else but color. With every day the thinking among black youth becomes more antihistorical, more metaphysical, and more superstitious and therefore more vulnerable to manipulation by unscrupulous demagogues and the mass media. The reality, the very sad reality today is that most of our young people have no basis for making decisions except their own momentary feelings, their own immediate selfish interests or their desire not to be unpopular with their peers. Every day black youth are becoming more individualistic, more pleasure-seeking, more unable to tell the difference between correct and incorrect ideas and principles.

That is why the responsibility of black intellectuals, and especially those of you who are in the field of political science, is so great. You have the responsibility to acquire, to develop a method of thought that is based upon the historical developments and contradictions of this society in this country. You now have the tremendous advantage of the experiences of the last twenty years—both good and bad—to evaluate. In this sense you are very fortunate.

Not all black intellectuals are going to be ready to accept this responsibility. Many, perhaps most of them, will continue to be prisoners of bourgeois thought, i.e., they will be concerned only with advancing their own careers and the careers of their cronies, just as white intellectuals have been. More and more black politicians are going to win elections in the next few years; therefore, it will seem to most of you foolish not to jump on their bandwagons or create a bandwagon of your own. But in thinking and acting this way, you will only become like so many black prime ministers in the West Indies and in the tiny African nations of our time—enjoying their own pomp and circumstance and begging whites to come to your city to spend their tourist dollars so that you can entertain them with African dances as the Native Americans entertain tourists with Indian dances.

My hope, however, is that some of you will be ready to accept the challenge I put to you—to be ready to struggle to think dialectically. That is, we must be ready to recognize that as reality changes, our ideas have to change so that we can project new, more advanced aspirations worth striving for. This is the only way to avoid becoming prisoners of ideas that were once progressive but have become reactionary, i.e., have been turned into their opposite. The only struggles worth pursuing are those that advance the whole society and enable all human beings to evolve to a new and higher stage of their human potential.

Knowledge must move from perception to conception; in other words, knowledge and struggle begin by perceiving your own reality. But it must have the aim of developing beyond what you yourself or your own group can perceive to wider conceptions that are based upon the experiences of the whole history of mankind. The only way that anyone can take this big step of moving beyond perception to conception is by recognizing and struggling against your own internal contradictions and weaknesses. Of these weaknesses, the most fundamental and most difficult to overcome, as a result of the specific history of U.S. society, is the tendency not to think at all but simply to react in terms of individual or ethnic self-interest.

Beginning in the mid-1970s, James and Grace Lee Boggs spoke every November to James Chaffers's class on urban redevelopment and social change in the School of Architecture and the Center for Afroamerican and African Studies (CAAS) at the University of Michigan. "Toward a New Concept of Citizenship" is the text of James Boggs's presentation to the class on November 9, 1976, just days after the election of Jimmy Carter as president. The National Organization for an American Revolution (NOAR) subsequently issued the text as a pamphlet.

Toward a New Concept of Citizenship

Last year when I spoke to this class, I talked about how, in the pursuit of individual success, millions of Americans have chosen the road of getting ahead in the economic arena. Therefore, we have become a nation of individualists who believe the further we get away from the communities or areas where we grew up, the more successful we are. In other words, the greater the distance we put between ourselves and other individuals from our past, the more we have achieved. Most Americans believe this—even if it means that we have to move every two or three years and live and work among strangers most of our adult life; even though it means that we, particularly women, have no relatives or childhood friends on whom we can depend for babysitting and day-to-day advice; and even though it means that we cannot depend upon our neighbors or others in the community to help raise our children or in emergencies.

I went on to show how our tendency to evaluate ourselves and other people by the status that we have achieved in our so-called progress on the ladder of success has now led to serious objective and subjective contradictions in our society. Our cities are mushrooming at the expense of the countryside; our economy is run by monstrous multinational corporations headed by executives and specialists who have no loyalty to this country or to any community. With every year, more and more of our old people and our young people, especially the black, the uneducated, and the unskilled, are reduced to parasites. And we have become more afraid of one another than people used to be of wild animals. Each person has become a lonely individual, narrowed down to a cog in a machine, with no individuality and no sense of citizenship. That is, we have no sense that our actions and decisions matter or that each of us has a responsibility for the whole society.

I explained that we are presently in this very dangerous situation because we have for so long believed that all our social and human problems could be solved by economic growth and advancing technology, and because we have left all the decisions with regard to our economy and the government to the professional politicians. That is why we got trapped in the war in Vietnam, that is why we had Watergate, and that is why we are totally alienated from one another as human beings even though, technologically, we are so advanced.

The Presidential Election

What has happened in recent weeks during the election campaign for the presidency has made all of this much clearer. Last week, the American people participated in another sweepstakes or horse race in which we went to the polls or racetrack to cast lots for our next president. By a mere shift in a few votes in each state, one man, Carter, won over another man, Ford, in a race one man had to win and whose outcome had been predicted by pollsters before we even went to the polls. Now the analysts and the pollsters are writing hundreds of articles on why Carter won over Ford but nothing about why millions of Americans continue to participate in this kind of sweepstakes every four years.

All of us witnessed the two conventions during the summer. We saw how a grand coalition of blacks, hardhats, women, project directors, and labor leaders, representing the outsiders in this society, came together and selected Carter to be the Democratic candidate because, out of all the Democratic horses, they felt he was the one who could win and therefore make it possible for them to get closer to the trough where the goodies of this society are distributed. On the other hand, we saw how the middle classes came together at the Republican convention and defeated the Reaganites who spoke for the big farmers, oil magnates, utilities, etc., because they felt Ford, as the incumbent who was closer to the center than Reagan, could win for the Republican Party.

In each group there were people who were antagonistic and competing with one another. But they put aside their differences long enough to draw up a party platform so that they could get to the main business—selecting a candidate who could win for the party. Therefore, after all the hullabaloo of drafting the party platform, this platform was never referred to again the day after the selection of the ticket. Neither candidate ran on the party platform. Nor was the convention ever referred to again during the whole campaign. It is as if the convention had never taken place and as if the platform adopted by the convention had been put through a paper shredder. So now we know, or should know, that the convention and all the so-called debates on the party platform were just another spectacle, a show that had been put on to entertain the American mass audience and to provide some suspenseful "happenings" around which the commercials could be telecast.

The result is that today we have a new president, but no one in the country knows what he stands for or what he will advocate in government policy. The president is only a personality who does not represent a body of political ideas and a party platform. He is an individual who will react to issues as they arise, wavering from one side to the other in making his decisions in accordance with how he and his staff estimate these decisions will help or hurt his chance for reelection. We did not elect a person representing a party to which he is accountable and which is accountable to him, a party that had developed a body of ideas and a program we could discuss, take sides on, and help implement. All we did was elect an individual who, we can be sure, will say the most popular thing at the right time and will avoid saying anything that will embarrass him or alienate too many sections of the population because this will endanger his reelection.

Thus, in essence, the presidential campaign was not a political campaign. It was not a campaign to make clear the mounting contradictions of this society and the choices *we* will have to make in order to resolve these contradictions. It did not give us any opportunity to develop ourselves politically through discussion and struggle over fundamental issues. All we did was go to the polls to vote for a personality the way that we might have gone to the racetrack. And now that the race is over, we have no role to play in making or in carrying out decisions.

In the meantime, while some people are speculating on *who* is going to get appointed to this and that post and what the president will not do on this or that issue, and *while* the sociologists are analyzing why and how people voted in order to provide the professional politicians with the date with which to figure out how to win the next elections, the system, that is, the government, the economy, and the society, is continuing on its not-so-merry way.

Bureaucracy as Usual

In Washington, the military-industrial complex and the welfare state are going ahead full steam. Military contracts are being negotiated and renegotiated, and the industries that are dependent upon these contracts are operating and tooling up, in complete confidence that they will continue to be an integral part of the economy. The housing, education, and welfare bureaucracy, which administers billions of dollars in construction contracts and social services, is continuing to administer these billions of dollars. The network of building contracts and real estate operators and education and welfare bureaucrats are going about their business as usual, confident that their part of the system will continue without fundamental change.

The only difference is that one group of individuals at the top of this bureaucracy— Republicans—will be displaced by another group of individuals—Democrats. In other words, Democrats and friends of these Democrats will now have a good chance to replace Republicans in the well-paying jobs that this bureaucracy controls from top to bottom. But nothing about government or the economy, what it does and how it works, will change. It will continue to be a warfare and welfare state because ever since the depression of the 1930s, it has been clear that the American economy would collapse if it were not for military production and for the billions of dollars handed out yearly in building contracts and various forms of benefits by the national government. The multinational corporations will continue to expand and the gulf between elite specialists and the unskilled mass will continue to grow. The main difference between Carter and Ford is that Carter will probably create more projects than Ford did because he has to placate the unions and the various minority groups that made his election possible. So, with Carter, the government and the system will become more of what it is already—a government and a system that is continually reducing more and more Americans to subjects and making a mockery of citizenship.

Now that elections are over, most people are saying that they are sick of politics, just as when the pro football or pro basketball seasons are over they say that they are tired of football or basketball and are ready for another sport. This is because, every year, politics in this country has become like professional sports or a huge spectacle in which the voters are passive spectators at a multimillion-dollar game between two teams, each competing to win so that the thousands of individuals who make up their staffs can control the big prize of hundreds of billions of dollars the government spends each year. Which team wins the presidency makes no more difference to the American government or the American economy. One president may have a different style than the other. For example, Carter's style is obviously more activist than Ford's, just as Princess Margaret's style is more flamboyant than Queen Elizabeth's. But whichever one is in the White House, the military-industrial complex and the welfare state continue to go ahead at full steam. The only difference is that more blacks and members of minority groups will now be drawn into the career of politics to become part of the apparatus of a half-million professional elected politicians, because electoral politics is one of the country's growth industries.

What Are Our Human Needs?

Now if this analysis is accurate—and it is an analysis everyone can verify from their own experience—what does it mean for the future? Does the future have to be just a continuation of the present or just more of the same? If so, are we ready to settle for a future in which each of us is constantly and increasingly being reduced to a subject or a cog in a machine? Are we ready to settle for a society in which each of us acquires more material things each year but is only a consumer and a contributor to the gross national product? Can we be satisfied that each of us can earn 10 percent more next year than this year? If so, how will we be able to judge when we have enough? Are we so greedy and arrogant that we are ready to say, as one of our leading tycoons said a century ago, "I will have enough only when I have it all and control it all." What is this "enough" we consider so important?

I raise these questions because nowadays most Americans have completely lost sight of the most fundamental qualities of living that any society must treasure and struggle to enhance if that society is to long endure. It has never been difficult to mobilize people to struggle for material needs because people know very well when their bellies are empty or when they are freezing because they lack shelter and clothing. But it is much more difficult to mobilize people to struggle for human needs because human needs reflect spiritual hungers that are much more difficult to articulate and make clear to oneself, let alone to other people. For example, in order to be human, we need to feel that we can walk the streets without fearing each other, that we don't need to spend millions of dollars each year on police dogs and security locks and electronic gadgets to protect our homes and our personal possessions, and that our security doesn't come from policemen or from police dogs but from the value and concern each of us has for the others because we value and cherish human beings more than we cherish material things and individual success.

In order to be human, we need to feel that we belong to a community where people of different ages and interests have grown to depend upon one another because over the years our personal lives and the life of the community have become interdependent. We need to feel that we can look to our neighbors for help in keeping the streets clean, in raising our children, in looking out for each other. In order to be human, we need to feel that the work we do is useful and that we are doing it not just for pay or profit but because it is socially necessary. That is, we are making things that people really need. In order to be human, we need to feel that we are in control of our lives. We need to believe that our decisions and actions make a difference in how we and our co-citizens live, in making our community one that we can be proud of, and in how our country is run.

Up to a few years ago, all over the world and even in the United States where economic success and individual social mobility have been more highly valued than anywhere else, people did value their social relations more than they valued material things. We did feel that we belonged to communities—to rural communities in the South and Midwest and to ethnic communities in the cities. We took pride in our work in the foundry, on the assembly line, and elsewhere, even when this work was dirty and unskilled, because we thought that it was socially necessary and that it was helping meet the real material needs of the people. We felt that our decisions and our actions and our struggles made a difference not only to our own lives but to the improvement of the whole country. So there was meaning to our economic struggles and political and social struggles.

It is only since the technological explosion made possible by World War II that all this has begun to change.

Today, as a result of our modern technology, we are an expanding mobile society of consumers, buying the products as fast as they can be produced and made known to us by advertising. Instead of being people, we have become masses, that is, individuals who believe that consumption and possession are what life is all about and therefore believe in ways that can be easily predicted by market researchers. The technology that we continue to develop is intervening with Nature itself, with the result that we live in constant danger of the whole planet being destroyed. The atmosphere and vegetation we depend upon for our sustenance are being fundamentally altered and even the chemistry of our bodies is being changed by such technological creations as the "pill." Meanwhile, as the quality of life continues to decline and the dangers to our planet increase, the only solutions that we can think of are in the form of more technology.

Yet as the recent election demonstrated, none of those who claim to be giving us political leadership thought these questions important enough to raise during the campaign. And most Americans continue to believe that some more of the same is what we need most. We have for so long been taught to believe that technology and economics or the creation and possession of more goods are the solution to all of our problems. Therefore, each of us continues to pursue this goal and to support political leaders who promise more of the same.

Here at the university, where you might expect that there would be some fundamental rethinking on these profound questions, we find the same thing taking place. Our universities are each year turning out more and more students with all kinds of degrees and skills to fit into and expand the existing system. Meanwhile, as the universities grow bigger and bigger, the ability of the students to make socially responsible decisions continues to decline. Instead of wondering about the need to develop people who are able to govern this country, the faculty and administration of the university continue to function in accordance with the pragmatic and utilitarian philosophy that if they equip students with the tools to earn a good living, they have done their job, despite the fact that all around the university and on campus itself, all of the students are being reduced to cogs in the machine of American economic and technological advancement; each student continues to think only of his or her individual ambitions and not of the needs of the whole society. So there is no movement on the campuses that is making a fundamental challenge to this system and this philosophy.

What Kind of Technology Do We Need?

The only difference between last year and this year is that the questions we raised last year have become more pressing and more obvious. This year we should know better than we did last year that we can't solve the problems of crime with more policemen and more locks, any more than we can build a sense of community with some new houses or shopping centers or Renaissance Centers. We can't solve the crisis of energy by the development of more technology because this new technology uses up as much energy in its production as it might save later and because there is only so much fossil fuel created by Nature. We can't solve the problems of pollution by building anti-pollution technology because the production of this new technology itself creates pollution. We can't resolve the question of national defense by producing more advanced types of bombs and bombers to kill more and more people more quickly because the people we seek to intimidate into submission by this technology are as capable of developing technology as we are. In other words, strange as it may seem to us today, the quality of life in our country cannot be fundamentally altered by more technology or more production. Technology does not and cannot substitute for the choices that we as human beings have to make as to what kind of society we want to live in and how much we are ready to struggle to bring that kind of society into being.

In fact, one of the main decisions that we have to make in this country is "What kind of technology should we develop?" and "Do we really want to keep some of the technology that we developed?" (e.g., the pill). Or "Should we repudiate the dictatorship of the technologically possible, which is the dictatorship under which we live today?" One of the most important things that we have to understand is that the technology we have is not value-free. It is a technology that has come out of a class society that has been more concerned with economic growth than it has been with human values and development, and which, therefore, has been producing more and more people at the bottom of the society and at the top of the age scale who have had no useful work to do, even if it means the destruction of communities and the countryside.

In a recent article of the local newspaper, I read that the head of the Department of Philosophy at the University of Michigan said that there are no great philosophers today because all philosophers today are pragmatists. That the head of a philosophy department of a great university could say this is a reflection of how little we in the United States understand about the role of philosophy in any society. What I think he was saying is that in the United States today we have accepted the philosophy of economic determinism. That is, we no longer believe in the capacity of human beings to determine the course of the society but instead accept the philosophy that human consciousness is determined by economic conditions. At the same time we in the United States also accept the philosophy of individualism. We have no idea of the power that is within us as human beings to struggle together to resolve contradictions that are in every society. We believe that the individual should strive to get ahead materially regardless of what is happening to the society and to others in the society.

It was this philosophy that enabled people of the United States to go their own way for so many years, pursuing economic development and material needs and wants even when they knew that this was taking place at the expense of blacks and other minorities. It was this philosophy that made it possible for us to go into Asia and into Latin America, supporting dictatorial regimes, regardless of how these regimes were trampling on the dignity of their peoples, as long as they gave us ready access to their raw materials and were ready to join our cold war with communism.

It is this philosophy that enables our oil consortiums to make deals with so many Arab rulers to exploit the oil resources even though they can see all around them that the people in these countries are like feudal subjects without any role in making decisions as to what is going to happen to their national resources.

WE CAN'T GO HOME AGAIN

What we are discovering is that this pragmatic philosophy is catching up with us. The joy ride we were on, having things more or less our way, is coming to an end because of the standing up of the third world and because of the limit of the world's natural resources. We face these new problems, which are the result of the solutions we made in the past. In resolving or negating the problems, however, those solutions created new contradictions, many of which serve as dehumanizing factors in our society. Everything we are and have become is based on decisions we make and have made in the past. We live in a society that was created by the ideas and deeds of us as human beings. Our forefathers and foremothers, as we are doing now, made the choices and decisions that made us Americans, and we must continue to do so, as we struggle to become more human human beings. Nothing can be the same any more. We are at a transition point in the whole world and in our own country, and yet, because we have not tried over the years to develop standards for our actions based upon human values, we today have no standards by which to make the decisions that have become so vital to our continuing existence.

We can't decide what should be and what should not be because we have taken so many things for granted as our due. We don't know what is criminal and what is not criminal, what is exploitative and what is not exploitative, what is racist and what is not racist, sexist or nonsexist. All we know is that life itself is becoming more insecure everyday even though we have more of the material things we thought would provide us with security than any human beings ever had. We have more industry than any country in the world, and yet we have millions of unemployed who are completely outside these industries. We have more hospitals than any country in the world and yet we have millions of mentally deranged individuals, alcoholics, drug addicts, and chronically ill persons. We have more individual houses than all the world yet we have millions living in dilapidated, unsanitary houses. We have more jails and detention institutions than any other country in the world, and yet we still have millions outside these institutions, committing antisocial acts. But we can't incarcerate them in these institutions because there is no room. We have more school building and learning institutions than any country in the world, and a larger percentage of our population attends these institutions than that of any other country; yet we have millions of semiliterate Americans. And even those who have gone to these institutions only know something about their own little field and have no idea of how to think about the whole society.

When questions of this profundity are raised, most Americans resort to blaming our problems on the politicians—or on the "system." They do this because Americans today think so much like victims. We find it easier to blame somebody else rather than to ask ourselves what is it that *we* have done or have not done to bring this situation into existence.

Changing Ourselves First

However, we can't just continue to shift the burden onto somebody else's shoulders, expecting those people to change when they are the ones who benefit most by the situation.

What we must begin to do is what we find hardest to do—confront our own individualism and materialism, our own going along with the system, which has made possible the strengthening and expansion of the system. When we do this, we are ready to begin the struggle for the new theory and practice of citizenship so urgently needed in the United States today. Most Americans think citizenship is a question of where you were born or of going to the polls to vote for politicians. Few of us realize that this nation was founded by a great revolution which inaugurated an age of revolutions all over the world because it gave men and women a new concept of themselves as self-governing human beings, i.e., as citizens rather than subjects. Instead of looking to kings and bishops to make the difficult decisions necessary to the functioning of any society—as the masses in Europe and elsewhere were doing at the time—the men and women of America who made the American Revolution said that people could and should think for themselves and should and could accept responsibility for making social, economic, and political decisions. Instead of looking at history as that which can be made only by elites, they believed that people who are ready to work with their minds and hands could build a new world.

In other words, instead of being masses, who think of themselves as victims and only make demands on others, they were ready to make demands on themselves. Based on this new concept of citizenship and these new principles of the fundamental worth of human beings, they were able through revolutionary struggle to transform themselves into a people, i.e., human beings ready to unite with others to struggle for a better future for themselves and their children.

As you continue your schooling in order to acquire skills to get a job—and I am not suggesting that you quit this—I hope you will give serious thought to this question of the responsibilities of citizenship.

Today as a result of developments over the last two hundred years, the concrete questions we face are completely different from and infinitely more complex than those faced by the men and women who made the first American Revolution. The coming American revolution will not be made to complete the first revolution (as most radicals and liberals believe) but to answer new questions that have been created by the successes that we have had in developing our economy of abundance and our incredible technology in the last two hundred years. But the fundamental decision remains the same—to believe in the inherent power of human beings to begin afresh, to put public good over private interests, and to become active participants in the ideological and practical struggles necessary to rid ourselves of an economic and political system that reduces us to subjects so that as active citizens, together, we can create a better society for ourselves and our posterity.

This country is still in its infancy. The ancestors of the overwhelming majority of today's Americans were not among the few millions who founded this nation two hundred years ago and established the political and social patterns that have brought us to our present crisis. The ancestors of today's blacks were here—but they were excluded from participation in the political and social process, even though their labors were building the infrastructure that made possible this country's rapid economic development. Thus the people now living in the United States have had no real experience of the great revolutionary struggles by which any great nation is created.

That political and humanizing experience still lies before us all!

"The Next Development in Education" is a speech delivered at Wayne State University in Detroit on February 28, 1977.

The Next Development in Education

I want to thank you for inviting me here to speak to you, especially since I have not come here to extol you for the sacrifices you are making in the pursuit of knowledge. Actually, I believe that the way most of you are pursuing knowledge is incorrect because you are pursuing what I call "received" knowledge. That is, you are trying to absorb information, facts, theories, etc., which have already been discovered or created by others, in the belief that if you can just absorb enough of this knowledge, you will qualify as "educated." This means that you think of education as a "thing" that is stored up somewhere. All you have to do is open the Pandora's box, get a good look at its contents, and, presto, you are educated.

Now I used to think that way myself—so don't feel so guilty or unfinished for thinking that way. When I was growing up, my mother kept urging me to get an education, just as so many mothers and fathers do today. In fact, in a book I wrote in 1963, called *The American Revolution: Pages from a Negro Worker's Notebook,* I described how my mother wanted me to go to school down South to get the ability to read and write, which was what at the time she considered an education. In order to inspire me to do so, she told me time and again how, if only she had been able to read and write, she could have gotten a job cooking for some very rich white people because rich white people at that time wanted a cook for whom they could leave a note saying what to prepare for dinner that night. Thus, for my mother, education was the ability to read and write. Not only people like my mother down in Alabama used to think that way. For many years in this country, reading and writing were viewed by most poor people and even some middle-class people as the essence of education. Even today, when many people say to their children, "You'd better get you an education," what they are thinking of, first of all, is being able to read and write enough to fill out an application form and, after that, enough skill to hold down a job. In other words, for most Americans, black or white, education is for the sake of getting a good job, meaning one that requires the least amount of manual labor. If you drive around most cities, you see signs everywhere, "Go to school to get a job" or "Go to college to get a job." The main difference between yesterday and today is that to get a decent job, it is not enough to be able to read, write, multiply, and divide. Now you need at least four years of college to get a job held by people who in the 1930s were ninth- or tenth-grade dropouts from high school because prior to World War II—which brought on the boom in college education with the GI Bill of Rights—most teenagers dropped out of school to go to work.

Only the elite children of the upper-middle class and rich people went on to college. So a college graduate was looked upon by most people in the community as something very special. Today everyone of college age who has the desire to go to college and the stamina to stay is in college. We have begun to tie our whole identity to the degrees we have acquired in college and to the status job these degrees entitle us to. People say, "I am a lawyer, or a doctor, or a teacher, or a scientist," meaning that they have the certificate or degree that entitles them to call themselves such. We have reduced our identities to the lowest possible denominator of what degrees we have that license us to work. In other words, if you are a ditchdigger, you are no more than a ditchdigger because you didn't go to school to become something else.

On the other hand, I believe that a human being is much more than what he or she does for a living and that your job or profession (which is what people call a job with a title) says very little about the person behind the job or profession. I always said, when I worked at Chrysler—and I worked there on the line for twenty-eight years—that I was a factory worker, but I was much more than a factory worker because I was concerned about the society I lived in and I was determined to play a part in shaping the minds of the people I related to because I believe that the world we live in has been made by people and therefore that it can be changed by people who accept responsibility for advancing humankind.

When we here today identify a person by what he or she does for a living, we have to be very careful not to be so narrow-minded as to assume that a person is limited by what he or she does for a living. It makes sense to have a limited view of an animal like a fox or a squirrel because animals live by instincts and shortly after birth are able to do all that they will ever be able to do as long as they live. Human beings, on the other hand, are born with fewer abilities than any other animal. But because they have a mind, they can think and develop their minds. They can reflect on the past and project ideas of what they think the future should be. They can change their minds. If they have been moving in an incorrect way, they can evaluate their mistakes and change course. In other words, what others in the past have decided and what we may have gone along with without questions up to now, does not have to continue. The world we live in is in a process of constant change. The material base is constantly shrinking in some ways and constantly expanding in others. People are constantly changing as they discover that ideas that once worked now only cause deeper and deeper crises. You and I are constantly changing. Everyone of us is a different person from what we were last year at this time, and the world we live in today as we approach the 1980s is very different from the world we struggled to change in the 1960s. Change, then, is the order of society whether we like it or not. We can sit back and just let it happen to us, or we can decide that we are going to decide what changes are made.

The concept of education has gone through many changes in the last few thousand years as human beings moved from one stage of development to another. When the

Greeks used the word "education" 2,500 years ago, they thought of education as the development of young boys to become philosophers who could then govern over those whose entire lives were spent in making a living, in other words, what we would today call "the masses." Because it took so much time and human energy in those days to provide for the material necessities of the society, people thought that only a relatively few could rule; therefore, the elite concentrated on imparting wisdom to those few so that they could rule wisely. The same concept of education prevailed among the Romans, who thought of education as leadership. In fact, the Latin "to lead" is at the root of our word "education." Much the same practice of examination in the classics was used to select individuals who would become members of the bureaucracy or what they called mandarins.

In Europe during the feudal period, rule depended more on the military or warlike skills, which enabled one feudal lord to protect his domain from another. So the offspring of kings and queens, lords and barons, only received a smattering of what we would today call culture, while their main training was in skills like swordsmanship and horse riding. No one even thought of education for the common people. They were only "masses," that is to say, serfs who had not yet arrived at the plateau of believing that they had the ability to determine their own destiny—or a sense of peoplehood.

In the sixteenth century a change took place in the concept of education with the Reformation, which launched the idea that ordinary people had the right to interpret the Bible for themselves and should not be dependent on priests and bishops. The people who launched this idea and made it a reality were people who could read and write. So reading and writing became terribly important to people because if you couldn't read the Bible, you couldn't govern yourselves in the congregations, which were the main social life in the communities, and you had no voice in the church, which had enormous power.

However, the greatest leap in the concept of education came with the American Revolution, which proclaimed to the world the idea of self-government or citizenship for ordinary people. In other words, if people were to participate in the ideological and practical struggles that led to the American Revolution, they had to be able to read and write the pamphlets and broadsides that flooded the colonies. If the Committees of Correspondence were to become a serious factor in the struggle to unify the colonists around common goals, people had to be able to write and read the letters that were dispatched from one colony to the other as fast as horses could take the carriages and their riders.

Thus, we can see that for over two thousand years the concept of education has been tied to the purpose of governing. Not until the nineteenth century in the United States, with the speed-up of the Industrial Revolution, side by side with the tremendous surge in immigration into this country of people from all over the world, did the concept of education become tied to strictly economic goals. For the first time, education was conceived as teaching the illiterate masses and their sons and daughters to read and write so they could work in factories. And for the first time we began to create a huge cast of teachers whose own livelihood came from teaching the illiterate masses to read and write so that they could get and hold a job.

For the purpose of rapid industrialization and the Americanization of immigrants, teachers had to be turned out like sausages, so there was a rapid expansion of teacher colleges or what were then called "normal schools." At first these teachers were mostly the sons and daughters of the lower-middle classes, skilled workers, farmers, and shop-keepers, and usually of northern European or Jewish descent. Not until the Great Depression does emphasis begin to be placed upon keeping millions of Italian, Slavic, and Afro-American children of the working class in school because industry no longer needs their labor in the factory. In 1900, only 6 percent of high school age young people graduated from high school. Now the majority are expected to stay in high school until graduation and considered failures if they don't. To keep these children from the working classes—who were not considered material for higher education—in school, a major part of the curriculum is devoted to sports. And young people of Slavic, Italian, and Afro-American descent begin to see the prospects for a good livelihood for themselves in becoming teachers.

During the 1930s, people still believed that a high school education was enough to get you a decent job. However, with the end of World War II and the introduction into the factories of the technology that had been developed during the war, industry was automated to the point that there were relatively few jobs for the millions of children from the lower classes, black and white. Therefore, a host of junior colleges and community colleges were built all over the country. Now high school young people were persuaded that a high school diploma was not enough to get a decent job. You need a college education. To get the job of a salesman or a mechanic or even a ditchdigger or hundreds of other jobs that had formerly been done by people who could barely read and write, you needed a certificate saying that you had completed a course in that field.

Therefore, we have created today the second-largest industry in the nation, a network of institutions called schools and colleges, in which hundreds of thousands of teachers and administrators have a vested interest. These schools and colleges are for the purpose of sorting out the winners from the losers, just as football and basketball tryouts at the beginning of the school year sort out the winners from the losers.

Now we all realize that if you have thousands and thousands of high school students who are local stars on the high school teams, only a few will make it to the "pros" because there is just so much room at the top. But few people stop to think about what happens to the hundreds of thousands of losers who don't make it. Having spent most of their young lives preparing to become "pros" to the point that they can't even read the name of the street they live on, they suddenly find themselves rejected. Then we wonder why they turn to any form of "making it" that they can find, including pimping off the young girls who flocked around them in high school stardom or just vandalizing the communities in which they still live.

Meanwhile, with millions coming out of college every year, we find that it isn't just those who put all their eggs into the basket of sports who are rejects. Thousands of those who were sifted out as winners and went on to get degree after degree from college find themselves out of jobs as the military-industrial complex changes defense contracts. Today even teachers find themselves looking for work, any kind of work.

But few people are ready to recognize that the contradiction of unemployment in the United States is not due to the lack of schooling among the unemployed but is rooted in a capitalist system that has put the goal of rapid economic development and expanding profits over human development. In other words, as long as this society is based upon giving priority to economic development and higher profits over human development, we will continue to install automation to replace human beings any-where and anytime and justify this by calling it progress, even though it makes losers out of at least 25 percent of young people, black and white. Meanwhile, just as for years the white ruling class in this country justified the racial and economic exploitation of black people by insisting that we were inferior, the ruling class and the education establishment, which now include administrators and teachers of all ethnic groups, will continue to tell young people that they are out of work because they do not have enough schooling.

We must be clear that the bourgeoisie has not brought this situation on all by itself. Most Americans accepted the idea that education is for the purpose of getting a job and that if you don't have a job, it is because you haven't gotten yourself an education. The fundamental assumption in most people's minds is that if you get enough knowl-edge and skill to perform a paying job, you can earn enough money to solve all other problems, so the goal of education is reduced to money, and money becomes the key to solving all other social and political problems.

Now I should not have to remind you that this is not true, because most of you can remember a time when you didn't have as much money or as good a job as you have now, and yet there was not the same deterioration in all social and political relations as we have today. Most Americans are better-off financially than we were forty years ago; yet all around us we are experiencing a total crisis in our families, our communities, and our local, state, and federal institutions as each American goes his or her individual way, trying to get enough dollars to purchase happiness.

Everyday it is becoming more painful for us to cope with the deterioration of our society because we continue to believe in concepts that were created by people at an-other state of history for completely different purposes—for example, in this case the concept of education to get a job, which was begun in the late nineteenth century at the height of the Industrial Revolution. Now we have come full circle on the concept of education. Not only do we believe that education is something like money in the bank that you go to school and get, but we have lost touch with our own reality because we believe that what was true at one time in history remains true for all time instead of recognizing that truth like everything else is relative and that what was true at one stage in history is not necessarily true at another stage. In fact, there are very very few absolute truths and no static ones. Because most of us believe that concepts created in the past are forever valid and that all we have to do is keep acting in accordance with those concepts even if they don't work, we don't even try to exercise our own capacities for creating new truths, new ideas, and new concepts. So we don't use our minds creatively and after a while, we find that they don't even work to absorb "received" knowledge because they have wasted away from lack of use in the creative and reflective arena, which is what keeps our minds healthy and alive.

Today all we hear from parents and administrators and teachers is that we need to extend the right to education to more people and that in order to pursue this goal we need more money. In other words, we need more of the same even if it is not working. We don't stop to ask ourselves whether what we are doing is correct or incorrect, whether it meets the needs of our times or doesn't meet the needs of our times. Thus we never face the reality that there is contradiction in all things, or that there is a bad side even to good things, and that therefore if you continue to pursue any one thing, single-mindedly, you are bound to end up in crisis.

Today we have to ask ourselves some very different questions if we are to find new answers that can be the basis for the solution to our crisis. The questions we ask are going to be very difficult for us to ask because we have gone on believing for so long that education is the road to economic success that we have not even begun to evaluate what happens to a people who treasure economic benefits and economic development more than they treasure human relations and human benefits.

Today I would like to suggest to you that we need to change our concept of education from the concept of education for earning to the concept of education for the purpose of governing. Now I hope that when you hear this, you don't just jump to the conclusion that I am proposing that we need education for the purpose of becoming or electing mayors or state senators. Because as we should be able to see today, we have all kinds of mayors and state senators who are not prepared for governing, and we have all kinds of electors whose only concept of governing is the mechanical one of going to the polls every few years to elect somebody else to look out for their interests. By governing, I mean the activity of governing, that is, the continuing exercise of our distinctively human capacity to make meaningful choices that human beings can make: between policies that will benefit our communities and our posterity and those that serve only our immediate self-interest. In other words, I am talking about preparing ourselves to use that all-around capacity that only human beings have: to think about the society we live in, determine what will advance our society, and then join with others to make the politically conscious and socially responsible decisions that will help mold and shape our society in the direction that we believe it should go.

Before we can entertain the idea of a new philosophy of education, we have to be very clear that American education for nearly a hundred years has been based upon the philosophy of individualism. According to this philosophy the ambitious individual of average or above-average ability from the lower and middle classes is encouraged to climb up the social ladder out of his or her class and community, leaving behind those who are less ambitious or less unscrupulous or less able. If in this process they conduct themselves in a way that meets the social standards and value-free philosophy of those in power (who are always observing them and grading their behavior), they will be rewarded by promotion into higher echelons of the system. Thus, in the final analysis, the American system of education, like all systems of education, has served to perpetuate the present system by constantly absorbing new individuals into it.

If we recognize that this is what American education has been, then we won't just blame the system. Instead we will be wondering how we can change it, since we see that it no longer works, and how we can create another system, another reality, which will be a better way to advance humankind. That is the starting point of all philosophy.

In order to develop the concept of education to govern, we have to begin with the recognition that the foundation of good government is the moral development of young people. This moral development must begin in the home or family where the child learns in practice and in face-to-face relations certain values and principles, such as the importance of telling the truth and of doing one's share of work around the house—because truth telling and doing one's share are the basis of trust and cooperation, without which no family and no community can long survive. The school must uphold these values and not see itself as a value-free institution. But the instilling of these values must begin in the family.

Next comes the development in the child of the skills that are necessary for people to make a productive contribution to the whole society. Particularly in a highly technical society such as we live in today, it is necessary that young people, female and male, be trained in technical skills. But training in technical skills should not take place as it does today, chiefly through books and in the schools. Instead, young people, from an early age, should have the opportunity to do some kind of productive work that will contribute to the overall society both because this is the best way to learn and because it is impossible to keep young people as parasites in school for fifteen to twenty years and then expect them to be responsible citizens.

After we have understood clearly the need for these two essentials, i.e., the need for moral development of young people and the need to train them in technical skills through the process of actual work, we can then begin asking ourselves some more concrete questions as to how to reorganize our schools.

Questions

How do we reorganize our schools so that we can develop our youth not only in theory but in practice so that in the process of work they will learn how important workmanship is to their development as human beings?

Should all schools have gardens and greenhouses so that young people can learn how to grow food as well as restore their relationship to nature, and should all the children have to cook and serve their own food in the course of this learning more about nutrition and budgeting?

Why shouldn't the young people in each school have the responsibility for caring for the trees, the playgrounds, and roads in their neighborhoods?

Should all students at colleges and universities be on a work-study program that involves them in the labor and creative work around the university, including the construction and design of new buildings, the management of the university finances, the legal work, and the running of the schools' health clinics? Why shouldn't those studying social work be working in the community with young people and old on projects to clean and fix up the community, including rehabilitating old houses, cleaning up alleys, and turning vacant lots into playgrounds for the recreation of the community?

Why shouldn't students in the sciences be given real problems to solve, such as the best ways to conserve energy sources, like water, coal, and oil, and to discover new ways to utilize old energy sources like coal and solar energy?

Should we consider closing down TV to about six hours a day so that we can begin to have serious discussions among ourselves as to the future of our society, get to know our families, friends, and neighbors again, and learn to use our minds instead of becoming like vegetables because we have kept our eyes glued to the idiot box for so long?

What human purposes should sex serve now that we no longer need to reproduce so many children in order to perpetuate the species and to maintain us in our old age, and now that contraception enables us to separate sex from pregnancy? How can we keep sex from being used as a means for the most unscrupulous exploitation and corruption of young people? This has now become a very real question for all levels of education today.

What kind of political system do we need that will involve all citizens in a process of responsible social decision making that will take the place of the kind of sweepstakes or lottery in which we are now asked to engage every few years? What is politics anyway?

These are just some of the questions we must now begin to ask ourselves. We have never asked them before, not because our minds were not capable of answering them but because we didn't realize that our minds were for the purpose of asking and creating the answers to questions like these. Instead we thought that our minds were like cameras, only reflecting theories, facts, and information that had already been created by others. Now we must recognize that knowledge is not something static. It is something that human beings like ourselves create through our reflections and practice.

Of course, I can't begin to raise all the questions that we have to ask ourselves as we approach the end of the twentieth century and the beginning of the twenty-first. What I would suggest to you is that after the discussion, you look at some of the materials that my comrades and I have brought with us. We are members of Advocators[*] and in the last few years have been asking ourselves some of these fundamental questions because we recognized that after a society has begun to rebel against old values on the scale of the rebellions of the 1960s, it is useless to try to build a new society unless you are ready to think seriously about the next development of humankind.

---

[*] A group of black radicals in Detroit formed by James and Grace Lee Boggs in 1970. The group's original name was Committee for Political Development (CPD), but by the mid-1970s CPD renamed itself Advocators. In 1978 Advocators joined with similar groups across the country and evolved into a new multiracial organization called the National Organization for an American Revolution (NOAR). —Ed.

"Liberation or Revolution?" is a speech delivered at Stanford University in March 1978 during a symposium titled "What Is Black Liberation?" In 1980 the National Organization for an American Revolution (NOAR) issued the speech as a pamphlet that featured images created by artist Tom Feelings.

Liberation or Revolution?

I want to thank you for inviting me to speak to you. I also want to warn you that what I am going to say may not please you. But it has to be said if I am to discharge my responsibility to speak the truth on what liberation is and what it is not.

In every period of history, there are those few who try to define the state of the particular society and the principal contradictions around which those who are concerned about the society should mobilize themselves at that particular time.

Any understanding of where we are, in the United States today, in the year 1978 must, *at the very least,* begin with an understanding of where the world was right after World War II. At the same time, the old Western alliance had been shattered by Hitler and Tojo. The British Empire, having crumbled, was being liquidated. The people in the colonial countries were beginning to stir.

The United States had come out of the war as the world's most powerful nation. But a few questions were already being raised as to the purpose of our existence as a nation.

For a brief period during the Eisenhower years of the 1950s, it seemed that these questions were premature. To most people, preoccupied with the pursuit of goods that were pouring off the nation's production lines, it seemed that the United States could continue on its merry and not-so-merry way dominating the world.

Then, suddenly, a giant within our nation, which had lain dormant for years, began to stir. Black people, especially southern black people who had been systematically damned by racism, began to ask what should be the relationship between one set of human beings—black—and another set of human beings—white. It was no mystery that the stirrings of black people within the United States coincided with those people of color in Asia, Africa, and Latin America. People of color inside the United States and people of color outside the United States had not only been *participants* in World War II. They had also been *observers.* They were aware that World War II had been a struggle between two blocs for world mastery. But they were also aware that it had been a struggle for the minds of people all over the world as to what should be our way of life in the twentieth century. People of color recognized that Europeans who had dominated the world for four centuries were now in deep crisis. So both in the United States and outside the United States they began to feel and to believe that there could be another way of life for them. They began to *dare to dream* that they could shape their own future.

How Movements Have Developed

When human beings begin to question existing reality in this way, they are at the starting point of all philosophy. They may or may not go on to create a new philosophy. But when they question the philosophy that has up to now justified their oppression, their questioning contains the opportunity for them to create a new philosophy. Most movements, however, do not begin with recognizing the need to create a new philosophy. Instead, those who participate in the movement believe that if they only exert enough pressure on those in power, they can make them share the rights and privileges they have been denied. In other words, they believe that all they have to do is reform the system to make it serve their needs.

To understand the black movement *after* World War II, it is helpful to compare and contrast it with the labor movement that erupted during the Great Depression *before* World War II. The black movement set out to establish the dignity of blacks as the labor movement had established the dignity of labor. But the contradictions faced by the black movement or the civil rights movement were far more complex than those of the labor movement.

In the 1930s, millions of Americans were living a Tobacco Road existence. They were ill fed, ill clothed, and ill housed. People of working age wandered from one part of the country to another, seeking employment where there was no employment, glad when they could get a crust of bread at the back door from a sympathetic housewife in exchange for cutting the grass or chopping some wood. At that time, the population of the United States was about 150 million. One-third of these were without the elementary means of survival. There was no welfare state and none of the social services to which we have become so accustomed today. Fifty million Americans were dependent upon the bread lines set up by the Salvation Army or other charitable institutions.

This was the common condition and experience that united Americans of all ethnic groups and in every section of the country, making it possible for the labor movement to rise so spontaneously and almost overnight establish the dignity of labor.

The black movement, on the other hand, faced the contradiction that Americans of all ethnic groups and all classes had been directly benefiting for centuries by systematically keeping blacks at the bottom so that every other group in American society could climb up the social and economic ladder on their backs. The black movement faced not only class and economic contradictions but class *and* race contradictions, with race playing the principal role. So when the black movement began to struggle for inclusion of blacks in the American way of life, it represented a threat to the way of life that had become possible for Americans through the exclusion of blacks.

Yet, despite these contradictions, blacks were able to create a self-developing movement that for more than ten years constantly gained momentum and rallied behind it not only blacks but every progressive individual and group in our country. That is because it was *not just a pressure group for the rights of blacks.* Equally important, and in fact more important as we look back today, it confronted every American on the fundamental question of what should be the relationship between human beings. It made every white American question his or her humanity as they had never been forced to question before.

In the course of challenging the consciousness of every American in this way, the movement was also able to challenge every institution in our society and shatter all the truths and traditions that had been holding these institutions and our entire society together.

Having thus disrupted the old social order, it laid the basis for the anti–Vietnam War movement to emerge and expose the war in Vietnam as a war to reinforce colonialism and commit genocide against a people of color. Like its predecessor, the abolitionist movement of the pre–Civil War period, the black movement also aroused women to consciousness of *their* oppression. It thus helped bring into being the modern women's movement in raising the most fundamental question of what should be the relationships between human beings in a technologically advanced society, as well as the need for everyone, men and women, to struggle to become a more complete human being. As a result, our society today on every level is grappling with the *oldest* oppression in human history—the oppression of women—*and also the newest questions* that are unique to an advanced country like the United States—our psychic needs as human beings.

Most of us here today have no trouble recognizing that the black movement of the 1950s and the 1960s did more than any movement in the history of this country to enlarge the consciousness of Americans. *However,* what most of us hate to admit is that *that movement has now become history. It is over.* And therefore, we are confronted today with new and more challenging questions brought about partly because we once dared to ask new questions and partly because the questions that we asked were not profound enough.

We did not realize (how could we have realized this since it was our first experience with a movement that went so deep into the contradictions of our society) that once a movement is launched with the aim of resolving one set of contradictions and is powerful enough to shatter the truths and traditions that had previously held the society together, *then* we are confronted with new and more complex contradictions.

THE BLACK MOVEMENT NO LONGER EXISTS

Most of us are aware that the black movement of the 1960s has splintered into various tendencies since the rebellions of 1967 and 1968. These tendencies range all the way from those who think that all blacks have to do is support the continuing expansion of American capitalism and catch the crumbs as they trickle down to us to the Pan-Africans who talk about going back to Africa while they continue to enjoy the comforts of the American way of life, particularly around the universities.

Today, the many programs the Johnson administration created to prevent further rebellions have achieved their purpose of pacification. Millions of blacks today have been incorporated into the electoral machinery of bourgeois politics, into the universities, and into the administration of the welfare state at every level. Today the lifestyle and the goals of these blacks for themselves and for their children are no different from the individualistic and materialistic goals of white middle-class Americans. Whatever Johnson left undone has been completed by Carter, who took advantage of the Watergate scandals of the Republican administration to pull everybody together into one big pacification package at the Democratic Convention in 1976. Each group, labor, blacks, women, liberals, and conservatives, smelling victory for the Democratic Party, was able to submerge differences long enough to get Carter elected. As a result, blacks have become just another self-interest group like labor, concerned only with what benefits them and the hell with everybody else.

Thus, a movement that had aroused the hopes and changed the consciousness of so many millions and inspired every progressive individual in our country to believe that at last we could create a new way of life that would put people above things has been reduced to a bunch of little sects, spouting slogans such as liberation, affirmative action, Pan-Africanism, etc., slogans they have picked up from revolutionary struggles in other parts of the world and have no meaning in our country because they are not based upon *our* reality and *our* history as Americans.

In this situation, when confusion is so rampant among those who consider themselves part of the movement or would like to be part of the movement, the question is no longer what the capitalists or the Democrats or the Republicans or anybody else have done or didn't do or are doing to us. It is *what we are doing to ourselves* that we must investigate. It is our confusion that needs clearing up.

New and More Complex Questions

First of all, we have to understand that we live in a country with extraordinary material resources. In addition, the United States has enough power to take what it needs from other countries to pacify its own population for some time to come. We also have to be very clear in our minds that American capitalism is so productive that it has made it possible and indeed finds it necessary today to encourage those on welfare to consume on a scale that Marx and the Marxists never thought would be possible under capitalism. Moreover, since the rebellions, capitalism has promoted blacks to positions of foremen, school superintendents, principals, and mayors of cities to a degree that ten years ago would have sounded like science fiction.

So if you are waiting for the capitalist system to collapse because of the demands you make on it for more of this or that, *you are living on illusions.* In every crisis, American capitalism has been flexible enough, resourceful enough, and expedient enough to negate the most pressing contradiction it faced. In each case, the negation by capitalism of the most pressing contradiction achieved the objective of keeping power in the hands of the state, which is the main objective of any capitalist power or even of any socialist power when it is in crisis. (I think that it is important for us to recognize that socialist states also want to keep power because more people today live under socialist states than under capitalist states and this trend toward socialist states will undoubtedly continue in other parts of the world.)

The questions we have to ask ourselves, therefore, are much more complex than the simple ones most radicals ask. The questions we have to ask ourselves are not just the questions of how to end discrimination or bring about greater job equality between blacks, Chicanos, Asians, and whites. The kinds of questions we ask will determine the kinds of answers we are satisfied with. If we ask simple questions, we will be satisfied with simplistic answers.

As I said earlier, in our society today as a result of the movements of the 1960s, all past truths about the most fundamental ingredients of human life, the meaning of freedom, of work, of the family, of politics, have been shattered. Only if we struggle to create new truths about these fundamentals will we be seeking the kinds of answers that have now become necessary to build a society where we can live together in relationships of mutual respect, cooperation, and responsibility.

LIBERATION GROUPS ARE PRESSURE GROUPS

It is very easy to spout phrases like affirmative action and liberation if you are satisfied with quick and simplistic answers. Since the black movement became defunct in the early 1970s, all kinds of groups are talking about liberation. Gays demand liberation, prisoners demand liberation, blacks demand liberation, radical feminists demand liberation. These groups call themselves movements but they are pressure groups, not movements. Each one wants to do its "own thing" and puts pressure, especially on other groups, to make its particular "own thing" the most urgent thing for everybody else. That is what each of these groups means by "liberation": the opportunity and the support from others to help them achieve some form of rights for their particular group—like civil rights, which is rapidly becoming to mean freedom *from responsibility* to society rather than the ability to be freed from something that has held you back in order to be able to make a contribution to the advancement of the whole.

If you reflect on what is happening, you would realize that if all these groups achieved the liberation they demand, our society would be in even deeper crisis and chaos than it is today because in essence, each group is talking about freedom without responsibility. They refuse to recognize that freedom is not a *thing* that somebody can give you like a watch or a car. *Freedom is an opportunity to build relationships* with others. You struggle for freedom from one kind of relationship, for example, discrimination and segregation, so that you will be free *to* build other relationships that will advance not only yourself but the whole society. That was the original concept of freedom that inspired the black movement and gave it enormous power to mobilize others.

However, since the decline of the black movement of the early 1970s, blacks and all those who pattern themselves after the black movement have lost this concept of freedom. Instead, blacks and others have been thinking and acting like victims. They have no concept of why blacks struggled for freedom down through the years. They have no concept of the power within even the most oppressed individual to make decisions that will advance the rest of society. They have no idea of the way in which blacks, down through the years, despite the most degrading conditions human beings have ever endured, refused to see themselves only as victims but continued to affirm and instill in their children the sense of their unconquerable human identity and dignity. Today, black militants have only contempt for their parents and grandparents and great-grandparents. Having lost any belief in their own selves as human beings, they go around blaming everybody but themselves. They see the cause of their condition only in external forces or external enemies.

Why is it that, having lived through one of the most momentous periods in human history, a period when millions of people were out in the streets, demonstrating their belief that there is another way for human beings to live together, most people today are far more empty, far more cynical, far more full of self-doubt than our parents were despite their worse condition? There are two main reasons for our present demoralization. On the one hand, once the system began handing out more crumbs and liberals began to win elections for themselves by encouraging people to ask for more crumbs, most people began to look to those in power to solve our problems rather than look to ourselves for solutions.

On the other hand, those who consider themselves "movement people" began to grab political ideas that had worked for revolutionary struggles in other countries instead of doing the patient theoretical work necessary to work out the political ideas and political solutions that are based on *our* situation, *our* history, and *our* country.

WHERE DO IDEAS COME FROM?

Now political solutions do not come out of the air. To arrive at political solutions, you have to know where your political ideas come from. For example, the concept of the third world was evolved at the Bandung Conference in 1955 when the colonial peoples of Asia, Africa, and Latin America met and announced that a new force had emerged in the world made up of those who had been systematically damned into underdevelopment by colonialism and imperialism. There were black Americans at the Bandung

Conference but they were more like observers than representatives. They were people of color like most of the people of the third world but they lived in the most highly industrialized and powerful country in the whole world.

Yet, over the last few years, every ethnic group of color in this country—blacks, Chicanos, Asians, Native Americans—has been calling itself "third world" and lumped together as "third world" peoples. At many colleges and universities, even women's studies is included under third world studies! But the only people in the United States today who are third world peoples are those who are foreign students or diplomatic representatives from colonial or neocolonial countries. The rest of us, whatever our color, are living in *this* country, which benefits from the exploitation of the third world.

In the same way, people in the black movement call themselves "Pan-Africans," ignoring the historical fact that Pan-Africanism is a concept that evolved out of the struggle of the colonized peoples in Africa to unify themselves so that they could struggle more effectively against colonial and imperialist domination.

These Pan-Africanists go around spouting catchwords and slogans such as "Black Americans can never be free until the African nation is free," which appeal, just like TV commercials, to the gullible or those who are satisfied with easy answers. But Africa is a continent, not a nation. Since 1963, most African countries have achieved their political independence, and today the African continent is made up of dozens of nations in the same way as the continents of Asia and Europe are made up of independent nations. These African nations still have to struggle against neocolonialism. But each has its own history and tradition, its own language, its own political identity. The ancestors of Alex Haley, the author of *Roots,* didn't just come from the continent of Africa. They came from a particular section of Africa that is now struggling to develop its nationhood. There is no such thing as the country or the nation of Africa. A Nigerian is not a Ghanaian and a Ghanaian is not an Ethiopian. Each is as different from the other as a Swede is from an Italian or a Pakistani is from a Japanese.

No Liberation from Struggles and Decisions

I emphasize this because if you keep mixing up political concepts, you end up in a situation where you have no grasp of reality. You become *paranoid,* which is what most blacks are today, living in a world of fantasy where you are only reacting to real or imagined grievances. If you don't know where the ideas in your head came from, you never know where you are going and you certainly will never be able to give leadership to anybody else.

For example, people often get up in a meeting and ask me what I think about Marx. When they ask me this question, I recognize that they are usually the same kind of people who ask whether you believe in God and who will then quote from a Bible written thousands of years ago to prove their point about what we should be doing today. I usually reply that I believe in the method of dialectical thinking Marx developed that stresses the need to see the connection between your ideas and the social contradictions of the society in which you are living. So I do not look to Marx, who lived in nineteenth-century Europe, for answers to our problems in twentieth-century America. Marx lived in an era when capitalism was still struggling for survival against feudalism and when the European economy was still an undeveloped economy. He had no idea of consumerism because the capitalism of his day was too underdeveloped to need the consumer for its own survival, as American capitalism needs the consumer today. So, anybody who looks to Marx for answers to our present contradictions is a dogmatist and his or her mind is stuck in a world that no longer exists.

So when I received the invitation to speak at this symposium on black liberation, I had to ask myself some questions. What do they mean by liberation? Liberation for what? Liberation to do what? Do they mean liberation from racism, liberation from capitalism, liberation from a class society? Do they want liberation from this country? If that is what they want, all they have to do is get on a plane. But wherever they land, *they still will not be liberated from the difficult struggles and decisions that are part of life.*

If you were by some miracle liberated from capitalism or racism, what kind of society would you put in the place of our present racist and capitalist society? Some of you would probably say that you would replace our present society with socialism. But what do you mean by socialism? Marx meant by socialism a society that would develop the productive forces to the point where everybody could have according to his needs. But U.S. capitalism has already developed the productive forces to the point where everybody could have according to his or her needs. So what do *you* mean by socialism?

I have to ask you these questions because all these groups talk about liberation. Yet most of them are just as materialist, just as caught up in the pursuit of more things and more pleasures as the average American. They do not realize that they are still living better than the vast majority of people in the rest of the world and that this country is consuming over one-third of the world's resources. Just as only a few years back whites were living much better than blacks at the expense of blacks, today, all Americans, black and white, are living at the expense of the vast majority of people in the rest of the world.

So socialism in *this* country would mean a society in which most of us would be satisfied with *less* goods rather than *more* goods and in which we would employ a much simpler, less energy-consuming technology than the highly advanced technology we have today.

So what is liberation? And where did this word come from? And does it apply to us in the United States today?

INDEPENDENCE, LIBERATION, REVOLUTION

Historically, the concept of liberation, like the concept of political independence to-day, comes from the revolutionary struggles in the third world: *countries* want independence; *nations* want liberation; people want revolution. Each of these struggles is a protracted one, but each is different from the other. A *country* in the third world consists of people living together in a definitive geographical area who have been deprived of their political independence. A *nation* in the third world today is no longer only a country because it has already achieved its political independence. But it is still under neocolonial or economic domination by imperialism and multinational capitalism. Therefore, its goal is liberation from economic subjugation so that it can develop the kind of economy that will serve the needs of its people.

When people want revolution, the only revolution they can make is a revolution in accordance with their own history and the stage of economic, political, and social development they have reached as a people. For *countries* that have been deprived of their political independence by colonialism, revolution means the struggle for political independence. For *nations* that are deprived of their economic independence by neocolonialism and multinational capitalism, revolution means the struggle to liberate themselves from economic domination by foreign capitalism.

WHAT DOES REVOLUTION MEAN FOR US IN AMERICA?

So, what does revolution mean for us who are Americans, living in the world's most technologically advanced society, exploiting the rest of the world so that we can maintain our economy of abundance rather than being exploited by the rest of the world?

We can't be struggling for political independence or liberation because we achieved these in the American Revolution. The colonists freed themselves from British domination of both our government and our economy and they proceeded to develop this country over the last two hundred years into a society that is the marvel of the whole world, a country where technology has advanced to such a degree that even those who are on welfare live better than the middle class in the rest of the world. In the United States, there is no such alternative as black liberation or women's liberation or the liberation of any other special interest group. Rather, the only political resolution to the present contradiction facing blacks, women, and all ethnic groups is a total socialist revolution in capitalist America.

There is no mystery about how this country was able to develop its economy so rapidly. From the beginning, we had the advantages of a rich and fertile continent stretching three thousand miles from east to west. The people who have come to this country *by choice* over the last four hundred years have been those who were most enterprising from the point of view of economic material advancement for themselves. In addition, millions of blacks were brought here in chains and kept in slavery in order to clear the land and grow the crops that could be sent to Europe in exchange for machinery and capital.

In the past, the rapid economic and technological development of the United States took place chiefly at the expense of blacks, immigrant workers, and the land itself. But today, this development has reached the stage where it is taking place at the expense of the human development of *all* American people.

As the direct result of constantly advancing technology, we have a permanent army of unemployed who have never worked and will probably never work, many of them the second generation of adults who have never held a job. Those who are still employed work at fragmented, meaningless jobs that could just as easily be done by robots and often produce socially unnecessary and socially destructive commodities and services. As a result of the mechanization of agriculture and the growth of agribusiness, not only are we destroying the soil and deepening our dependence upon declining supplies of fossil fuels, we also have driven millions of Americans off the land into the inner cities where they live on handouts from the welfare state without any hope of ever controlling their lives or their communities. At the same time, millions of others who are taxed for this welfare grow increasingly resentful. Blacks have moved and been removed from the rural South where they were oppressed, powerless, and terrorized to the urban ghettos where they were equally helpless in the face of the huge bureaucracies of the welfare state.

Our small towns and communities, in which neighborliness and character were more important than money and status, have been replaced by suburbs, which are little more than dormitories, ringing the inner cities like a noose and depending upon constantly increasing supplies of energy for the cars that take people to work and to shopping centers. Women have been transformed into sex objects. Our families are falling apart. Our atmosphere, rivers, and lakes are polluted. Mass transportation scarcely exists and for the first time in American history we face the realities of shortages in energy, food, and other commodities and the realization that prices will never go down as long as the present system continues.

Meanwhile, as a result of constantly advancing technology and constant expansion for the sake of expansion, American capitalism has reached the stage of multinational or global cooperation. In the past, most capitalists regarded production at home as center and their operations abroad as adjuncts. Now modern technology has made distance no obstacle to the rapid movements of goods, capital, and ideology. So, the multinational cooperation shifts capital, production, and jobs to places like Taiwan, Hong Kong, the Philippines, or wherever the maximum profit can be made. Then it sells the goods back here in the United States. These corporations have no loyalty to the United States and they are too powerful to be controlled by any government, even a government as a powerful as that of the United States. As a result, they are transforming our country from a nation of producers into a nation of consumers. We have become *guts* who eat and drink until we are overweight but who have little opportunity for productive or creative work and have no control over our communities or our government.

Thus, the revolution that we, the American people, now need is not the same as that which is needed by third world countries and nations. *We don't need rapid economic and technological development. We need to stop the capitalist drive toward economic and technological development* so that we can develop our human relationships with one another and our capacity to make socially responsible decisions for our communities and our country.

This is the American revolution all Americans now need, no matter where our ancestors came from or whether they came by choice or chains. Black people, whether we like it or not, are now an integral part of this technologically overdeveloped nation, and any revolution that will advance black people to a higher plateau of human development must also advance all Americans to a higher plateau of human development. This is the reality blacks have tried to evade ever since the black nationalist stage of the movement. This is because blacks still have a slave mentality in the sense that they can't see themselves as part of the leadership that will revolutionize all of American society. So they fall back on hoping that the American pie will get bigger so that more crumbs will dribble down to them, or they retreat into romantic dreams of going back to Africa. Therefore, they are unable to provide meaningful projections for the United States as we approach the twenty-first century.

THE CHOICE BETWEEN TWO ROADS

In one speech I cannot raise with you all the complex questions that we must answer in the next twenty years as we move toward the twenty-first century. That is why I have asked some of my comrades out here on the West Coast to bring some of our literature, which will give you some insight into the awesome challenges facing every American today.

However, I realize that those who invited me to speak and most of you in this audience are young people with the rest of your lives before you. The next twenty years are crucial years in your lives. You have a lot of decisions in front of you as to where you are going to work, what kind of families you want to raise, what kind of social and political relationships you are going to establish with all the various ethnic groups that make up the American people. You have a lot of freedom in making these decisions compared to your parents and grandparents, whose decisions were for the most part determined by economic necessity and social pressure. Therefore, it is important that you have some concept of the political alternatives that in the next twenty years will be before the American people as a whole.

In essence, we, the American people, now have only two alternatives. Either we can continue to drift as most people are doing, continuing to hope, despite all the evidence around us, that if capitalism continues its material and technological expansion, the benefits from this expansion will dribble down to us, hoping against hope that the politicians we elect will solve the problems of our society for us or that somehow things will get better for us even if they get worse for somebody else. This alternative means that our society will continue our present drift into barbarism. Hate, suspicion, and antagonism will continue to rule the relationships between the classes, the races, the sexes, and the generations. Determined to remain free of our responsibilities to one another and to our nation as a whole, we will increasingly lose the freedom even to go outdoors at night.

Or we can recognize that in this country we have come to the end of a historical epoch that lasted nearly four hundred years and that we are entering into a new era—the era when human beings will derive their happiness *not from* moving onward and upward but from realizing a new concept of citizenship based on the social and political responsibilities we assume for our communities, our nation, and our planet. On the basis of that new vision, we can create a new America.

A New and Enlarged View of Citizenship

There is no blueprint for that new America. It will have to be built, as was yesterday's America, by our hard work, ingenuity, and creativity as Americans. But the new America we create will be a different and better America because it will come from a new and *enlarged vision of citizenship.* Recognizing how much we have wasted and destroyed of the humanity of others and ourselves in the past because of racism, sexism, individualism, and materialism, we will have a new sense of the value we should place on the mutual respect, responsibility, and cooperation we develop with one another in our families, our communities, and our nation. Recognizing the arrogance and irresponsibility we have shown in our efforts to *conquer* nature, we will then begin to see ourselves as part of nature and begin to live by the principles of nature, the most fundamental of which is to give back what is taken out.

On the basis of this new set of values, we can then begin to reverse drastically the present trend toward ever bigger institutions and concentrations of capital. We will find ways and means to build communities and industries, small and decentralized enough so that the average citizen can participate in continuous and meaningful decision making and thus acquire at a lower and local level the experience in social and political responsibility that will enable us to create a national government that can be held accountable to other nations and to future generations.

In order to build this new America, we will eventually have to take power from the American capitalists who in their drive for more profits and greater control of capital all over the globe are destroying the rights and responsibilities that we as Americans have for our own self-government and for making meaningful choices. But there is no

point in trying to mobilize or organize Americans for a revolution against the capitalists as long as the great majority of Americans are still dominated by the same capitalist
vision of material and scientific expansion, struggling only to get for themselves the
material goods that other Americans have. If by some miracle, tomorrow or in the
near future, the oppressed in American society were able to take power away from the
American capitalists without having overcome our own individualism and materialism, the new America would not be any different from the old.

Like every great historical crisis, the present crisis represents not only a danger but
an opportunity. The ancestors of most of us were not among those who founded this
country only two hundred years ago and established the political, economic, and social
patterns by which we have developed to our present state. The American people as a
whole have never really engaged in the revolutionary struggles by which any great nation is created. That great humanizing experience still lies before us.

The American people are today confronted with the choice between two roads: the
capitalist road of constantly expanding economic and technological development by
which this country has developed its unique strengths and weaknesses, or the socialist
road by which we can begin the struggle to develop ourselves as new human beings
who welcome the challenge of taking responsibility for our communities, our nation,
and our planet.

This socialist road is not a Thing. It is a direction, a constitution of the struggle
to become more human, which human beings have been carrying on for the last fifty
thousand years. The new America we must build is not a Promised Land in which everybody gets all that he or she wants, once the oppressed take power. Being an American is and always has been a complex fate in the sense that our identity is something
that we must create for ourselves. It is a challenge to the creativity and commitment of
each of us. Each of us, each of you, must decide for yourself whether during the next
twenty years you are going to be part of the problem of part of the solution.

"The Challenge Facing Afro-Americans in the 1980s" is the text of a presentation made in a colloquium at the Center for Afroamerican and African Studies (CAAS) at the University of Michigan on October 31, 1979.

The Challenge Facing Afro-Americans in the 1980s

Not too many years ago blacks from every strata of the population were engaged in great struggles to eliminate the racism that had for nearly four hundred years kept blacks out of the mainstream of American society. Most blacks, whether they actually participated in these struggles or cheered them on from the sidelines, conceived racism as the principal and fundamental contradiction of American society. They reasoned that if only this contradiction could be resolved, all our problems would be resolved. We would no longer be systematically relegated to the bottom of society, we would no longer feel inferior to other Americans, and we would be free to pursue happiness as we saw other Americans pursuing it all around us.

Particularly in the South, it seemed obvious that if only the barriers of racism could be lifted—so that blacks could go any place that whites went, live any place that whites lived, develop the skills that whites had—everything in capitalist America would be all right for blacks and whites. The dream dominating black thinking was the same as that dominating white thinking. It was the dream of America as the land of opportunity where everyone could become as rich as Rockefeller. Most blacks believed that if any whites didn't realize this dream, it was their own fault. The only reason why it hadn't become a reality for blacks was the barrier of racism.

Today, as the result of the courage and sacrifices of hundreds of thousands of Americans, including whites, we can go anyplace we want to. Blacks now hold all kinds of high positions, making $25,000 and up a year. There are black mayors, black judges, black school superintendents, black police chiefs, black university presidents, black foremen. In every TV commercial, on every TV newscast, there are as many black personalities as white ones.

Yet our neighborhoods are falling apart; in every block where blacks live, there are two and three boarded-up houses. Our schools are like jungles and security guards are everywhere—in our stores, in our hospitals, even in our churches. Blacks live in fear and trembling of one another, and most of us feel safer walking after dark in white neighborhoods than in our own neighborhoods.

All around us we can see the many changes that have taken place in the last ten years for the better, in the sense that blacks now enjoy the same civil rights as other Americans, and for the worse, in the sense that blacks are now doing even more vicious things to one another than whites used to do to blacks. Yet most blacks insist that "nothing has changed," particularly when they try to justify to themselves or to others the rapid deterioration that is taking place in all our institutions and all our social relationships.

Why do so many blacks—including, I am sure, some of you—insist that nothing has changed? I believe that it is because most blacks do not want to give up the dream of capitalist America as the land of opportunity where everybody can get to the top. We have not taken the time to reflect on the fact that so many white Americans were able to get to the top only because they were climbing on the backs of blacks and other people of color as well as workers and the colonial peoples of the world. Because we have been kept out of the American Dream for so many centuries, we think we have a right to enjoy this dream now—even though practically everything in the world has changed as a result of our own struggles and the struggles of other oppressed peoples of the world. Largely because of the great struggles of the 1960s the American Dream has been exposed as a nightmare, and the moral authority and legitimacy of all American institutions have been destroyed. But we are not willing to accept the responsibility for creating a new vision and new institutions for America so that all Americans can begin to live new and more meaningful lives on the basis of new relationships of responsibility and respect between the races, for one another and for other peoples of the world. So we keep insisting that "nothing has changed," not realizing that by so doing we are belittling the great struggles of the 1950s and 1960s and demoralizing our young people.

What Do We Mean by Freedom?

Ever since World War II millions of people in the third world, taking advantage of the crisis of Western civilization, have been engaged in tremendous struggles against colonialism and neocolonialism. They have been struggling not only for political independence but to liberate their natural resources and their economies from the control of Western imperialism and neocolonialism. As these struggles have evolved, many of the natural resources that those of us living in the advanced capitalist countries have taken for granted as our right to enjoy how and when we want have become scarcer and more expensive. Not only has the economic basis of the American Dream, with all its wastefulness, been eroded, but the moral authority the West once enjoyed has collapsed, making it necessary for us to reexamine the American way of life that once seemed so desirable and accessible.

The turning point for us as Americans came with the defeat of the United States in Vietnam. When all the advanced technology of the West was unable to win out against the political and moral determination of the Vietnamese to control their own destiny, the time had come for all of us in the West to abandon the illusion that advanced technology is the solution to human questions. But we hold tight to this illusion, and so we have our Three Mile Islands and our continuing energy crisis.

The defeat of the United States in Vietnam was brought about not only by the military and political genius of the Vietnamese but by the antiwar movement here at home and the crisis the black movement created in all American institutions. Ever since then, no institution in American society has had any legitimacy or moral authority—all the way from the president in the White House down to the teacher in every school and the parents in every home. As a result, every individual now feels justified in doing anything that serves his or her self-interest. Every ethnic group or special interest group feels that it is their right to get anything that they have enough clout or power to get. Everyone is engaged in a war or competition with everyone else to get a larger portion of the goodies of our society—and the devil take the hindmost. Individualism or the absolute right of every individual to do what he or she pleases has become the norm in every respect of our daily lives.

Up until a few years ago it was mostly the capitalists who interpreted freedom to mean the right to pursue profits and material gain regardless of the social impact of their actions, for example, regardless of the number of people they threw out of work or the rivers and atmosphere they polluted with industrial waste. Most Americans (even though we also believed in individualism and materialism) were restrained by the pressures and the moral authority of our families, our communities, and our institutions. Today, however, as a result of the breakdown of all our institutions, the average American interprets freedom to mean the absolute right of every individual to pursue personal pleasures and material gains, no matter what this costs in terms of destroying our neighborhoods, our schools, our homes, and our respect and trust for one another.

Meanwhile, in the pursuit of profits, American capitalism has been setting up multinational corporations all over the world so that they can exploit cheap labor and the natural resources of the third world. Not only are they taking away the opportunity for Americans to engage in productive labor, but they are flooding the country with consumer goods that have been manufactured abroad and using the electronic media to whet the appetites of Americans for these goods.

Because as Americans we have not replaced the American Dream of becoming as rich as Rockefeller with another vision of how human beings should live, we are now at the mercy of these multinational corporations and their commercials. Most Americans now have no other purpose in life but the unlimited accumulation of consumer goods and the unlimited pursuit of immediate pleasures. Even though all around us our institutions, our families, our communities, our schools, our economy, and our government are falling apart, all we can think of is what we are going to buy next, or what we are going to wear to the newest disco joint, or how we are going to make a killing in the lottery or at the racetrack or on *Beat the Clock.* Most people, whether they are middle class or poor, live by credit cards, owing as much money as they earn. In every walk of life, in every ethnic group, beating the system by becoming part of it has become the driving force that keeps Americans going from one day to the next.

Until a few years ago blacks were very critical of the individualistic and materialistic values of white Americans because it was so obvious that the high standard of living enjoyed by white Americans was largely at the expense of blacks and other people of color. The black community prided itself on the trust and respect that blacks had for one another, contrasting it with the way that whites would do anything for a buck. However, since the barriers of racism have been lifted to let blacks into the system, the individualistic and materialistic values that were always at the heart of the American Dream have become as much a part of black relationships as they are of the relationships among other Americans.

Meanwhile, however, most black Americans, even though we have adopted the values of the system, still continue to see ourselves as victims of the system, looking to the government or to somebody else to solve our problems for us. That is why the disintegration of blacks is taking place faster than any other section of American society. We have lost all confidence in ourselves and in one another.

Toward a New Social Order

However, it is not just a question of black disintegration. Our total society is in a state of chaos. This is because once those who have been at the bottom of a society erupt in massive rebellions, it is impossible for any system to proceed any longer in an orderly fashion. At this point there is nothing *any* government that exists to defend the system can do to restore order, no matter how many handouts or concessions it makes to those demanding rights or reparations for past or present grievances. Once the bottom of a society has heaved itself up, no relationships can continue on their old basis. The question then is no longer the rights of any group but whether there are any new forces in the society who are ready to assume responsibility for bringing into being a new social order based on new principles and new relationships.

That is the nature of the period we are living in now. It is a revolutionary period because no matter how many rights any group demands or the government concedes, our society will continue to disintegrate and disorder will continue to escalate until some new forces are ready to take responsibility for reorganizing our whole society.

In every revolutionary period, in any country, it is necessary for some new forces to take responsibility for reorganizing the nation. What is unique about the revolutionary period in our country today is that this reorganization will have to take place not around the question of rights but around the question of responsibility.

Our country was founded at the beginning of the age of rights, four hundred years ago, when Europe was moving away from the feudal social order and capitalism was just beginning to emerge as a new social order. For the last four hundred years most progressive struggles, not only on this continent but around the world, have been about the question of rights: the right to self-government, the right to free speech and free assembly, the right of labor to organize, the rights of blacks and other people of color, the rights of women, the right of every citizen to food, clothing, and shelter. In some parts of the world the struggle for rights is still progressive. People in the third world still have to struggle against colonialism—for the right to self-government or political independence. They still have to struggle for liberation from neocolonialism—or the right to control their own economies and natural resources.

But in the United States today the struggle for the rights of special ethnic or special interest groups is no longer progressive or revolutionary. All it does is increase the fragmentation and disorder in our society. All it does is increase our tendency to see ourselves as outsiders and victims, dependent on government agencies for our identity. The only revolutionary struggle today is the struggle to restore our society on the basis of our mutual responsibility for one another, for our planet, and for our posterity.

Thus, the black movement—which started out to resolve one contradiction, racism—has ended up creating new contradictions not only for blacks but for everyone else in American society. Even though racism still exists, it is no longer the principal contradiction of our society. Therefore, today, those who want to carry on the heroic tradition of the 1950s and 1960s must be ready to ask themselves new questions that neither they nor any other Americans have ever asked before.

This poses a real dilemma for all the groups that have been looking at the contradictions of our society chiefly in terms of self-interest and rights—which means practically all Americans. It poses a particular dilemma for blacks, who have been the most oppressed by and in American society. How can those who have been deprived for so long of their elementary rights give leadership to those who have been their oppressors? How can we conceive of ourselves as Americans when for so long we have been kept out of American society? Why should we take responsibility for this society when for so long this society has acted as if we were less than human?

These are the kinds of questions that people ask when they are unclear about their historic role. Black people, whether we like it or not, have been and always will be pivotal to the development of American society. Without our labor, there would never have been the infrastructure that enabled the United States to develop its economy so rapidly. Down through the years blacks have been the conscience or the soul of America, constantly reminding Americans of the principles of equality and citizenship on which this nation was founded, and acting as a counterforce to the prevailing materialism and individualism. That is why American jazz, which was created by blacks, remains to this day the greatest contribution of this nation to world culture.

Now that by our struggles and our rebellions we have destroyed the moral authority and legitimacy of all American institutions, we have no alternative but to tackle the new contradictions that we have created by our rebellions and struggles. Our future is tied up with the future of this country just as the future of this country has always been and always will be tied up with our future. If we just stand by and allow the situation to drift into deeper chaos and decay, we will not escape the chaos and decay. We will not be free. As Martin Delaney pointed out many years ago, "No people can really be free unless they constitute a part of the leadership and ruling forces of the country they live in."

The Choice between the Two Roads

Black Americans today are faced with the choice between two roads. We can drift into the twenty-first century, bemoaning and complaining about the wrongs that have been done to us and are still being done to us and viewing ourselves in the way that whites have always viewed us, the adjuncts and outsiders. Or we can be in the forefront and an integral part of the revolutionary leadership that is now needed to take our country into the twenty-first century.

The contradictions that face our society today are no longer black questions but human questions that all Americans have to face—just as the question of racism was not only a black question but a human question on which every American was forced to take a stand by the civil rights and black movements of the 1950s and 1960s. The twentieth century in which the main line was the color line is coming to an end. This does not mean that racism has ceased to exist; it still exists in many forms. But the struggle for the twenty-first century is the struggle for new relationships not only between the races but between ourselves and Nature, between the advanced countries and the third world, between men and women. The struggle for the twenty-first century is the struggle to create new relationships in all these areas on the basis of new principles of mutual responsibility, respect, and cooperation.

The main or principal contradiction facing Americans today is the absence of a revolutionary leadership that has a vision of a new America built on these new principles and is willing to make the tremendous effort required to win the hearts and minds of the American people to struggle for this new America.

By revolutionary leadership with vision, I do not mean people who continue to think that political struggle is mainly a clash between special interest groups or classes for a piece of the capitalist pie or who think of revolutionary struggle chiefly in terms of whetting the appetite of the have-nots for a redistribution of goods. The first thing that revolutionary leadership for the twenty-first century has to recognize is that a new America can only be built by people who have rejected the philosophy of individualism and materialism that has dominated Western society for the last four hundred years and who recognize that life in the twenty-first century will only be worth living if we take responsibility for each other, for our planet, and for people in the rest of the world. Having come to this decision, those of us who are ready to accept the responsibility for revolutionary leadership then have to ask ourselves and other Americans some very profound and difficult questions.

First and foremost, what is life all about? Does man/woman live by bread and possessions alone? Or will our lives have meaning only when we are ready to strive continuously to create more harmonious relationships between individuals in our communities, between communities, between our nation and other nations in today's interdependent world that is made up of people from so many different ethnic and cultural backgrounds.

What kind of government and leaders do we need as we move toward the twenty-first century? Do we need governments and leaders who act only as transactional leaders, winning elections because they promise to satisfy our greed and our wants? Or do we need governments and leaders who are committed to transforming and uplifting us into the kinds of new women and new men who can take responsibility for one another and for our planet, and who are themselves living examples of these new women and new men?

What kinds of relationships do we now need to create with other nation-states who are all different from the United States? Do we continue to view other nations and other peoples as competitors with us for the world's resources, or do we start by recognizing them as members of the human family with whom we must live in harmony and cooperation and mutual respect, trading and sharing the resources of the planet and our differing cultural backgrounds, struggling with one another as members of a family will always do! How will we divest ourselves of the many possessions we have appropriated all over the world, whether these be military bases or factories and mines owned by American-controlled multinational corporations, so that other nations can develop their own economies and resources?

How do we take responsibility for the continuing survival of Planet Earth? How long can we continue to think about national security in terms of nuclear weapons when we know that even to contemplate our security through the extermination of millions of people is dehumanizing us and turning us into international terrorists? Why can't we dispose of all our atomic bombs unilaterally and thus set an example to the rest of the world?

How do we begin to challenge all Americans to recognize that we have come to the end of the epoch when expanding production was progressive and help them understand that our main capital is in Nature, so that we must no longer view ourselves as conquerors of Nature but as trustees and stewards, responsible for conserving Nature for ourselves and our posterity?

How do we take advantage of our good fortune that our nation is more like a world than a nation, including people from every country and culture in the world, to create a society in which all ethnic groups live in harmony and cooperation with mutual respect for one another and of the diversity that enriches us all?

How do we reorganize our industries on a decentralized and human scale so that they can be controlled by human beings and local communities? How do we reorganize agriculture so that millions of Americans who now live in asphalt jungles can go back to the farms—not just for the sake of their own health but for the health of all the people in our country? Only when we create new relationships between industry and agriculture, between city people and country people, can we produce food that is not contaminated by chemicals and preservatives because it has to be transported thousands of miles from the farm to the consumer. Only in this way will we begin to renew our relationship to and respect for Nature.

How do we reorganize our housing both for the purpose of conserving energy and for the purpose of creating community? We can no longer afford the luxury of separate dwellings in the way that we take for granted nowadays. We need to organize ourselves to use less energy, not more, even if it becomes feasible to get more energy. But we also need the kind of housing units that enable several families and several generations to live closely together within the community so that the raising of children can be shared and so that our children can get the sense of the continuing evolution of humankind that comes from growing up around grandparents.

How do we reorganize what we now call our education system? We must recognize that the first stage of education begins in the home where parents teach children in practice how to act morally and ethically in relationship to others and that both the home and the school must be rooted in the community if children are to have the living models that are absolutely essential to education. Education in schools should be not only to develop skills but to teach children how to make the life decisions that will enable them to become good citizens. This means that education must give children a respect and appreciation for their communities, for Nature, for the universe, and for people in the rest of the world. At the same time it must give children an understanding of what has been the history of our nation, both its achievements and its shortcomings, so that they feel they have a tradition to build on and to go beyond.

And last but not least, how do we encourage the leadership capacity of women so that they can bring their nurturing qualities and sensitivity to the creation of a new America? How do we at the same time encourage men to struggle against their male chauvinisms and in the process become new human beings with the nurturing qualities and sensitivity all of us need to create a new America together?

We cannot live truly human lives as long as we evade discussing and deciding difficult questions like these in terms of what will advance the human development of our country and of the human species. Only through political struggles over questions of this profundity can we as Americans begin to bring meaning back into our lives and begin to create a new nation out of these United States that all Americans—regardless of race, class, sex, or creed—will be proud to call our own.

We will not always make the correct decisions, and even when we do, new contradictions will constantly arise, requiring new struggles and new decisions, because man/womankind and this nation are still evolving. There is no "final solution," no "Promised Land." But not until those who call themselves progressive and/or revolutionary are ready to pose questions of this magnitude to the American people are we thinking about making the kind of American revolution that will take us into the twenty-first century, confident that we are part of the continuing evolution of humankind.

PART IV

COMMUNITY BUILDING
AND GRASSROOTS LEADERSHIP
IN POST-INDUSTRIAL DETROIT

Introduction to Part IV

This section presents writings from 1984 to 1993, the last ten years of James Boggs's life. Though he battled cancer during the latter half of those years, first bladder cancer and then lung cancer, to which he succumbed on July 22, 1993, Boggs nonetheless continued his writing, speaking, and organizing throughout this period. As Grace Lee Boggs recalled, he remained "alert and active almost to the very end."[1] The specific character of his activism and the contours of his thinking during this final stage of his career are documented in this group of writings, which include a letter to fellow activists, a guest editorial in the *Detroit Free Press*, three speeches, and several short articles from the SOSAD newsletter.[2] Five concerns animate this group of writings: empowering local communities; repairing social relationships; rebuilding crisis-ridden cities (with particular attention to the unique challenges of urban youth); facing internal contradictions; and finding new ways to meet basic economic and human needs. As this list of concerns suggests, Boggs's writings during this period focused squarely on local conditions. His activism had always been rooted in local experience, but during the 1980s and 1990s the specific crises facing Detroit took on a particular urgency and primacy in his thinking. At the heart of these writings is a firm commitment to grassroots efforts to meet the urgent challenges faced by black communities in post-industrial Detroit in the aftermath of the Black Power movement.

This local turn and the specific concerns it called forth clearly mark this group of writings as a new period in Boggs's career, but this should not be taken as a sharp departure from the radical vision that drove his activism and his writing during the preceding decades. The goal of revolutionary change remained, but the context in which he sought it and the shape or form in which he envisioned it shifted. During the previous three decades he wrote in connection to progressive social movements or organized political spaces—the labor movement, the Marxist left, the civil rights movement, and the Black Power movement—giving his work specific contexts. Each such context furnished concrete political questions to address, intellectual spaces to engage, even venues in which to publish. No such context existed in the 1980s and 1990s. Thus, the writings in this section are not, as we have seen in his work from previous periods, interventions into an ongoing movement. For the first time in Boggs's political life, the country faced no significant mass movement or other form of collective social protest. Thus, his writings of the 1980s and early 1990s took a slightly different character because they were not, as all of his previous work had been, designed to interject an ideology or develop a program for an existing or fully articulated struggle. Rather, in this period he sought to cultivate or call forth a new movement. There is, however, some continuity in that these writings build on or develop further ideas first articulated in previous periods. Moreover, this group of writings demonstrates how Boggs's method of analysis and political practice continued to be guided by his belief in the need to "think dialectically," that is, to recognize that social struggles create new conditions and new contradictions. A recurring theme in these writings is Boggs's insistence that the social and political challenges facing African Americans in the 1980s and 1990s must be approached differently than they had been during the 1960s.

Broadly speaking, two sets of conditions speak most dramatically to the changed social and political reality of 1980s and 1990s Detroit. One was the ascendency of black political power.[3] As Boggs had predicted, the struggle for Black Power coupled with urban demographic shifts created black political power in many cities, with African Americans constituting majorities and assuming control of municipal government in cities like Detroit, which elected Coleman Young, its first black mayor, in 1973. By the 1980s, Detroit was the archetypal black city—African Americans constituted nearly 80 percent of the city's population, and municipal power firmly rested with black politicians and other officials.[4] The arrival of a post-industrial economy constituted the second set of conditions. The insidious impacts of deindustrialization—the decades-long process of automating, relocating, and closing factories—resulted in massive job elimination and the virtual gutting of the city's industrial economy.[5] As Boggs had decried in *The American Revolution*, this process began in the 1950s and was quite evident in the 1960s, but few heeded the warnings of the devastation to come. By the 1980s and early 1990s, it was clear that the city's severe economic decline had produced crisis levels of unemployment and poverty and contributed to harrowing and increasingly lamented conditions of social decay in black communities.

Detroit's post-industrial landscape, more than anything else, activated Boggs's analyses and projections in this period. The components of the city's crisis are by now well-known: a shrinking tax base and mounting fiscal deficits; persistent unemployment and chronic poverty (the 1990 census reported one-third of Detroit citizens in poverty, the highest rate in the nation);[6] a crack cocaine epidemic devastating individual lives, families, and communities; a faltering public school system; and an epidemic of gun violence, especially among black youth (earning for the city the moniker "Murder Capital U.S.A.").[7] Of course none of these conditions was unique to Detroit, but the severity and accumulated intensity with which they existed in the Motor City compelled grave concern.

The practice of community building assumed a central place in Boggs's vision for revitalizing Detroit. He saw in these post-industrial conditions not only the culpability of runaway corporations and the malfeasance of unscrupulous political leaders but also a crisis at the level of human relationships: "The residue of the last hundred years of rapid technological development," he wrote, "is alienation, hopelessness, self-hate and hate for one another, and the violence that has created a reign of terror in our inner cities."[8] To reverse this, that is, to repair social relationships and restore a sense of community, Boggs envisioned a collective commitment to transform *neighborhoods* into genuine *communities*. Neighborhoods, he said, were places "where people live together physically and have common problems," but they lack meaningful connections to each other. Communities, by contrast, are characterized by people who not only live in the same geographical area but also "have created social ties with one another" and "recognize their dependence upon one another."[9] To build these community connections, he proposed a range of support networks and other collective endeavors, such as community gardens and greenhouses, recycling projects, daycare networks, neighborhood responsibility councils, repair shops, skills banks, panels to resolve disputes between neighbors, and community bakeries. These and other community-building activities, Boggs believed, would create a pattern and practice of collective self-reliance through which citizens would rely on themselves—and not city (or state or national) government or big corporations—to revitalize Detroit and other cities.[10]

Two selections in part 4 showcase Boggs's ideas about community building. Each one argues for an understanding of community building as part of a fundamental rethinking of social relationships. In "Going Where We Have Never Been: Creating New Communities for Our Future," a speech given in Oakland, California, in 1986, Boggs traced the shifting meanings of community in the context of urban change over the past half century, and he proposed a new way of looking at cities: "[T]he city must be seen as the place where you create social ties with the people you live with and not just with a place to which you come to get a job or to make a living."[11] The other speech, "Community Building: An Idea Whose Time Has Come" delivered at an African American leadership conference in Detroit in 1987, focuses on the social alienation, violence, and insecurity within black communities. "Every day," he told the audience, "I wake up feeling the devastation of this city and what is happening to our people on my back."[12] Boggs said that the situation required African Americans to "become new men and women" committed to forging a "life-affirming culture" that rejected capitalist values and was instead based on social responsibility and respect. The first step, he said, was "the rebuilding or regenerating of our communities because it is in community that human beings have always found their personhood or their human identity."[13] Both speeches end with the same sentence: "I believe the next great movement in the United States must be the community-building movement, which is also a people-building movement. It is an idea whose time has come."

Boggs interjected his ideas about community building into citywide debates around how best to redevelop Detroit. For example, in 1988 Mayor Coleman Young proposed the legalization of casino gambling as a way to stem the city's economic slide. Detroit voters had already rejected proposals for legalizing casino gambling in referendums in 1976 and 1981. Yet, as the decade wore on, Young became increasingly desperate to find a way to bring jobs to the city. By 1988, with the continued erosion of the city's economic base (the city lost one hundred thousand manufacturing jobs between 1976 and 1986),[14] staggering unemployment, and the dramatic increase in crime, drugs, and violence, Young again proposed casinos as a means of job creation and economic redevelopment. "Rebuilding Detroit: An Alternative to Casino Gambling" is the text of Boggs's remarks in opposition to the proposal during a public speak out against casino gambling in June 1988. The speech not only argues against casino gambling but also projects a grassroots vision for the city's economic recovery and revitalization. He argued that the idea, like Young's redevelopment agenda more generally, was based on "the illusion that we can bring back the good old days"[15] when Detroit was a center of manufacturing that provided mass employment and economic security. Boggs urged the citizens of the city to consider a competing vision and a different path: "We have to get rid of the myth that there is something sacred about large-scale production for the national and international market. . . . Instead, we have to begin thinking of creating small enterprises that produce food, goods, and services for the local market."[16] Boggs argued with some urgency that such local enterprises—if they took advantage of natural resources in the area, utilized the existing and potential skills of local people, and created opportunities for the productive involvement of young people—offered the most promising and sustainable path for the city's economic future.

Boggs again challenged Young's redevelopment agenda and his vision of the city's future in 1991.[17] The mayor backed a ballot proposal to give the city authority to tear down Ford Auditorium and rezone public space on the riverfront along the Detroit River, opening it up for private development. Boggs flatly opposed the measure and worked for its defeat.[18] In a guest editorial for the *Detroit Free Press,* Boggs argued that a vote against the proposal would be a turning point for the city: "For too long, our city has been the victim of the giveaway mentality of the mayor and his economic development advisors. Dangling the promise of jobs before Detroiters, they promote mega-projects that have been shown to eliminate jobs and enrich developers."[19] Boggs sharply criticized Young for using highly visible development projects that masked rather than reversed economic decline and which, most important, ignored community development. "Those Detroiters who still believe in the mayor's empty promises," he wrote, "should look around them to see how the same kind of benign neglect of Ford Auditorium is at work in our neighborhoods. Just as the number of vacant buildings keeps growing downtown, so the number of vacant lots keeps growing in our neighborhoods."[20]

The question of Detroit's future not only revolved around economic matters but also focused on violence and the city's youth. Amid the dire circumstances confronting many young people in 1980s Detroit—poverty, the crack cocaine epidemic, a crumbling school system—grew a heartbreaking crisis of gun violence and homicide. In 1985, thirty-two young people were shot and killed by other youth. The next year this number rose to forty-one. "In the mid 1980s," writes historian Richard Thomas, "the black youth population was declaring war on itself" as the "larger black community looked on helplessly."[21] It was in this context that Clementine Barfield, whose sixteen-year-old son was killed in the summer of 1986, began meeting with other mothers of slain children to find ways to go beyond mourning and build alternatives to violence. In early 1987 they founded Save Our Sons and Daughters (SOSAD), a pathbreaking organization that spearheaded a movement to reduce youth violence and create peaceful pathways for youth development. The Boggses soon became involved with SOSAD. Among other things, Grace edited the monthly SOSAD newsletter and Jimmy wrote a regular column.

Several of his SOSAD columns are presented in this section. With passion and urgency, they probe the life chances of the city's black youth and call on adults to make a radical reevaluation of their ideas, values, and practices. A common thread in most of these columns is Boggs's insistence on the need to examine internal contradictions, that is, to be self-critical, as individuals and as communities, and to recognize the internal changes that need to be made. As he saw it, to uproot violence and other problems affecting black communities required that we "admit and struggle against our own weaknesses."[22] Many of these pieces pose questions designed to challenge existing patterns of social interaction with black communities (for example, "Why Are We at War with One Another," "What Can We Be That Our Children Can See?" "Why Are Our Children So Bored?"). Some stress the need for African Americans to break out of old modes of thinking ("We Must Stop Thinking Like Victims," "What Time Is It in Detroit and the World?" "We Can Run But We Can't Hide," "Beyond Civil Rights"). Others propose specific strategies, such as an appeal to create community standards that uphold the responsibilities of fatherhood ("What Does It Mean to Be a Father?").

Two of Boggs's SOSAD columns ("Time to Act Like Citizens, Not Subjects" and "Why Detroit Summer?") discuss Detroit Summer, the youth volunteer program he, Grace Lee Boggs, and a few others started in 1992. Inspired by the historical example of the Student Nonviolent Coordinating Committee (SNCC) and Freedom Summer, the program embodied Boggs's concern for Detroit youth as well as his vision for rebuilding Detroit. More broadly, it was an extension or continuation of his and Grace's growing belief in the need and possibility for a movement of grassroots urban revitalization across the nation. As he wrote in "Time to Act Like Citizens, Not Subjects," their goal in creating Detroit Summer was to

foster among young people, both outside and inside Detroit, a sense of citizenship and the kind of social consciousness that was expressed by the youth of the 1960s. . . . We were also aware that the devastation of Detroit is a symbol of the crisis facing all American cities east of the Mississippi. For most of the twentieth century Detroit was a mecca luring people from the country into the city seeking to become industrial workers, earning enough money to become homeowners and send our children to college. Now, having been abandoned by the corporations that lured us here, we and our children and our grandchildren are trapped in a city that is beginning to resemble a nineteenth-century ghost town.[23]

The program brought college students from across the country together with Detroit teenagers for three weeks of community building and service activities. They turned vacant lots into parks, planted community gardens, rehabilitated houses, painted murals, interviewed people in the neighborhoods in which they lived and worked, and shared intergenerational dialogues with longtime activists. Boggs wrote in "Why Detroit Summer?" that through these activities the participants in the inaugural year of Detroit Summer "won the respect of grassroots Detroiters and seeded the idea that together we can build a movement to rebuild, redefine and respirit Detroit from the ground up."[24] Created a year before Boggs's death, Detroit Summer stands as a telling expression of his continued and evolving activism and his efforts to create new visions for the twenty-first century.[25]

Boggs wrote this letter to fellow activists on September 20, 1984.

Letter to Friends and Comrades

Dear Friend and Comrade:

GREETINGS! In a few weeks the hoopla of the 1984 presidential campaign will be over and we will be faced not only with four more years of Reagan but a counterrevolutionary movement emboldened by success.

It should now be clear to all who are for human progress that all great advances must be based on social and political struggles outside the electoral arena. Having lived through the demise of the movements of the 1960s and early 1970s, we should also be clear that once any movement allows itself to be incorporated into electoral politics, it cannot be resurrected. A new and different movement must be built on much broader and deeper foundations and issues.

Today the high technology that made possible the nuclear bomb has become a cancer threatening to destroy every institution humanity has created down through the ages to protect itself. Those at the bottom of our society, particularly young blacks, Hispanics, and Native Americans, have been made expendable to the point where they cannot even build families. Our communities have been turned into wastelands. Public transportation is not only constantly breaking down but its cost has become prohibitive. Crime has become so normal that we fear one another more than we used to fear wild beasts. Our earth, waters, and air have become so contaminated by industrial waste that if the bomb doesn't kill us first, dioxin will.

Yet, instead of challenging the system, most Americans are collaborating with it. Rather than recognize that the American Dream of unlimited economic expansion has become a nightmare, even those most victimized by it are trapped in pursuing wants and fantasies. Millions, pressed to the wall even to meet basic needs, are putting their hopes into catching the lottery. More and more people are using not only drugs but religion to escape from making the hard choices between right and wrong that have now become critical. Thus the corruption is not only in our oppressors but in ourselves.

I believe the time has come for those who recognize the need to create a just and humane society to begin building a new movement not only against the system but for the transformation of those who are being destroyed by their collaboration with the system.

If you agree, I hope you will want to join me in issuing a call that summons the American people to chart a new and different course. This call should be issued before the election in order to make clear that our perspectives for a new movement are not dependent on the results of the election.

Please let me hear from you as soon as possible. Please feel free also to suggest others you think may be interested and whether, where, and/or when we should meet to prepare this call and to plan its promotion and distribution.

COMRADELY,
JAMES BOGGS

"Going Where We Have Never Been: Creating New Communities for Our Future" is a speech delivered at St. Philip's Lutheran Church in Oakland, California, on October 18, 1986.

Going Where We Have Never Been: Creating New Communities for Our Future

When we talk about communities, we are usually referring to people who live together in a particular geographical area, who have created social ties with one another, and who recognize their dependence upon one another. In that sense, except on some Native American reservations, there are few communities; we are talking about what used to be or what we would like to be rather than what exists at present.

Today we have neighborhoods where people live together physically and have common problems. But few of them recognize their dependence upon one another except in extreme circumstances, for example, a hurricane or a tornado. In an emergency people tend to come together and act like a community because they are forced to. But as soon as the emergency is over, people return to their isolation and alienation from one another.

At the same time many people, particularly those over forty, say that what is wrong today is that we no longer have a sense of community. These people sense that we have lost something that we need to recover or re-create.

Communities in the United States have always been in a state of flux. People have tended to move out when a particular company moved to another city, when new opportunities presented themselves, or when they moved up the social and economic ladder. However, in the past when one community broke up because the residents had begun to "do better," it was usually replaced by a community made up of members of another ethnic group who weren't doing as well.

Most people would agree that up to World War II our major cities were made up predominantly of working-class communities, most of them bound together by ethnic and kinship ties. This gave people a tremendous sense of security. You lived near your kith and kin; there were usually three generations living close to one another: grandparents, parents, children, aunts and uncles, cousins, nephews and nieces. So the community was like an extended family, with a sense of caring and the continuity between the past, present, and future. Women carried the major responsibility for this caring, but their work was undervalued.

The main difference between communities in the city and those in the country was that city people usually went outside the community to work—although not very far, as a rule. Meanwhile, in most communities there were still small shops: bakeries, fruit and vegetable markets, butcher and barber shops, shoe repair shops, variety stores, taverns, etc. Today, however, most people not only earn their living outside the community, they travel many miles to get to their jobs. And they also spend most of their income outside the community at supermarkets and shopping centers that are usually owned by huge national and multinational corporations selling merchandise that has been manufactured outside the country—in the Philippines, Taiwan, South Korea.

In every city communities have had their own history of development. How they came together had a lot to do with what was happening in agriculture and industry. Usually something had happened, like the mechanization of agriculture, which drove people off the land, or the starting up of a factory in a certain area, which lured people to that area. So in the beginning of most urban communities there has been both a negative and a positive: the negative being that people were driven off the land and the positive that new jobs had opened up in the city.

During World War II a tremendous change took place in our cities, mainly because so many factories opened up or expanded in order to produce for the war. For example, Oakland became a great center for shipping and shipbuilding. World War II came in the midst of a Great Depression during which farms had become mechanized, driving millions to the cities of the South and the Midwest. Up to that time the economy of the West Coast had been based primarily on agriculture and food production. But the millions who poured into the cities of the West during World War II—except those from Mexico—came not to work in farming but in heavy industry or service trades in the city. For most of these—Texans, Oakies, blacks, Latinos—war industry offered machines, on the assembly line, in packing, textiles, and shipbuilding. From the human point of view this kind of work was challenging and exciting. People, especially women, who up to that point had only done domestic work or worked in the fields, got an opportunity to work with complex machinery, to learn new skills, and to meet new kinds of people. Most of them had come from a rural or folk culture, so this represented a cultural widening that was stimulating and educational. The unions had just been organized, so there was also a respect for the dignity of labor inside and outside the shop. Workers were needed to produce for the war, so everyone felt a sense of pride in being part of the "arsenal of democracy." Thus, despite the racial and ethnic segregation especially in housing, workers in the city during World War II saw themselves progressing not only materially but also as human beings. At the same time within the urban community respect for the elderly and high hopes for the young continued.

However, with the end of the war, urban communities began to disintegrate. During the war we had gotten used to moving around the country. Then, under the GI Bill of Rights, war veterans from working-class backgrounds got a chance to go to college and thus to move upward on the social and economic ladder. As more and more people bought cars, they became more mobile, buying houses in the suburbs, traveling twenty to thirty miles to work, leaving behind them in the inner cities those who were unemployed or could only find cheap jobs—blacks and the elderly. Convinced that every individual could realize the American Dream as an individual, most people began to view where they lived as only a temporary stopping place until they could move further upward on the capitalist ladder.

At the same time, in order to keep the economy going, the corporations mobilized to create a mass consumer culture. Over the radio, in newspapers, and then on television, the American public was persuaded that our human identity depended upon our purchasing new refrigerators, cars, furniture, clothes, and appliances. Americans were ready to buy all these things because of a decade of depression and war shortages.

Hence by the 1960s the main communities that still existed in our cities were black communities because blacks, regardless of their class or economic status, were still restricted to black areas, still forced to live together by their common racial oppression. But after the movement of the 1960s forced the breakdown of legalized segregation, the black community also began to disintegrate. The black middle classes, following the same capitalist path of upward social mobility whites have been traveling, have been moving out of the inner city into the suburbs, in the process destroying the class and age diversity that had contributed so much to the cultural creativity of the black community. In this sense we can say that the black community in the American city was the last to break up. Now we all have to face the reality that the community relationships, which throughout U.S. history have been deepest at the bottom of American society, that is, among the workers and people of color, no longer bind people together. All of us, from the top to the bottom of our society, are now trapped in the individualistic and materialistic culture of the United States, which from the very beginning has operated to destabilize and uproot U.S. communities.

At the same time, whole cities are now being devastated because they are being abandoned by runaway multinational corporations that owe no allegiance to any community, any city, or any state, or even to the United States. As plants close down, not only do blue-collar workers lose their jobs but small businesses go bankrupt and the tax base for city services dries up. Having devastated American cities, these multinationals are now exporting manufacturing jobs to other countries to destroy their communities. Meanwhile, back in the United States more and more jobs are being eliminated by the robots that have been introduced into industry in the name of efficiency and to make the United States more competitive on the world market. So the millions who flocked to the cities lured by job opportunities can no longer depend upon capitalist industry to provide the jobs that were supposed to make them into self-sustaining individuals and responsible citizens.

So here we are today at the end of the rainbow. Millions of people live on the edge of survival in every city. Their hope that through wage labor they could achieve the

American Dream has turned into despair. Not only the unemployed and those who have never held a job but the underemployed—that is, the working poor who live from hand to mouth trying to provide for their shelter, food, and transportation on minimum wages—begin asking themselves, "Why struggle to survive on welfare or on $3.35 an hour when I could push dope?" We are experiencing in our cities a depth of barbarism that is unprecedented in human history.

For the great majority of those who live in the inner city of Detroit, Oakland, and all over the United States, there is no other place to go. There are no new industries coming to our cities to employ them now that capitalism has reached the multinational stage. Therefore, if we are thinking about a future for our people in the cities, if we are to give hope to our young people, we have to break with the ideas about what it means to be a human being that we have accepted in the past and start with new basic principles.

First of all, we must recognize that we are coming to the end of the era when we could think of citizenship only in terms of voting for politicians who make promises to the electorate based upon the concessions and bribes they make to corporations to provide jobs. City governments and state governments have no power to make multinational corporations stay in any city or state. All they can do is offer tax breaks and other concessions to these corporations, knowing full well that they will pick up and leave when they see the opportunity to make more profits elsewhere. People need to believe in and depend upon themselves and not on governments or corporations, which obviously don't care a hoot about us. Difficult as it is, we must give up the illusion that we can count upon corporations to provide jobs for us.

Many people will continue to wander to other towns or cities where they hope there are job opportunities, in the process destroying their own potential for creating social and political ties to one another in a particular city or community. Today you may run but you can't hide; soon everyone and particularly the poor will have to stop running and face reality.

The reality is that efficiency in production can no longer be our guiding principle because it comes at the price of eliminating human creativity and skills and making millions of people expendable. In the name of progress we are eliminating the role of people, competing to see how rapidly we can make them superfluous or killing them the fastest through the arms race. The reality is that the culture we have considered progressive for the last four hundred years is now revealing itself to be a culture of death and destruction.

Thus the rapid mechanization of agriculture with chemicals and machinery has tremendously increased the output of food, but it has also been destroying our topsoil and using up our groundwater, displacing millions of people from the land and in the process destroying the basis of a culture based upon respect for Nature and for natural processes. The same result has been achieved by automation and cybernation in the production of goods.

Rapid technological development has caused the city to become a graveyard. The residue of the last hundred years of rapid technological development is alienation, hopelessness, self-hate and hate for one another, and the violence that has created a reign of terror in our inner cities.

The question therefore becomes, is there another way of envisaging the city? Another way of looking at human relationships? Another way of looking at decision making that serves the needs of those who have been made obsolete by the rapid technological development we call progress? Another way of looking at the relationship between production and consumption?

It isn't going to be easy to create that new way of looking. But we must make a start, being very clear that there are no simple answers and that it is going to take a lot of imagination, cooperation, and experimentation to reverse the direction in which we are going today.

To begin with, the city must be seen as the place where you create social ties with the people you live with and not just a place to which you come to get a job or to make a living. We have to see the power that is in people and not see people as existing only to create capital for production or as dependent upon capital for their livelihood. The foundation of our cities must be people living in communities who have come to realize from their experiences that they can no longer leave the decisions as to their present and their future to the marketplace or to industrialists and capitalist politicians— regardless of their race or ethnic background. Our power lies in taking responsibility and caring for one another. We will begin to overcome our powerlessness and regain our humanity only as we begin to develop our neighborhoods into communities in which all residents see themselves as the creators and controllers of all institutions and services—and not just as users or consumers. A house is not just a place to sleep in. Keeping the streets clean is not just a job for the sanitation workers. The city is not just what is artificial, that is, what human beings have manufactured. It is the people, the land, and different species of plant and animal life. A neighborhood becomes a slum not just or mainly because of poverty but because people in that neighborhood have accepted the concept of themselves as slum dwellers—or, as the capitalists think of them, only as a means to an end. People are responsible for their communities, and our social ties are more important than our material wealth. By creating processes and local institutions for our mutual support we create respect for each other and security for ourselves.

A community is made up of people of all ages and classes who have a stake in the community. Special attention needs to be paid to the youth and the elders in every community so that they can contribute to the community and see it as their own.

Young people should work as part of their schooling and on weekends and after school to keep up and improve the community, to beautify the streets and parks and playgrounds, and to do services for older residents.

Young people and older people especially need public transportation so that they can move about and create and maintain social ties. Young people and older people especially need neighborhood stores within walking distance of their home so that they are not dependent upon a car to take them to the shopping mall or the supermarket with a lot of money in their pockets once a week. To build communities our streets must come alive with people walking to the store and to the corner to take the bus. To build the community we must scale down our dependence on private cars.

In every community there must be shops where the goods that people need are being produced. Small enterprises should be encouraged both to produce food for the community and to produce goods for community use so that young people can develop a sense of the relationship between efforts and results and as they grow older acquire skills and themselves contribute to the goods and services needed in every community, at the same time learning how to work with other people and gaining pride in what the community produces. We need to expose the myth that large-scale production is necessarily cheaper or more efficient—a myth that is maintained by covering up the tremendous waste involved in advertising, long-distance distribution, and bureaucracy.

Neighborhood responsibility councils should be created in every community. Public buildings and especially schools should be places for workshops and meetings where the members of the community meet to discuss and decide the issues and problems facing the community and the city.

Our concept of schools needs to be fundamentally changed. The school needs to be seen as an integral part of the whole community and not just as a place where young people are educated so that they can advance outward and upward out of the community. Youth must be given opportunities to play meaningful roles in the community: providing child care; performing small repairs and maintenance in their homes, schools, and communities; and keeping the school grounds and the neighborhood clean and attractive. All high schools should have home economics departments where food and clothing are produced for people in the community, as well as health clinics in which all youth participate. Not only in classes but in community projects young people should be learning how to make socially responsible decisions and thereby preparing themselves for citizenship. Scholarships should be established at every high school so that those who show leadership in contributing to the improvement of the community are guaranteed an opportunity to go to college, not as a way out of the community but in order to acquire skills that they can bring back to serve the community. However, the most meaningful education for young people must come from within the community, in young people working with elders, learning from them and opening up vistas of the future to their elders.

In every community or within a few miles of every community there must be farms or greenhouses where food for the community is grown in and out of season, not only to assure healthier food but so that young people can grow up with a respect for Nature and natural processes.

New communities like these are not going to be created overnight. It is going to take a lot of time and a lot of struggles to create them. But in cities all over our country taking responsibility for creating communities like these—out of what today are only geographical neighborhoods—is fast becoming the only realistic perspective.

We can no longer depend—as most of us are still doing—upon runaway multinational corporations to provide jobs for our young people. We can no longer depend upon the schools as they are today to educate our young people. That would be idealistic. It would also be idealistic to expect the government or corporation to pay us to do the work that is needed to keep up our communities and to provide for our elementary safety and security. We can no longer depend upon voting for politicians. We must now begin to practice doing for ourselves—or collective self-reliance. And as we do this, starting with relatively simple things—like creating support networks to look out for each other and moving on to community gardens and greenhouses, community recycling projects, community repair shops, community daycare networks, community mediation centers—we will discover that we are not only controlling and improving our space but that we are also transforming ourselves and our young people from faceless masses who are afraid of one another into socially responsible, mutually respecting, and politically conscious individuals who are systematically building the power to change our whole society.

In the nineteenth century the few Americans who rejected the mainstream culture had to leave the city to create communities like Brook Farm. In the late 1960s and early 1970s young people who saw the need to create a counterculture created communes and collectives made up mainly of their peers and those who agreed with them philosophically. But today creating communities wherever we are, of all those who live in the same neighborhood, of varying ages and ethnic backgrounds and regardless of ideological differences, has become a necessity for our survival.

That is why I believe the next great movement in the United States must be the community-building movement, which is also a people-building movement. It is an idea whose time has come.

"Community Building: An Idea Whose Time Has Come" is a speech delivered on April 5, 1987, in Detroit to an African American Leadership Conference titled "Return to the Source II," which was a follow-up to a conference two years earlier to which Boggs gave a "State of the Nation Address." The title of this speech appears in the last line of the preceding selection as well as this one. While the two speeches share the same subject—community building—and contain some similar language and ideas, they take different approaches to the topic and pose distinct questions and challenges to their audiences. The two speeches, therefore, are more complementary than duplicative and together provide a rich picture of Boggs's thinking about the importance of community building during the 1980s.

Community Building: An Idea Whose Time Has Come

Good morning. I start this way because I will always remember that when I first came to Detroit in 1937, I went over to Hastings and Theodore and said "Good Morning" to every old person I saw on the street. But nobody said anything back to me. When I told my auntie what happened, she said, "Boy, you are from the country. Folks up North don't say 'Good morning.' They take care of their own business." This seemed to me to violate everything human because my mother had always taught me that saying "Good morning" was the way you initiated relationships of humanity with old people and everybody else.

Over the last few days we have been grappling with the many profound contradictions facing African Americans today, nearly twenty years after the great struggles that enabled us to overturn a way of life that was accepted as normal and natural by the majority of Americans. In this session I do not intend to review the issues we have discussed. Rather what I hope to do at this point is to take some of the major ideas that have emerged and the unity and collectivity I have sensed and pull these together into an overall strategy so that as we go out from this conference, each of us, individually and collectively, in our various organizations and the many different areas where we function, can begin to see our struggles as part of the overall struggle we must now embark on to turn our communities and our lives around.

As I have listened to and participated in the discussions and in the workshops, I have two main impressions. On the one hand, it is clear to me that there is a high degree of black consciousness among the participants in this conference—for which I am profoundly grateful. In other words, most of you are proud of the great contributions to the evolution of humanity that have been made by African civilizations in the past, by Africans in the present (during the very moving ceremony with which we opened this morning I kept thinking of Nkrumah and Cabral), and by African Americans on this continent. It was on our backs that the infrastructure of this country was created; we were the first major labor force. An integral part of that black consciousness is the sense of solidarity and identity you feel with the millions of people in the third world who are also victims of U.S. capitalism and imperialism. Most of you also realize that blacks were not born with this consciousness but that it is the result of the great struggles that blacks have carried on over the centuries, culminating in the civil rights and Black Power struggles of the 1950s and 1960s—all of which have made you aware of the power that resides within you to change this whole society.

At the same time it is also clear to me that we are still groping for the spiritual vision and the political strategies that will enable us to meet the much more complex contradictions of this period—or, in the words of the conference call, the "assaults on our communities, our families, our children and our very souls, both from within and without."

Today, far more than twenty and thirty years ago, we live from crisis to crisis, both internally and externally. Every day I wake up feeling the devastation of this city and what is happening to our people on my back. Today the unity we once enjoyed no longer exists among us. We are now more afraid of one another than we used to be of white folks. We live in fear not only of strangers but of our neighbors and even the members of our own families. Even our churches are no longer safe places. While we are praying and singing and amen-ing the preacher, someone may be lifting our car from the parking lot. While we are taking up the offering, someone may come in and liberate the collection. The undertaker has to keep the doors of the funeral parlor locked so that someone doesn't come in and rob the deceased. Our older people are afraid to leave their homes after dark—that's why Detroiters for Dignity* has to meet in the daytime—and we are not safe even in our homes because most killings today are done by those close to us.

At the same time the blacks who are "making it" or those whom we used to call our "Talented Tenth" have run off or are planning to run off to Southfield or Bloomfield Hills, hoping to escape inner-city schools and inner-city crime. It isn't just "white flight" that is taking place. Let's not pretend that white folks won't know about this if we keep quiet about it. They know it and we know it.

Meanwhile, our lives externally are also a nightmare. We are not sure of our jobs; at any time we may be replaced by a robot; or the plant or office where we work may be moved to another city or country where workers can be hired to do the work for one-fourth of what we are getting. Most of the economic and social gains we won by the labor struggles of yesteryears are being taken away. Wages are being cut left and right. Seniority is no longer a guarantee against layoff. Even city and state jobs are no longer secure because the tax base is being eroded as multinational corporations abandon this country. So the cities to which your fathers and mothers were lured in the hope of making a better life for themselves and their children (I am one of those; I

---

* An organization of seniors, mostly women, formed to demand better treatment in the provision of city service. —Ed.

came North because I heard everything was so good up here) have become reservations on which our young people are trapped, with no opportunity to develop their skills and their humanity through useful and productive work; where the only way they can spend their time is by watching TV, making babies, taking drugs, and hustling. Every year everything that lured us to the cities is leaving the city. Every year the rich get richer and the poor, the homeless, and the hopeless become more abundant.

For four hundred years we have believed—and this is the philosophy of this country and of every Western capitalist country—that if we could create enough material abundance through rapid economic and technological development, everybody—even those who had been kept at the bottom so that others could rise to the top—would benefit; in other words, that a rising tide would lift all boats. Now we are faced with the reality that living by this materialistic and exploitative philosophy has resulted in the creation of a permanent underclass in our cities, the pollution of our atmosphere, the erosion of our soil, the threat of nuclear destruction, the withering away of our human identity, and worst of all, the loss of our freedom to make meaningful and principled choices—in other words, a culture of death.

Today we are living in a society where capitalist culture-or a culture organized around making profit—is destroying everything that is necessary to our identity as human beings. (Even though you may say, "this culture isn't mine," let's be clear that the culture we are living in is a capitalist culture and it rubs off on you.) Because our culture is organized around making profit, it gives priority to economic development over human relationships and over everything that is sacred to human beings. As a result, it has developed technologies and strategies on a global scale to turn the people of the whole world into a gigantic cheap labor pool, pitting individuals against one another and the workers of one country against those of other countries. The U.S. government is not going into Central America to bring democracy. We want to control Central America so that we can exploit cheap labor down there. We couldn't care less about the democratic rights of the Nicaraguan people—or we wouldn't have supported Somoza for so long. In fact, we have to be very clear about democracy itself. It was under democracy that we had slavery in the United States; it was under democracy that we exterminated the Native Americans and drove them onto reservations.

The level of our human relationships has never been so low. We live in a social environment where there is little or no respect for human or natural life; where violent crimes against those close to you and the abuse of women, children, the old, the blind, and the crippled have become almost normal; and where even those who have increased their access to material things and to high position resort to drugs and alcohol because they are so spiritually impoverished. Human beings cannot live by bread alone—as should be obvious from how many of our sports stars who have become millionaires also become junkies. I'm talking about us now. But it is not only us. You would be surprised how many members of old New England families get drunk every night, as do a lot of our senators and congressmen. Material abundance and high technology have not advanced either our humanity or our security.

That is why the main question before us is "How can we become new men and new women?" willing to accept the challenge to live by the vision of another culture, a new culture we still have to create, a culture based on social responsibility and respect for one another instead of individualism and materialism and on a love for and kinship with the land and with Nature, instead of viewing Nature as something to be conquered and land as a commodity to be owned? How do we create a culture that is life affirming rather than life destroying, which is based on caring and compassion rather than on the philosophy of the "survival of the fittest"?

In order to create this new life-affirming culture, our first priority must be the rebuilding or the regeneration of our communities because it is in community that human beings have always found their personhood or their human identity as persons. You can't find your human identity out there by yourself. It is in the community that our human identity is created because it is in the community that love, respect, and responsibility for one another are nurtured. At the present time our human identities are being destroyed mainly because our communities are destroyed by the relentless economic development of capitalist culture. Up to now we have depended upon the corporations to create communities for us—in the sense that we came to wherever the corporations had built their factories or their mines and raised our families to meet the needs of the company. Up to now we have not depended upon ourselves to build community. But now that the corporations are abandoning and destroying our communities, it is up to *us* to build the community. That means we need a two-pronged approach. On the one hand, we must resist the efforts of the corporations to destroy our communities by closing down our places of work and of the urban planners who are working for the mayor to turn Detroit into a tourist center and develop the riverfront to lure back those folks who have abandoned the city. (One day we will have to deal with Coleman Young. Don't be fooled by the black face because race isn't good enough. You need something else besides skin color.) But at the same time we must be building the communities necessary for the human identity of ourselves and our children.

What I am talking about is what the Chinese call "walking on two legs" and Cabral called "building as we fight." This is very difficult to do. It is much easier to focus your energy on the external enemy—even though meanwhile we are losing something inside. It is especially difficult now because we are so fragmented.

It means that we will need to have continuing faith in people when all around us we see so many of our brothers and sisters without faith, without hope, and living such empty lives. It is very hard to wake up each morning and see what is happening on your street and still have faith in people. Each morning I have to rededicate myself or I would go nuts. It is much easier to vilify the racist and capitalist exploiters than to have faith in the ability of people to transform themselves into new, socially responsible, cooperative human beings. That is why so many blacks have abandoned the inner city and are doing their own selfish thing. These blacks are abandoning us the same way that the labor leaders who came out of the great labor struggles abandoned the workers in the plant and joined the company. They have lost faith in us. They say, "Chile," how can you fault me for leaving Detroit? Only a fool would want to stay down there with all that crime." It is much easier to cross over than to live day after day with what is going on in our neighborhoods.

Most people are not going to join you to build the community in the beginning. As in every great struggle you have to start with the few to get to the many. My experience is that the many only come running after the few have gotten things started. Nor will it be easy to choose the issues to start with. The issues that seem most pressing only hold the attention of most people for a few days or a few weeks, whereas building community takes quiet and patient work over many years. For example, when Bishop Tutu came to town, everybody wanted to be there. But now there are only a handful of preachers here in Detroit who are saying anything about South Africa. On February 8 there were two thousand people at the memorial for the forty-three kids killed in Detroit in 1986. At the next meeting to create a working organization two hundred kids showed up—and now only about a hundred people are still meeting, even though the crisis hasn't gone away and our kids are still shooting and killing one another.

Therefore, what we need is a profound belief that every human being, each of us, needs community as the foundation of our human identity. For example, our young people were not born junkies or criminals. The main reason why so many of them resort to drugs and crime is because we have not been able to demonstrate to them in practice that their personhood, their self-respect and respect for others, can only be achieved through their being part of a community.

How do we carry on a two-pronged struggle? How do we combine the struggle against the internal enemy with the struggle against the external enemy? First of all, we must recognize that it is much easier to cuss out and blame somebody else out there or to resist the shutting down of a hospital than it is to change our way of living so that we are practicing preventive health care—even though we know that if we are not healthy we won't be able to struggle at all. So our first serious struggle should be to stop eating junk food, which pollutes our bodies, and stop littering our neighborhoods with garbage and junk cars and start working with our neighbors to clean up our alley so that we and our young people will stop believing that the only good neighborhoods are those where white folks live. Drive across Detroit any day or night, drive east or west, north or south, and if you are not depressed by what you see, then there is something wrong with you. Detroit is a floating garbage dump. Let's face it. We can't wait for somebody else to clean up our neighborhoods. We have to create a healthy environment for ourselves. We live here and our kids live here. If garbage and litter are everywhere, what are they going to have pride in?

But at the same time we also have to mount a campaign from coast to coast for a national health program that will entitle everyone to complete medical care. We black people have the highest mortality rates from cancer and high blood pressure.

Our infant mortality rate is staggering. But everyone in this country also needs a national health service because so many workers now only work part-time without benefits and so many corporations are cutting back on health insurance. In fact, in the next contract negotiations GM and Ford have that as their main goal.

But it doesn't do much good to live in a healthy environment if we don't have good relationships with the people in our community. What models can we set for our young people in creating respectful relationships? We can start by struggling for a radical change in the way that black men relate to black women. We know that sexually males are different from females, but being different doesn't make you superior. Any black male who has to discover his manhood through dominating females—and a lot of black males (and also white males) believe this—needs to be criticized and challenged openly. I struggle with this, too. In fact, one of the most important steps we can take in our community to create more self-respect and respect for others among our young people is to struggle openly and in public places for more equal and more human relationships between black males and black females. We need to insist that this question of more equal and more human relationships between the sexes be taken up in our schools as a major subject. Let's bring some real humanities into our schools. We also need to challenge our preachers to face up to the fact that the black church is one of the most sexist institutions in the whole country. Right now one of the most difficult questions the pope is facing on his tours to different countries is the role of women in the Catholic Church. If he doesn't straighten up on this question, Catholic women all over the world are going to leave the church. We can't continue to say that we cannot resolve the question of sexism until we have gotten rid of capitalism and racism—as I heard some folks saying in yesterday's workshop. That is a crutch we have to get rid of, if only because women need to be holding up their half of the sky for any serious struggle against racism and capitalism.

We say that our youth are our future. Yet we are losing over 50 percent of our youth each year in school dropouts and to prisons, drugs, and the military. It is much easier for us to demand that the corporations or the government provide jobs for our youth or classes and schools to train them for jobs because we think that if they are in school or at work, they won't be stealing, getting hooked on drugs, or killing one another. But men and women with jobs are also hooked on drugs and killing one another because it is not jobs or money in our pockets that makes us human. We are making too many things depend on jobs. We excuse someone for stealing or becoming a junkie because "he can't find a job." Or we say it's OK because white folks also do it, even though we know how many incorrect things are done by whites.

In the past teenagers didn't have jobs—jobs for youth is a post–World War II phenomenon. Before World War II there were so many socially useful things for young people to do around the house or in the community that they were glad to have time to play. Young people were proud of themselves because they felt themselves a necessary part of the community. We need to find ways to make our youth feel needed or a necessary part of the community. If we don't, then we are in effect saying to them, "If you don't have a job, if you are not bringing home a paycheck, you are nobody." That is a terrible thing to be saying to any human being. In every community we need youth-building programs in which adults work with young people to plan youth activities of all kinds and in which we give awards to youth for good deeds like helping the elderly, planting gardens, and scholastic achievement. We need to organize events that will raise scholarship funds for neighborhood youth to go to college and return to live and work in the community. We need neighborhood newsletters that report the activities and achievements of our young people. They don't have to be expensive or elaborate. In our schools we should insist on programs that enable older students to work with younger ones, encouraging them to excel. Fifty years ago males, especially black males, dropped out of school to go to work to help support their families. That is what my two older brothers did. Today they drop out and end up in jail—every year there are fewer black males who have the skills or the literacy that would make them suitable candidates as mates for black women. Let's face it: we are losing our black males at a terrible rate. It is hard enough for black women to be mothering and supporting black males. Yet that's what's happening.

Most important of all, we need to be talking and listening to our young people so that together we can decide on a course for developing our communities. We must stop thinking that all knowledge and wisdom are up at the schoolhouse. We might start by discussing with them the purpose of having children. If you ask them this question, you'd be surprised how many think the purpose is just self-gratification. We are probably the first generation in human history facing this question because historically our ancestors had children to help do the chores around the farm or the house or in the hope that they would take care of you in your old age. Entwined in the answer to this question is how much hope or perspective our young people have in the future.

Yesterday we talked about a new vision for our cities that is based not upon commerce but upon community. We all know or we should know that the houses we live in were built primarily to house us so that we could go to work for the company. Even if we built the house ourselves, that was our main purpose. It is not only that we as black people have inherited the leavings of other ethnic groups but that we ourselves don't think of our houses as homes or homesteads. Instead we believe that we can let our houses deteriorate and then move on to other areas of the city where the housing is better. The result is that more and more of our neighborhoods are turning into plain old slums. That is why we need to set into motion a movement to preserve our neighborhoods as places where we can put down our roots and to which our children will be proud to return to raise their own families. At the same time we should struggle to make absentee landlords fix up our houses—or turn the property over to us. We must demand that city and state governments provide the materials for people in the neighborhoods to fix up our houses and to build new homes so that all age groups can live together in the same community. We can't continue to allow old folks to live over there and young folks to live over here because that kind of fragmentation and segregation of the generations (which used to happen more with white folks than it did with us) robs a people of the experience and wisdom of their elders and therefore guarantees they will become more backward with each generation. They are constantly reinventing the wheel. If we older ones do not treasure our youth and our youth don't treasure their elders, we will break the continuity that is necessary for the survival and continuing evolution of a people.

At the rate that housing is deteriorating in the inner city and with no new housing programs on the horizon, Detroit and every major city in this country are going to experience an acute housing shortage in ten years. In Detroit we lose five houses for every new one that is built or fixed up. One-third of all black people who have a roof over their heads are very close to homeless; the roof just hasn't fallen off yet. One-third of Detroit housing is worse than the cotton-patch houses we lived in down South during the 1930s. The high gas bills we pay go to heat the air more than to heat our bodies. That is because even though we have been saying "the city is the black man's land," we have yet to see the city as ours because we still see "ours" in terms of money and property rather than stewardship. We should be creating plans to make this city really ours in terms of the human values that will tie us together in mutual respect. That means that we have to struggle against the urban planners who see the development of our city in terms of fancy waterfront apartments, convention halls, and gambling casinos.

Now I have not even taken up the question of jobs because I believe we need a much fuller discussion of the present crisis and of the future than we have been able to have up to now. But there are certain realities we have to face. None of your sons and daughters—and very few sons and daughters of whites and other ethnic groups, such as Mexican Americans, Arab Americans, Native Americans—will ever work in the plants of Ford, Chrysler, and GM unless they are engineers or designers, and they are going to need fewer and fewer of those all the time. That means we have to rethink totally how we are going to make our livings in a society that is being rapidly deindustrialized. Nor can we continue to delude ourselves that we can keep moving on to greener pastures. Today's boomtown is next year's bust town. So, as Booker T. Washington said, we have to put our bucket down where we are, put down some roots, and begin struggling to make where-we-are the kind of community where we and our descendants will want to live. That means we have to break with most of the ideas that we have held in the past about what it means to be a human being and start with some new principles.

First of all, we must recognize that we are coming to the end of the era when we can think of citizenship only in terms of voting for politicians who make promises to us based upon the concessions and bribes they make to corporations to provide jobs. That is what every mayor is—someone who woos and bribes corporations to come or to stay in his or her city. We must recognize that city and state governments have no power to make corporations stay in any city or state. All they can do is offer tax breaks and reduce worker benefits to corporations, knowing full well that these corporations will pick up and leave when they see the opportunity to make more profit elsewhere— as Parke-Davis did, as Stroh's did, and as GM will do with Poletown. Don't think Poletown is always going to be there just because so much money was spent and because the community was bulldozed to build it. Chrysler built a new foundry, so did Ford, and now they're both blowing in the wind.

We also have to recognize that we have come to the end of the era when we could count upon the corporations to provide jobs for people. Also, we can no longer count upon the schools as they are to educate our young people. It would also be unrealistic to expect the government or the corporations to pay us to do the work needed to build and maintain our communities and to provide for our elementary safety and security. Therefore we must now begin to practice doing for ourselves: collective self-reliance. But as we do this, starting with relatively simple things, like support networks to look out for each other, and moving on to

> community gardens,
>
> community recycling projects,
>
> community repair shops,
>
> community daycare networks,
>
> community panels to resolve disputes between neighbors,
>
> community skills banks,
>
> community greenhouses and community bakeries, etc., etc.

we will discover that we are not only controlling and improving our space but also transforming ourselves and our young people from faceless masses who are afraid of one another into what Jim Chaffers[*] spoke of in yesterday's "Creating Safe Communi-

---

[*]This is a reference to a previous session of the conference. See pp. 374–75n2 and the headnote on p. 274 for Chaffers and his relationship to Boggs. —Ed.

ties" workshop as "public families" who are building the power to change our whole society.

That is why I believe the next great movement in the United States must be the community-building movement, which is also a people-building movement. It is an idea whose time has come.

"Rebuilding Detroit: An Alternative to Casino Gambling" is the text of remarks made during a public speak-out concerning a ballot proposal to allow casino gambling in the city of Detroit. The event took place at the First Unitarian-Universalist Church in Detroit on June 24, 1988.

Rebuilding Detroit: An Alternative to Casino Gambling

Monday night I went to the graduation for one of my grandsons in Ford Auditorium at which Mayor Young was the main speaker. The student who introduced Young said, with a smile, that he was the only mayor she had ever known. Young then said in the same joking vein that maybe some students should come back in ten years and run for mayor because by then he would probably have retired. Everyone laughed, but it is no joking matter. The sad truth is that his honor has been mayor for so long he thinks he owns the town and seems to have forgotten that the people elected him and may one day retire him before his vision of Detroit leads us into even deeper chaos.

Coleman Young was elected mayor of Detroit fifteen years ago because the city was majority black and the time had come for a black mayor. Also, blacks were furious with STRESS,* the decoy system that the Gribbs administration had created to catch street criminals. When he was elected, Young had no program for stopping crime. All he could propose in his inaugural speech was that the criminals should hit Eight Mile Road. But he did have a dream, the dream that he could get the corporations to stay in Detroit by bribing them with tax abatements.

Today Young's dream has turned into a nightmare. Crime has not hit Eight Mile Road,† but industry has. Parke-Davis, Stroh's, the Mack Ave. Chrysler plant are all gone. Young promised us 6,000 jobs if we allowed him to bulldoze 1,500 homes, 600 businesses, and 6 churches for a new GM plant in Poletown. Today our taxes are still going to pay for Poletown, but there have never been more than 2,500 workers at the Poletown plant and most of those are from GM plants that have been closed down in other parts of the city, creating a wasteland in once thriving communities, especially on the southwest side of the city. At the same time the east side around the Chrysler Jefferson plant has been bulldozed so that it looks like a moonscape. Despite protests small businesses have been forced to leave, as in Poletown.

---

*The acronym for Stop the Robberies, Enjoy Safe Streets, a police unit begun in 1971 as a secretive, elite section of the Detroit Police Department's undercover assault squads. In its first thirty months, STRESS officers conducted five hundred raids without search warrants and killed twenty people. —Ed.

† Eight Mile Road serves as one of the city's borders, separating Detroit from its northern suburbs. During his inaugural address, Young declared: "I issue a warning to all those pushers, to all rip-off artists, to all muggers: It's time to leave Detroit; hit Eight Mile Road!"—Ed.

The reason Coleman Young's dream has turned into a nightmare is that it was based on the illusion that we can bring back the good old days when Detroit was the auto capital of the world and hundreds of thousands of workers came to the city to do manufacturing jobs at the decent pay that had been won through the organization of the union. But today cars are being built all over the world, not only in Japan and West Germany but in South Korea and Yugoslavia, and multinational corporations have exported manufacturing jobs to the third world where they can make more profit through cheaper labor. Coleman Young knows, as we all do, that large-scale industry is not coming back to Detroit. That's why he is now calling casino gambling an "industry" and trying to force it down our throats, promising us it will bring 50,000 to 80,000 jobs, as the auto industry once did.

The workers, who came to Detroit during World War II, particularly from the South, had a lot of hope. They also brought with them a sense of family and a sense of community or of people living in harmony with one another. Working in the plant, they developed a sense of solidarity, at the same time earning enough money to buy homes and raise their families. As a result, Detroit became known as one of the best organized and disciplined cities in the United States, with the highest percent of working-class homeowners north of the Mason-Dixon Line.

Today, however, the great majority of Detroiters no longer have any hope or solidarity with one another. Born and raised in the city, they have no experience of the culture that was second nature to those who had lived close to the land in small southern communities. At the same time, they can no longer look forward to the well-paying manufacturing jobs that enabled their parents and grandparents to buy their own homes and raise their families. So rather than accept the minimum-wage jobs that offer no hope for the future, an increasing number of our youth are attracted to the fast money and big bucks that come from selling dope. The result is that instead of being the auto capital of the world, Detroit has become the murder capital of the world.

However, instead of calling upon Detroiters to embark on a collective reassessment and exploration of how to rebuild Detroit, Young is becoming more arrogant and more stubborn every day. We, the people, he is convinced, are too dumb to know what's good for us. So he set up a commission stacked with his friends and appointees to study casino gambling. Unable to win a majority in the city for casino gambling, he created his own majority.

Today a person has to be really socially conscious and farsighted to care about the people of Detroit or, for that matter, the people of any of our big cities. I emphasize this because we are living today in a society where most people only care about the here and now. To rebuild Detroit we need a long-range perspective and not just a quick-fix solution. We need to think of human beings as more than just bodies to be clothed and housed or bellies to be filled. Most of all, we need a philosophy that gives young people the basis for the kind of hope that their grandparents had: the philosophy that people and the relationships between people are more important than material things and instant self-gratification and the confidence that we can create a better tomorrow if we live by this philosophy. We know that the welfare state has failed to give them this perspective. We also know that big industry is not coming back and that from now on, large-scale industrial jobs will be done in the developing countries or the third world. Historically, capitalism has always made sure that the people on the bottom get the leavings, and in this day and age the large-scale industrial jobs are the leavings and the people in the third world are at the bottom. We also know that a free marketplace economy only serves the interests of the capitalists and that the capitalists are in business not to serve the human needs of working people but to make profit. Therefore, when we think about rebuilding Detroit, we have to think of a new model of production based upon serving human needs and the needs of the community and not any get-rich-quick schemes.

The question Detroit and other industrial cities are now facing is "What is the purpose of a city?" Up to now, because it has been our historical experience for the last seventy-five years, most Americans have thought of the city as a place to which you go for a job after you have been driven off the land by mechanization. But now we know that the large industrial corporations are not going to provide those jobs in our cities.

What, then, is going to happen to the one million people who still live in Detroit, half of them on some form of public assistance, not only blacks but Chicanos, Arab Americans, Asians, and poor whites? For most of them, Detroit is the end of the rainbow. They can't go back to the farms from which their parents and grandparents came because these have been wiped out by agribusiness. There are no new industries coming for Detroiters. So if we are going to create hope, especially for our young people, we are going to have to break with most of the ideas about cities that we have accepted in the past and start with new basic principles.

To begin with, we have to stop seeing the city as just a place to which you come to get a job or to make a living and start seeing it as the place where the humanity of people is enriched because they have the opportunity to live with people of many different ethnic and social backgrounds. In other words, we have to see that our capital is in the people and not see people as existing to make capital for production or dependent on capital to live.

The foundation of our city has to be people living in communities who realize that their human identity or their love and respect for self is based on love and respect for others and who have also learned from experience that they can no longer leave the decision as to their present and their future to the marketplace, to corporations, or to capitalist politicians, regardless of ethnic background. We, the people, have to see ourselves as responsible for our city and for each other, and especially for making sure that our children are raised to place more value on social ties than on material wealth.

We have to get rid of the myth that there is something sacred about large-scale production for the national and international market. Actually, our experience over the last seventy-five years has demonstrated that large-scale production, because it is based on a huge separation between production and consumption, makes both producer and consumer into faceless masses who are alienated from one another and at the mercy of economic forces and the mass media. Instead, we have to begin thinking of creating small enterprises that produce food, goods, and services for the local market, that is, for our communities and for our city. Instead of destroying the skills of workers, which is what large-scale industry does, these small enterprises will combine craftsmanship, or the preservation and enhancement of human skills, with the new technologies that make possible flexible production and constant readjustment to serve the needs of local consumers.

In order to create these new enterprises, we need a view of our city that takes into consideration both the resources of our area and the existing and potential skills of Detroiters.

Detroit itself is in the Great Lakes region, so we should think of how we can take advantage of this resource. We can start by developing a fishing fleet. This would mean training young people to fish for a living as they do in New England and along the West and East coasts. It would also mean building docks and cleaning facilities along the riverbank in order to supply fresh fish for the whole area.

Michigan also has the best sand in the world. In the past this sand has been used mostly in foundries. We can use it to produce glass—glass to replace the broken windows that we see all around us; glass for the storm windows that will enable us to save energy and use the sun to heat our homes and our water. We can also use glass for greenhouses all over the city so that we can grow vegetables for the local market year-round. During the spring and the summer we should "Green Detroit" by planting gardens in the thousands of vacant lots all over the city.

Every day on the expressway we see hundreds of trucks and vans equipped with ladders, electrical tools, and lumber bringing carpenters, electricians, and other skilled workers into Detroit to do the work of repairing Detroit homes. Meanwhile, inner-city youth, black and white, stand around doing nothing and waiting for the dope man. Our community colleges should be organizing crash programs to train our youth to use their hands and heads so that they can be doing this work to improve our communities and our city instead of depending on suburbanites.

Detroit has raised many talented clothes designers, but they have all left for New York or California because we have only been able to think in terms of large-scale industry and haven't recognized that Detroit could become a clothes-producing center for the state of Michigan.

Over the years Detroiters have become locked into the mentality that a party store is the only small business that the average person can create and that shopping malls in the suburbs are where you go to buy most things. We need to be creating all kinds of locally owned stores in our communities so that we can buy our necessities locally and our young people can see stores not just as places where you spend money to buy what you want but as places where people are working to meet the needs of the community. In every neighborhood there should be a bakery where families can purchase freshly baked bread and children can stop by after school to buy their sweets. In every neighborhood there should also be food shops where working people can purchase whole meals to take home to eat together, instead of living off McDonalds and Kentucky Fried Chicken. This has been a common practice in other countries.

We also need a fundamental change in our concept of schools. Since World War II our schools have been transformed into custodial institutions where our children are warehoused for twelve years, with no function except to study and get good grades so that they can win the certificate that will enable them to get a job. What kids learn from books in school has little if any relationship to their daily lives. While they are growing up, they are like parasites doing no socially useful work, spending their time playing and watching TV. Then when they become teenagers, we blame them because they have no sense of social responsibility. We have to create schools that are an integral part of the community in which young people naturally and normally do socially necessary and meaningful work for the community, for example, keeping the school grounds and the neighborhood clean and attractive, taking care of younger children, growing gardens that provide food for the community, etc., etc. Connections should be created between schools and local enterprises so that young people see these as an integral part of their present and future. Our goal should be to make Detroit the first city in the nation to use our schools to support the community rather than as places where our young people are upgraded to leave the community.

Because of our declining population many school buildings in Detroit have been abandoned or are about to be abandoned. These schools can be turned into daycare centers to care for the children of working mothers and fathers. They can be developed into political and cultural centers for the community; the place for town meetings or for a local museum where the arts and crafts are proudly exhibited.

These are only a few examples of the kinds of things we can do to rebuild Detroit once we realize that we can no longer depend upon the corporations or the politicians to save us and begin thinking for ourselves about what we can do and must do. At this point, what we need to do is to begin discussing how we are going to rebuild our city, in every block club, every church, every school, every organization, and every home because for the rest of this century and most of the next, the major question in this country is going to be "How will we live in the city?" Up to now we have come to the city expecting somebody else, meaning the corporation, to provide us with a livelihood. Now we are stuck here and we can't run or hide anymore. We can't go back to the farms, we can't keep running from city to city. We must put down our roots where we are and put our hearts, imagination, minds, and hands to work so that we can empower ourselves and one another to create an alternative to casino gambling. Coleman Young's crisis is our opportunity. Let us start the discussion here tonight.

"We Must Stop Thinking Like Victims" appeared in the June 1990 issue of the *Save Our Sons and Daughters Newsletter.*

We Must Stop Thinking Like Victims

Seldom a day goes by that I don't hear someone say, "If it wasn't for racism, I'd have everything under control. I'd have a good job and I'd be living in a good neighborhood." What gives them this idea? There are a lot of whites and people of other ethnic groups in this country who don't have jobs and don't have their lives under control. What reason do they give?

There is no question that most, if not all, African Americans have been handicapped by racism. Anyone who knows the history of the United States knows that it was practically founded on African slavery and Indian dispossession. But anyone who knows the history of the United States knows that millions of African Americans, even in the cruelest and most ruthless days of slavery and Jim Crow, never stopped struggling to overcome and to achieve. In fact, some of the most important developments in this country were the fruit of African American struggles at a time when the United States was ten times more racist than it is today.

When I, along with millions of other African Americans, was growing up in the South, lynchings were taking place all around us. But that didn't keep us from daring to fight to change and to do the things we knew white Americans didn't want us to do. We tried to get a good education even though we went to inferior schools. Against overwhelming odds we found ways to acquire skills in mechanics and other trades from which we were excluded. Often we would work at jobs and in positions far below our skills because we had so much confidence in our own ability to perform.

Most of us were like Jackie Robinson in spirit. Because we knew how racist this society is, we also knew that in order to advance in our field, we had to be the very best. So striving for excellence became second nature for us. We were determined to "make a way out of no way." That is how our parents raised us.

That is why we read books and acquired skills. We knew whites didn't want us to have this knowledge or these skills, but we weren't going to allow them to dictate our actions. We learned these skills even when we knew we were not going to be given a fair chance or an equal opportunity. We believed that if at first we didn't succeed, we could try and try again.

That is the spirit and the drive that used to pervade the African American community from top to bottom. That is the spirit and the drive that distinguished our best leaders from Sojourner Truth and Paul Robeson to Martin Luther King and Malcolm X. That is the spirit and the drive that gave birth to the struggle against slavery and to the civil rights movement.

Today one of the main reasons why our children are not learning in school and why our neighborhoods are so devastated is that we have lost that spirit and that drive. Meanwhile, those who claim to be our leaders, instead of trying to inspire us with that drive and that spirit, encourage us to blame everything on racism. So all around us young people are filled with despair.

There is no question that the United States remains a racist society. But there is also no question in my mind that if African Americans spent as much time struggling to develop our skills and working together to improve our neighborhoods as we do blaming racism and bemoaning our fate, our children would have much more hope and neighborhoods would be much friendlier.

The worst thing that can happen to someone who has been a victim of oppression—whether of class or race—is to think like a victim.

"What Does It Mean to Be a Father?" appeared in the July 1990 issue of the *Save Our Sons and Daughters Newsletter*.

What Does It Mean to Be a Father?

In the past, when most Americans lived in rural communities or small towns, the value system of the community shaped the relationship between men and women. If a man impregnated a woman, the unwritten code of the community practically guaranteed that they would get married. People who conceived children were ashamed not to take responsibility for them. Also, men were viewed as the head of the household, so they were more ready to get married.

But now that most of us live in big cities, all the powers of the police and the courts are not enough to make men take responsibility for raising their children. Also, women have evolved to the point that they no longer view men as the head of the family. In 1988 more than 21 percent of all American children lived in families headed by women; 60 percent of black fathers and 47 percent of white fathers had not seen their children at all in the past year. So our children grow up emotionally and morally deprived of the support and guidance that comes from being raised by both a male and a female parent. They are the ones that suffer the most.

In recent years we have cheapened the words "fatherhood" and "self-esteem" by using them so loosely. We call men "fathers" when they are little more than studs or baby-getters. We talk about "self-esteem" as if you can get it from a workshop or a lecture. Fatherhood and self-esteem have to be earned. And they are earned when a person takes responsibility for his or her actions.

There are millions of males in the United States today who are evading the responsibilities of fatherhood because people in the community allow them to. Parents no longer raise their male children with the understanding that if they impregnate a woman they will have to take financial and moral responsibility for raising the child. Instead of ostracizing a man who evades this responsibility, his friends joke about it and continue to accept him as a friend. And too many women are also ready to conceive a child by a man they know is not going to be around to raise the child.

So we all have to take a good look at ourselves. What standards are we ready to create in the community as the foundation for raising our children, male and female? What commitments do we believe men and women should make to raising children before they bring them into the world? Are we ready to ostracize men who boast about how many children they conceive but do not accept the financial and moral responsibility of fatherhood? Should we publish their names on a dishonor roll?

And how serious are women about this issue? History tell us about communities where women got so sick and tired of raising their male children to adulthood and then seeing them sent off to be killed in war that they refused to have sex with their lovers and husbands. Can we ask women today to stop being sex objects and baby-getters for men they know are only using them?

In the South we used to boycott merchants who refused equal treatment to blacks. Today this issue of fatherhood is as important as civil rights. We cannot save our sons and daughters until we summon up the courage to face it and to make sacrifices in the struggle to resolve it.

"Why Are We at War with One Another?" appeared in the October 1990 issue of the *Save Our Sons and Daughters Newsletter*.

Why Are We at War with One Another?

Fifty residents on Field Street near Mack Ave.* joined SOSAD, WE-PROS, and the DETROIT GREENS on September 17 to plant a tree in memory of the three little children killed in the firebombing of their home over Labor Day weekend. We held hands, sang, prayed, and pledged to start caring for one another and to nurture this tree as a symbol of life. Neighbor Maxine Sharpe lifted our spirits with "Amazing Grace" and Pastors V. B. Washington and Skip Wachsmann of Trinity Deliverance and Genesis Lutheran churches led us in prayer. Both churches are only about a hundred feet from the site of the tragedy.

After the ceremony some of us discussed what is happening in Detroit. We wondered why people only get aroused if there is a conflict between the races (e.g., a white person kills a black person or vice versa) but don't get too disturbed if the killing takes place within one ethnic group.

We spoke about the serious decline that has taken place in our value system and felt that until we grapple with this phenomenon, we will go right on holding funerals and our young people will keep on thinking that it is beyond their ability to change the killing climate and that somehow it is God's will that we are burying so many of our children.

I said that we have to recognize that this is not because of God's will. There is an evil force loose in our community. We have lost the belief that people have the power to change our conditions in life. We seem to have lost all the most valuable lessons from our history as a people. We need to look within ourselves and ask what has happened to and in our culture in the United States that we can have more than twenty thousand homicides each year and not recognize that we are at war with one another.

There are some two thousand churches in the city of Detroit. Why have they had so little impact on the killing climate of our city? If only 10 percent of these two thousand churches would declare a drug-free, crime-free zone in a four-block area around the church, it would achieve miracles in overcoming the hopelessness in our neighborhoods.

Why do African Americans in Detroit still think of ourselves as a minority when we are over 70 percent of the population? Why do we still think that we have been

---

*This is near the Boggses' home at 3061 Field Street on Detroit's east side. —Ed.

abandoned? Why do we still cling to the hope that some outside force (the state or federal government or some big company) will come to our aid? Has the tendency to blame everything on "racism" destroyed the self-esteem of our young people so that they no longer believe they can use their minds and talents and struggle together to make this a better world?

We can't keep evading these questions. Examining the internal contradictions in and among the people will always be difficult and painful, but it is a necessary step toward discovering a higher form of being. The lives of our children who are our future depend upon some new thinking among us. Do you agree or disagree? I would like to hear from SOSAD readers.

"A 'No' Vote Will Say Detroiters Want to Save What's Left" appeared in the Other Voices section of the *Detroit Free Press* on April 23, 1991, the day voters ultimately rejected Proposal A, a ballot initiative that would have allowed public land to be rezoned for commercial development. Boggs's piece, which opposed Proposal A, ran alongside a piece in favor of the proposal. The two opposing views appeared under the banner "A Proposal to Build On?" with this introductory statement: "Detroit voters go to the polls today to vote on whether to give the City of Detroit the authority to tear down Ford Auditorium and rezone public space along the riverfront for private development. Today we present two views of Proposal A, by David Baker Lewis, a Detroit Attorney who specializes in municipal bonds, and by James Boggs, a retired Chrysler worker, author, and community activist."

A "No" Vote Will Say Detroiters Want to Save What's Left

A "no" vote on Proposal A will be a turning point for the city of Detroit. It will let the world know that the people of Detroit are determined not to give away Ford Auditorium, Belle Isle, or Hart Plaza to commercial developers.

For too long, our city has been the victim of the giveaway mentality of the mayor and his economic development advisors. Dangling the promise of jobs before Detroiters, they promote mega-projects that have been shown to eliminate jobs and enrich developers and contractors.

These developers and contractors have no interest in our city's past or future. They are interested only in how much money they can make by tearing down old buildings and constructing new ones. So they make generous contributions to the mayor's coffers, and he uses our tax money to construct new office buildings, even though Detroit has forty-six vacant office buildings downtown. The result is further blight and a shrinking tax base as companies move from older buildings to newer ones, creating more vacancies and more vacant buildings.

Voting no on Proposal A will make clear that Detroiters can no longer be fooled by the mayor's propaganda (paid for by friendly contractors) that his economic development schemes will create thousands of new jobs.

Poletown, the People Mover, Chrysler Jefferson—each has been touted as key to Detroit's economic development. But each has ended up costing us more and leaving us with fewer jobs. Each has made a few developers rich while saddling the rest of us with tax abatements, higher taxes, bond issues payable until the year 2040, and the increasing devastation and depopulation of our city, leaving ever fewer people to bear the burden. To pay for these "development" schemes that have actually undeveloped Detroit, we have borrowed from the next three generations.

And now on the eve of the election, the mayor has once again come up with a scheme that he hopes will defeat the grass roots movement to save Ford Auditorium: a new hotel on the Ford Auditorium site. Once again, he uses the promise of jobs to try to pull the wool over our eyes. And, once again, he says nothing about how a new hotel will affect the already dangerously low occupancy rates of the Pontchartrain, the Omni, and the St. Regis hotels, threatening them with the same fate as the boarded-up Statler and the Book Cadillac.

Detroiters who still believe in the mayor's empty promises should look around them to see how the same kind of benign neglect of Ford Auditorium is at work in our neighborhoods. Just as the number of vacant buildings keeps growing downtown, so the number of vacant lots keeps growing in our neighborhoods. The mayor likes to boast that "I own more property than any mayor in the country." Well, the time has come to make clear to him that it is the citizens of Detroit, and not the mayor, who own this city.

Ford Auditorium, like Hart Plaza and Belle Isle, is not the property of any administration or elected official. No elected body has the right to sell them to or dispose of them for private or commercial use. They are public property, the property of Detroit's citizens.

For much too long, the mayor has been "yeasaying" the developers and "naysaying" the people of Detroit. Voting no on Proposal A says "yes" to the people of Detroit and "no" to the developers.

The time has come for the people of Detroit to reclaim our city and to let every elected official and every city appointee know that they are the servants and not the masters of the people. They were elected to serve the people and not their self-interests or the interests of developers and contractors. We will not sit idly by while our city declines and the things we love about our city are given away.

"How Will We Make a Living?" appeared in the June 1991 issue of the *Save Our Sons and Daughters News-letter.*

How Will We Make a Living?

Every June millions of young people come out of high schools and universities hoping that someone, some business or institution, private or public, will give them a job. Ever since they were kids they have been told, "Stay in school and get an education so that you can get a job."

But today there are millions of Americans of all colors, ages, and skills who are out of work because so many jobs have been eliminated by high-tech or exported out of the country. So after you finish high school you discover that you have to go on to college if you want something better than a job at McDonalds. And after you finish college, you have to continue on to graduate school to acquire skills and credentials.

In the 1950s and 1960s racism was the main issue in the United States because segregation and discrimination were legal, and every African American was very conscious of the blatant and often dangerous effects of racism. But unemployment was not a serious problem at that time. A young person could drop out of school and get a job in the plant.

Today, because of the struggles of the 1960s, a few African Americans can get the kinds of middle-class jobs that enable them to realize the American Dream of a house in the suburbs. But for everyone who achieves this dream, there are ten others for whom the only options are minimum-wage jobs, welfare, engaging in some kind of illegal activity, or joining the military. For all too many the price for making a living is making a killing or taking the chance of being killed.

At the same time social programs and government spending at all levels are being cut because the upper and middle classes have made up their minds that they are not going to pay any more taxes to support the poor.

So the question that we face has become "Do we continue to depend upon big corporations to provide us with jobs when it is obvious that these corporations are eliminating more jobs than they are creating, or do we begin to create jobs for ourselves?"

This is the question that we can no longer evade because the way things are going, there will be fewer jobs every year—and therefore more unemployed, poor, homeless, and hungry people.

In the 1950s and 1960s we had to overcome our own fears and the sense of inferiority a fascist society had instilled in us in order to create the civil rights and Black Power movements.

Today, it is going to take much more courage, cooperation, and ingenuity to confront the question of how we are going to make a living. This is something we have always left to "the man." But, as I said in my last article, the only one who can save us now is us.

The longer we evade this question, the more desperate and cynical our young people will become. On the other hand, the sooner we put our minds, hearts, hands, and imaginations together to begin creating solutions, the sooner we can begin to create hope, self-esteem, and self-confidence in ourselves and in our youth.

"Why Are Our Children So Bored?" appeared in the summer 1991 issue of the *Save Our Sons and Daughters Newsletter.*

Why Are Our Children So Bored?

When I was growing up in the South before World War II, I had no time to be "bored." I had so many things to do around the house: taking out the ashes, emptying the pan under the icebox, running to the store. Every day I looked forward to finally finishing my chores so that I could go out to play with my friends or go walking in the woods.

But today the most common complaint among children is "I'm bored. There's nothing to do around here." So parents worry about how they are going to make life more entertaining for their children to keep them out of trouble. They take them shopping to buy fancy clothes and give them money to go to the show and to concerts, never asking themselves what kind of adults and what kind of society we are creating by raising our children to believe that life should be fun and full of goodies.

The family used to be a place where children were needed to do things. Children had a sense of their value (or what we now call "self-esteem") because they knew they were making a contribution. But today there is little in the way of useful activities that the average family has to offer children. In single-parent or two-parent households, adults go off to work and send the kids off to school or to a babysitter. Then when the parents come home, they feel they ought to offer the kids something to amuse them.

The family used to be a place where children learned that to be a full human being you need to do your share of the work that is necessary to maintain the household. By working around the house children learned early in life what it means to belong and to be socially responsible. That is what was meant by raising children.

But after we came to the city we stopped doing things for ourselves and began depending on others to do for us. In the process we lost our understanding of the relationship between the family, work, and raising children. We no longer see the role of the family as raising the next generation to become responsible adults. Instead folks have children to satisfy their personal need for someone to love or to prove they are a man or a woman. We don't see work as a way to develop our distinctively human capacities to produce goods and services and to cooperate with one another. We only see work as a "job" or something that is done to make money. We have reduced everything to material benefits and to making money.

Instead of providing kids with opportunities to be useful, we struggle to "give them the things I didn't have when I was growing up."

We try to get kids out of our way by sitting them down before the TV set or by sending them out to play. If we need them to do something around the house, we pay them. Then we complain when, like workers in a factory, they want to be paid more.

We don't think of education as a process by which children expand their capacities. We tell children to stay in school so that eventually they can get a job making a lot of money. Then we are surprised when many of our young people say, "Why should I stay in school so that I can eventually get a job making a lot of money when I can make a lot of money selling dope?"

Most people think that the solution to "boredom" is to provide more entertainment and recreation. My own view is that our children would be less bored and their self-esteem would be higher if we gave them more opportunities to be useful.

It isn't going to be easy to turn this situation around in today's cities. But we can start by involving children, beginning at a young age, in work around the house and in the community.

"What Can We Be That Our Children Can See?" appeared in the fall 1991 issue of the *Save Our Sons and Daughters Newsletter.*

What Can We Be That Our Children Can See?

In the last ten years Americans in general and Detroiters especially have been concerned about our youth. Here in Detroit it seems that more teens are killing each other, using drugs, committing crimes, having babies, dropping out of school, going to jail, and more devoid of a purpose in life than at any other time in our history. Different people give different reasons for this crisis that is wasting the lives of so many young people: breakdown in the family structure, poor schools, not enough time spent by adults with children, lack of self-esteem.

I don't think there is one single root cause, but one thing I do know. Our children were not born the way they are. The way they are is the result of the way they were raised. So it is adults who need to look at how we have been raising our children.

Most adults today have lost the sense of the role and purpose of youth. When I was growing up, people had children more out of a sense of necessity: to take care of them when they got old or to carry on the family. Today most parents seem to have children to satisfy their ego, to prove that I am a man or woman or to have someone to love.

In the past most people understood that human beings, unlike animals, are born with very little ability to do for themselves. They need a lot of care and raising. Therefore, what they are taught, how they are raised, is critical.

Today, however, there is so much emphasis put on schools that parents seem to believe that their children will get knowledge, understanding, wisdom, and even common sense from school.

So we have to ask ourselves whether common sense can come from schools, or is there another more important source for common sense? In asking this question, we should bear in mind that many of our parents didn't have a chance to go to school, couldn't read or write "good English." Yet they raised children who were outstanding citizens.

There is an important lesson for us in this history. Most children in this country do not do the same kind of work their parents did. But their character or what kind of human beings they become depends a lot on how their parents and other adults behave and what they see around them in the community.

So when we see children not caring about anyone else but themselves or about anything else except money, fancy cars, and fancy clothes, when we see them using violence to settle conflicts, we have to ask, what kind of examples have we set for them? I like to think that if Malcolm X were alive today, that is the question he would be asking us. Malcolm knew how to chide and challenge us to look at our own weaknesses and struggle to overcome them. I can still see people in his audience laughing and shouting, "Tell it like it is." That is what we should be doing today.

"Time to Act Like Citizens, Not Subjects" appeared in the summer 1992 issue of the *Save Our Sons and Daughters Newsletter.*

Time to Act Like Citizens, Not Subjects

Back in 1991, when we started thinking about Detroit Summer, our great goal was to foster among young people, both outside and inside Detroit, a sense of citizenship and the kind of social consciousness that was expressed by the youth of the 1960s. We especially had in mind the SNCC (Student Nonviolent Coordinating Committee) youth who left college to go South and join with local residents in the civil rights struggle. Their energy and commitment played a key role in forcing Congress to pass the Civil Rights Act of 1964 so that not only African Americans but many poor whites were able to vote for the first time. As a result, the United States came closer to being a "democracy" than it had ever been. In that sense "democracy" came to this country not in 1787 but in 1964.

We were also aware that the devastation of Detroit is a symbol of the crisis facing all American cities east of the Mississippi. For most of the twentieth century Detroit was a mecca luring people from the country into the city who wanted to become industrial workers, earn enough money to become homeowners, and send their children to college. Now, having been abandoned by the corporations that lured us here, we and our children and grandchildren are trapped in a city that is beginning to resemble a nineteenth-century ghost town, with this difference: today's multinationals have left not only Detroit but the whole country, to which they feel no allegiance.

Two generations have come of age since the 1960s and most young blacks accept the freedoms of today as if they had always been there, not recognizing that they were won by the struggles of their forebears over the years. Also, most people today, including young people, can't conceive of doing anything in their community, even something as simple as picking up litter in front of their house, unless they are paid. So, in addition to the devastation created by corporate abandonment, we are also suffering the devastation created by an absence of a sense of social responsibility.

We cannot expect today's young people to be just like those of the past because they have been raised in a different age. We also can't expect corporations like Ford, GM, and Chrysler to come back and rescue us by providing jobs. These corporations exist only to make profits, and as long as they can make more profit by producing in places like Mexico they are going to do it.

Therefore, in a city like Detroit we are confronted with the challenge of creating another way of life for ourselves and our children. The question we have to ask ourselves is: How can the million people now trapped in a city like Detroit make a living?

How can we ourselves rebuild Detroit? What kind of an economy can we create, since we know very well that we can't depend upon Ford or GM to do it for us? Can we come together and create an economy of small enterprises that will provide for our needs and also provide us with jobs?

These are now life-and-death questions for the people of Detroit. Working people like ourselves have never been confronted with this kind of challenge before. We know that big corporations today are eliminating more jobs than they create by exporting them out of the country and/or by introducing high-tech. We also know that small enterprises now provide more jobs than big ones. But it is still hard for us to put these two facts together and act on them. We are still waiting for the "master" to come and rescue us. We are still not thinking like full-fledged or first-class citizens. We are still not thinking like a community that has to save itself.

That is because African Americans are still trapped in old modes of thinking. We are still thinking like a "minority" even though today we make up over 75 percent of the population of Detroit. And we are still thinking in terms of blacks vs. whites and not multiculturally even though the population of Detroit, like that of most big American cities, now includes large numbers of people of Hispanic, Arab, and Asian descent.

Just as we are still hoping that the corporations will come back and provide us with jobs, we are still hoping whites will come back and save us. So we keep blaming them for our plight.

The time has come for us to stop playing "blame politics" and to take on the responsibility for rebuilding Detroit. Historically in this country the ethnic group that becomes the majority in a city has always taken on the responsibility for political power and leadership of that city, including the responsibility for living in harmony with all the different ethnic groups who provide city life with its rich texture.

These are some of the ideas that went into the creation of Detroit Summer '92. I hope and believe that, like the SNCC youth who went South in the 1960s, the young people of Detroit Summer '92 will be advancing the civilization of this country to another plateau.

"What Time Is It in Detroit and the World?" appeared in the fall 1992 issue of the *Save Our Sons and Daughters Newsletter.*

What Time Is It in Detroit and the World?

In the last fifteen to twenty years a lot of African Americans have been living on ideas from the past that have become myths and have even created new myths in order to evade facing the reality that, like every other ethnic group in the world, we have contradictions within and among ourselves. As a result, these contradictions are beginning to catch up with us.

For example, when we are around people of another ethnic group we shut up about the negative things happening in our community because we don't want to expose ourselves to criticism. We think that if we don't talk about our weaknesses in public, others won't know about them. We think that we are fooling others but we are actually fooling ourselves.

Or we make a big hullabaloo when a person of another ethnic group uses racist terminology in talking to or about a black person even though everyone knows that in this country people from all ethnic groups, including African Americans, talk that way all day long.

In the United States today there is so much talk about black-white relationships that you would think that blacks and whites are the only two races in this country. In fact, the United States was never only a black-white country. It only appeared to be so because until twenty years ago the main contradictions, and therefore the main struggles, of this country were, first, against the enslavement of African Americans, which culminated in the Civil War, and then the struggle for civil rights, which culminated in the Civil Rights Act of 1964.

However, because of our indigenous Native American and Hispanic populations, the United States has always been more like a United Nations than just an African American–European American nation. In the last twenty to thirty years this multicultural diversity has been enriched by the huge immigration of peoples from Asian, Latin American, and Arab countries.

Historically in this country when any ethnic group became the majority in a city, it began to assume the responsibility for governing that city. Today African Americans are 74 percent of Detroit's population while Euro-Americans are only 15 percent. But African Americans in Detroit still have not accepted responsibility for rebuilding Detroit. We are still thinking like a minority, still looking to whites to come back and save us. A lot of African Americans are even still pursuing school integration, even though Detroit Public Schools are now 80–90 percent African American. So we have all these yellow buses transporting African American children from neighborhood schools to other schools that are predominantly African American. And when a city erupts, as L.A. did this spring, some African Americans still talk about integration when there is very little left for them to integrate into.

At a time when millions of college graduates are unemployed or underemployed we are still trying to persuade our children that if they want to get a good job and make a lot of money, they should stay in school. Then we wonder why so many of them say, "Why go to school to make a lot of money tomorrow when you can make a lot of money rollin' today?"

I emphasize these points because I believe that until we change our thinking to relate to the new stage of development in this country and the world, we are creating frustration and demoralization in our young people. Because we are ourselves confused about what time it is in the United States and the world, we are unable to challenge them to live up to their potential. Because we are living on myths and trying to pass these on to our young people we are encouraging them to think like victims who are always reacting to how others treat us instead of setting positive goals for ourselves and working to achieve them.

As we approach the twenty-first century the United States is no longer the greatest country in the world either in terms of production or social relations. We are number one only when it comes to violence and killing one another over material things.

For the first time in the history of this country we are faced simultaneously with the two most basic and challenging questions of life: How do we make a living? How do we live in harmony with one another and with Mother Nature?

The world is not out there just waiting for us with jobs and a bright future. It is waiting for us to design and create new and different ways to make our livings and to live together.

When we challenge our young people to get involved in creating and designing these new and different ways to make our livings and to live together, I believe we will also see a decline in the level of violence in our communities and among our young people.

"We Can Run But We Can't Hide" appeared in the winter 1993 issue of the *Save Our Sons and Daughters Newsletter.*

We Can Run But We Can't Hide

Detroiters have been living so long by the slogan "They won't let us" that we now have two generations who blame everything on "the system" or "the man" and don't believe that we can do anything ourselves. We can only see the external contradictions and we forget that as human beings what we do depends upon both external and internal contradictions.

Throughout our history in this country African Americans in particular have had to endure both class and race oppression. But until the civil rights period thirty years ago we were clear that we couldn't expect any help from the external enemy. Therefore, any change for the better had to come from mobilizing our inner selves to struggle and to overcome.

Today we still face external contradictions and enemies, but our main contradictions and enemies are internal and we don't know how to struggle against them. So when all around us blacks are robbing and killing, all we can say is, "Child, everything has gotten out of hand. I just don't know what we're going to do."

What we're saying in essence is that if a white person or a person of another ethnic group disrespects or beats or kills an African American, we know what to do. Within an hour we're out there, organized to protest, march, fight back. But when an African American does the same thing to another African American, we're immobilized. All we can say is, "It's crazy."

That is because we have a set of principles for how the external enemy should conduct itself. But we have not developed a set of principles for ourselves. So in our neighborhoods African Americans kill, rob, and terrorize one another and we are afraid to get involved. "Child, they might burn up my house," we say. The fear we now have of one another is like that we used to have of the white man.

We were able to summon up the courage to stand up against the external enemy. We sent our little children to schools from which we had been excluded. We sat in at "his" lunch counters and "his" libraries. But today we escort or drive our children to "our" schools to protect them from African American terrorists. And many of us shop in the suburbs because we feel safer there and dream of making enough money so that we can move there to live.

In 1993 we have to face up to some very painful realities that we wish we could keep from other ethnic groups and that we are ashamed to face ourselves.

The reality is not only that our young people are killing and terrorizing each other.

The reality is also that we are now more afraid of one another than we are of white people. The reality is also that we are afraid to admit and struggle against our own weaknesses. We don't get together to shut down the crack house next door because we are afraid that one of our own children is running it. We don't get involved in stopping our youth from rolling and robbing and killing one another because it could be one of our own children who is doing the rolling, robbing, and killing, and some of us are even sharing in the loot. Our schools are in such turmoil that the children who want to learn can't even study and our children take guns to schools because we haven't summoned up the courage to challenge and transform the youth who are doing the terrorizing.

Who do we expect to bring about the changes in our schools and in our neighborhoods that we so desperately need? Who are we waiting for to change our families, our youth, our communities, and our schools from the way they are now to the way they have to be if we and our children are to have a future? Until we face and overcome our internal contradictions, the enemy within, we can't even face, let alone overcome, our external enemies.

Back in the 1950s and 1960s, we were so confident of ourselves that we used to tell whites, "You can run but you can't hide." That's what we need to tell ourselves today. Until we face our internal contradictions, all we're doing is running.

"Beyond Civil Rights" appeared in the spring 1993 issue of the *Save Our Sons and Daughters Newsletter.*

Beyond Civil Rights

In 1926 historian Carter Woodson started Negro History Week so that we could evaluate where we had come from, where we were, and where we still had to go. At that time hundreds of Negroes were being lynched every year. Most did not graduate from high school. Few people had indoor toilets, electric lights, or telephones. We had to go to the back door of restaurants run by whites, sit in the back of the streetcar or bus, and ride up front on the train immediately behind the locomotive.

Because we had so far to go, Woodson believed we needed a time each year to measure our progress or lack of progress, and project the areas where we needed to struggle in order to obtain a better way of life for ourselves in this country, for which we had done so much to build.

After the social upheavals of the 1960s Negro History Week became Black History Month and then African American History Month. In the course of the name changes from colored to Negro to black to African American and extending the period to a month, we began to lose sight of the original purpose of Negro History Week. So this year African American History Month in Detroit started in February and was still going strong in the middle of March. We were still talking about our achievements during our four-hundred-year history in this country, which most Americans don't know. The trouble, however, is that we are not evaluating where we are in relation to where we have been and where we have to go. We celebrate the struggles of the 1960s but we do not understand those struggles. So we are still talking about discrimination and segregation even though anyone looking seriously at our conditions can see that the major issues facing the majority of blacks are not issues of racial oppression but economic.

Thirty years ago most African Americans had jobs and better housing than we have today. Before the Civil Rights Act of 1964 we may have had the money but we couldn't go into most hotels or buy a home outside the ghetto. Today the only reason why we can't go to a hotel or buy a decent home is because we don't have the money.

But we are still focused on the question of race and it is paralyzing us. For example, when one black person kills another, we don't see it as a violation of that person's humanity. But if a white person just calls a black person a name, we are shouting racism and ready to march. All we do about the black person who was killed by another black person is to take the body to the church and say, "God has called him home."

It is obvious that things have changed, but we don't know how to move the struggle to another level. So we keep whipping up excitement about civil rights and organizing civil rights rituals when the most serious issues facing most African Americans today are economic. We still believe we can use the U.S. Constitution as a way to solve our economic problems when there is nothing in the Constitution guaranteeing jobs and housing and medical care because this country was founded on the capitalist system and in the agricultural era when most whites lived on farms and blacks were slaves on plantations.

The time has come for us to move our struggle beyond civil rights. We have to face the reality that the corporations have abandoned cities like Detroit and that if we want jobs we have to create them for ourselves. We have to organize the kinds of struggles that will make our neighborhoods viable. We have to engage our young people in struggles that will make them proud of themselves and what they can accomplish.

It is much easier to shout racism and discrimination than it is to organize the kinds of struggles that will meet our basic economic and human needs. As long as we keep insisting that the issues are race and discrimination, we can maintain the illusion that if we raise enough sand, someone else will solve our problems for us. To meet our economic and human needs we must rely on ourselves. The longer we evade this challenge, the more we demoralize ourselves and frustrate our young people.

"Why Detroit Summer?" appeared in the May 1993 issue of the *Save Our Sons and Daughters Newsletter*.

Why Detroit Summer?

Last summer we made a good beginning toward involving out-of-town youth with local youth in the struggle to build Detroit. We now know that there are some young people who can be counted on to join a cause that requires commitment to a vision larger than themselves. Creating parks out of vacant lots, rehabbing houses, planting community gardens, painting murals, and marching against crack houses, Detroit Summer '92 Youth Volunteers won the respect of grassroots Detroiters and seeded the idea that together we can build a movement to rebuild, redefine, and respirit Detroit from the ground up.

When all around us so many people are drowning in the politics of blaming others, when most people refuse to grapple with hard questions because they are afraid of failure (not recognizing that failure is often the mother of success), it is heartwarming to know that there are people who care enough about the future of our city, our country, and the world that they are ready to engage in the struggle to create new relationships between the generations and new ways to build community.

Like most cities Detroit today is at a historic point. At one time it was a crowning jewel of the Industrial Revolution. Millions of young people were lured here to pursue their dream of finding a job. Today that dream has evaporated as corporations replace human beings with robots and export jobs overseas where they can make more profit with cheaper labor. So we, the citizens of Detroit, are faced with new problems no previous generation has had to solve. We have to ask ourselves new questions that human beings like ourselves never had to ask. We have to create new dreams for the twenty-first century.

How can the million people now trapped in Detroit make a living? What kind of an economy can we create since we know very well that we can't depend upon Ford or GM to do it for us? Can we create the kinds of local enterprise that will provide for our basic needs and at the same time provide meaningful jobs for all citizens? How can we put our hearts, minds, hands, and imaginations together to redefine and create a city of community, compassion, cooperation, participation, and enterprise in harmony with the earth?

I do not have the answers to these questions. At this juncture in history no one has the answer to the future. All we know is that we are living at one of the most challenging times in human history, at a time when the people not only of this city but also of the country and the world are in need of new direction and new visions of social, political, and economic responsibility toward one another and to our planet.

Historically, new methods of thinking have come out of young people. Just as in the early 1960s SNCC youth spearheaded a new direction in the struggle for civil rights in the South, young people today can inspire Detroiters to pioneer in building the city of the twenty-first century—as we pioneered in the struggle for the dignity of labor in the 1930s and for black political power in the 1960s and 1970s.

Afterword

Grace Lee Boggs

In the weeks following Jimmy's death on July 22, 1993, I received many messages and articles about him from different people. On August 11, after reading a tribute to him in *Race & Class,*[*] I wrote this note to myself.

HOW ROOTED Jimmy was in the reality of Detroit, this country, and the world.

HOW SECURE he was in his concept of himself (a) as a worker who had lived through agriculture, industry, and automation and (b) as a revolutionary theoretician.

HOW HE COULD FIX ALMOST ANYTHING WITH HIS HANDS (cars, plumbing, etc.).

HOW HE REFUSED TO GIVE UP HIS "ALABAMESE."

HOW GOOD HE WAS AT DEVISING CONCRETE STRATEGIES FOR STRUGGLE.

HOW MUCH HE ENJOYED PICKETING, LEAFLETING, MARCHING AGAINST CRACK HOUSES.

HOW VISIONARY—YET NOT IDEALISTIC—HE WAS ABOUT THE FUTURE.

HOW HE LOVED TO READ. He read the daily paper from cover to cover and loved history, most recently, Paul Kennedy's *Rise and Fall of the Great Powers* and *Preparing for the 21st Century* and Robin Kelley's *Hammer and Hoe.*

HOW QUICKLY AND CONFIDENTLY HE TOOK SHARP CONTROVERSIAL POSITIONS ON CURRENT POLITICAL ISSUES—in a meeting or to reporters, over the phone or at a demonstration.

HOW HE LOVED TO TALK. He carried on long, laughing, daily phone conversations with family and friends, mostly folks raised like him in the South. In response to a simple question, he would give an extended historical answer (e.g., going back to feudalism to explain capitalism). Over the years in our living room on Field Street, he held forth to hundreds of individuals: activists, students, writers—local, national, and international. Over the years he also spoke to scores of university classes all over the country (also in Italy in 1968), always trying to expand the minds of young people by raising new questions.

---

* A. Sivanandan, *Race and Class* 35, no. 2 (1993).

HOW PROUD HE WAS OF HIS JAZZ COLLECTION, his Duke Ellington, Dinah Washington, Count Basie et al., and how often he would surprise me with songs and verses from his childhood and from the Harlem Renaissance.

HOW OPENLY AND HONESTLY HE EXPRESSED HIS POLITICAL VIEWS in any company, regardless of race or class, yet not aggressively except under extreme provocation.

HOW EASILY AND FLUENTLY HIS PEN FLEW ACROSS THE PAPER. In later years he got careless with his spelling, punctuation, sentence structure, and penmanship. But I can still see him coming home from work in the early 1960s, lying on his stomach on the living room floor and writing *The American Revolution*. The original manuscript is around somewhere, and some of his handwritten letters are in the Wayne State University Labor Archives.

HOW FEARLESSLY HE CHALLENGED BIOLOGICAL THINKING, CULTURAL NATIONAL-ISM, THE ROMANTICIZATION OF AFRICA, BLACK POLITICIANS, SEXISM, etc., in the 1970s and 1980s when "blackness" was in fashion—and power.

HOW RIGOROUSLY HE STUCK TO STRUGGLE OVER IDEAS and refused to get involved in personalities or attacks on individuals.

HOW STRUGGLING FOR PRINCIPLES was more important to him than winning. He used to say that he had never won a victory—which wasn't completely true.

HOW HE REGARDED C. L. R. JAMES as his mentor—yet didn't hesitate to clash with CLR in 1962 on Marxism and what was happening to the American worker.

HOW AFTER MALCOLM'S BREAK WITH MR. MUHAMMAD, William Worthy thought he should come to Detroit and spend a year with us preparing for the next stage of struggle.

⊙ ⊙ ⊙

IF EVER THERE WAS AN "ORGANIC INTELLECTUAL" JIMMY WAS ONE. He was well on the way to being one long before we met. How? Why? Why him—and not his brothers or other African Americans who came north from the cotton fields of Alabama to work in the auto plants during World War II? What role do organic intellectuals play in building a movement? What role do private intellectuals play in stopping a movement? What can we learn from Jimmy's life to encourage and nurture other potential organic intellectuals?

Notes

Preface

1. During the early 1930s, Italian Marxist Antonio Gramsci articulated the concept of organic intellectual to describe those who arise from a particular class and direct ideas in the interest of that class. Rather than see intellectuals as a distinct social category, Gramsci argued that a range of people classify as intellectuals, and he identified two categories of intellectuals. Traditional intellectuals derive their status from professional position, formal recognition, and employment as an intellectual. Organic intellectuals, on the other hand, are characterized by their function, that is, their role in developing ideas, organizing, and providing leadership for the class to which they belong. See Antonio Gramsci, *Selections from the Prison Notebooks,* ed. Quintin Hoare and Geoffrey Nowell Smith (New York: International Publishers, 1971), 1–14. In a brief memorial statement published in the British journal *Race and Class* 35, no. 2 (1993), A. Sivanandan described Boggs as "that rare and miraculous combination: a working-class organiser and an organic intellectual." For examples of scholars applying the concept of organic intellectual to black thinkers, see George Lipsitz, *A Life in the Struggle: Ivory Perry and the Culture of Opposition,* rev. ed. (1988; Philadelphia: Temple University Press, 1995), especially the introduction and chapter 5; Barbara Ransby, *Ella Baker and the Black Freedom Movement: A Radical Democratic Vision* (Chapel Hill: University of North Carolina Press, 2003), introduction and chapter 12; Cornel West, "Prophetic Christian as Organic Intellectual: Martin Luther King, Jr.," in *The Cornel West Reader* (New York: Basic Civitas Books, 1999), 425–34; Thabiti Asulkile, "J. A. Rogers: The Scholarship of an Organic Intellectual," *The Black Scholar* 36, no. 2–3 (2006): 35–50; and Manning Marable, *Black Leadership* (New York: Columbia University Press, 1998), chapter 7. Anthony Bogues argues that the concept of organic intellectual cannot satisfactorily describe and explain the work of black radical intellectuals. See his *Black Heretics, Black Prophets: Radical Political Intellectuals* (New York: Routledge, 2003), 5–7, 71–72.

2. Perhaps the most sophisticated analysis of black thinkers' confrontation with Marxism is in Cedric Robinson, *Black Marxism: The Making of the Black Radical Tradition* (Zed Press, 1983; Chapel Hill: University of North Carolina Press, 2000). Robinson devotes a chapter each to three thinkers—W. E. B. Du Bois, C. L. R. James, and Richard Wright—whose lives and work, he argues, serve as exemplars of the black radical tradition. "For all three," Robinson writes, "Marxism had been the prior commitment, the first encompassing and conscious experience of organized opposition to racism, exploitation, and domination. As Marxists, their apprenticeships proved to be significant but ultimately unsatisfactory. In time, events and experience drew them toward Black radicalism" (5). While my understanding and analysis of black radicalism have been informed by Robinson's exceptional text, I differ with his assessment of C. L. R. James; in my estimation James's work and thought remained solidly Marxist. *Black Marxism* also contains insightful commentary on the work of Oliver C. Cox, situating him within the black radical tradition as well. Robinson develops his analysis of Cox further in his "Oliver Cromwell Cox and the Historiography of the West," *Cultural* Critique 17 (Winter 1990–91): 5–20. For an elaboration of Cox's ideas, see his *Capitalism as a System* (New York: Monthly Review Press, 1964). For assessments of Cox's work, see Christopher A. McAuley, *The Mind of Oliver C. Cox* (Notre Dame, IN: University of Notre Dame Press, 2004), and Herbert M. Hunter and Sameer Y. Abraham, eds., *Race, Class, and the World System: The Sociology of Oliver C. Cox* (New York: Monthly Review Press, 1987). For Hubert Harrison,

see Jeffrey B. Perry's illuminating study, *Hubert Harrison: The Voice of Harlem Radicalism, 1883–1918* (New York: Columbia University Press, 2008); Hubert Harrison, *When Africa Awakes* (1920; Baltimore: Black Classic Press, 1997); and Jeffrey B. Perry, ed., *A Hubert Harrison Reader* (Middletown, CT: Wesleyan University Press, 2001). Tony Bogues builds upon Robinson's framework in his *Black Heretics*. See also *Race and Class* 47, no. 2 (2005), a special issue devoted to an assessment of Robinson's work titled "Cedric Robinson and the Philosophy of Black Resistance," with guest editor Darryl C. Thomas. For the study of black radicalism, the works of Robin D. G. Kelley are essential. See, in particular, *Freedom Dreams: The Black Radical Imagination* (Boston: Beacon Press, 2002).

3. Perhaps the most influential of these studies is Thomas Sugrue, *The Origins of the Urban Crisis: Race and Inequality in Postwar Detroit* (Princeton: Princeton University Press, 1996), which identifies deindustrialization, racial discrimination, and struggles over urban space during the two decades following World War II as the central causes of urban decline and persistent, racialized poverty.

4. Examples of such scholarship are Robert Self's *American Babylon: Race and the Struggle for Postwar Oakland* (Princeton: Princeton University Press, 2003), and Matthew J. Countryman, *Up South: Civil Rights and Black Power in Philadelphia* (Philadelphia: University of Pennsylvania Press, 2006).

5. In his 1984 study of the post–World War II black political movements, Manning Marable wrote: "Perhaps the most radical interpretation of Black Power was made by black socialist theorist James Boggs." See Manning Marable, *Race, Reform, and Rebellion: The Second Reconstruction and Beyond in Black America, 1945–2006*, 3rd ed. (Jackson: University Press of Mississippi, 2007), 95. More recently, Boggs (along with his wife and political partner, Grace Lee Boggs) has been identified in the following works as a central figure in Detroit radical politics as well as an influential Black Power theorist and mentor to a younger generation of activists: Peniel E. Joseph, *Waiting 'Til the Midnight Hour: A Narrative History of Black Power in America* (New York: Henry Holt, 2006), 54–59; Peniel E. Joseph, "Dashikis and Democracy: Black Studies, Student Activism, and the Black Power Movement," *Journal of African American History* 88, no. 2 (2003): 190; James Edward Smethurst, *The Black Arts Movement: Literary Nationalism in the 1960s and 1970s* (Chapel Hill: University of North Carolina Press, 2005), 80, 186–92; Bill V. Mullen, *Afro-Orientalism* (Minneapolis: University of Minnesota Press, 2004), chapters 3–4; Michael C. Dawson, *Black Visions: The Roots of Contemporary African-American Political Ideologies* (Chicago: University of Chicago Press, 2001), 200–202; Van Gosse, *Rethinking the New Left: An Interpretive History* (New York: Palgrave Macmillan, 2005), 51, 114. In April 2005, Boggs was among the forty Detroiters whose names were inducted into the Ring of Genealogy of the Charles H. Wright Museum of African American History. As part of the museum's fortieth anniversary celebration, brass plates bearing the names of the "Detroit 40" were installed in the museum's rotunda floor.

6. James Boggs, *Racism and the Class Struggle: Further Pages from a Black Worker's Notebook* (New York: Monthly Review Press, 1970), 7.

Introduction

For their careful readings of drafts of this introduction, I am especially grateful to Richard Feldman, Melba Boyd, Cedric Johnson, Grace Lee Boggs, Nyanza Bandele, and the two anonymous reviewers.

1. This interview is in the *Detroit Committee for the Liberation of Africa Newsletter* 1, no. 4 (1975): 1–3.

2. These quotations are from the fall of 1991 when James and Grace Lee Boggs spoke to Professor James Chaffer's Urban Redevelopment and Social Justice class at the University of Michigan (videotape in the author's possession). The Boggses had visited this class nearly every year since the early 1970s, when they met Chaffers through his work with a community group in Detroit called the Grass Roots Organization of Workers (GROW). Usually James would lead the presentation, but on this occasion, with James weak from his illness, Grace spoke to the students while James sat, looking on. After her presentation, she and James fielded questions from the students, during which he instructed the students on a range of topics. For example, after detailing the persistence of racism in American culture—"that ol'

skin game" of "divide and conquer"—he exhorted blacks not to accept the concept of a minority or to abdicate their political responsibility as citizens and members of communities. He said, in part, "You better . . . get out of this, 'I'm a minority,' cuz when you [are] a minority you think like an underling, you don't believe you [are] capable of doing something and you begin to think all of the white folks or people of superior something can do things."

3. James Boggs and Grace Lee Boggs, *Revolution and Evolution in the Twentieth Century* (1974; New York: Monthly Review Press, 2008), 19.

4. Quoted in Nkenge Zola, John S. Gruchala, and Grace Lee Boggs, eds., *James Boggs: An American Revolutionary* (Detroit: New Life Publishers, 1993). This is a booklet of messages received after James Boggs's death in 1993. This booklet will hereafter be cited as James Boggs memorial booklet. It is not paginated.

5. James Boggs memorial booklet.

6. Ibid.

7. Ibid.

8. Ibid.

9. Ibid.

10. Kenneth Snodgrass, "James Boggs Lives," *Michigan Chronicle*, August 4–10, 1993, 1-A. Portions of this article are reproduced in the James Boggs memorial booklet.

11. James Boggs memorial booklet.

12. Grace Lee Boggs, *Living for Change: An Autobiography* (Minneapolis: University of Minnesota Press, 1998), 146.

13. James Boggs memorial booklet.

14. Ibid. (emphasis in original).

15. G. Boggs, *Living for Change*, 91.

16. Ibid., 92–93. In January 2007, Grace Lee Boggs served as the keynote speaker at Eastern Michigan University's Martin Luther King Jr. Day Celebration. After the address, Michael Abner, one of the young men Jimmy had counseled, who was by then fifty-seven years old, thanked Grace for Jimmy's help in successfully obtaining conscientious objector status for him and thus enabling him to avoid fighting in the Vietnam War. See Rod Podell, "Longtime Social Activist Boggs Finds MLK's Words Still Relevant Today," *Focus EMU Online*, January 17, 2007, www.emich.edu/focus_emu/011607/mlkwrap.html (accessed April 20, 2007).

17. Darrell Dawsey, "An American Revolutionary," *Detroit News*, April 21, 1992, 4C.

18. Quoted in ibid.

19. Certificate of Birth, State of Alabama, Bureau of Vital Statistics, copy in author's possession. The program for his memorial service gives May 28 as his birthdate.

20. Boggs made these remarks during a community celebration for him and Grace in Detroit in 1990 (videotape in author's possession). His remarks are also cited in G. Boggs, *Living for Change*, 228. The "About the Author" page at the end of his *American Revolution: Pages from a Negro Worker's Notebook* (New York: Monthly Review Press, 1963), reads in part: "James Boggs, born in Marion Junction, Alabama, forty-four years ago, never dreamed of becoming President or a locomotive engineer. He grew up in a world where the white folks are gentlemen by day and Ku Klux Klanners at night. Marion Junction is in Dallas County where even today, although Negroes make up over 57 percent of the total county population of 57,000, only 130 Negroes are registered voters."

21. William M. Tuttle Jr., *Race Riot: Chicago in the Red Summer of 1919* (New York: Atheneum, 1970), 14, 22.

22. The biographical information in this section is drawn from the following sources: James Boggs oral history in Elaine Latzman Moon, ed., *Untold Tales, Unsung Heroes: An Oral History of Detroit's African American Community, 1918–1967* (Detroit: Wayne State University Press, 1994); the text of Boggs's statement during the "Pendle Hill Seminar/Search: Martin Luther King, Jr. and the Modern Freedom Movement," led by Vincent Harding and Rosemarie Freeney Harding, dated July 18, 1979, 1 (in author's

possession); Xavier Nicholas, *Questions of the American Revolution: Conversations with James Boggs* (Atlanta: Institute of the Black World, 1976); James Boggs interview in *Detroit Committee for the Liberation of Africa Newsletter;* G. Boggs, *Living for Change,* chapter 4; and the author's interviews with Grace Lee Boggs.

23. *Detroit Committee for the Liberation of Africa Newsletter,* 3; G. Boggs, *Living for Change,* 84, 92.

24. In her book titled *A Way out of No Way: Claiming Family and Freedom in the New South* (Charlottesville: University of Virginia Press, 2002), Dianne Swann-Wright cites the following "African American folk saying" on the page facing the table of contents: "Our God can make a way out of no way. . . . He can do anything but fail."

25. This quotation comes from the 1990 community celebration cited in note 20. See also G. Boggs, *Living for Change,* 227–28.

26. For further discussion, see Joyce A. Ladner, *The Ties That Bind: Timeless Values for African American Families* (New York: Wiley, 1998), chapter 11. Reflecting on her memory of Martin Luther King Jr., Marian Wright Edelman, herself a veteran of the civil rights movement, a child of the South, and a longtime activist, writes: "I also remember him as someone able to admit how often he was afraid and unsure about his next step. But faith prevailed over fear and uncertainty and fatigue and depression. It was his human vulnerability and his ability to rise above it that I most remember. In this, he was not different from many Black adults whose credo has been to make 'a way out of no way.'" See Marian Wright Edelman, *The Measure of Our Success: A Letter to My Children and Yours* (New York: Harper Perennial, 1992), 11.

27. J. Boggs, "Pendle Hill Seminar/Search," 1; G. Boggs, *Living for Change,* 93.

28. J. Boggs, "Pendle Hill Seminar/Search," 1.

29. Quoted in Dawsey, "An American Revolutionary."

30. Nicholas, *Questions of the American Revolution,* 1. This is a pamphlet published by the Institute of the Black World in 1976 consisting of Nicholas's extended interview of Boggs.

31. This description of Boggs's arrival in Detroit is drawn from his oral history in Moon, *Untold Tales, Unsung Heroes.* The quotations appear on page 150.

32. Detroit population statistics from *United States Census of Population, 1910–1970,* cited in Sugrue, *Origins of the Urban Crisis,* 23.

33. Steve Babson, *Working Detroit: The Making of a Union Town* (Detroit: Wayne State University Press, 1986), 18; Olivier Zunz, *The Changing Face of Inequality: Urbanization, Industrial Development, and Immigrants in Detroit, 1880–1920* (Chicago: University of Chicago Press, 1982), 292–93.

34. Babson, *Working Detroit,* part 2; B. J. Widick, *Detroit: City of Race and Class Violence,* rev. ed. (Detroit: Wayne State University Press, 1989), 43–66; Roger Keeran, *The Communist Party and the Auto Workers Unions* (Bloomington: Indiana University Press, 1980), chapter 3.

35. Sidney Fine, *Sit-Down: The General Motors Strike of 1936–1937* (Ann Arbor: University of Michigan Press, 1970); Widick, *Detroit,* 67–78.

36. For the Ford organizing drive and its consolidation of the labor movement's gains, see Babson, *Working Detroit,* 103–10. See also August Meier and Elliott Rudwick, *Black Detroit and the Rise of the UAW* (Oxford: Oxford University Press, 1979), for an analysis of the 1941 campaign as an impetus for increased black participation in industrial unionism and as a turning point in the relationship between black Detroiters and the UAW.

37. Black Bottom earned its name from the area's dark, fertile soil, on which Detroit's early settlers farmed, but the name took on new meaning as African Americans came to inhabit the area in the first half of the twentieth century. As literary scholar and poet Melba Boyd explains, "during the Great Migration, that name [Black Bottom] acquired additional symbolic meaning as black southerners crowded into a neighborhood situated on the bottom of the city's social strata." See Melba Joyce Boyd, *Wrestling with the Muse: Dudley Randall and the Broadside Press* (New York: Columbia University Press, 2003). As African American migrants continued to arrive in the city and settle in the lower east side during the 1930s and 1940s, housing pressures extended the residential district northward into Paradise Val-

ley, thus blurring the boundaries between the original residential district and commercial district. The names Black Bottom and Paradise Valley are now frequently used interchangeably to describe the entire black neighborhood.

38. For businesses along Hastings, see Sunnie Wilson with John Cohassey, *Toast of the Town: The Life and Times of Sunnie Wilson* (Detroit: Wayne State University Press, 1998), 104–5, and various selections in Moon, *Untold Tales, Unsung Heroes.*

39. Examples include Detroit Count, "Hastings Street Opera"; John Lee Hooker, "Boogie Chillen"; and Dudley Randall, "Hastings Street Girls."

40. Moon, *Untold Tales, Unsung Heroes,* 150–51.

41. "Not that I was for Hitler and Tojo," Boggs added, "but it was they who gave blacks the opportunity to work in the factories en mass[e]." Boggs, "Pendle Hill Seminar/Search," 2.

42. J. Boggs, *The American Revolution,* 133 (in this book). The entire text of *The American Revolution* is reprinted as part 2 of this book.

43. Sugrue, *Origins of the Urban Crisis,* 26.

44. For an insightful analysis of black protest politics (especially the efforts of African American workers) in Detroit during World War II, see Beth T. Bates, "'Double V for Victory' Mobilizes Black Detroit, 1941–1946," in *Freedom North: Black Freedom Struggles Outside the South, 1940–1980,* ed. Jeanne F. Theoharis and Komozi Woodard (New York: Palgrave Macmillan, 2003), 17–39. A fuller exposition of Bates's argument regarding black workers' struggle for economic rights and full citizenship is in her *Pullman Porters and the Rise of Protest Politics in Black America, 1925–1945* (Chapel Hill: University of North Carolina Press, 2001).

45. August Meier and Elliott Rudwick, *Black Detroit and the Rise of the UAW* (New York: Oxford University Press, 1979); Richard W. Thomas, *Life for Us Is What We Make It: Building Black Community in Detroit, 1915–1945* (Bloomington: Indiana University Press, 1992), chapter 8; Widick, *Detroit.*

46. Widick, *Detroit,* 72. Boggs recalled to an interviewer years later that the role of the flying squadron was to make people join the union, both during strikes and otherwise: "Our job was to force folks to join up to the union, threaten them and certain things. More people joined the union because forced them in the union than joined automatic[ly]. Because they didn't want to pay no dues. We told them they had to pay. . . . That was a part of organizing." Quotations from Detroit Urban League Oral History Transcript, James and Grace Lee Boggs Papers (hereafter Boggs Papers), box 16, folder 9, Archives of Labor and Urban Affairs, Walter P. Reuther Library, Wayne State University, Detroit (hereafter ALUA), 9, and Moon, *Untold Tales, Unsung Heroes,* 152.

47. Moon, *Untold Tales, Unsung Heroes,* 153. "Goon squads" refers to UAW flying squadrons.

48. Nicholas, *Questions of the American Revolution,* 4.

49. Two important biographical studies of influential black Detroiters insightfully illustrate the ways in which the labor movement helped fashion the unique and rich political culture of black Detroit: Boyd, *Wrestling with the Muse,* and Angela D. Dillard, *Faith in the City: Preaching Radical Social Change in Detroit* (Ann Arbor: University of Michigan Press, 2007). Taking unique approaches to biographical writing, these works are at once powerful studies of historical figures (Dillard's book is organized around the Revs. Charles A. Hill and Albert B. Cleage Jr.) and exceptional analyses of black political, religious, and artistic dynamics of Detroit through much of the twentieth century. As such, they each make a signal contribution to our understanding of Detroit history and the study of black intellectual life.

50. "Jim Crow Broken" and "Discrimination Action Committee" in Ernest C. and Jessie M. Dillard Papers, box 1, folder 44, ALUA. Sidney Fine reports that the Diggs Act was an upgrading of the state's 1885 civil rights law; see his *Expanding the Frontiers of Civil Rights: Michigan, 1948–1968* (Detroit: Wayne State University Press, 2000), 105. For a related discussion of the DAC as part of a dynamic black activist community in 1950s Detroit, see Dillard, *Faith in the City,* 213–15. The timing of the DAC in Dillard's account differs slightly from mine. This may reflect the fact that there were multiple attempts by various groups at different times to challenge discrimination in restaurants. Thomas Sugrue shows that activism directed at restaurant discrimination was widespread and significant in Detroit and other cities during

World War II and into the 1950s in his *Sweet Land of Liberty: The Forgotten Struggle for Civil Rights in the North* (New York: Random House, 2008), 148–54.

51. Dillard interview in Moon, *Untold Tales, Unsung Heroes.*

52. Another figure who exemplifies this overlap and collaboration is Simon P. Owens, who wrote under the pen names Matthew Ward and Charles Denby. Like Boggs and Dillard, Owens was a black auto worker who migrated to Detroit from the South, and like them he was a member of the SWP (in the early 1950s he was also a member of the Correspondence, discussed later in the introduction). In his memoir *Indignant Heart,* Owens writes about his experiences in the South, the auto industry and the labor movement, Detroit's black community, and the SWP. The book was first published in 1952 under the name Matthew Ward. It was reprinted by South End Press in 1978 and as Charles Denby, *Indignant Heart: A Black Worker's Journal* (Detroit: Wayne State University Press, 1989).

53. Nicholas, *Questions of the American Revolution,* 9.

54. For example, in 1950, Boggs, Dillard, and Owens were selected as captains in the NAACP Membership Drive "working in the labor division." They were among at least a dozen auto workers representing their local unions. This information is recorded in a document listing the results of an April 1, 1950, meeting of "about 45 persons present representing various locals in the UAW" found in the Ernest C. and Jessie M. Dillard Papers, box 1, folder 44, ALUA. Note that this occurred in the midst of the DAC activity but apparently with no direct connection.

55. There is a relatively voluminous literature on C. L. R. James and (to a lesser extent) the Johnson-Forest Tendency. For an introduction to this literature, see Anna Grimshaw, ed., *The C. L. R. James Reader* (Cambridge: Blackwell, 1992); Anna Grimshaw and Keith Hart, eds., *American Civilization* (Cambridge: Blackwell, 1993); Martin Glaberman, ed., *Marxism for Our Times: C. L. R. James on Revolutionary Organization* (Jackson: University Press of Mississippi, 1999); Paul Buhle, ed., *C. L. R. James: His Life and His Work* (New York: Allison Busby, 1986); Paul Buhle, *C. L. R. James: The Artist as Revolutionary* (New York: Verso, 1988); Kent Worcester, *C. L. R. James: A Political Biography* (Albany: State University of New York, 1996); Selwyn R. Cudjoe and William E. Cain, eds., *C. L. R. James: His Intellectual Legacies* (Amherst: University of Massachusetts Press, 1995); and Scott McLemee, ed., *C. L. R. James on the "Negro Question"* (Jackson: University Press of Mississippi, 1996).

56. "Statement of the Editor," *Correspondence,* October 3, 1953, 1.

57. Kevin Boyle, *The UAW and the Heyday of American Liberalism, 1945–1968* (Ithaca: Cornell University Press, 1995); Keeran, *The Communist Party,* 250–91.

58. To avoid confusion, when referring to either James Boggs or Grace Lee Boggs I will at times identify them by their first names (using "Jimmy" for James Boggs).

59. These changes in part reflected the difficulties of building a radical organization during the height of McCarthyism. C. L. R. was detained on Ellis Island and forced to leave the United States in 1953 because of his immigration status. In 1955 the U.S. attorney general's office placed Correspondence on its list of subversive organizations. This precipitated a dispute among members of the group over how to respond, leading to a split in the organization, with Raya Dunayevskaya and about half of the members (including Simon Owens) leaving to form a new group, News and Letters. See G. Boggs, *Living for Change,* 99–103.

60. Grace Lee Boggs recalls that Jimmy was "the comrade chiefly responsible" for recording or reporting the views and concerns of people in Detroit's auto plants and neighborhoods for the "Reader's Views" section of the paper; see G. Boggs, *Living for Change,* 99.

61. Al Whitney, "Negro Challenge," *Correspondence,* August 7, 1954, 8. Boggs wrote: "It has been over 100 years since Margaret Garner, a Negro mother, tossed her son into the Ohio River, giving him back to his maker rather than give him to slavery." However, the incident occurred in 1856, slightly less than a hundred years earlier. Also, the child was Garner's daughter, not son as Boggs says, and Garner did not throw the child into the Ohio River, which they crossed in their attempt to escape; she used a knife to kill the child. Despite these inaccuracies, Boggs's knowledge of the event is noteworthy.

62. Detroit Urban League Oral History Transcript, ALUA, 17.

63. James Boggs, "The First Giant Step," *Correspondence*, June 3, 1961, 1, and reprinted in this book, p. 67.

64. About four months earlier, in a letter to the executive board of his union local dated January 25, 1961, Boggs had made a similar call for the UAW to more actively support the civil rights movement. The letter explained that the local's Fair Practices Committee (FPC) had received "a communication from the Negro-American Labor Council announcing a special conference to be held in Washington," and he was writing to request that the executive committee authorize the entire active membership of the committee to attend the conference. This was justified, he argued, because the "Negro question is the No. 1 question in the country today, and is particularly acute in the City of Detroit because of the present tension between the races." Furthermore, the full participation of the local's FPC was necessary because the UAW-CIO "can no longer afford to measure its concern with the [Negro] question in dollars and cents as has been its past practice in this field." James Boggs to the members of the Executive Board of Local 7, January 25, 1961, in author's possession.

65. "End of an Era: State of the Union," *Correspondence*, April 22, 1961, 1. There is no byline to this article, but the next page carries an announcement for a "Detroit Public Meeting" that lists James Boggs as the speaker on the subject "The State of the Union—The End of an Epoch in the UAW." Moreover, the style, tone, and specific language are consistent with his other writings.

66. Jeremy Rifkin, *The End of Work: The Decline of the Global Labor Force and the Dawn of the Post-Market Era* (New York: G. P. Putnam's Sons, 1995), 81; Amy Sue Bix, *Inventing Ourselves Out of Jobs? America's Debate over Technological Unemployment, 1929–1981* (Baltimore: Johns Hopkins University Press, 2000), 254–74.

67. J. Boggs, *The American Revolution*, 109 (in this book).

68. James Boggs, "A Workless Society in a World of Want," *Correspondence*, February 1963, 3.

69. Nicholas, *Questions of the American Revolution*, 34.

70. James Boggs, "'Full Employment Is as Reactionary Today as 'Rugged Individualism' Was in the 1930s," *Correspondence*, March 1963, 3.

71. Of course, he was not alone or the first in making such an argument. Earlier in the twentieth century, black radicals including W. E. B. Du Bois, Hubert Harrison, and Oliver C. Cox similarly critiqued Marxism on these grounds, all of them rejecting the idea that the industrial working class must be the agent of revolution. Contemporary to Boggs, though coming from a different personal trajectory and political framework, was Harold Cruse, who made an equally forceful critique of American Marxism for its inability to see past the standard Marxist vision of revolutionary change.

72. The book first appeared as the special summer double issue of the socialist journal *Monthly Review* in August 1963 and the next month as a Monthly Review Press paperback. It is reprinted in this volume in part 2.

73. Jimmy to "Dear Friends," December 30, 1961, Martin and Jessie Glaberman Papers, box 6, folder 12, ALUA.

74. Boggs, *The American Revolution*, 106 (in this book).

75. Ibid., 105–6 (in this book).

76. Ibid., 113 (in this book).

77. Ibid., 111 (in this book).

78. Ibid.

79. Ibid., 136 (in this book).

80. Ibid., 137 (in this book).

81. Ibid., 139 (in this book).

82. The book has recently been reissued in the Monthly Review Press Classics Series with a new introduction by Grace Lee Boggs: Boggs and Boggs, *Revolution and Evolution*.

83. For insightful treatments of GOAL, the Henry brothers, UHURU, and especially Cleage, see Dillard, *Faith in the City*, chapter 6, and Angela D. Dillard, "Religion and Radicalism: The Reverend Albert B.

Cleage Jr., and the Rise of Black Christian Nationalism in Detroit," in *Freedom North: Black Freedom Struggles Outside the South, 1940–1980,* ed. Jeanne Theoharis and Komozi Woodard (New York: Palgrave, 2003).

84. On Williams, see Timothy B. Tyson, *Radio Free Dixie: Robert F. Williams and the Roots of Black Power* (Chapel Hill: University of North Carolina Press, 1999), and Robert F. Williams, *Negroes with Guns* (1962; Detroit: Wayne State University Press, 1988).

85. Reginald Wilson, interview by the author, February 13, 2006 (audiotape).

86. For a broader and thoughtful discussion of Williams's relationship to this community of activists in Detroit throughout the decade, see Mullen, *Afro-Orientalism,* chapter 3.

87. Foreword to "Monroe, North Carolina . . . Turning Point in American History" (*Correspondence* pamphlet, n.p.) and reprinted in this book, p. 72.

88. In 1966, French publisher François Maspero released French translations of *The American Revolution* and *Negroes with Guns* in one volume under the title *La révolution aux Etats-Unis? Traduit de l'américain et présenté par Guillaume Carle* (Paris: Librarie Francois Maspero, 1966). Robert Williams was among the many activists and former comrades who had worked with the Boggses at various times and in different movements who came together for a community celebration in 1990 honoring the Boggses. Upon James Boggs's death three years later, Robert and Mabel Williams sent the following message: "We add our voices and spirit to the ranks of freedom fighters who pause to pay tribute to a mighty Brother, fallen from our midst. We memorialize Brother James Boggs for his vast contributions and we pledge that we will keep his spirit alive by heightening our struggle against all forms of oppression and social injustice. We will miss his devoted and faithful voice" (James Boggs memorial booklet). When Robert Williams died three years later, Grace Lee Boggs joined with other activists in Detroit to form the Robert Williams Tribute Committee, which organized a program of remembrance and celebration honoring Williams. The event was originally planned for November 1, 1996, as the "Honor Our Heroes While They're Alive" celebration, but after Williams's October 15 death it was changed to "A Legacy of Resistance."

89. G. Boggs, *Living for Change,* 125, 134; Grace Lee Boggs to Paul [Sweezy], May 13, 1964, Boggs Papers, box 1, folder 18, ALUA. On RAM, see Muhammad Ahmad, *We Will Return in the Whirlwind: Black Radical Organizations, 1960–1975* (Chicago: Charles H. Kerr Publishing Company, 2007), chapter 3, and Robin D. G. Kelley, *Freedom Dreams: The Black Radical Imagination* (Boston: Beacon Press, 2002), chapter 3.

90. The essay is reprinted in this volume. It also appeared in Boggs's second book, *Racism and the Class Struggle: Further Pages from a Black Worker's Notebook* (New York: Monthly Review Press, 1970).

91. J. Boggs, *Racism and the Class Struggle,* 163 (in this book).

92. Ibid.

93. Jennifer Jung Hee Choi, "At the Margins of the Asian American Political Experience: The Life of Grace Lee Boggs," *Amerasia Journal,* UCLA Asian American Studies Center, 25, no. 2 (1999): 39n25.

94. J. Boggs, *Racism and the Class Struggle,* 116.

95. Constitution of the Inner City Organizing Committee, Boggs Papers, box 5, folder 7, ALUA.

96. Ibid.

97. Dillard, *Faith in the City,* 220–92; Joseph, *Waiting 'Til the Midnight Hour,* 53–63, 73–76, 81–84, 87–92; Smethurst, *The Black Arts Movement,* 224–26; Mullen, *Afro-Orientalism,* 73–111.

98. Larry Neal, *Visions of a Liberated Future: Black Arts Movement Writings* (New York: Thunder's Mouth Press, 1989).

99. The press, government officials, and many citizens called this event a riot, but many activists and other black Detroiters labeled it a rebellion. My reading of the event suggests that rebellion is a more accurate description, and I have chosen to use the label that Boggs and others used. It may be even more precise to understand the disorder as two events: the initial rebellion (perhaps the first day or two) and the official response, which could be characterized as a "police riot."

100. Sidney Fine, *Violence in the Model City: The Cavanagh Administration, Race Relations, and the Detroit Riot of 1967* (1989; East Lansing: Michigan State University Press, 2007).

101. Louis Lomax, "Anatomy of a Riot," *Detroit News,* July 30, 1967, 1.

102. Grace Lee Boggs, "My Philosophical Journey" (unpublished paper, 1998, in author's possession), 7.

103. Ibid.

104. G. Boggs, *Living for Change,* 141.

105. Kwame Nkrumah to Mr. and Mrs. James Boggs, September 23, 1967, Kwame Nkrumah Papers, box 154-1, folder 19, Moorland-Spingarn Research Center, Howard University.

106. Grace Lee Boggs, "Coming Full Circle," 4 (paper presented to the North American Labor History Conference, Wayne State University, October 19, 2001, in author's possession).

107. James Boggs, Grace Lee Boggs, Freddy Paine, and Lyman Paine, *Conversations in Maine: Exploring Our Nation's Future* (Boston: South End Press, 1978); G. Boggs, *Living for Change,* 143–50.

108. James Boggs, *Manifesto for a Black Revolutionary Party* (Detroit: Advocators, 1969).

109. Patricia Wendolyn Coleman-Burns, "A Rhetorical Analysis of the National Organization for an American Revolution" (Ph.D. diss., Wayne State University, 1987), 32, 35–36, 48–61; G. Boggs, *Living for Change,* 160–67; Grace Lee Boggs, introduction to Boggs and Boggs, *Revolution and Evolution,* vii–x.

110. Boggs and Boggs, *Revolution and Evolution,* 140.

111. Ibid.

112. For a discussion of NOAR's founding, ideology, and activities, see Coleman-Burns, "A Rhetorical Analysis," and G. Boggs, *Living for Change,* 171–84.

113. Coleman-Burns, "A Rhetorical Analysis," contains a bibliography of NOAR literature on 203–9.

114. Ibid., 46.

115. Grace Lee Boggs discusses the collapse of NOAR, including a critical assessment of its structure and practices, in *Living for Change,* 184–89.

116. Ibid., 185.

117. G. Boggs, *Living for Change,* chapter 8, discusses the organizations listed in this paragraph.

118. For more on SOSAD, see Richard Thomas, "The Black Community Building Process in Post–Urban Disorder Detroit, 1967–1997," in *The African American Urban Experience: Perspectives from the Colonial Period to Present,* ed. Joe W. Trotter, Earl Lewis, and Tera W. Hunter (New York: Palgrave MacMillan, 2004).

119. In the mid-1990s a proposal for casino gambling finally passed, opening the way for the casinos now operating in downtown Detroit.

120. Bernard L. Brock and Sharon Howell, "Leadership in the Evolution of a Community-Based Political Action Group," in *Group Communication in Context: Studies of Natural Groups,* ed. Lawrence R. Frey (Hillsdale, NJ: Lawrence Erlbaum Associates, 1994), 151.

121. G. Boggs, *Living for Change,* 232; James Boggs, "Why Detroit Summer?" (in author's possession).

122. G. Boggs, *Living for Change,* 232.

123. SOSAD Movement Building Workshop, "Think Dialectically, Not Biologically," Detroit, Michigan, March 19, 1993 (videotape in author's possession).

124. Grace Lee Boggs, "Remembering James Boggs (1919–1993)," *Third World Viewpoint* (Fall 1993): 12; G. Boggs, *Living for Change,* 235–38.

125. Program of James Boggs Memorial, October 23, 1993, First Unitarian-Universalist Church, Detroit (in author's possession).

126. Ruby Dee quoted in James Boggs memorial booklet. Also see G. Boggs, *Living for Change,* 237–38.

127. The quotation is from the back of the James Boggs memorial booklet. Several of the tributes mention Boggs making such a statement.

Introduction to Part I

1. Grace Lee Boggs, interview by the author, April 6, 2005 (videotape).
2. For a brief discussion of the Johnson-Forest Tendency, see the introduction, 14–15.
3. The full arc of *Correspondence*'s history has yet to be articulated. The most thorough treatments are Rachel Peterson, "Correspondence: Journalism, Anticommunism, and Marxism in 1950s Detroit," in *Anticommunism and the African American Freedom Movement: Another Side of the Story,* ed. Robbie Lieberman and Clarence Lang (New York: Palgrave Macmillan, 2009), which focuses on the paper's early years; Worcester, *C. L. R. James: A Political Biography,* 124–29, 139–40; Smethurst, *The Black Arts Movement,* 187–92; and Buhle, *C. L. R. James: The Artist as Revolutionary,* 119–22. Also very valuable for understanding *Correspondence* is G. Boggs, *Living for Change,* 67–68, 99–100, 103.
4. Peterson, "Correspondence," 130. During its first year, the editors reported 3,000–4,000 regular readers ("Sameness in the Paper," *Correspondence,* August 7, 1954, 6).
5. Peterson, "Correspondence," provides an excellent discussion of this repression and the organization's response to it.
6. On the postal service's decision, see the October 1955 issue of *Correspondence.* The postal service apparently used this designation to delay the paper's application for second-class mailing rights. The February 1956 issue has a short piece announcing that the paper had, after a two-year delay, received second-class mailing rights. On the attorney general placing the group on the subversive list, see Martin Glaberman to Friends and Supporters of Correspondence, December 1954, Frances D. and G. Lyman Paine Papers, box 2, folder 11, ALUA.
7. Beginning in the summer of 1961, Reggie Wilson regularly wrote articles on the civil rights movement and its ideological development. The others wrote articles intermittently throughout most of this period. Additionally, by October 1962, Reggie Wilson was managing editor and Dolores Wilson was business manager, and starting in February 1963 Conrad Mallet served as art director.

Introduction to Part II

1. After a long period of being out of print, *The American Revolution* has recently been reissued by Monthly Review Press with short introductory essays by Grace Lee Boggs and six other Detroit-based activists. Each essay addresses how the book contributed to the writer's conceptions and practice of grassroots activism and social change. Together, these introductions give a vivid picture of the book's legacy. Another statement on the book's influence comes from Dan Georgakas's personal reflections on Detroit radical politics from the late 1950s through the 1960s. *The American Revolution* "was widely admired in Detroit radical circles," he writes. "I believe it was read by almost every person who later became a member of the [League of Revolutionary Black Workers'] Executive Committee." See Dan Georgakas, "Young Detroit Radicals, 1955–1965," in Buhle, *C. L. R. James: His Life and Work,* 193.
2. The languages were French, Italian, Spanish, Japanese, Catalan, and Portuguese.
3. The members who left with James Boggs were Grace Lee Boggs, Freddy Paine, Lyman Paine, and Filomena Daddario. See G. Boggs, *Living for Change,* 109.
4. Just weeks before publication, the title was still in question. In April 1963 Boggs confessed to Huberman and Sweezy that he was having "a very hard time trying to arrive at a title because of the varied nature of the book. If it were just about race, the title would be easier to find; the same if it were just a question of work. But what the book does, in my estimation, is make an analysis of the economic, industrial, social, and political changes that have taken place in the United States and in its relations to world changes, and the effect that these changes are having on the people in molding them into the pattern that they are at present." Explaining his thinking on the title to that point, Boggs said that with his most recent revisions to the manuscript he felt that "a drive has now been injected into the book that will make it quite a controversial piece and that regardless of which side one is on, it will strike

home to a lot of people. It is perhaps for this reason that I am tentatively entitling the book 'But Only One Side Is Right'" (James Boggs to Mr. Huberman and Mr. Sweezy, April 30, 1963, Boggs Papers, box 1, folder 18, ALUA). At one point Boggs considered as an alternative title "Rights Are What You Take" (Table of Contents, Boggs Papers, box 1, folder 6, ALUA). Each of these discarded titles made their way as phrases into the book's introduction, in the opening and closing sentences, respectively. Sweezy suggested *The American Revolution: Pages from a Negro Worker's Notebook* (Paul Sweezy to Jim Boggs, May 27, 1963, Boggs Papers, box 1, folder 18, ALUA).

5. *Monthly Review* 15, no. 5 (September 1963). The statements appear in the "Notes from the Reader" section on the inside cover of the issue.

6. Bertrand Russell to James Boggs, August 20, 1963, Boggs Papers, box 1, folder 20, ALUA. By 1963 Russell had developed a strong interest in and concern for the plight of African Americans, leading him to read widely both in the history African Americans and contemporary material on America's racial conflict. He received newly published works from editors and writers, such as James Baldwin, who sent Russell a copy of *The Fire Next Time*. In the summer of 1963 *Monthly Review* editors Leo Huberman and Paul Sweezy sent *The American Revolution* to Russell. See Barry Feinberg and Ronald Kasrils, eds., *Bertrand Russell's America*, vol. 2, *1945–1970* (Boston: South End Press, 1983), chapter 17, and G. Boggs, *Living for Change*, 115.

7. Ossie Davis, *Life Lit by Some Large Vision: Selected Speeches and Writings* (New York: Atria Books, 2006), 196. This passage comes from Davis's remarks at a memorial service for Boggs on October 23, 1993, in Detroit. As Davis recounted in his remarks, his reading of *The American Revolution* was the first in a series of times through their three-decade association that Davis reported this feeling: "One of the biblical passages I always loved was Christ's response to Nicodemus: 'You must be born again'—not going back to the womb, of course, but undergoing some fundamental change if you are going to save your life. There were several moments when, because of Jimmy, I was indeed born again" (195–96).

8. G. Boggs, *Living for Change*, 114. See also Ruby Dee's note prefacing Davis's statement in *Life Lit by Some Large Vision*, 195.

9. Wyndham Mortimer to Mr. James Boggs, August 12, 1963, Boggs Papers, box 1, folder 22, ALUA.

10. Wyndham Mortimer to Mr. Boggs, September 1, 1963, Boggs Papers, box 1, folder 22, ALUA.

11. Minnie Livingston to Mr. James Boggs, October 15, 1963, Boggs Papers, box 1, folder 22, ALUA; James A. Kennedy to Mr. Robert Harris, August 2, 1963, Boggs Papers, box 1, folder 22, ALUA.

12. Williams, *Negroes with Guns*. Originally published in 1962, the book tells the story of Williams's 1961 forced exile after leading the black community of Monroe, North Carolina, in organizing and arming itself in defense against racist violence.

13. A. B. Spellman, "The View from Harlem," *The Nation*, June 29, 1964.

14. Ibid.

15. L. M. Meriwether, "From Cover to Cover," *Los Angeles Sentinel*, September 5, 1963.

16. Ernie Allen and Kenn M. Freeman, "Notes on James Boggs' *American Revolution*," *Soulbook* 1, no. 3 (1965): 221, 224.

Introduction to Part III

1. James Boggs, "Black Power: A Scientific Concept Whose Time Has Come," in *Black Fire: An Anthology of Afro-American Writing*, ed. LeRoi Jones and Larry Neal (New York: William Morrow, 1968); James Boggs, "The Revolutionary Struggle for Black Power," in *The Black Seventies*, ed. Floyd B. Barbour (Boston: Porter Sargent, 1970); James Boggs, "The Myth and Irrationality of Black Capitalism," *Review of Black Political Economy* 1, no. 1 (1970): 27–35. The first and last are reprinted in this book.

2. Angela Dillard calls this the "second civil rights community in Detroit." See Dillard, *Faith in the City*, chapters 5–6, and especially 251–85.

3. On Randall, see Boyd, *Wrestling with the Muse*. On the Black Arts movement in Detroit, see Smethurst,

The Black Arts Movement, chapter 4.

4. I am referring here to the civil disturbance that shook Detroit during the end of July 1967. It was the most deadly and destructive such disturbance of the "long hot summers" of the period and sparked President Johnson to empanel the National Advisory Commission on Civil Disorders, known as the Kerner Commission.

5. J. Boggs, "The American Revolution: Putting Politics in Command," 238 (in this book; the remaining notes to this part's introduction cite pages from James Boggs's essays included in this book).

6. J. Boggs, "Liberalism, Marxism, and Black Political Power," 160–61.

7. Ibid., 161.

8. The first statement appears on p. 176 of J. Boggs, "Black Power: A Scientific Concept Whose Time Has Come"; the second is on p. 172.

9. J. Boggs, "Culture and Black Power," 184.

10. J. Boggs, "Beyond Rebellion," 251.

11. J. Boggs, "The Myth and Irrationality of Black Capitalism," 189.

12. J. Boggs, "The American Revolution: Putting Politics in Command," 243.

13. Ibid.

14. Ibid., 245.

15. Ibid.

16. Ibid., 221.

17. Ibid., 223.

18. Ibid., 223–24.

19. This is the title of chapter 3 of the *Manifesto.*

20. J. Boggs, *Manifesto,* 212.

21. James Boggs and Grace Lee Boggs, "The Role of the Vanguard Party," *Monthly Review* 21, no. 11 (1970): 22.

22. J. Boggs, "Beyond Nationalism," 258.

23. J. Boggs, "Liberation or Revolution?" 296.

24. Ibid.

25. "The Black Movement No Longer Exists" is a subheading on page 295 of "Liberation or Revolution?"

26. J. Boggs, "Liberation or Revolution?" 296.

27. "New and More Complex Questions" is a subheading on page 296 of "Liberation or Revolution?"

28. J. Boggs, "The Challenge Facing Afro-Americans in the 1980s," 309.

29. Ibid., 310.

30. Ibid.

31. Ibid., 311.

32. Ibid., 308–9.

33. J. Boggs, "Toward a New Concept of Citizenship," 278–79.

34. Ibid., 280.

35. J. Boggs, "The Next Development in Education," 289–90.

Introduction to Part IV

1. G. Boggs, *Living for Change,* 241. She describes his activities during his final weeks and days on pages 235–39. See also G. Boggs, "Remembering James Boggs," 12.

2. SOSAD is described below.

3. For an overview of the history of black political power in Detroit, see Joe T. Darden, Richard Child Hill, June Thomas, and Richard Thomas, *Detroit: Race and Uneven Development* (Philadelphia: Temple University Press, 1987), 202–20.

4. In 1990 blacks were 77.8 percent of the population in Detroit; in 2000 that figure was 82.8 percent. On

Coleman Young and the changes in Detroit's politics, see Wilbur C. Rich, *Coleman Young and Detroit Politics: From Social Activist to Power Broker* (Detroit: Wayne State University Press, 1989); Heather Thompson, "Rethinking the Collapse of Postwar Liberalism: The Rise of Mayor Coleman Young and the Politics of Race in Detroit," in *African American Mayors: Race, Politics, and the American City,* ed. David R. Colburn and Jeffrey S. Adler (Urbana: University of Illinois Press, 2001); and Coleman Young and Lonnie Wheeler, *Hard Stuff: The Autobiography of Mayor Coleman Young* (New York: Viking, 1994).

5. For the causes and impacts of deindustrialization in Detroit, see Sugrue, *Origins of the Urban Crisis.*

6. Reynolds Farley, Sheldon Danziger, and Harry J. Holzer, *Detroit Divided* (New York: Russell Sage Foundation, 2000), 1.

7. Widick, *Detroit,* 236.

8. J. Boggs, "Going Where We Have Never Been: Creating Communities for Our Future," 328.

9. Ibid., 324.

10. It is worth noting that today, twenty-five years later, we see some of these very ideas—particularly community gardens but also others—in full bloom throughout Detroit, making up part of the fabric of a vibrant grassroots activism that is creating a model of alternative, community-based urban revitalization. Moreover, the work of James and Grace Lee Boggs inspired or is directly linked to some of these contemporary initiatives and organizations. For example, the early Detroit Summer groups and the Boggses' relationship to a group of Detroit elders called the Gardening Angels contributed to the growth of the now quite large urban agriculture movement in the city. The Hub of Detroit (formerly Back Alley Bikes), which was started by Detroit Summer volunteers, is an example of Boggs's idea for repair shops (www.thehubofdetroit.org). Avalon International Breads, which was in part inspired by a speech Boggs delivered to a University of Michigan class, is an example of the type of local enterprise he called for. Avalon is a popular bakery successfully carrying out its vision of a local, community-minded business with the express purpose of effecting community revitalization (see Nicole Ray, "Avalon Rising: Eating Well and Doing Good in Detroit," *Edible Wow* [Winter 2010], http://www.ediblecommunities.com/wow/winter-2010/feeding-the-community.htm; Lisa M. Collins, "On a Roll: Avalon International Breads Isn't Just about Making Dough," *Metro Times,* September 4, 2002; and Patricia B. Gray, "A Bakery on the Rise: Two Partners Try to Expand Their Food Business without Losing Momentum," *Fortune,* March 24, 2008). Ron Scott, a longtime Detroit activist who worked with Boggs during the 1980s and continues to work with Grace Lee Boggs, mediates conflicts as part of his activist work with the Detroit Coalition Against Police Brutality, including the creation of Peace Zones for Life, which is in line with the spirit of Boggs's idea for community panels to resolve disputes. Boggs's vision of community building and urban revitalization also called for a new vision of education and of the function of schools in his speeches on community. Five Detroit educators, one of whom was one of the original members of Detroit Summer (see note 24 below), are planning to launch the Grace Lee Boggs Educational Center, which is inspired by the Boggses' ideas about education (www.boggseducationalcenter.org). The idea for the Boggs Educational Center grew directly from a Freedom Schooling initiative of the Boggs Center to Nurture Community Leadership (BCNCL), which was created in 1995, following James Boggs's death, by fellow activists and friends of the Boggses to "honor and continue their legacy as movement activists and theoreticians" (www.boggscenter.org; www.boggsblog.org). These and other innovative community-based efforts are associated with Detroit City of Hope (DCOH), a coalition of organizations and people putting into practice a grassroots vision of transforming the city (www.dcoh.org). See also the online publication FLYP Media (issue 23, February 13–26, 2009), "Breath of Hope: Stories from Detroit" (www.flypmedia.com). This community of grassroots activists was instrumental in bringing the U.S. Social Forum to Detroit during the summer of 2010.

11. J. Boggs, "Going Where We Have Never Been," 328.

12. J. Boggs, "Community Building: An Idea Whose Time Has Come," 332.

13. Ibid., 334.

14. Widick, *Detroit,* 236.

15. J. Boggs, "Rebuilding Detroit: An Alternative to Casino Gambling," 341.

16. Ibid., 344.

17. For a thorough, critical assessment of Young's redevelopment agenda, see June Manning Thomas, *Redevelopment and Race: Planning a Finer City in Postwar Detroit* (Baltimore: Johns Hopkins University Press, 1997), chapter 7. For a decidedly more favorable assessment, see Rich, *Coleman Young,* chapter 6. See also Darden et al., *Detroit;* and Jon C. Teaford, *The Rough Road to Renaissance: Urban Revitalization in America, 1940–1985* (Baltimore: Johns Hopkins University Press, 1990).

18. Grace Lee Boggs describes their organizing efforts that defeated the proposal in G. Boggs, *Living for Change,* 231.

19. J. Boggs, "A 'No' Vote Will Say Detroiters Want to Save What's Left," 353.

20. Ibid., 354.

21. Richard Thomas, "The Black Community Building Process in Post-Urban Disorder Detroit, 1967–1997," in *The African American Urban Experience: Perspectives from the Colonial Period to the Present,* ed. Joe W. Trotter, Earl Lewis, and Tera W. Hunter (New York: Palgrave MacMillan, 2004), 231.

22. J. Boggs, "We Can Run But We Can't Hide," 366.

23. J. Boggs, "Time to Act Like Citizens, Not Subjects," 361.

24. J. Boggs, "Why Detroit Summer?" 369. The phrase "rebuild, redefine, and respirit Detroit from the ground up" was commonly used to describe the program. See, for example, G. Boggs, *Living for Change,* 232.

25. For the reflections of a Detroit Summer volunteer on the program and on Boggs's impact, see Julia Pointer-Putnam, "The Call to Detroit Summer," in the new edition of James Boggs, *The American Revolution: Pages from a Negro Worker's Notebook* (New York: Monthly Review Press, 2009). The program continued in its original form for about a decade. It now exists as an activist collective and its members participate in various dimensions of Detroit's activist community. As described on its Web site, "Detroit Summer is a multi-racial, inter-generational collective in Detroit, working to transform ourselves and our communities by confronting the problems we face with creativity and critical thinking" (www.detroitsummer.org). On the evolution of Detroit Summer, see Jeanette Lee, "The Outsiders Practicing Transformation," in the new edition of *The American Revolution.*

Index

Abner, Michael, 375n16

abolitionist movement, 295

A-bomb, 120, 121

absentee landlords, 338

Addes, George, 15

Ad Hoc Committee on the Triple Revolution in Cybernation, Weaponry, and Human Rights, 79

Advocators, 27, 292

AFL, 99

AFL-CIO, 116; merger, 92

Africa: Balkanization of, 184; independence of nations, 61–62, 299

African American History Month, 367

agribusiness, 302

agricultural research institutes, 192

agriculture: mechanization of, 302, 325, 327; need for reorganization, 313

Algerian Revolution, 136–37

Allen, Ernie, 81

American Indian dispossession, sanctified by ideology, 186, 202

American Marxists, 106–7, 121; and automation, 103–4; idea that industrial working class must lead social revolution in America, 104, 138, 159–60, 174, 379n71; and problem of socialist revolution in U.S., 130–31; reinforcement of "victim mentality," 199; split and decline after Russian Revolution, 108; view of black Americans in race terms, 137, 159–60

American Motors, 94, 95

American Revolution, and political independence, 301

The American Revolution: Pages from a Negro Worker's Notebook (Boggs), 11–12, 18–21, 41, 172, 269, 284, 318, 382n4; "The American Revolution," 139–43; and argument that Marxism could not account for new stage of capitalism, 78; and Boggs's reputation as theorist and activist, 77; "The Challenge of Automation," 100–106; and civil rights movement as revolutionary force, 19; "The Classless Society," 106–9; concept of full unemployment, 84, 118; "The Decline of the United States Empire," 126–30; on economic and social implications of automation on black labor, 77; editor's foreword, 83–84; on growing group of people with no place in economic order, 19; on implications of deindustrialization, 19; indictment of American labor movement, 77–78; "Introduction," 84–85; "The Outsiders," 109–19; "Peace and War," 120–25; "Rebels with a Cause," 130–39; response from readers, 79–80; reviews, 80–81; "The Rise and Fall of the Union," 85–99

Americans: choice between material goods and political freedom, 141; consumer culture, 63–64, 303, 325, 326; interpretation of freedom as right to pursue material gain without consideration of social costs, 308–9; need to change from individualists and materialists to socially and politically conscious people, 233. *See also* white America

American socialists: failure to understand burden of capitalism on workers, 140; refugees in theory from American Revolution, 140

American Trotskyism, 14

anti-Vietnam War movement, 295, 308

Aristotle, 165

armed struggle, 225

assembly line, 9

Asulkile, Thabiti, 373n1

atomic scientists, questioning of war as way of life, 122

Attica prison uprising, 27

Attucks, Crispus, 44

automation: in auto plants, 57–58; and black labor, 77, 175, 208, 235; and conflicts among sectors of the population, 103; and end of unions, automation (*continued*)

17; and growth in unemployment, 93, 102–3, 109–12, 288; impact of, 79, 100–106, 328; and need for radical approach to society, 111

auto plants: "Big Three," 94; cutbacks and layoffs due to automation, 57–58; ex-foremen one-third of workforce, 101; physical rating codes, 98; "scheduling," 95. *See also* labor unions; workers, industrial

Avalon International Breads, 385n10

Back-to-Africa Movement, 259

back-to-Africa schemes, 165, 181, 236, 251, 257, 267

Baldwin, James: *The Fire Next Time*, 80, 383n6

Bandung Conference of 1955, 298–99

Barfield, Clementine, 30, 320

Bargain of 1877, 130, 132, 158

Batista, Fulgencio, 126, 127

"Battle of the Overpass," 10

"Beyond Civil Rights" (Boggs, James), 367–68

"Beyond Nationalism" (Boggs, James), 153–54, 253–63

"Beyond Rebellion" (Boggs, James), 150, 251–52

"Big Three," 94

biotechnology, 231

Birmingham, Alabama, demonstrations of summer of 1963, 163, 207, 251

black Americans: adoption of individualistic and materialistic values, 309; conscience of America, 310; disillusionment with northern democracy after WWI, 132; and effects of Bargain of 1877, 130, 132, 158; employment in education and social and public service, 164; exploitation for economic development of U.S., 209, 233, 255, 310; greatest revolutionary potential in U.S., 72, 138, 174, 200, 205; inability to be integrated into industrial structure, 164; infant morality rate, 336; and inseparability of racism and capitalism, 205; internal contradictions, 365–66; lack of confidence in capacity to rule, 249; lack of political power as greatest weakness, 138–39; large proportion of working class, 87; as majority of inner-city population, 8, 175; need for education and mobilization, 164–65; opening of defense industry jobs to, 133, 160; post–Civil War segregation, 130; revolts among soldiers and sailors during WWII, 133; sensitivity of, 48–49; separation from traditional relationship to

economy, 208; underemployment, 164; value of identification with African past for sense of identity, 176

"Black and White, Unite and Fight," 136

black and white power, and war for American cities, 163

Black Bottom, Detroit, 10–11, 376n37

black capitalism, 151, 236, 251–52; as delusion, 209; and enslavement of black labor force, 187. *See also* "The Myth and Irrationality of Black Capitalism" (Boggs, James)

black Christian nationalism, 26, 148

black church: and killings in cities, 351; sexism, 336

black college students, challenge to racism structured into higher education, 224–25

black consciousness, 331

black cultural separation, 236

black culture, 180–82, 184

Black Economic Development Conference, Detroit, 1969, 150–51, 185

Black Fire, 147

Black History Month, 43, 367

black industrial workers: formation of Dodge Revolutionary Union Movement (DRUM), 26; impact of WWII on, 12, 114, 133, 160; simultaneous involvement in civil rights and labor movements, 13–14. *See also* workers, industrial

black leaders, 247–49; charismatic, 248; incorporation into system through pacification programs, 197, 209–10, 221, 268–69

black liberation movement, 163

"Black Manifesto" (Forman), 151, 185

black mayors, 28, 271

black men: need for improved human relations with black women, 336; in prison system, 336, 337

black movement: arousal of women to consciousness of their oppression, 295; began with establishment of dignity of blacks, 294; destruction of moral authority of American institutions, 310; division over goals, 240; many different stages of, 235, 236, 251–52; move from defensive to offensive in battle for rights, 134, 248; nationalist and anti-colonial character of struggle, 172; race and class struggle, 50–51, 73, 130–31, 158–59, 294; splintering into various tendencies, 295–96; struggle for equal rights, 45; struggle for self-determination, 206. *See also* Black Panther Party; black political mobilization; Black Power movement; black revolutionary movement; civil rights movement

black Muslims, 135, 136, 158

black nationalism, 61, 135, 161, 207, 257; and Black Power movement, 153–54; cannot be separated from history of black Americans in U.S., 258; as second stage of black movement, 237, 251, 257, 270; view of as end in itself, 258

black-on-black violence, 351–52, 365, 367

Black Panther Party, 23, 24, 27, 148, 151–52; began as defense organization, 263; failure to develop revolutionary ideology, 197–98; first attempt to form vanguard party, 198, 245, 262–63; historical importance, 247; and *Little Red Book,* 247; philosophy of violence and adventurism, 247; reaction against nonviolent philosophy and opportunism of many black organizations, 246–47; revolutionary force of black school and street youth, 243, 247; as small mass party, 246, 263; social services programs, 246; Ten-Point program, 245

black political mobilization: after assassination of Dr. King, 201; ascendency of in 1980s and 1990s, 318; in Chicago, 14; in post-WWII Detroit, 11–14; as revolutionary force in American scene, 136; rise of, and decline of labor movement, 136; and struggle for classless society, 137–38. *See also* Black Power movement

"Black Power: a Scientific Concept Whose Time Has Come" (Boggs, James), 24, 150, 171–79

Black Power: Boggs's writings on: "The American Revolution: Putting Politics in Command," 229–50; "Beyond Nationalism," 153–54, 253–63; "Beyond Rebellion," 150, 251–52; "Black Power: a Scientific Concept Whose Time Has Come," 24, 150, 171–79; "The Challenge Facing Afro-Americans in the 1980s," 306–14; "The City Is the Black Man's Land" (Boggs and Boggs), 22–23, 150, 153, 162–70; "Culture and Black Power," 24, 150, 180–85; "Liberalism, Marxism, and Black Political Power," 157–61; "Liberation or Revolution," 154, 293–305; *Manifesto for a Black Revolutionary Party,* 27, 152–53, 186–87, 195–228; "The Myth and Irrationality of Black Capitalism," 150–51, 185–

94; "The Next Development in Education," 155, 156, 284–92; *Racism and the Class Struggle: Further Pages from a Black Worker's Notebook,* 23, 24, 151; "Think Dialectically, Not Biologically," 150, 264–73; "Toward a New Concept of Citizenship," 155, 274–83

Black Power movement, 20, 147, 207; beginning of, 165–66; Black Power slogan, 23, 148, 196, 241, 242; as cadre organization, 168, 178; call for black Americans to replace white people in power, 176, 212; challenge to precepts of civil rights movement, 23–24, 176–77; concept shaped by media, 242; creation of excitement and expectation among masses, 242; efforts to define concept, 251; and emergence of nationalism, 153–54; end of by mid-1970s, 5, 28, 153; energized in Detroit by rebellion of 1967, 26; interpretation of by individual spokesmen, 242; key to black liberation and economic emancipation of masses, 169, 177; and new relationship of government to people and property, 168–70; and principle of independent black political action, 22; revolutionary social force in black belt of South and urban ghettos of North, 176; seeking of solution only for blacks, 238; split between romantics and realists, 176, 177; steps in revolutionizing of America, 212–20; theory and practice of building, 167–68

black revolutionary movement: addresses concrete grievance of masses, 223; all-black in membership, 226; avoidance of black male chauvinism, 222–23; based upon vanguard party, 196, 199–200, 221; and black self-determination, 206; creation of parallel power structures, 223–24, 246; development of, 245–46; development of political consciousness of black youth, 222; embodiment of revolutionary humanist values, 222; fear of challenge, 267; and long-range strategy, 226; must accept historical reality of black Americans in U.S., 259–60; must overturn every institution of American society, 234, 238, 240; must support national liberation struggles in Asia, Latin America, and Africa, 226; possibility of, 219–20; rejection of philosophy of individualism and materialism, 222, 311–12; roles of, 220; tenets of, 201–2; and united front of all classes within black community, 226; white objections to, 249 black revolutionary movement, community development: based on comprehensive five-year planning, 193–94; based on large-scale social ownership, 191; from bottom up, 189; and community control of police, 192; and community control of public services and funds, 191–92; educational programs, 191; and land reform and acquisition, 192–93; and preparation of blacks for bright-future jobs, 190–91; rapid pace, 190; and social ownership and control, 193; struggle to stimulate crisis learning, 189–90

The Black Scholar, 147

The Black Seventies, 147

"black thought," 272

black underdevelopment: and capitalist development, 185, 187, 188, 189; and exclusion from decision-making roles, 188; and exclusion from higher education, 188

black urban communities, growth of, 8

black youth: alienation, 164, 197, 206–7; as cannon fodder in counterrevolutionary wars, 175; drift through various tendencies of black movement, 236; easily provoked to violence, 221–22; mass uprisings in late 1960s, 196; need for participation in planning and development of black community, 192; need for programs to challenge imagination and potential of, 191, 337; prey upon one another or members of the black community, 197, 211; as revolutionary social force, 192, 208, 243–44; separation from economic system, 72, 208, 210–11, 235

Boggs, Ernest, 7

Boggs, Grace Lee, 2, 37; editorship of *Correspondence,* 16, 39; insight into James's political activism, 6; on James's reporting on auto plants for *Correspondence,* 378n60; keynote speaker at 2007 Eastern Michigan University's Martin Luther King Jr. Day Celebration, 375n16; notes on James Boggs, 371–72; and Robert Williams Tribute Committee, 380n88. *See also* Boggses, James and Grace Lee

Boggs, James: on antidotes for corrupting influences of society, 155–56; in black radical political circles in mid-1960s, 21–26; break with Marxist orthodoxy, 18, 20, 78, 148–49; centrality of revolutionary change in his political practice, 1–2; compassionate engagement of people, 3–7; concept of revolution, 19; and *Correspondence,* 16, 37–41, 78; dialectical thinking, 17–18, 32, 300, 318; early life, 7–8; early years in Detroit, 8–11; impact and legacy, 31–34; intellectual confidence, 1, 31; job at Chrysler assembly plant, 11; and Johnson-Forest Tendency (JFT), 14–15; locally based activism, 2–3; love of political work, 3; memorial, "Celebrating a Life," 32; mentorship of younger activists, 4; as organic intellectual, 372; political development, 13; relationship to Robert Williams, 20–21; rhetorical style, 12; self-described revolutionist, 1, 7–8; and Socialist Workers Party (SWP), 13, 14; speeches throughout the 1970s, 26, 81, 154–56; understanding of political struggle, 31

Boggs, James: and Black Power movement, 147–56; on Black Power as new stage in black struggle, 150; on Black Power as vehicle for revolution, 149; call for Leninist vanguard party, 149, 152; concern with clarifying meaning of Black Power, 147, 149–50; and contradiction of economically advanced but politically backward country, 153; and "parallel power structures," 152–53; on political choices in wake of Black Power movement, 155; rejection of Marxist scenario of revolution, 148–49; on role of black revolutionary party, 152; work on theoretical and practical framework for Black Power movement, 19, 24, 148–49. *See also* Black Power: Boggs's writings on

Boggs, James: and labor movement: call for UAW to more actively support civil rights movement, 379n64; and Chrysler Local 7 of UAW, 12; criticism of UAW and labor movement, 77; and employment of black workers during war years, 133, 160; and NAACP Membership Drive, 378n54; on significance of decline of labor movement and upsurge of civil rights movement, 18; simultaneous involvement in black activist and labor movements, 13–14; "The State of the Union—The End of an Epoch in the UAW," 17–18; telegram to Walter Reuther urging support for Freedom Rides, 16–17, 67–68; UAW as platform for activism, 13

Boggs, James: writing, speaking, and organizing from 1984 to 1993, 313–21; "Beyond Civil Rights," 367–68; centrality of community-building, 318–19; "Community Building:

An Idea Whose Time Has Come," 319, 331–40; focus on local conditions, 317; "Going Where We Have Never Been: Creating New Communities for Our Future," 324–30; "How Will Me Make a Living?", 355–56; insistence on different approach from 1960s to challenges facing black Americans, 318; "Letter to Friends and Comrades," 322–23; and local enterprises, 320; "A 'No' Vote Will Say Detroiters Want to Save What's Left?", 353–54; "Rebuilding Detroit: An Alternative to Casino Gambling," 319–20, 341–46; Save Our Sons and Daughters (SOSAD) columns, 320–21; "Time to Act Like Citizens, Not Subjects," 321, 361–62; "We Can Run But We Can't Hide," 365–66; "We Must Stop Thinking Like Victims," 347–48; "What Can We Be That Our Children Can See?", 359–60; "What Does It Mean to Be a Father?", 349–50; "What Time Is It in Detroit and the World?", 363–64; "Why Are Our Children So Bored?", 357–58; "Why Are We at War with One Another?", 351–52; "Why Detroit Summer?", 321, 369–70

Boggs, Lelia, 7

Boggs Center to Nurture Community Leadership (BCNCL), 385n10

Boggses, James and Grace Lee: and Advocators, 27, 292; black nationalist politics, 61; break with Correspondence and C. L. R. James, 20, 78, 372; call for black people to claim control over administration functions of cities, 22–23; community organizing, 30; concept of "two-sided transformation," 29–30; and Detroit Summer, 31–32, 321; efforts to develop revolutionary program for Black Power movement, 27; evolving concept of revolution, 30; formation of Committee for Political Development (CPD), 27; formation of National Organization for an American Revolution (NOAR), 29–31; formation of Organization for Black Power (OBP), 22, 152; formation of WE-PROS (We the People Reclaim Our Streets), 31; and Freedom Now Party (FNP), 22, 41; friendship with Ossie Davis and Ruby Dee, 80; grassroots activities in early 1960s, 40; groundwork for emergence of Black Power, 24; ideological and political collaboration, 23; intellectual and political trajectory, 20; and Kwame Nkrumah, 26–27; leadership of

Correspondence, 16, 152; leadership of Detroit Committee to Aid the Monroe Defendants (CAMD), 20–21; lecture series "On Revolution," 28; local grassroots organizing, 24–25; and Michigan Committee to Organize the Unemployed, 30; as movement intellectuals, 20; and Northern Negro Grassroots Leadership Conference, 22; organization of Grassroots Leadership Conference, 40–41; reciprocal relation between theoretical work and political activism, 23; relationship to Robert Williams, 20–21; revolutionary study groups, 27; and Save Our Sons and Daughters (SOSAD), 320; visits to James Chaffer's Urban Redevelopment and Social Justice class, University of Michigan, 374n2

Bogues, Anthony, 373n1, 373n2

Bolsheviks, 232

Boyd, Melba Joyce, 376n37, 377n49

Britain, ban-the-bomb movement, 123

Broadside Press, 148

Brook Farm, 330

Brotherhood Week, 43

Brown, H. Rap, 27, 247

Brown v. Board of Education, 52, 73, 134

Bulletin of the Atomic Scientists, 122

bureaucracy, 276–77

Cabral, Amilcar, 237, 331

cadre organization. *See* vanguard party

capitalism, American, 18, 186; antagonism between those who have to be supported and those who support them, 103; based on treating blacks as scavengers, 265; and black plight, 185; built upon exploitation of blacks and Indians, 209, 255; connection to racism, 205, 266, 269; contradictions of, 97, 140; control of two-thirds of world's resources, 209; creation of politically dispossessed classes, 214; different development from other capitalisms, 265–66; economic exploitation required by, 202; encouragement of consumption, 296; forced the worker to work in order to live, 216; incorporation of ethnic groups, 268–69; negation of contradictions, 297; priority to economic development over human relationships, 333; pursuit of profits regardless of social impact, 308; stage of multinational cooperation, 302; welfare statism, 199

capitalist colonialism, 185

capitalist society: policy to never mention blacks who do not accept their "place," 43

Carmichael, Stokely, 2, 23, 27, 171, 196, 241, 247

Carter, Jimmy, 154, 274, 275, 277, 296

Carver, George Washington, 43, 102

Castro, Fidel, 127

Catholic Church, role of women, 336

Center for the Study of Democratic Institutions, 79

central cities, devastation of, 28–29

Central Congregational Church, Detroit, 26

Central High School, Little Rock, Arkansas, 54

Chaffers, James, 274, 339–40

"The Challenge Facing Afro-Americans in the 1980s" (Boggs, James), 154, 155, 306–14

"Change Yourself to Change the World," 30

Charles H. Wright Museum of African American History, "Detroit 40," 374n5

Chiang Kai-shek, 121

Chicago, black political mobilization, 14

children: expanding the capacities of, 357–58; setting examples for, 359–60

Chinese Revolution, 120, 142, 174–75, 232, 239

Chrysler, 94; strike of 1950, 91; Twinsburg, Ohio, stamping plant, 95

CIA, 142

cities, American: abandonment by corporations, 326, 327, 330, 334, 343, 361–62, 368; breeding places of senseless violence by black youth, 162; disintegration of after World War II, 325–26; foundation of must be people living in communities, 328; idea of black self-government in, 164; methods for mass black removal, 175; need for self-government of by black majority, 22–23, 163; as police states, 163; tradition of largest ethnic minorities running the cities, 175, 204, 363; war of black and white power for, 163

citizenship, new theory and practice of, 282–83, 304–5

city governments, concessions and bribes to corporations to stay in cities, 339

"The City Is the Black Man's Land" (Boggs and Boggs), 22–23, 150, 153, 162–70, 178, 269

Civil Rights Act of 1964, 363, 367

civil rights movement, 16, 148, 185, 251; arousing of mass consciousness, 241; attempt to separate struggle against racism from struggle against capitalism, 257; black workers' transfer of interest to from union work, 16; challenging of consciousness of Americans, 295; goal of integration through confrontation, 207; move to the North, 207–8; philosophy of essential dignity of every human being, 265, 294; quest for higher form of human relationships between people, 264, 293, 295; raising racism to national rather than regional struggle, 266; as reform movement, 203, 256, 266–67; as self-developing movement, 256; transformation into Black Power movement, 20, 21

Civil War, and American industrialization, 130

"Class Consciousness and Revolution" (Boggs, James), 154

classless society, 106–9, 137–38

class struggle: post–Civil War shift of, 132; theory of, 86

Cleage, Albert, Jr., 2, 20, 24, 25, 26, 147, 148, 377n49

"Clear it with Sidney, 90

Cold War, 121, 122, 134

collective bargaining, 17

collective self-reliance, 319, 339, 345

colonialism and neocolonialism, 178, 307

Committee for Political Development (CPD) (later Advocators), 27

"Committee on Social and Political Implications," 122

Communist Party, mobilization of in Detroit, 10

communities: black communities last to break up, 326; composed of people of all ages and classes, 328–29; as extended families, 324; foundation for human identities, 334, 335; in a state of flux in America, 324; working-class communities, 324

community-building, 318–19, 362; collective self-reliance, 319, 339, 345; housing, 337–38; integration of generations, 338; local enterprises using natural resources, 344; locally owned stores, 324–25, 345; neighborhood responsibility councils, 329; new vision of how to make a living, 338, 355–56, 364, 368; public transportation, 329; schools as integral part of community, 329, 345; small enterprises, 343, 362; use of abandoned school building for community activities, 345; youth-building programs, 337

"Community Building: An Idea Whose Time Has

Come" (Boggs, James), 319, 331–40
community colleges, and youth training, 344
community gardens, 330, 344, 385n10
Congo, Republic of (Democratic Republic of Congo), 61
Congress of African People (CAP), 154
Congress of Industrial Organizations (CIO), 10, 18, 86, 87, 90, 99, 114, 133, 136; failure to solve problem of unemployment, 89; first use of contractual language, 89; framework by which blacks and women could fight for equality in workplace, 96–97; idea of human relations in workplace, 96; pressure on for advancement of blacks, 50–51; promise of worker racial solidarity of 1930s, 16; realization of Marxian perspectives, 105; and social change, 139
Congress of Racial Equality (CORE), 23–24, 158
Constitution of the United States, extension of definition of manhood to blacks, 173
consumer culture, 303, 325, 326
consumption goods, production for market created by manufacturers, 115, 296
"Correcting Mistaken Ideas about the Third World" (Boggs, James), 154
Correspondence, 14, 15, 16, 37, 378n59
Correspondence, 15, 20–21, 382nn3, 4, 6; cessation of publication, 41; and foundation of Black Power movement, 40; increasing coverage of African Americans and civil rights movement, 39; interim phase of journal of commentary and political theory, 39; as journal of black activist politics, 40; and McCarthy-era repression, 38–39; "Readers' Views" section, 38; role in James Boggs's intellectual and political development, 37–41; "Special Negro News," 38; stages of history, 38–40; as vehicle for expression of workers, women, youth, and African Americans, 37; "Viewing and Reviewing," 38
Correspondence (Boggs's columns): "FBI Asks Me about Rob Williams," 70–71; "The First Giant Step," 67–68; "Foreword to 'Monroe, North Carolina . . . Turning Point in American History,'" 72–74; "Land of the Free and the Hungry," 60; "Negro Challenge," 44; "New Orleans Faces We Still Haven't Seen," 65–66; "The Paper and a New Society," 46–47; "A Report on the March on Washington, 52–53; "Safeguarding Your Child's Future," 59; "Sensitivity," 48–49; "The Stage That We Have Reached," 50–51;

"Talent for Sale," 42; "Viewing Negro History Week," 43–44; "A Visit from the FBI," 69; "The Weakest Link in the Struggle," 57–58; "What Makes Americans Run," 63–64; "Who Is for Civilization," 56; "Who Is for Law and Order," 54–55; "The Winds Have Already Changed," 61–62
counterculture, 330
counterrevolutionary movement, U.S., 103, 175, 219, 220, 221, 223, 229–30, 235–36
Countryman, Matthew J., 374n4
Cox, Oliver C., 373n2, 379n71
crack cocaine, 30, 318, 320
Crocket, George, 42
Crusader, 20
Cruse, Harold, 379n71
Cuban crisis, 124, 129
Cuban Revolution, 127–28, 129, 232
"Culture and Black Power" (Boggs, James), 24, 150
cyber-cultural revolution, 164
cybernation, 111, 208, 235, 328

D'Addario, Filomena, 4
Davis, Angela, 27
Davis, Ossie, 33, 79–80, 383n7
Dawson, Michael C., 374n5
Dee, Ruby, 33, 79–80
dehumanization, 227
Delaney, Martin, 311
Democratic Convention of 1976, 154
Denby, Charles (Simon Owens), 38
Detroit: archetypal black city by 1980s, 318; automobile industry, 9; Avalon International Breads, 385n10; Belle Isle, 354; black Americans as 75 percent of population in 1992, 362; black radicalism in, 11–14; Boggs Center to Nurture Community Leadership (BCNCL), 385n10; as center of Black Arts movement, 25, 148; Chrysler Jefferson, 353; City of Hope, 385n10; community-based urban vitalization, 385n10; Detroit Coalition Against Police Brutality, 385n10; economic development planners, 353; effect of labor unions on political culture of black community, 377n49; Ford Auditorium, 353–54; GM Poletown plant, 341, 353; Grace Lee Boggs Educational Center, 385n10; growth of black and white migrants from South, 9; growth of industrial economy, 9; Hart Plaza,

Detroit (*continued*)
354; Hastings Street, and black Detroit, 10–11; Hub of Detroit, 385n10; local enterprises using natural resources, 344; major center of wartime production, 12; most active center of Black Power movement, 147–48; network of black activists, 20; Peace Zones for Life, 385n10; People Mover, 353; population on public assistance, 343; post-industrial landscape, 30, 318; Proposal A, 353–54; proposed casino gambling, 319, 342; as union town in 1930s, 10

Detroit City of Hope (DCOH), 385n10

Detroit Coalition Against Police Brutality, 385n10

Detroit Committee to Aid the Monroe Defendants (CAMD), 20–21

Detroiters for Dignity, 30, 332

Detroiters Uniting (DU), 31

DETROIT GREENS, 351

Detroit Public Schools, 80–90 percent black American, 363

Detroit rebellion of 1967, 25, 26, 148, 381n99, 384n4

Detroit Summer, 2, 31–32, 321, 361–62, 369–70, 386n25

dialectical thinking: Boggs, James, 17–18, 32, 300, 318. *See also* "Think Dialectically, Not Biologically" (Boggs, James)

Diggs Act (Michigan public accommodation statute), 13, 377n50

Dillard, Angela D., 377n49, 378n54, 384n2

Dillard, Ernest, 13

Dixiecrats, 134

Dodge Revolutionary Union Movement (DRUM), 26

Dominican Republic, 129

drug traffic, legal and illegal, 231, 342

Du Bois, W. E. B., 373n2, 379n71

Dulles, John Foster, 122

Dunayevskaya, Raya (Freddie Forest), 14, 16, 38–39, 378n59

Dykes, Jimmie, 60

Eastern bloc, 128

Eaton, Cyrus, 122

economic determinism, 280

Edelman, Marian Wright, 376n26

Edison, Thomas, 181

education: benefits of black community control, 224; changes over time, 285–86; current goal of sorting winners from losers, 287–88; current system based on philosophy of individualism, 290; current system robs blacks of self-knowledge and dehumanizes whites, 217; greatest change in with American Revolution, 286; junior and community colleges, 287; new developments in, 284–92; pragmatic and utilitarian view of, 279, 284–85; and received knowledge, 284; socially responsible human beings as end of, 217, 313; tied to economic goals after industrial revolution, 286–87, 288–89; tied to purpose of governing historically, 286, 289–90; of working-class children, 287

Einstein, Albert, 120

Eisenhower, Dwight, 54, 66, 92, 134, 142, 293

emerging nations, 106

eminent domain, to acquire land for black community, 192–93

energy crisis of 1970s, 27

Engels, Frederick, 18

Ethiopia, role in thinking of black Americans, 253–54

European Marxists, 107, 172–73; "Workers of the World Unite" philosophy, 173

Executive Order 8802, 12, 133

fascism, 173

fatherhood, meaning of, 349–50

Faubus, Orval, 54

FBI: as political police, 142; and Robert Williams, 69, 70–71

Federation for Independent Political Action, 166

Feldman, Rich, 5

Ferry, W. H. "Ping," 79

feudalism, 254

Fine, Sidney, 377n50

Flint sit-down strikes, 80

Ford, Gerald, 275, 277

Ford, Henry, 9, 102

Ford Auditorium, Detroit, 320, 353–54

Ford Hunger March of 1932, 10

Ford Motor Company, unionization of, 88, 133

Ford River Rouge plant, 10, 88

Foreman, Lloyd A., 65

Forest Club, Detroit, 11

"For James, Writer, Activist, Worker" (Dee), 33

Forman, James: "Black Manifesto," 151, 185

Forum '65, '66, '67, 25

Franck, James, 122

Franco, Francisco, 121

freedom: American interpretation of as right to

pursue material gain without consideration of social costs, 308–9; illusion of, 141; as opportunity to build relationships, 298; without responsibility, 297–98

Freedom Now Party (FNP), 22, 24, 41, 148, 149, 166

Freedom Rides, 16, 39, 67, 135, 136

Freedom Summer, 321

Freedomways, 40

Freeman, Kenn M., 81

free time, 218–19

full unemployment, 84, 118

"The Future Belongs to the Dispossessed: King, Malcolm, and the Future of the Black Revolution" (Boggs, James), 24

Gabrielle, Jimmy and Daisy, 65

Gagarin, Yuri, 123

Garner, Margaret, 16, 44, 378n61

Garvey, Marcus, 132, 165, 259

General Motors, 95; escalation clause, 91; five-year contract, 92; plant in Poletown, 341; strike of 1945–46, 91

generations, segregation of, 338

Georgakas, Dan, 382n1

Ghana, 62, 209

GI Bill of Rights, 325

Gibson, Richard, 81

Glaberman, Marty, 39

"Going Where We Have Never Been: Creating New Communities for Our Future" (Boggs, James), 324–30

Goodman, Paul: *Growing Up Absurd*, 84

Gordon, James, 52

Gordon, Theresa, 52

Grace Lee Boggs Educational Center, 385n10

Gramma, 232

Gramsci, Antonio, 373n1

Grant, Jim "Mudcat," 60

Grassroots Leadership Conference, 1963, 147–48, 241

Great Depression, 294, 325

Great Migration, 8, 9

greenhouses, 330, 344

Gregory, Dick, 136

Group on Advanced Leadership (GOAL), 20, 25, 147

Gruchala, John, 32

gun violence, 318, 320

Haley, Alex: *Roots*, 299

Hampton, Fred, 248

Harding, Vincent, 4, 375n22

Harlem uprising, 163

Harrison, Hubert, 373n2, 379n71

H-bomb, 121, 122

Henderson, Errol, 6

Henry, Milton, 20, 25, 26

Henry, Richard, 20, 25, 26

higher education: black exclusion from, 188; challenge to racism by black students, 224–25

Hill, Charles A., 377n49

Hillman, Sidney, 90

Hiroshima, 120

Hitler, Adolph, 130, 133, 160, 293

Ho Chi Minh, 248

home improvement associations, 160

House, Gloria (Aneb Kgositsile), 4–5

House Un-American Activities Committee hearings, 124, 142

housing, 215–16, 337–38

"How Black Power Will Revolutionize America" (Boggs, James), 212–20

Howell, Sharon ("Shea"), 5–6

"How Will We Make a Living?" (Boggs, James), 355–56

Huberman, Leo, 79, 84, 382n4, 383n6

Hub of Detroit, 385n10

human needs, 277–79

human relationships, 333

Humphrey, Hubert, 163

Hungarian Revolution, 128

Hunter, Herbert M., 373n2

Illustrated News, 25, 40

imperialism: and South African apartheid, 209; Western, 307; working class defense of, 204

individualism: adoption of by black Americans, 309; American values of, 233; black revolutionary movement rejection of, 222, 311–12; current system of education based on, 290

infant morality rate, 336

Inner City Organizing Committee (ICOC), Detroit, 24–25, 148

"instant revolution," 240

integration: appeal to older black Americans, 236; sabotaging of revolutionary struggle against oppression, 173

intercontinental missiles, 121

James, C. L. R., 2, 3, 16, 39, 78, 373n2, 378n59; and Johnson-Forest group, 14

James, Selma, 3–4

James Boggs: An American Revolutionary (Zola, Gruchala, and Boggs), 32–33, 375n4

jazz, 310

Jim Crow, 7, 16

Johnson, Lyndon B., 268, 296

Johnson-Forest Tendency, 14–15, 37. *See also* Correspondence

Joseph, Peniel E., 374n5

Jung Hee Choi, Jennifer, 23

junk food, 335

Kasavubu, Joseph, 61

Kelley, Robin D. G., 374n2

Kennedy, John F., 64, 67, 104, 111, 123

Kerner Commission, 268, 384n4

King, Martin Luther, Jr., 24, 79, 80, 136, 158, 163, 247, 347; assassination of, 27, 151, 196, 201, 243, 251; idea that whites could be reformed by moral appeals, 239; nonviolent tactics, 135, 207; at Prayer Pilgrimage for Freedom, 52–53

Korean War, 92, 142

Ku Klux Klan, 7, 133, 135, 160, 174

labor unions: "Black and White, Unite and Fight" concept, 136, 138, 173, 174; conflict over available work, 115–16; confusion in face of Black Power concept, 173; cooling-off period, 94; corruption, 90–91; decline of, and rise of black movement, 136; discrimination, 160; failure to take control from capitalists, 96; growth in bureaucracy, 89–90; inability to face issues of 1960s, 115; inability to organize workers in South, 99; inability to solve problem of unemployment, 89, 112, 114, 115; incorporation into capitalist system through economic concessions, 204, 268; initial goal of establishing dignity of labor, 294; lack of support of civil rights movement, 16, 67–68; little support for militant workers, 116–18; no-strike pledge, 89, 90; opposition to foreign imports, 116; outlawing of actions by unemployed workers, 94; partnership with management, 115; pension as method of silent firing, 98; Political Action Committee, 91; and profit-sharing, 95; program to ease workers out of plants, 95; sapping of revolutionary

potential, 15; "security clause," 91; "Sliding Scale of Socialism" strategy, 91; "Solidarity Forever" philosophy, 115; space for black activists, 12–13; view that man must work in order to live, 114; weakness of, 57–58; "Workers of the World Unite" philosophy, 116, 173

Latin America: revolution, 128–29; rule by U.S., 126–27

League of Revolutionary Black Workers (LRBW), 26, 81, 148

Lee, Grace Chin (Ria Stone): and Johnson-Forest Tendency, 14–15; marriage to James Boggs, 15. *See also* Boggs, Grace Lee

Lenin, Vladimir, 86, 172, 195, 248, 262

"Letter to Friends and Comrades" (Boggs, James), 322–23

Lewis, John L., 90, 166

"Liberalism, Marxism, and Black Political Power" (Boggs, James), 149–50, 157–61

liberated areas, 223, 224, 225

liberation groups, 299–300

"Liberation or Revolution" (Boggs, James), 154, 293–305

Liberator, 40, 147

Lincoln, Abraham, 133

Lipsitz, George, 373n1

Little Red Book, 247

Little Rock nine, 54

Little Rock school riot, 54–55, 56

Livingston, Minnie, 80

Lomax, Louis, 25–26; *The Negro Revolt*, 149–50, 157–61

Louis, Joe, 43

Louisiana: purging of black children from state welfare rolls, 60; restriction of voting rights, 60

Lumumba, Patrice, 61

lynchings, 7, 70, 132, 133, 347

Lynn, Conrad, 21, 72

majority rule, myth of, 249

"making a way out of no way," 7, 376nn24, 26

Malcolm X, 2, 24, 79, 169, 208, 247, 251, 347, 359–60; assassination, 171; "black liberation by all means necessary," 208; "Message to the Grassroots," 22, 40–41, 165, 241; split from Nation of Islam, 165, 207

Mallet, Conrad, 20, 40, 382n7

Mallet, Gwen, 20, 40

Manifesto for a Black Revolutionary Party (Boggs, James), 27, 152–53, 186–87, 195–228, 250; "The Black Revolutionary Party," 220–28; "How Black Power Will Revolutionize America," 212–20; introduction to the fifth printing, 196–200; preamble, 200–202; "Racism and Revolution," 202–4; "Who Will Make the Revolution?", 204–12

"The Man Who Would Not Be King (for James Boggs)" (Williams), 3

Mao Tse-Tung, 174–75, 184

Marable, Manning, 374n5

March on Washington, 12, 14, 52–53, 79, 133, 166

Marco Polo, 184

Mardi Gras, 65

Marion Junction, Alabama, 375n20

Marx, Karl, 18, 86, 104–5, 117, 300; choice of England as basis of class struggle analysis, 172; concept of workers' power, 172, 176; socialism as transitional society between capitalism and communism, 107; "socialized labor," 105

Marxism: black thinkers and, 373n2; Boggs and, 18, 78, 148–49

Marxists: European, 170, 173–74. *See also* American Marxists

McAuley, Christopher A., 373n2

McCarthyism, 15, 92, 120–21, 378n59

McCone Commission, 163

McKinley, Annie, 11

medical care, 214–15

medical research, 215

Meredith March, Student Nonviolent Coordinating Committee (SNCC), 23, 25

Michigan Committee to Organize the Unemployed, 30

military-industrial complex, 142, 233, 276, 277

minority rule, 182

Mississippi Freedom Summer, 32

"Monroe, North Carolina . . . Turning Point in American History," 21

Monroe, North Carolina black community, 21, 135, 383n12

Monroe defendants, 72

Monroe Doctrine, 126

Montgomery bus boycott, 67, 134, 135

Monthly Review, 79; editors' foreword to *The American Revolution*, 83–84

moral development, as foundation of good governing, 290

Morrison, Toni: *Beloved*, 16

Mortimer, Wyndham, 80

mothers with dependent children, 214

Mubutu, Joseph, 61

Muhammad, Elijah, 165

Mullen, Bill V., 374n5

multicultural diversity, 363

multinational corporations: abandonment of American cities, 326, 334; exploitation of cheap labor and resources of third world, 308, 342; exportation of jobs to other countries, 302, 326; sell goods made outside the U.S., 325

"The Myth and Irrationality of Black Capitalism" (Boggs, James), 150–51, 185–94

National Association for the Advancement of Colored People (NAACP), 42, 52, 54–55, 136; birth of, 132; Discrimination Action Committee (DAC), 13, 377n50; failure as offensive organization, 158; founded as organization to defend black Americans, 157–58

National Black Economic Development Conference, 1969, 150–51

National Conference for Community and Justice, 43

national health program, 335

nationalism. *See* black nationalism

National Labor Relations Board (NLRB), 89

National Organization for an American Revolution (NOAR), 2, 5, 28–31, 274, 292

Nation of Islam, 165

Neal, Larry, 25

Negro History Week, 43–44, 367

neighborhood responsibility councils, 329

neighborhoods vs. communities, 318, 324

neocolonialism, 259

neutralist bloc, 128

Newark uprising, 26, 163

New Deal, 86, 112

New Orleans school desegregation battle, 65–66; "the cheerleaders," 66

"The Next Development in Education" (Boggs, James), 155, 156, 284–92

Nixon, Richard M., 64, 127

Nkrumah, Kwame, 2, 26–27, 61, 209, 331

"No Contract, No Work," 90

Northern Negro Grassroots Leadership Conference, 22

no-strike pledge, 17

"A 'No' Vote Will Say Detroiters Want to Save
What's Left" (Boggs, James), 353–54
nuclear weapons, 121, 312

Oakland, 325
Obadele, Gaidi and Imari (Richard and Milton
Henry), 26
Oliver, Bill, 42
"open shop," 10
organic intellectual, xi, 372, 373n1
Organization for Black Power (OBP), 22, 23, 148,
152; founding conference statement, 166–67
Organization of American States, 129
outsiders: alienated from society, 112; development
of creative abilities and responsibility, 119;
need for new concept of how to live, 113; need
for organization, 114
Owens, Simon, 38, 39, 378n52, 378n54, 378n59

Pacesetters, 27
Paine, Freddy and Lyman, 27, 39
Pan-Africanism, 252, 258–59, 267, 295–96, 299
Paradise Valley, Detroit, 11, 376n37
parallel power structures, 29, 152–53, 223–24, 246,
250
paranoia, 299
Pauling, Linus, 122
peace movement, 123–24
peacetime army, dumping ground for unemployed,
98
Peace Zones for Life, 385n10
people of color, as majority of people who have
been deprived of self-government, 176
permanent underclass, 333
Perry, Jeffrey B., 373n2
Perry, Joe, 9
Philadelphia uprising, 163
philosophy: pragmatic and utilitarian, 279, 280, 281;
starting point of, 294
police power, 182–83, 231, 236
political ideas, genesis of, 298–99
political independence, 300
politics, American, as multimillion-dollar game, 277
pollution, 230
post-industrial economy, 19, 318; of Detroit, 30, 318
Powell, Adam Clayton, Jr., 52
power, defined, 172
Prayer Pilgrimage for Freedom, 52–53
presidential election of 1976, 275–76

preventive medicine, 215
production: creative work of, 112; myth of efficiency
of large-scale, 329, 344; sufficiently developed
to meet material needs, 212
protest movement vs. revolution, 260
public transportation, 213, 230
Pugwash Conferences, 122

Quislings, 162

Rabinovitch, Eugene, 122
racialism, 253
racism: of American working class, 163, 204;
connection to American capitalism, 205, 257,
266, 269; of higher education system, 224–25;
history of in U.S., 173; and inability to recognize
idea of black political power, 162; structured
within every American institution, 186–87, 202,
203; totalitarian system for dehumanization of
one people by another, 227. See also white
power structure
Racism and the Class Struggle: Further Pages from
a Black Worker's Notebook (Boggs, James), 23,
24, 151
Randall, Dudley, 148
Ransby, Barbara, 373n1
Reagan, Ronald, 29, 275, 322
rebellion, as stage in development of revolution,
198
"Rebuilding Detroit: An Alternative to Casino
Gambling" (Boggs, James), 319–20, 341–46
received knowledge, 284
Reconstruction, 130
"Red Summer" of 1919, 7
"Relevant Philosophy for the Late 20th Century"
(Boggs, James), 154
reparations, 151, 185
Republic of New Africa (RNA), 21, 26, 148
Reuther, Walter, 42, 67, 68, 92; "Open the Books"
slogan, 91
Review of Black Political Economy, 147
revolution: ability of leadership to impart vision of
new society, 240; begins with mass concern
over structure and conditions of society, 139;
clashes among segments of population, 139;
in economically undeveloped countries, 232;
legitimacy of new ruling power based on
replacement of old system with new one that
benefits all, 249; made by specific people in

specific countries, 262; meaning of in America, 301–3; no precedent for in U.S., 232; success dependent on working people, 140; vs. rebellion, 198–99. *See also* black revolutionary movement

Revolution and Evolution in the Twentieth Century (Boggs and Boggs), 2, 19–20, 27, 28

Revolutionary Action Movement (RAM), 21, 22, 25

revolutionary humanism, 227

Revolution magazine, 81

Ricks, Willie (Mukasa Dada), 23, 171

Robeson, Paul, 121, 347

Robinson, Cedric, 373n2

Rochester uprising, 163

Roosevelt, Franklin D., 90, 141–42

Russell, Bertrand, 2, 79, 383n6

Russell, Theresa, 60

Russia: explosion of A-bomb, 120; nuclear testing, 123

Russian Revolution, 107, 108, 128, 132, 172, 177, 232, 255–56

Save Our Sons and Daughters (SOSAD), 6, 30, 320, 351

scabs, 88

scarcity, 108

school desegregation battle, 54–55, 134; New Orleans, 65

schools: as integral part of community, 329, 345. *See also* education

scientific community, humanitarian party vs. government party, 122

Scott, Ron, 385n10

Scottsboro Case, 132

segregationists, barbarism of, 56, 65–66

Selassie, Haile, 254

Self, Robert, 374n4

self-governing America, call for, 30

self-respect, 343

seniority system, in reverse, 119

Sharpe, Maxine, 351

shopping centers, 325

Shrine of the Black Madonna Church, Detroit, 26

sit-down strikes, 88

Sivanandan, A., 373n1

SLA (Symbionese Liberation Army), 197

slavery: and economic development of British America, 186, 202; sanctified by ideology, 186, 202

small enterprises, 343

Smethurst, James Edward, 374n5

Snodgrass, Kenneth, 5

socialism, in United States, 300

socialist class consciousness, 262

socialists. *See* American socialists

socialist states, 297

socialist thought vs. bourgeois thought, 261

Socialist Workers Party (SWP), 13, 14, 37

socialized labor, 105

social order, new, 309–11

social revolution, and classless society, 108–9

Sojourner Truth, 347

Soulbook, 80–81

Southern Christian Leadership Conference (SCLC), 52–53, 158

southern repression, 8

South Side Tenants Organization, Chicago, 14

Spellman, A. B., 80

Springfield, Illinois, riot of 1908, 132

Sputnik, 122

Stalin, Josef, 96, 102, 174

Stanford, Max (Muhammad Ahmed), 22

"State of a Nation: 1962" (Boggs, James), 78–79

"The State of the Union—The End of an Epoch in the UAW" (Boggs, James), 17–18, 379n65

Stop the Robberies, Enjoy Safe Streets (STRESS), Detroit Police Department, 341

Strickland, Bill, 4

Student Nonviolent Coordinating Committee (SNCC), 4, 151, 171, 207; conclusion that integration and democracy were myths, 242–43; direct-action group, 158; discovery of powerlessness of black people, 241; historical example for Detroit Summer, 321, 361, 370; intellectualism, 247; Meredith March, 23, 25

student sit-ins, 39, 134–35

suburbs, 302, 325

Sugrue, Thomas, 12, 374n3, 377n50

Swann-Wright, Dianne, 376n24

Sweezy, Paul, 79, 84, 382n4, 383n6

Taft-Hartley Act, 92

"Talented Tenth," 332

taxation without representation, 162

technology, 233, 279–81; and permanent army of unemployed, 302; produced expanding mobile society of consumers, 278–79

Teller, Edward, 122

"Think Dialectically, Not Biologically" (Boggs, James), 150, 264–73
third world, concept of, 298–99
Thomas, R. J., 15
Thomas, Richard, 320
Till, Emmet, 21, 70, 72, 134
time-study specialists, 93
"Time to Act Like Citizens, Not Subjects" (Boggs, James), 321, 361–62
Tito, Josip Broz, 121
Tojo, Hideki, 133, 160
Touré, Sékou, 237
"Toward a New Concept of Citizenship" (Boggs, James), 155, 274–83
Trotsky, Leon, 86
Trotskyites, 91, 96
Trujillo, Rafael, 126
Truman, Harry, 92, 133–34
Tutu, Bishop, 335

UHURU, 20, 25, 26, 147
underclass: permanent, 333; world, 172, 173
underdeveloped countries: and colonialism, 164, 187–88; and technological underdevelopment, 188
Unemployed Councils, 10
unemployment: among black youth, 72, 235; inability of labor unions to solve, 89, 112, 114; as result of automation, 93, 102–3, 109–12, 288. See also outsiders
union shop contract, 90
United Auto Workers (UAW), 10, 89, 376n36; contribution to CORE, 68; failure in eyes of black workers during 1950s, 16; Fair Practices Department, 42, 68; flying squadrons, 12, 377n46; giving up of rights won in 1930s and war years, 95; "Guaranteed Annual Wage" contract, 92; and jobs for black workers during war years, 12; left-wing caucus, 15; Local 7 Fair Practices Committee, 12; model for labor movement, 92; pension scheme, 91–92; as platform for black activism, 12–13; sit-down strike against GM, 10
United Detroiters Against Gambling (UDAG), 31
United States: capitalism based on dispossession and enslavement, 173, 186; citadel of world capitalism, 140; concentration of economic and political power in hands of a few, 234; continuation of slavery through denial of equal rights, 158; dependence on war economy, 142; economic overdevelopment and political underdevelopment, 233–34, 260; and Fascism, 173; foreign policy during Cold War, 121; humane pretensions and antihuman practices, 231; illusion of freedom, 141; multicultural diversity, 363; in need of political and social revolutionary change, 232; political alternatives, 303–4; preservation of white supremacy, 231; racism as integral part of capitalist development, 205, 257, 266, 269; rapid urbanization, 175; regarding of black problem as race problem, 131–32; subordination of human to economic values, 233; subversion of revolutionary movements abroad, 142, 218; worldwide hatred of, 203. See also Americans; white America
urban crises, 28–29
urban rebellions of 1960s, 26, 27, 148, 152, 208, 223, 242, 256
urban renewal, as method of black removal, 175, 192, 215–16
U.S. Rubber, 93

vanguard party (cadre organization), 29, 168, 178, 196, 197, 198, 199–200, 221, 245, 246, 260, 262–63
Vaughn, Ed, 25
Vaughn's Bookstore, Detroit, 25
Venezuela, 127
victim mentality, 199, 261, 347–48
Vietnam War, 167, 175; as international political struggle, 229; protests of, 211, 295, 308

Wachsmann, Skip, 351
Wagner Act, 88
war contracts, 111, 118
warfare state, 108, 276
War Labor Board, 89, 90
War on Poverty program, 165
Washington, Booker T., 43, 338
Washington, V. B., 351
Watergate, 27, 296
Watts uprising, 22, 26, 163, 167, 251
Weathermen, 197
"We Can Run But We Can't Hide" (Boggs, James), 365–66
welfare state, 276, 277, 302
"We Must Stop Thinking Like Victims" (Boggs,

James), 347–48

WE-PROS (We the People Reclaim Our Streets), 31, 351

West, Cornel, 373n1

Western bloc, 128

Western Europe, mass labor parties, 131

"What Can We Be That Our Children Can See?" (Boggs, James), 359–60

"What Does It Mean to Be a Father?" (Boggs, James), 349–50

"What Is Black Liberation?" (Boggs, James), 154

"What Time Is It in Detroit and the World?" (Boggs, James), 363–64

White, Walter, 42

white America: acceptance of philosophy of economic development as key to social progress, 234; characterization of black struggle as racist, 169

White Citizens Councils, 65, 160, 174

white liberals: assumption that blacks want integration into white society, 159, 160; incorporation into system, 197

white power structure, 168–69, 171–72; built on exploitation of colored peoples of world, 170; conviction that people of color are subhuman, 170, 227; co-option of black leaders, 221; pacification programs, 209–10, 268–69, 270, 271, 296; re-enslavement of black people through black capitalism, 187

white supremacy, 7, 170, 227, 231

white university students, as potential revolutionary force, 211–12

"Why Are Our Children So Bored?" (Boggs, James), 357–58

"Why Are We at War with One Another?" (Boggs, James), 351–52

"Why Detroit Summer?" (Boggs, James), 321, 369–70

Widick, B. J., 12

wildcat strikes, 89, 90, 92, 93

Wilkins, Roy, 52, 80

Williams, Mabel, 20, 380n88

Williams, Robert F., 20, 21, 39, 69, 70–71, 72, 135, 380n88; *Negroes with Guns*, 80, 383n12

Williams, Willie, 3

Wilson, Dolores, 382n7

Wilson, Doris, 20, 40

Wilson, Reginald, 20, 40, 382n7

Wilson, Sunnie, 11

women: employment in war industry, 325; need for development of leadership capacity, 313

women's movement, 295

women's studies, 299

Women Strike for Peace committees, 123, 124

Woodson, Carter G., 43, 367

work, belief in necessity of, 111, 114, 119

workers, industrial: average wage in 1945, 91; concern for work conditions over wage raises, 94; and control over production, 216–17; development of political experience, 97; disillusionment with union, 95–96; and fully company-controlled plants, 93; and new relations to work, 101–2, 204; "Specific Local Grievances," 92; struggle for control of production from 1935 to 1941, 88–89; support for system in exchange for standard of living, 173; transformation by changes in production, 87; wildcat strikes, 89, 90, 92, 93

Workers Party (WP), 14

working class: racially divided, 130–31; and racism, 163, 204

working-class communities, 324

work layout specialists, 93

workless people. *See* outsiders

workless society, 110, 118–19

Works Progress Administration (WPA), 11

world revolution, 262

world underclass, 172, 173

World War II: changes in American cities, 325–26; changes in American economy, 11; impact on black workers in Detroit, 12, 114, 133, 160; social melting pot at union plants, 89

Worthy, William, 166, 372

Wright, Richard, 373n2

Young, Coleman, 31, 318, 319, 320, 334, 342; proposal to bring casino gambling to Detroit, 342, 381n119

Young, Whitney, 79

Yugoslavia, 127

Zola, Nkenge, 32

Zupan, Johnny, 38, 39

CPSIA information can be obtained
at www.ICGtesting.com
Printed in the USA
BVHW012218191021
619375BV00020B/217

9 780814 332566